Fodor's 2015

WASHINGTON, D.C.

WELCOME TO WASHINGTON, D.C.

With its neoclassical government buildings and broad avenues, Washington, D.C. looks its part as America's capital. Majestic monuments and memorials pay tribute to notable leaders and great achievements, and merit a visit. But D.C. also lives firmly in the present, and not just politically; new restaurants and bars continually emerge, upping the hipness factor in neighborhoods from Capitol Hill to U Street. Fun museums and tree-shaded parks make it a terrific place for families. You may come for the official sites, but you'll remember D.C.'s local flavor, too.

TOP REASONS TO GO

★ **Cherry Blossoms:** For a few weeks in spring, D.C. is awash in glorious pink blooms.

★ **The White House:** 1600 Pennsylvania may be the best-known address in the U.S.

★ **Memorials:** The lives of soldiers, presidents, and political figures are commemorated.

★ **Museums:** For every taste—whether you like spies, airplanes, history, or art.

★ **Globetrotting Cuisine:** Diverse cultures support restaurants with authentic flavors.

★ **The Mall:** Ground zero for museums, picnics, festivals, and performances.

917.53
FOD
2015

Fodor's WASHINGTON, D.C. 2015

Publisher: Amanda D'Acierno, *Senior Vice President*

Editorial: Arabella Bowen, *Editor in Chief;* Linda Cabasin, *Editorial Director*

Design: Fabrizio La Rocca, *Vice President, Creative Director;* Tina Malaney, *Associate Art Director;* Chie Ushio, *Senior Designer;* Ann McBride, *Production Designer*

Photography: Melanie Marin, *Associate Director of Photography;* Jessica Parkhill and Jennifer Romains, *Researchers*

Maps: Rebecca Baer, *Senior Map Editor;* David Lindroth, Mark Stroud, Moon Street Cartography *Cartographers*

Production: Linda Schmidt, *Managing Editor;* Evangelos Vasilakis, *Associate Managing Editor;* Angela L. McLean, *Senior Production Manager*

Sales: Jacqueline Lebow, *Sales Director*

Marketing & Publicity: Heather Dalton, *Marketing Director;* Katherine Punia, *Senior Publicist*

Business & Operations: Susan Livingston, *Vice President, Strategic Business Planning;* Sue Daulton, *Vice President, Operations*

Fodors.com: Megan Bell, *Executive Director, Revenue & Business Development;* Yasmin Marinaro, *Senior Director, Marketing & Partnerships*

Copyright © 2015 by Fodor's Travel, a division of Random House LLC

Editorial Contributors: Mike Lillis, Will O'Bryan, Robert Michael Oliver, Elana Schor, Cathy Sharpe

Editors: Kristan Schiller, Penny Phenix
Production Editor: Jennifer DePrima

ISBN 978-0-8041-4274-8

ISSN 0743-9741

All details in this book are based on information supplied to us at press time. Always confirm information when it matters, especially if you're making a detour to visit a specific place. Fodor's expressly disclaims any liability, loss, or risk, personal or otherwise, that is incurred as a consequence of the use of any of the contents of this book.

SPECIAL SALES

This book is available at special discounts for bulk purchases for sales promotions or premiums. For more information, e-mail specialmarkets@randomhouse.com

PRINTED IN THE UNITED STATES OF AMERICA

10 9 8 7 6 5 4 3 2 1

CONTENTS

CONTENTS

ABOUT
THIS GUIDE

Fodor's Recommendations

Everything in this guide is worth doing—we don't cover what isn't—but exceptional sights, hotels, and restaurants are recognized with additional accolades. **Fodor's Choice**★ indicates our top recommendations; and **Best Bets** call attention to notable hotels and restaurants in various categories. Care to nominate a new place? Visit Fodors.com/contact-us.

Trip Costs

We list prices wherever possible to help you budget well. Hotel and restaurant price categories from $ to $$$$ are noted alongside each recommendation. For hotels, we include the lowest cost of a standard double room in high season. For restaurants, we cite the average price of a main course at dinner or, if dinner isn't served, at lunch. For attractions, we always list adult admission fees; discounts are usually available for children, students, and senior citizens.

Hotels

Our local writers vet every hotel to recommend the best overnights in each price category, from budget to expensive. Unless otherwise specified, you can expect private bath, phone, and TV in your room. For expanded hotel reviews, facilities, and deals visit Fodors.com.

Restaurants

Unless we state otherwise, restaurants are open for lunch and dinner daily. We mention dress code only when there's a specific requirement and reservations only when they're essential or not accepted. To make restaurant reservations, visit Fodors.com.

Credit Cards

The hotels and restaurants in this guide typically accept credit cards. If not, we'll say so.

Top Picks
★ Fodor's Choice

Listings
- ✉ Address
- ✉ Branch address
- ☎ Telephone
- 🖷 Fax
- ⊕ Website
- ✉ E-mail
- 🎫 Admission fee
- ☉ Open/closed times
- Ⓜ Subway
- ✛ Directions or Map coordinates

Hotels & Restaurants
- 🏨 Hotel
- ↰ Number of rooms
- 🍽 Meal plans
- ✕ Restaurant
- 🍴 Reservations
- 👔 Dress code
- ⊟ No credit cards
- $ Price

Other
- ⇨ See also
- ✐ Take note
- ⛳ Golf facilities

EXPERIENCE WASHINGTON, D.C.

WASHINGTON, D.C. TODAY

Classically majestic and stunningly beautiful, the Capitol, the White House, and the Supreme Court stand at the heart of Washington, D.C., symbols of the stability and strength of the nation. But the city that revolves around this axis is in a constant state of change, lived on a more human scale.

A company town. Today's D.C. is a company town, and because that company is the federal government, business tends to be good even in the worst of times. At no point was this trend more apparent than during the recent recession, when the housing market tanked, private businesses struggled, and unemployment rates skyrocketed across much of the United States—yet D.C. emerged from the mess as one of the wealthiest cities in the country. The reason is no mystery. Federal employment tends to remain relatively stable even in times of economic turmoil, and with hundreds of thousands of federal employees living and working in and around D.C., the area was insulated from the downturn in a manner that most other locales could only dream about.

Demographic dance. Washington's postrecession economic boom has only accelerated the demographic face-lift that was already transforming the city in recent years. This shifting tide is highlighted by several recent population milestones: an increase in the number of residents, a decline in the District's black population to below 50% for the first time since 1960, and a median age that has fallen below 34—more than three years younger than the country as a whole (and it's still dropping!).

Hardly unrelated, the trends reveal that, after years of fleeing D.C. due to high crime rates and underperforming schools, more and more suburban families are opting to live in the city where they work. These younger professionals—mostly white, mostly drawn by the government and related industries—have helped bolster Washington's economy, but not without a price. Indeed, the gentrification—heightened by enormous stadium projects like Nationals Park—has reached deep into the traditionally black areas of Northeast and Southeast, stirring resentment, driving up costs, and pricing many longtime residents out of their childhood homes. (Indeed, for all the enviable economic gains Washington has seen in recent years, the city also has one of the widest income gaps between

WHAT'S NEW

Streetcars: More than 60 years after Washington retired streetcars from Downtown, residents celebrated their return in 2014 with the construction of a new rail line running east from Union Station to the Anacostia River. The 2.4-mile H/Benning line is designed to bring more traffic to one of D.C.'s fastest-growing commercial districts: the bustling H Street Corridor. And that's not all. Ultimately, the system is expected to boast 37 miles of track fanning into all parts of the city—a network that will put Washington in league with Portland, Oregon, and Seattle, Washington, when it comes to streetcar options.

Capital Observation Ferris Wheel: Launched in May 2014, this year-round attraction at Washington's National Harbor features 42 climate-controlled gondolas that ascend to 175

rich and poor in the country.) The changes have flown largely under the radar but are starting to get more attention as local officials seek ways to strengthen commercial interests without sacrificing decades of community and culture.

Favored by foodies. It ain't quite New York City, but Washington has made great culinary strides in recent years. No longer known only for stuffy steakhouses catering to lobbyists and Capitol Hill power brokers, D.C. now offers options to satisfy the most eclectic tastes. The trend is not limited to restaurants—the number of neighborhood farmers' markets rises each year—but it's in the city's eateries that the movement toward true foodie-dom has been most pronounced. And top-tier chefs from around the country have taken notice, with many descending on D.C. to catch their share of the wave.

Wolfgang Puck's The Source, adjacent to the Newseum, wows visitors with its posh, three-story dining room and offbeat Asian fusion menu. Top Chef's Mike Isabella has launched a mini-empire, featuring the Italian eatery Graffiato in Chinatown and the Mexican inspired Bandolero in Georgetown. Iron Chef competitor R. J. Cooper offers an ambitious 24-course menu at Rogue 24 in the Logan Circle neighborhood. And Johnny Monis, who won the 2013 James Beard award for the best chef in the mid-Atlantic, is at the helm of Komi and Little Serow.

These relative newcomers join D.C. pioneers like Robert Wiedmaier, whose Belgian roots are on full display at the awarding-winning Marcel's in Foggy Bottom, Nora Pouillon, whose namesake restaurant near Dupont Circle was the country's first to be certified organic; and José Andrés, the culinary powerhouse behind Zaytinya, Oyamel, and Jaleo, all near Chinatown.

Traffic turmoil. It's official: The roads around D.C. are among the most poorly planned in the country, snarling traffic at all hours and creating the nation's longest commute outside of New York. Spend an hour in gridlock on the Beltway—or 30 minutes in a cab just to get across town—and you'll understand why more locals are flocking to the Metro and to bike sharing to get around the city. Visitors to D.C., it is often suggested, can preserve both time and sanity by doing the same.

---

feet. Visitors enjoy views of the White House, Capitol, Arlington Cemetery, and Alexandria. Rides cost $15; VIP gondolas are more.

Smithsonian National Museum of African American History and Culture: This $500 million project, set to open on the National Mall in 2015, will examine all aspects of the African American experience, including slavery, the Harlem Renaissance, and the March on Washington.

The Wharf: Stretching east along the Washington Channel from the Maine Avenue fish market, this 47-acre project, slated to open in 2015, will include residential, office, and retail development wrapped around a waterfront promenade with restaurants, parks, boat slips, and a museum of maritime history.

WASHINGTON, D.C. PLANNER

Safety Tips

D.C. is a relatively safe city, but crimes do occur, even in typically "safe" neighborhoods. The best way to protect yourself is to stick to well-lighted and populated areas and avoid walking alone after dark.

Many of the city's business and government districts become deserted at night, but the public transportation system is exceptionally safe, with only a few incidents of crime reported each year.

When to Go

D.C. has two delightful seasons: spring and autumn. In spring the city's ornamental fruit trees are blossoming, and its many gardens are in bloom. Summers can be uncomfortably hot and humid. By autumn most of the summer crowds have left and you can enjoy the sights in peace.

Winter weather is mild by East Coast standards, but a handful of modest snowstorms each year bring this southern city to a standstill.

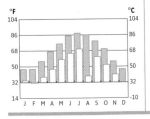

Getting Your Bearings

Four Quadrants: The address system in D.C. takes some getting used to. The city is divided into the four quadrants of a compass (NW, NE, SE, SW), with the U.S. Capitol at the center. Because the Capitol doesn't sit in the exact center of the city (the Washington Monument does), Northwest is the largest quadrant. Northwest also has most of the important landmarks, although Northeast and Southwest have their fair share.

Numbered Streets and Lettered Streets: Within each quadrant, numbered streets run north to south, and lettered streets run east to west (the letter J was omitted to avoid confusion with the letter I).

The streets form a fairly logical grid—for example, 900 G Street NW is the intersection of 9th and G streets in the northwest quadrant of the city. Likewise, if you count the letters of the alphabet, skipping J, you can get a good sense of the location of an address on a numbered street. For instance, 1600 16th Street NW is close to Q Street, Q being the 16th letter of the alphabet if you skip J.

In short, this means it's vital to know which quadrant you're headed to, because 14th Street NW is a long way from 14th Street NE—about 28 blocks, in fact.

Avenues on the Diagonal: As if all this weren't confusing enough, Major Pierre L'Enfant, the Frenchman who originally designed the city, threw in diagonal avenues recalling those of Paris.

Most of D.C.'s avenues are named after U.S. states. You can find addresses on avenues the same way you find those on numbered streets, so 1200 Connecticut Avenue NW is close to M Street, because M is the 12th letter of the alphabet when you skip J. Furthering the chaos, L'Enfant devised a number of traffic circles as well—aesthetically pleasing additions that can nonetheless frustrate even the best out-of-town drivers.

Getting Around

Car Travel: Driving in D.C. can be a headache. Traffic is usually congested, and the road layout is designed for frustration, with one-way streets popping up at just the wrong moment. Once you've reached your destination, the real challenge begins: D.C. must be among the most difficult cities in America in which to find parking. All of this means that you'd be wise to use public transit whenever possible.

Metro and Bus Travel: The Washington Metropolitan Area Transit Authority operates a network of subway lines (known locally as the Metro) and bus routes throughout D.C. Most popular tourist attractions are near Metro stops, though certain areas are accessible only by bus, most notably Georgetown and Adams Morgan in Northwest and the Atlas District in Northeast.

Metro fares depend on the distance traveled and the type of pass used. Holders of popular SmarTrip cards get steep discounts, with rides ranging from $2.15 to $5.90 during "peak" hours—which include the morning and evening commutes and the after-midnight hours of weekends—and from $1.75 to $3.60 at all other times. Those using paper fare cards will pay $1 more for each leg of the trip at all hours, providing travelers a real incentive to get SmarTrip cards if they plan to use Metro trains even just a few times during their stay. The rechargeable cards can be purchased for $5 online or at any Metrorail station. One day passes for unlimited Metro travel are also available for $14.50, while weekly passes cost $59.25 and monthly cards run $237.

Bus fares are $1.75 (exact change only) for regular routes, regardless if you use cash or a SmarTrip card. A special bus, the 5A, runs from D.C. to Dulles airport for $6. SmarTrip cards will grant users free transfers between buses and $0.50 discounts on transfers between buses and the Metro.

Washington Metropolitan Area Transit Authority
☎ 202/637-7000 ⊕ www.wmata.com.

Taxi Travel: Taxis in D.C. charge a $3.25 minimum base rate, which covers the first eighth of a mile, plus $0.27 for every additional eighth of a mile ($2.16 per mile). Riders stuck in traffic will pay more, as wait fees cost $25 per hour. Large bags stowed in the trunk cost $0.50, but smaller bags and groceries are exempt. A $2 charge applies to cabs hailed by phone.

Taxi Information District of Columbia Taxicab Commission
☎ 855/484-4966 ⊕ www.dctaxi.dc.gov.

Getting Here

D.C. is served by three airports: **Ronald Reagan Washington National Airport (DCA)** in Virginia, 4 miles south of Downtown Washington; **Dulles International Airport (IAD)**, 26 miles to the west; and **Baltimore/Washington International-Thurgood Marshall Airport (BWI)** in Maryland, about 30 miles to the northeast.

Amtrak trains arrive and depart from Union Station, in Northeast D.C.

Visitor Information

Washington, DC Convention and Tourism Corporation ⊠ 4th fl., 901 7th St. NW, Downtown ☎ 202/789-7000, 800/422-8644 ⊕ www.washington.org.

Motorcades

Among D.C.'s natural hazards, motorcades rank near the top. These inconvenient affairs—which mark every time Vice President Joseph Biden is whisked from the White House to the Naval Observatory or visiting dignitaries travel in the city—lead to street closings that span dozens of blocks. For pedestrians, proximity to prominent figures might prove exciting. For drivers, motorcades are a hassle and another reason to stick with the Metro during your stay.

WHAT'S WHERE

1 **The Mall.** This expanse of green is at the heart of D.C., stretching from the Capitol to the Washington Monument, and is lined by some of America's finest museums. D.C.'s most famous monuments are concentrated west of the Mall and along the Tidal Basin.

2 **The White House Area and Foggy Bottom.** There's great art at the Corcoran and Renwick galleries, as well as performances at the Kennedy Center, and a whiff of scandal at the Watergate.

3 **Capitol Hill and Northeast D.C.** The Capitol itself, along with the Supreme Court and Library of Congress, dominates this area. Follow Hill staffers to find restaurants, bars, and a thriving outdoor market. Also explore the ever-growing H Street Corridor, aka the Atlas District.

4 **Downtown.** The Federal Triangle and Penn Quarter attract visitors to museums and galleries by day. By night, crowds head to the Verizon Center and Chinatown's bars, restaurants, and movie theaters.

5 **Georgetown.** The capital's wealthiest neighborhood is great for strolling, shopping, and partying, with the scene centering on Wisconsin Avenue and M Street. The C&O Canal starts here, providing recreation in and out of the water.

6 **Dupont Circle and Logan Circle.** This hub of fashionable restaurants and shops is also home to the most visible segment of the gay community. The Kalorama neighborhood is an enclave of embassies, luxurious homes, and small museums. Moving east, beautiful Logan Circle is largely residential, though a few hip new bars and eateries are just a short block away.

7 **Adams Morgan.** One of D.C.'s most ethnically diverse neighborhoods has offbeat restaurants and shops and a happening nightlife. Grand 19th-century apartment buildings and row houses have lured young professionals here.

8 **U Street Corridor.** Revitalization has brought trendy boutiques and hip eateries to the area around 14th and U, which was a hotbed of African-American culture in the early 20th century.

9 **Upper Northwest.** This mostly residential swath of D.C. holds two must-see attractions: the National Cathedral and the National Zoo.

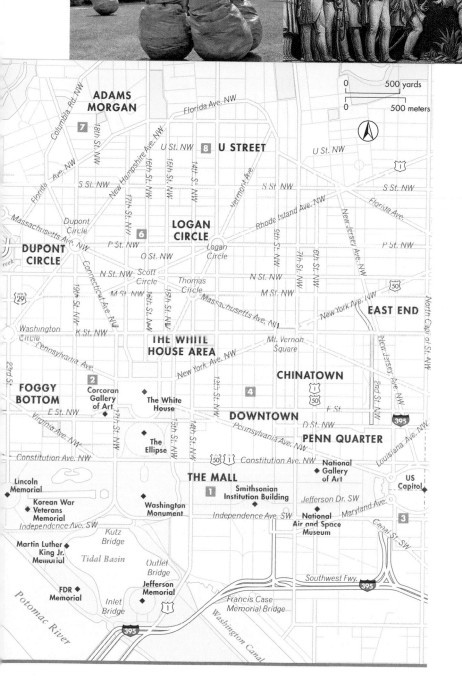

ADAMS
MORGAN

Florida Ave. NW

U St. NW · 8 · U STREET

U St. NW

S St. NW · S St. NW · S St. NW

LOGAN
CIRCLE

6

Dupont
Circle

DUPONT
CIRCLE

P St. NW · O St. NW · Logan
Circle · P St. NW

N St. NW · Scott
Circle · Thomas
Circle · N St. NW

M St. NW · M St. NW · M St. NW

Massachusetts Ave. NW

New York Ave. NW

EAST END

Washington
Circle · K St. NW

THE WHITE
HOUSE AREA

Mt. Vernon
Square

New York Ave. NW

CHINATOWN

FOGGY
BOTTOM

2

Corcoran
Gallery
of Art

The White
House

E St. NW

4

DOWNTOWN

F St.

The
Ellipse

Pennsylvania Ave. NW

D St. NW

PENN QUARTER

Constitution Ave. NW

Constitution Ave. NW

National
Gallery
of Art

US
Capitol

Lincoln
Memorial

THE MALL

1

Smithsonian
Institution Building

Jefferson Dr. SW

3

Korean War
Veterans
Memorial

Independence Ave. SW

Washington
Monument

Independence Ave. SW

National
Air and Space
Museum

Kutz
Bridge

Martin Luther
King Jr.
Memorial

Tidal Basin

Outlet
Bridge

FDR
Memorial

Inlet
Bridge

Jefferson
Memorial

Francis Case
Memorial Bridge

Southwest Fwy.

Potomac River

Washington Canal

0   500 yards
0   500 meters

WASHINGTON, D.C. TOP ATTRACTIONS

Capitol

(A) Home of the Senate and the House of Representatives, the marble Capitol is an architectural marvel filled with frescoes and statues. Tours begin at the new Capitol Visitor Center. The Capitol grounds are equally stunning—Frederick Law Olmsted, the landscape architect famous for New York City's Central Park, designed them. A tour of the interior is impressive, but nothing beats attending a live debate on the House or Senate floor.

Washington Monument

(B) This 555-foot, 5-inch obelisk is visible from nearly everywhere in the city. From the top, it also offers unparalleled views. Although damage suffered during a rare East Coast earthquake closed the monument in 2011, it reopened in 2014 after careful repairs. Ride to the top to see views of the District, Maryland, and Virginia.

Lincoln, Jefferson, and FDR memorials

(C) The key to these memorials is to stop, stand, and read the writing on the walls. There's nothing quite like reading the Gettysburg Address while the massive marble statue of Lincoln broods behind you. Ponder the first lines of the Declaration of Independence at the Jefferson Memorial, and remember the line "We have nothing to fear but fear itself" as you encounter the stark monuments to poverty and war at the FDR Memorial.

White House

(D) The best-known address in the United States may be 1600 Pennsylvania Avenue. Every president but George Washington has lived here, and many heads of state have passed through its hallowed halls. The self-guided tour lets you follow their footsteps through the historic rooms. Note that it takes advance planning to visit the White House.

National Cathedral

(E) Like its medieval European counterparts, this 20th-century cathedral has a nave, transepts, and vaults that were built stone by stone. Unlike those historic buildings, the National Cathedral has a gargoyle in the shape of Darth Vader.

Dumbarton Oaks

(F) If you enjoy formal gardens, visit the 10-acre grounds of Dumbarton Oaks in upper Georgetown, one of the loveliest spots for a stroll.

Arlington National Cemetery

(G) The hills across the Potomac from the Tidal Basin are the final resting place for some 340,000 members of the armed services. A visit here can be both sobering and moving.

Smithsonian museums

(H) Mostly flanking the National Mall, these illustrious galleries hold everything from Kermit the Frog to the *Spirit of St. Louis* and the Hope Diamond to Rodin's *Burghers of Calais*.

Martin Luther King Jr. Memorial

The newest addition to the Mall, this 30-foot sculpture of solid granite pays tribute to King, the giant of the civil rights movement killed by an assassin's bullet in 1968. President Barack Obama dedicated the memorial in October of 2011.

Vietnam Veterans, Korean War Veterans, and World War II memorials

Touch a name of a Vietnam vet, see your reflection alongside the statues of Korean War soldiers, search for the stories of those who lost their lives in World War II. These memorials are interactive and unforgettable.

National Zoo

The pandas may be the zoo's most famous attraction, but they're not the only highlight. Monkeys, elephants, lions, and other exotic residents never fail to delight.

GREAT ITINERARIES

ONE DAY IN D.C.

If you have a day or less (and even a dollar or less!) in D.C., your sightseeing strategy is simple: take the Metro to the Smithsonian stop and explore the area around the Mall. You'll be at the heart of the city—a beautiful setting where you'll find America's greatest collection of museums, with the city's monuments and the halls of government a stone's throw away.

Facing the Capitol, to your left are the **Museum of Natural History,** the **National Gallery of Art,** and the **National Archives.** To your right are the **Museum of African Art,** the **Hirshhorn Museum,** the **National Air and Space Museum,** and more. Head in the other direction, toward the **Washington Monument,** and you're also on your way to the **World War II Memorial,** the **Lincoln Memorial,** the **Vietnam Veterans Memorial,** and more monuments to America's presidents and its past. A lover of American history and culture could spend a thoroughly happy month, much less a day, wandering the Mall and its surroundings.

If you're here first thing in the morning: You can hit monuments and memorials early. They're open 24 hours a day and staffed beginning at 8 am. The sculpture garden at the Hirshhorn opens at 7:30, and the Smithsonian Institution Building ("the Castle") opens at 8:30. In the Castle you can grab a cup of coffee, watch an 18-minute film about D.C., and see examples of objects from many of the 19 Smithsonian museums.

If you have only a few hours in the evening: Experience the beauty of the monuments at dusk and after dark. Many people think they're even more striking when the sun goes down. National Park Service rangers staff most monuments until midnight.

FIVE DAYS IN D.C.

Day 1

With more time, you have a chance both to see the sights and to get to know the city. A guided bus tour is a good way to get oriented; if you take one of the hop-on, hop-off tours we recommend, you'll get genuine insights without a lot of tourist hokum. ⇨ *See Day Tours and Guides in Travel Smart Washington, D.C.*

Because you can get on and off wherever you like, it's a good idea to use a bus tour to explore **Georgetown** and the **Washington National Cathedral,** neither of which is easily accessible by Metro.

Day 2

Devote your next day to the Mall, where you can check out the museums and monuments that were probably your prime motivation for visiting D.C. in the first place. There's no way you can do it all in one day, so just play favorites and save the rest for next time. Try visiting the monuments in the evening: they remain open long after the museums are closed and are dramatically lighted after dark.

Keep in mind that the **National Museum of Natural History** is the most visited museum in the country, while the **National Air and Space Museum,** the **National Gallery of Art,** and the **Museum of American History** aren't far behind; plan for crowds almost any time you visit. If you visit the **U.S. Holocaust Memorial Museum,** plan on spending two to three hours. If you're with kids on the Mall, take a break by riding the carousel.

Cafés and cafeterias within the museums are your best option for lunch. Two excellent picks are the Cascade Café at the **National Gallery of Art** and the Mitsitam Café at the **National Museum of the American**

Indian, where they serve creative dishes inspired by native cultures. Just north of the Mall, the **Newseum** features a food court with a menu designed by celebrity chef Wolfgang Puck. If you have more time (and more money to spend), drop by The Source, a ritzy Puck-owned restaurant behind the museum.

If the weather permits—and you're not already weary—consider the healthy walk from the **Washington Monument** to the **Lincoln Memorial** and around the **Tidal Basin,** where you can see the **Jefferson Memorial,** the **FDR Memorial,** and the new **Martin Luther King Jr. Memorial.** Nearby, nestled north of the Mall's reflecting pool, is **"The Wall,"** a sobering black granite monolith commemorating the 58,272 Americans who never returned from the Vietnam War—a design that's "not so much a tombstone or a monument as a grave," in the somber words of writer Michael Ventura.

Day 3

Make this your day on **Capitol Hill,** where you'll have the option of visiting the **Capitol,** the **U.S. Botanic Gardens,** the **Library of Congress,** the **Supreme Court,** and the **Folger Shakespeare Library.**

Call your senators or congressional representative (or your country's embassy, if you are a visitor from outside the U.S.) for passes to see Congress in session. You can also venture into one of the congressional office buildings adjacent to the Capitol, where congressional hearings are almost always open to the public. (Visit ⊕ *www. house.gov* and ⊕ *www.senate.gov* for schedules.) Likewise, check the Supreme Court's website (⊕ *www.supremecourtus. gov*) for dates of oral arguments. If you arrive early enough, you might gain admission for either a short (three-minute) visit or the full morning session.

Day 4

Head to the **National Zoo** and say good morning to the pandas. If the weather is bad, you can still enjoy the numerous indoor animal houses. Then hop on the Metro to **Dupont Circle** for lunch. Walk west on tree-lined P Street NW to **Georgetown,** where you can shop, admire the architecture, and people-watch.

If you got a good dose of Georgetown on your first day, consider instead visiting the **International Spy Museum,** a Chinatown attraction that tends to be less crowded after 2 pm. From there you can easily walk to the **Smithsonian American Art Museum** and **National Portrait Gallery,** which stay open until 7.

Day 5

Spend the morning at **Arlington National Cemetery.** While you're there, don't miss the changing of the guard at the Tomb of the Unknowns, every hour or half hour, depending on the time of year. A short detour north of the cemetery brings you to the **Marine Corps War Memorial,** a giant bronze rendering of American soldiers planting the flag on Iwo Jima during World War II—one of the most famous images in U.S. military history.

After your contemplative morning, head back across the Potomac to spend the afternoon in **Adams Morgan** and **Dupont Circle.** Lunch at one of Adams Morgan's Ethiopian, El Salvadoran, or Mexican restaurants, and browse the Dupont Circle art scene—there are offbeat galleries tucked into the side streets, as well as the renowned **Phillips Collection.**

D.C. WITH KIDS

D.C. is filled with kid-friendly attractions. These sights are sure winners:

Bureau of Engraving and Printing
Any youngster who gets an allowance will enjoy watching bills roll off the presses. Despite the lack of free samples, the self-guided, 35-minute bureau tour is one of the city's most popular attractions.

DC Ducks
What do you get when you cross a tour bus with a boat? A duck—DC Ducks, that is. Tour the city by both land and water without leaving your seats aboard these unusual amphibious vehicles: standard 2½-ton GM trucks in watertight shells with propellers.

Discovery Theater
Within the Smithsonian's Ripley Center on the Mall, this lively theater began as a low-key puppet show before expanding to feature more than 300 programs a year exploring art, science, and global heritage—everything from robots to the Wright Brothers to African drums.

International Spy Museum
This museum takes the art of espionage to new levels for junior James Bonds and Nancy Drews. Even the most cynical pre-teens and teenagers are usually enthralled with all the cool gadgetry. This museum is best for older tweens and teens—if you bring along a younger sibling, you could be in for a workout: there aren't many places to sit down, and strollers aren't allowed in the museum. Also, there is an entrance fee.

Mount Vernon
Farm animals, a hands-on discovery center, an interactive museum, and movies about the nation's first action hero make George Washington's idyllic home a place where families can explore all day.

National Air and Space Museum
There's a good reason why this place is one of the most popular museums in the world: kids love it. The 23 galleries here tell the story of aviation and space from the earliest human attempts at flight. All three gift shops sell freeze-dried astronaut food—not as tasty as what we eat on Earth, but it doesn't melt or drip. If you've never crunched into ice cream, it's worth the experience.

National Museum of American History
Oh, say, you can see . . . the flag that inspired "The Star Spangled Banner," Oscar the Grouch, the ruby slippers from *The Wizard of Oz,* an impressive collection of trains, and more Americana than anyone can digest in a day.

National Museum of Natural History
Say hello to Henry. One of the largest elephants ever found in the wild, this stuffed beast has greeted generations of kids in the rotunda of this huge museum dedicated to natural wonders. Take your kid to the O. Orkin Insect Zoo, home to live ants, bees, centipedes, tarantulas, roaches (some as large as mice), and other critters you wouldn't want in your house. Did we mention the dinosaurs?

National Zoo
Known more for its political animals than its real animals, D.C. nevertheless has one of the world's foremost zoos. If your child is crazy about animals, this is an absolute must—it's huge!

Paddleboat the Tidal Basin
How better to see the Jefferson Memorial and the world-famous cherry trees—gifts from Japan—than from the waters of the tidal basin? The paddleboats get the kids and you off your feet and into the sun!

D.C. LIKE A LOCAL

To get a sense for D.C. as the locals know it, try these experiences.

Catch a Flick

Summers in D.C. add a refreshing twist to the typical dinner-and-a-movie date night. In July and August locals head to several outdoor venues to see classic films alfresco. The Mall's Screen on the Green is the most popular. But the MLK Memorial also hosts films, and NoMa's Summer Screen, just north of Union Station, pulls an ever-growing audience as well.

Dine on Ethiopian Food

The District's many Ethiopian expats have introduced the community to their unique African cooking. The best restaurants, such as Etete, have long been clustered in the U Street neighborhood, but Ethiopic, a relative newcomer in the Atlas District, is rewriting those rules. Meat and vegetarian dishes are ladled onto a large round of spongy *injera* bread, and diners eat with their hands, ripping off pieces of bread to scoop up the delectable stews. Using your hands instead of utensils adds to the sensual appeal of this cuisine.

Go for a Bike Ride

Your typical Mall-and-monuments tourist may not know that D.C. is home to several great bike trails—and the city's bike share program (🌐 *www.capitalbikeshare.com*), introduced in 2010, makes it easier than ever for visitors to take advantage. The Capitol Crescent Trail and Rock Creek Trail are popular routes between D.C. and Maryland. For more ambitious cyclists, the Custis Trail in Arlington links D.C. to the 45-mile Washington & Old Dominion (W&OD) trail in Virginia, while the Chesapeake & Ohio (C&O) towpath runs for nearly 185 miles between D.C. and western Maryland. From there, the most hardcore peddlers can catch the Great Allegheny Passage trail, which extends another 150 traffic-free miles to Pittsburgh. On a warm, sunny day, expect to find the local paths bustling with cyclists, rollerbladers, and strollers.

Hang Out on U Street

You won't find many tourists in the U Street neighborhood, and many locals have only recently discovered the area. During the day, browse through the unique boutiques that line 14th and U streets NW or read the *Washington City-Paper* at one of the many cafés. In the evening, select from trendy or ethnic restaurants, post up at a local bar like Dodge City, a newish hipster hangout, or catch a popular indie band at the 9:30 Club or some jazz at Bohemian Caverns.

Shop at an Outdoor Market

Instead of sleeping in on a Saturday morning, grab your trusty canvas bag and a wad of cash and head to one of D.C.'s outdoor markets. The best-known venue, Eastern Market on Capitol Hill, is gorgeous, and *the* place to buy a quick meal or picnic ingredients and mingle with residents. On weekends there are craft, flea, and produce markets. The Dupont Circle farmers' market and Georgetown flea market—both year-round venues—are also popular, while the Atlas District's Union Market attracts huge crowds eager to sample oysters, craft beers, and other local delicacies. Lastly, the Maine Avenue Fish Market in Southwest is a must-visit for seafood lovers. Get there early to see the fishermen unload their catch.

FREE IN D.C.

For the thrifty, D.C. is a dream come true. All Smithsonian museums and national memorials are free, as are many other top attractions like Ford's Theatre and Dumbarton Oaks. Summertime is heaven for budget travelers, with free outdoor concerts and festivals every week.

Free Attractions

Anderson House
Arlington National Cemetery
Dumbarton Oaks (free November 1 to March 14)
Folger Shakespeare Library
Ford's Theatre
Gravelly Point
Kenilworth Aquatic Gardens
Kennedy Center tours
Library of Congress
National Arboretum
National Postal Museum
National Zoo
Old Post Office Pavilion
Old Stone House
Phillips Collection (donations recommended)
Rock Creek Park
Sculpture Garden at the National Gallery of Art
Supreme Court of the United States
U.S. Botanic Garden
U.S. Capitol/Capitol Visitors Center
Washington National Cathedral
White House

Free Performances

The **Kennedy Center** hosts free performances every day at 6 pm on the Millennium Stage. Every September the Prelude Festival kicks off the Kennedy Center's fall schedule with many free events. Choral groups perform at the **National Cathedral,** often at no charge.

In summer, bands perform on Monday and Thursday nights atop **Fort Reno Park.**

You can hear jazz in the **National Gallery of Art's sculpture garden** on Friday evenings in summer—get there early if you want to secure lawn space. The Carter Barron Amphitheatre in **Rock Creek Park** hosts free events throughout spring and summer with tickets distributed at the facility's box office the day of the events. To catch free performances of the **Shakespeare Theatre Company,** sign up online for the group's Free-for-All lottery, which awards same-day tickets at the Sidney Harman Hall in Chinatown. From June through August the U.S. Navy Band, U.S. Air Force Band, U.S. Marine Band, and U.S. Army Band take turns playing concerts on the grounds of the **U.S. Capitol** weekdays at 8 pm. You can also see the U.S. Marine Band every Friday night May through August during the Evening Parade at the Marine Barracks.

Almost every day of the year, the **Politics and Prose** bookstore on Connecticut Avenue invites authors to the store for readings, talks, and Q&A sessions. **Busboys and Poets,** another bookstore, offers readings, films, and political discussions almost every night as well.

Free Festivals

D.C. is a city of festivals, many of which are free to the public. For a complete list of events, visit the Washington, D.C. Convention and Tourism Corporation at ⊕ *www.washington.org.*

Half-Price Tickets

TICKETPlace (✉ *407 7th St. NW, between D and E sts.* ⊕ *cutlurecapital.tix.com* ⊙ *Wed.–Sun., hours vary*) sells half-price tickets to D.C.'s theater and music events.

SIGHTSEEING TOURS

If ever there was a "do it yourself" city, it's D.C. The Metro system is safe and easy to navigate and most major sights and museums are concentrated in a single area. Armed with a Metro map, a guide to the Mall, and a comfortable pair of shoes, you can do it all by yourself.

Nevertheless, sometimes a guided tour makes more sense, especially when it comes to insider knowledge and a parking pass. So consider one if your trip falls into any of the categories below. ⇨ *See Travel Smart Washington, D.C. for more information.*

If this is your first trip

The Metro might be the most convenient way to get around, but it is notably lacking in city views. If you'd like to get the lay of the land with ease, **Old Town Trolley Tours** and **Tourmobile** buses operated by the National Park Service offer multiple routes, hop-on, hop-off convenience, and are perfect for your first day in the city.

A bike tour, with a company such as **Bike the Sights**, offers a gentle ride with show-stopping scenery. Visitors might also consider D.C.'s bike-share program, **Capital Bikeshare**. To use the program, you must first purchase a membership, available in increments of 24 hours (for $7), three days ($15), one month ($25), or one year ($75). Additional charges are added depending on how long you actually use the bike, but the system is best suited for short trips around the city—not long hauls on the surrounding bike trails—as the costs rise quickly beyond 90 minutes to between $12 and $16 per hour. For a more automated journey, **Capital Segway, City Segway Tours,** and **Segs in the City** offer guided rides around the major sights and average between $65 and $80 for a two-to-three-hour tour.

If you want an insider's look

Arranging constituent visits to the sessions of **Congress** is one of the duties of your representative and senators. Contact their offices (⊕ *www.house.gov* and ⊕ *www.senate.gov*) in advance. If you are a visitor from another country, your embassy in D.C. can make the arrangement for you with enough notice. Several other government buildings, like the **State Department,** require advance reservations for a tour.

If you just can't get enough

Hear the juicy bits from Washington's rumor mill with **Gross National Product's Scandal Tours.** Now entering its 27th year, the tour features stops at the Tidal Basin, where a powerful congressman and his stripper girlfriend ran afoul of the law, and the Watergate, where the country's most infamous burglary led to the fall of a president. For a walk through the battles and strategies that shaped Civil War history, take a multiday tour with **Smithsonian Associates.** Stops include such historic sites as Manassas National Battlefield Park in Virginia, Antietam National Battle Field in Maryland, and Harpers Ferry, West Virginia, site of John Brown's last stand.

If you want a new perspective

Have you ever seen the monuments from the Potomac River? **Thompson Boat Center** offers rentals on canoes and kayaks. Pack a lunch and paddle over to Roosevelt Island for a picnic. A double kayak rents for $20 per hour or $45 per day, while a canoe goes for $14 per hour and $35 per day. Sunfish sailboats are also available.

WASHINGTON, D.C. BLACK HISTORY WALK

A walk along U Street and the eastern rim of Adams Morgan gives a taste of D.C. that most tourists never get. This tour through "Black Broadway" bounces from lively commercial streets brimming with hip bars, cafés, and boutiques to quiet, tree-lined residential blocks, and highlights African-American culture and history.

"Black Broadway"—U Street Corridor

The **African-American Civil War Memorial** at 10th and U streets is the perfect place to start; it has its own Metro stop. More than 200,000 names of black soldiers who fought for their freedom surround the small memorial. A block west sits **Bohemian Caverns,** a landmark restaurant and lounge that once hosted such jazz greats as Louis Armstrong, Ella Fitzgerald, Billie Holiday, and native son Duke Ellington. You can still catch live jazz here; check the schedule and return in the evening. Across 11th Street is **Washington Industrial Bank,** which thrived by offering African-Americans a service that others in the city wouldn't: the option to borrow money. One block south and another west you'll find the **12th Street YMCA,** the oldest black Y in the country (1853). Head back to U Street to explore the **African-American Civil War Museum,** featuring wonderful photographs from the era and an extensive on-site database for searching individual soldiers. Next, grab a half-smoke at **Ben's Chili Bowl.** A D.C. landmark, Ben's refused to close its doors during the fierce riots that followed the 1968 assassination of Dr. Martin Luther King Jr. While most of U Street was being destroyed, Ben's fed the policemen and black activists trying to keep order. Next door is the **Lincoln Theater,** another exceptional jazz venue and, from 1922 until desegregation, one of the largest and most elegant "colored-only" theaters. Given the area's history, it's probably little wonder that 15th and U marked the epicenter of the spontaneous celebration that erupted in the streets following the 2008 election of Barack Obama, the country's first African-American president.

North of U Street

Venture north one block to marvel at **St. Augustine's Catholic Church**—a gorgeous, two-tower cathedral now home to a black congregation that seceded from its segregated church (St. Matthews) in 1858. Feel free to walk inside to glimpse the striking stained-glass portrait of a black St. Augustine and St. Monica. A few steps north is sprawling **Meridian Hill (or Malcolm X) Park,** where a number of civil rights marches have originated over the years. If you're lucky enough to be strolling through on a Sunday, don't miss the lively drum circle that forms spontaneously in the afternoon. Cutting through the park to 16th Street, you'll spot **Meridian Hill Hall,** Howard University's first coed dorm. Alumni of the elite African-American school include Thurgood Marshall and Toni Morrison. Continuing north, past some beautiful working embassies, you'll find **All Souls Unitarian Church.** Its pastor in the 1940s, Reverend A. Powell Davies, led the push to desegregate D.C. schools. President William Taft and Adlai Stevenson were once members, and the church bell was cast by the son of Paul Revere.

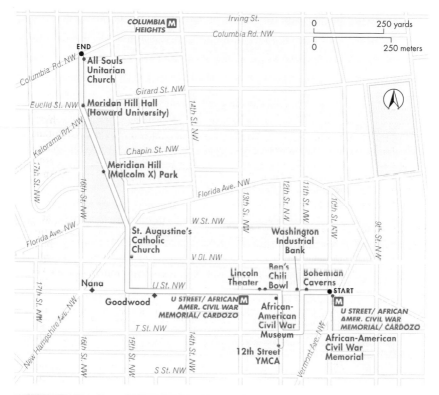

Highlights:	U Street was the center of black culture before Harlem was Harlem. See where Duke Ellington played, indulge in a half-smoke at Ben's Chili Bowl, and learn a bit about African-American history along the way.
Where to Start:	African-American Civil War Memorial on the Metro's Green or Yellow line
Length:	About 1½ miles; 1–2 hours, with window-shopping
Where to Stop:	All Souls Unitarian Church. The S1, S2, or S4 bus lines on 16th Street will whisk you back Downtown.
Best Time to Go:	While the sun is up, though the nightlife on U Street is an attraction in itself.
Worst Time to Go:	Avoid walking through Meridian Hill Park after dark.
Shopping Detour:	Check out Nana (✉ 1528 U St. NW between 15th and 16th sts., upstairs) for new and vintage women's clothing, and browse Goodwood (✉ 1428 U St. NW between 14th and 15th sts.) for antique wood furniture and estate jewelry.

I HEART LINCOLN WALK

President Abraham Lincoln spent the final four years of his life in the nation's capital. During his time here, he left a lasting imprint on the entire city, particularly on the buildings where he lived and worked and at the theater where he lost his life. Today, you can visit many of the sites that best preserve the memory and ideals of this American hero.

The Scene of the Crime

Start your tour at **Ford's Theatre,** the site of Lincoln's assassination. On Good Friday, April 14, 1865, John Wilkes Booth, an actor, shot Lincoln in the head while the president and the first lady were seated in the Presidential box. There's a museum below the theater that explains how Booth and his coconspirators planned the murder. Across the street is the **Petersen House,** where Lincoln died the next day.

The Road to the White House

Leave the museum and head right (south) on 10th Street NW. Turn right on E Street NW, which becomes Pennsylvania Avenue at 13th Street, and then continue walking past Freedom Plaza to the **Willard Intercontinental Hotel,** which has been on this location since 1847. Lincoln and his family stayed here prior to his first inauguration. In the hotel's History Gallery, the president's hotel bill is on display.

From the Willard, go north on 14th Street for six blocks. You'll pass the **White House Gift Shop** (⊠ *1440 New York Ave. NW*) on your right side, where you can stop to buy some Lincoln memorabilia, then continue north past Franklin Square on your right, and make a left on L Street NW, then a right on Vermont Avenue to the **Lincoln Restaurant** (⊠ *1110 Vermont Ave. NW*). This upscale diner has tables and floors embedded with more than a million Lincoln pennies. The menu includes the 16th president's favorite foods—oysters, gingerbread, and chicken fricassee.

After a rest, walk south on Vermont Avenue, and turn off onto 15th Street heading south. Walk three blocks, and turn right onto Pennsylvania Avenue; enter Lafayette Park to see **the White House.** Lincoln moved in on March 4, 1861, soon after his inauguration. His wife, Mary Todd Lincoln, extensively renovated and redecorated the "shabby" house when she moved in, running up some very high bills in the process.

"A government of the people, by the people, for the people . . ."

Leave Lafayette Park and the North Lawn of the White House to walk right (south) on 15th Street NW. Walk three blocks, with the grounds of the White House on your right, until you arrive at the **National Mall.** Go one block and enter the grounds of the Washington Monument. Walk up and over the hill toward the World War II Memorial, and continue along the Reflecting Pool toward the Greek temple–like **Lincoln Memorial,** at the other end. In this work, not dedicated until 1922, Lincoln sits immortalized. On the walls, Lincoln's Gettysburg Address is preserved in its entirety, facing his Second Inaugural Address.

If you arrive in the evening, you'll see the lights on the National Mall create some stunning vistas. Rest a while to reflect on Lincoln's achievements.

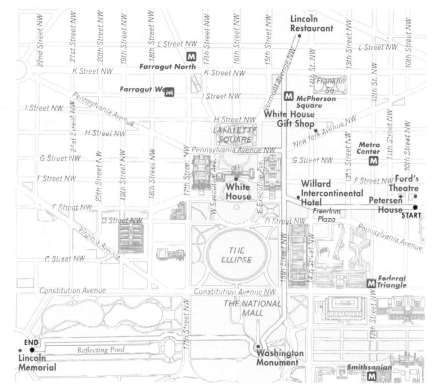

Highlights:	The fittingly majestic Lincoln Memorial is a must-see. It's a stunner even when measured against the many other grand structures on the Mall.
Where to Start:	Ford's Theatre, near Metro Center on the Metro's Orange, Blue, and Red lines; or Gallery Place–Chinatown, on the Green or Yellow line
Length:	3 miles; at least 2 hours, not counting additional time for lunch or a tour of Ford's Theatre
Where to Stop:	The Lincoln Memorial. From there either walk back east through the Mall or walk north on 23rd Street about ¾ of a mile to reach the Foggy Bottom Metro station.
Best Time to Go:	Schedule your visit around the timed-entry tickets needed for Ford's Theatre (final entry is 4:30), and try to end up at the Lincoln Memorial in the evening, when it's at its most impressive.
Worst Time to Go:	During a hot and humid summer afternoon
Lunch Stop:	Lincoln Restaurant

D.C.'S TOP FESTIVALS

For a look at yearly events, visit ⊕ *www. washington.org*, the website of the tourist bureau.

Winter

National Christmas Tree Lighting/Pageant of Peace (☎ *202/208–1631* ⊕ *www.the nationaltree.org* ⊗ *Dec.*). Each year in early December, the president lights the tree at dusk on the Ellipse, with concerts, a Yule log, and Nativity scene held later in the month.

Restaurant Week (⊕ *www.ramw.org/ restaurantweek* ⊗ *Jan. and Aug.*). More than 200 top restaurants offer lunch and dinner menus for around $20 and $35 respectively—often a steal.

Washington Auto Show (⊕ *www.washington autoshow.com* ⊗ *Late Jan.*). This yearly event showcases the latest offerings from the world of automobiles.

Spring

National Cherry Blossom Festival (☎ *877/44– BLOOM* ⊕ *www.nationalcherryblossom festival.org* ⊗ *Late Mar.–early Apr.*). D.C.'s most eye-catching annual festival opens with a Japanese lantern-lighting ceremony at the Tidal Basin.

Georgetown French Market (☎ *202/298– 9222* ⊗ *Late Apr.*). Shop, eat, wander, and enjoy strolling mimes and live musicians in one of D.C.'s most beautiful neighborhoods.

National Cathedral Flower Mart (☎ *202/365– 3222* ⊗ *Early May*). This 76-year-old free event on the Cathedral grounds features food, music, kids' activities and, of course, flowers.

Summer

Capital Pride Festival (☎ *202/719–5304* ⊕ *www.capitalpride.org* ⊗ *Early June*). This weeklong festival with parade celebrates gay, lesbian, bisexual, and transgendered citizens.

Washington Shakespeare Theatre Free for All (☎ *202/547–1122* ⊕ *www.shakespeare theatre.org* ⊗ *June*). For two weeks, the theater company mounts free nightly performances at the Sidney Harman Hall, near Chinatown. Tickets are required.

Smithsonian's Folklife Festival (☎ *202/633– 6440* ⊕ *www.folklife.si.edu* ⊗ *Late June– early July*). This two-week festival includes traditional dance and music, storytelling, and ethnic food.

Independence Day Celebration (☎ *202/619– 7222* ⊗ *July*). A parade fills Constitution Avenue, fireworks fly over Washington Monument and the NSO plays on the west lawn.

National Symphony Orchestra Labor Day Concert (☎ *202/416–8114* ⊕ *www.kennedy-center.org* ⊗ *Labor Day weekend*). This free concert is held on the grounds of the U.S. Capitol.

Fall

National Book Festival (☎ *202/707–1940* ⊗ *Late Sept.*). This two-day event attracts some of the world's top authors and poets to the National Mall, where visitors can get books signed.

Washington International Horse Show (☎ *202/525–3679* ⊕ *www.wihs.org* ⊗ *Late Oct.*). Held at Verizon Center, this annual show features jumping, dressage, barrel racing and more.

Veterans Day (☎ *703/607–8000 for Cemetery Visitor Center, 202/619–7222 for National Park Service* ⊗ *Nov. 11*). Services held at Arlington National Cemetery, Vietnam Veterans Memorial, and U.S. Navy Memorial with a wreath-laying at 11 am at the Tomb of the Unknowns.

NEIGHBORHOODS

Updated
by Robert
Michael Oliver

Washington is a city of vistas—a marriage of geometry and art. Unlike other large cities, it isn't dominated by skyscrapers. The result: The world's first planned capital is also one of its most beautiful.

HOW D.C. CAME TO BE

The city that invented American politicking, back scratching, and delicate diplomatic maneuvering is itself the result of a compromise. Tired of its nomadic existence after having set up shop in eight locations, Congress voted in 1785 to establish a permanent federal city. Northern lawmakers wanted the capital on the Delaware River; Southerners wanted it on the Potomac. A deal was struck when Virginia's Thomas Jefferson agreed to support the proposal that the federal government assume the war debts of the colonies if New York's Alexander Hamilton and other Northern legislators would agree to locate the capital on the banks of the Potomac.

George Washington himself selected the site of the capital, a diamond-shape, 100-square-mile plot not far from his estate at Mount Vernon, near the confluence of the Potomac and Anacostia rivers. To give the young city a head start, Washington included the already thriving tobacco ports of Alexandria, Virginia, and Georgetown, Maryland, in the District of Columbia. In 1791 Pierre-Charles L'Enfant, a French engineer who had fought in the Revolution, created the classic plan for the city.

It took the Civil War to energize the city first, attracting thousands of new residents and spurring a building boom that extended the capital in all directions. Streets were paved in the 1870s, and the first streetcars ran in the 1880s. The early 20th century witnessed the development of the city's monumental core: memorials to famous Americans such as Lincoln and Jefferson, along with the massive Federal Triangle, which includes the National Archives, the Internal Revenue Service, and the Department of Justice.

THE MALL
AMERICA'S TOWN GREEN

It could be said that the Mall—the heart of almost every visitor's trip to Washington—has influenced life in the U.S. more than any other expanse of lawn. The Mall is a picnicking park, a jogging path, and an outdoor stage for festivals and fireworks. People come here from around the globe to tour the illustrious Smithsonian museums, celebrate special events, or rally to make the world a better place.

The AIDS Memorial Quilt on the Mall in 1996.

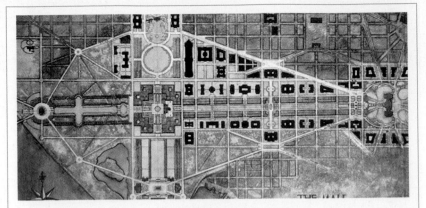

FROM TRASH HEAP TO TOURIST ATTRACTION:
A BRIEF HISTORY OF THE MALL

Even before becoming the birthplace of American political protest, the Mall was a hotly contested piece of real estate. More than a century of setbacks and debate resulted not in Pierre L'Enfant's vision of a house-lined boulevard, but rather the premier green space you see today.

In 1791, Pierre Charles L'Enfant designed Washington, D.C., with a mile-long Grand Avenue running west from the Congress building. According to his plan, the boulevard would be lined with homes for statesmen and open green spaces, including a central garden bordered by a dense grove of trees.

L'Enfant's grandiose plan took more than 100 years to become a reality. By 1850, the area we now know as the Mall had not become a park, but was used instead as a storage area for lumber, firewood, and trash. With President Fillmore's permission, a group of businessmen hired landscape designer Andrew Jackson Downing to plan a national park featuring natural-style gardening. Sadly, Downing was killed in 1852, and his plan was never fully implemented.

Despite this setback, progress continued. The first Smithsonian museum on the Mall, the National Museum (now the Arts and Industries Building), opened to the public in 1881, and after 35 years of construction, the Washington Monument was completed in 1884.

A victory for the Mall occurred in 1901, when the Senate Park Commission, or McMillan Commission, was created to redesign the Mall as the city's ceremonial center. The McMillan plan embraced L'Enfant's vision of formal, public spaces and civic art, but replaced his Grand Avenue with a 300-foot expanse of grass bordered by American elms. It also called for cultural and educational institutions to line the Mall. Finally, a modified version of L'Enfant's great open space would become a reality.

The National Park Service assumed management of the Mall in 1933. In the latter half of the twentieth century and into the twenty-first, new museums and monuments have opened on the Mall to create the public gathering place, tourist attraction, and tribute to our nation's heroes that we know today.

Above, McMillan Plan for the Mall, Washington, D.C., 1902.

HISTORIC RALLIES ON THE MALL

1894: Coxey's Army, a group of unemployed workers from Ohio, stage the first-ever protest march on Washington.

1939: Contralto Marian Anderson gives an Easter Sunday concert on the grounds of the Lincoln Memorial after the Daughters of the American Revolution bar her from performing at their headquarters.

1963: The Lincoln Memorial is the site of Martin Luther King Jr.'s inspirational I Have a Dream speech.

1971: The Vietnam Veterans Against the War camp out on the Mall to persuade Congress to end military actions in Southeast Asia.

1972: The first Earth Day is celebrated on April 22.

1987: The AIDS Memorial Quilt is displayed for the first time in its entirety. It returns to the Mall in 1988, 1989, 1992, and 1996.

1995: Nearly 400,000 African-American men fill the Mall, from the Capitol to the Washington Monument, during the Million Man March.

2009: The inauguration of President Barack Obama brings a record two million onlookers to the Mall.

Top, Matin Luther King Jr. delivers his I Have a Dream speech.

Center, Vietnam War Veterans protest.

Bottom, Million Man March.

WHAT ABOUT THE MONUMENTS?

Visitors often confuse the Mall with the similarly named National Mall. The Mall is the expanse of lawn between 3rd and 14th Streets, while the National Mall is the national park that spans from the Capitol to the Potomac, including the Mall, the monuments, and the Tidal Basin. To reach the monuments, head west from the Mall or south from the White House and be prepared for a long walk. To visit all the monuments in one day requires marathon-level stamina and good walking shoes. You're better off choosing your top priorities. ⇨ *For more about D.C.'s monuments and memorials, see Chapter 4.*

TOP 15 THINGS
TO DO ON THE MALL

1. Ride the old-fashioned carousel in front of the Smithsonian Castle.

2. Watch the fireworks on the Fourth of July.

3. See the original *Spirit of St. Louis,* and then learn how things fly at the National Air and Space Museum.

4. Gross out your friends at the Natural History Museum's Insect Zoo.

5. Gawk at Dorothy's ruby slippers, Julia Child's kitchen, Abraham Lincoln's top hat, and Lewis and Clark's compass at the American History Museum.

6. Twirl around the ice skating rink in the National Gallery of Art's sculpture garden.

7. View astonishing wooden masks at the Museum of African Art.

8. Taste North, South, and Central American dishes at the National Museum of the American Indian's Mitsitam Café.

9. Exercise your First Amendment rights by joining a rally or protest.

10. Peek at the many-armed and elephant-headed statues of Hindu gods at the Sackler Gallery.

11. Pose with sculptures by Auguste Rodin and Henry Moore at the Hirshhorn Sculpture Garden.

12. Learn how you make money—literally—at the Bureau of Engraving and Printing.

13. Follow the lives of the people who lived and died in Nazi Germany at the Holocaust Memorial Museum.

14. Eat, drink, watch, listen, and learn at an outdoor cultural festival.

15. Picnic and people-watch on the lawn after a hard day of sightseeing.

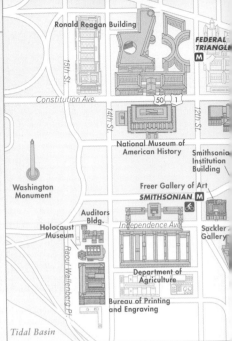

VISITING THE MUSEUMS ON THE MALL

MAKE THE MOST OF YOUR TIME

With 12 museums spread out along 11 city blocks, you can't expect to see everything in one day. Few people have the stamina for more than half a day of museum- or gallery-hopping at a time; children definitely don't. To avoid mental and physical exhaustion, try to devote at least two days to the Mall and use these itineraries (and our listings in Chapter 3) to make the best use of your time.

Historical Appeal: For a day devoted to history and culture, start with the **Holocaust Museum,** grabbing lunch at its excellent cafeteria. After refueling, the next stop is the **American History Museum.** Or, cross the length of the Mall to visit the **Museum of the American Indian** instead.

Art Start: To fill a day with paintings and sculptures, begin at the **National Gallery of Art.** Enjoy the museum's sculptures while you dine in the garden's outdoor café. You'll find a second sculpture garden directly across the Mall at the **Hirshhorn.** If you like the avant-garde, visit the Hirshhorn's indoor galleries; for a cosmopolitan collection of Asian and African art and artifacts, head instead to the **Sackler Gallery** and **Museum of African Art.**

Taking the Kids: The most kid-friendly museum of them all, the **National Air and Space Museum** is a must-see for the young and young-at-heart. There's only fast food in the museum, but the **Museum of the American Indian** next door has healthier options. If your young bunch can handle two museums in a day, cross the lawn to the **Natural History Museum.** This itinerary works well for science buffs, too.

THE BEST IN A DAY

Got one day and want to see the best of the Smithsonian? Start at the **Air and Space Museum,** then skip to the side-by-side **Natural History** and **American History Museums.** Picnic on the Mall or hit the museum cafeterias.

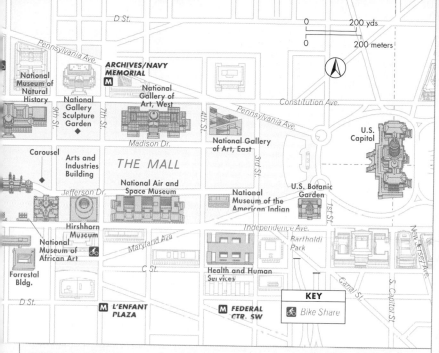

KEY

M L'ENFANT PLAZA

M FEDERAL CTR. SW

🚲 Bike Share

NOT ANOTHER HOT DOG! A Survival Guide to Eating Well on the Mall

Even locals wonder where to grab a decent bite to eat when touring the Smithsonian Museums. Hot dogs, soft pretzels, and ice cream from a cart don't make for a nutritious lunch. On a weekday, the streets north of Constitution Avenue offer easy-to-find lunch spots, but virtually all are closed on weekends.

Here are some places for better dining by the Mall, though several require a few blocks' walk.

On the Fly food carts offer eco-friendly, often organic snacks. Find one by the Sackler Gallery.

Museum of the American Indian: The Mitsitam Café—the name means "let's eat" in the language of the Delaware and Piscataway people—is one of the best museum cafeterias on the Mall. Food stations serve native-inspired sandwiches, entrees, soups, and desserts from five regions of the western hemisphere.

Pavilion Café: Located in the **National Gallery's Sculpture Garden,** this eatery offers indoor and outdoor seating with views of the artwork and fountain/ice rink outside. The menu includes salads, sandwiches, and pizzas. You'll also find more food options inside the National Gallery.

Pennsylvania Avenue SE: If lunchtime finds you on the east end of the Mall, head past the Capitol to Pennsylvania Avenue SE. Between Second and Fourth Streets, you'll find plenty of pubs, cafés, and sandwich shops. It's a bit of a hike, but well worth the shoe leather.

National Museum of Natural History: Three high-quality restaurants focus on healthy, seasonal food, drinks, and desserts.

Ronald Reagan Building and International Trade Center: The food court here is another option, but is closed on Sundays during the winter.

ANNUAL EVENTS

The Mall's spacious lawn is ideal for all kinds of outdoor festivals. These annual events are local favorites and definitely worth a stop if you're in town while they're happening.

St. Patrick's Day Parade

WINTER

Ice Skating: Whirl and twirl at the outdoor ice rink in the National Gallery of Art's Sculpture Garden. *Mid-November through mid-March*

St. Patrick's Day Parade: Dancers, bands, and bagpipes celebrate all things Irish along Constitution Avenue. *Mid-March*

SPRING

National Cherry Blossom Festival: When the cherry trees burst into bloom, you know that spring has arrived. Fly a kite, watch a parade, and learn about Japanese culture in a setting sprinkled with pink and white flowers. *Late March through early April*

Cherry Blossom Festival

SUMMER

Smithsonian Folklife Festival: Performers, cooks, farmers, and craftsmen demonstrate cultural traditions from around the world. *Around July 4*

Independence Day: What better place to celebrate the birth of our nation than in the capital city? Enjoy concerts and parades on the Mall, then watch the fireworks explode over the Washington Monument. *July 4*

Smithsonian Folklife Festival

Screen on the Green: Film favorites are shown on a gigantic movie screen on Monday nights. Bring a blanket and picnic dinner to better enjoy the warm summer evenings. *Mid-July through mid-August*

FALL

Black Family Reunion: D.C. celebrates African-American family values. Pavilions showcase businesses owned by African-Americans and events and performances feature black entertainers, celebrities, and experts. *September*

Independence Day Reenactment

National Book Festival: Meet your favorite author in person at the Library of Congress' annual literary festival. Over 70 writers and illustrators participate in readings, live interviews, and events for kids. *September*

Marine Corps Marathon: The "Marathon of the Monuments" starts in Virginia but winds its way around the entire National Mall. It's as fun to cheer as it is to run. *Late October*

Marine Corps Marathon

PLANNING YOUR VISIT

National Cherry Blossom Festival Parade

KEEP IN MIND

■ All of the museums on the Mall are free to the public.

■ Since September 11, 2001 security has increased, and visitors will need to go through screenings and bag checks, which create long lines during peak tourist season.

■ Two museums require timed-entry passes: the Holocaust Museum from March through August, and the Bureau of Printing and Engraving. If you've got a jam-packed day planned, it's best to get your tickets early in the morning or in advance.

GETTING HERE AND GETTING AROUND

Metro Travel: You can access the Mall from several Metro stations. On the Blue and Orange lines, the Federal Triangle stop is convenient to the Natural History and American History museums, and the Smithsonian stop is close to the Holocaust Memorial Museum and Sackler Gallery. On the Yellow and Green lines, Archives/Navy Memorial takes you to the National Gallery of Art. The L'Enfant Plaza stop, accessible from the Blue, Orange, Yellow, and Green lines, is the best exit for the Hirshhorn and Air and Space Museum.

Bus Travel: Walking from the Holocaust Memorial Museum to the National Gallery of Art is quite a trek. Many visitors take advantage of the Mall Express bus run by ANC Tours/Martz Gray Line (⊕ www.anctours.com/MallExpress.php), which run March through September, 9 to 6:30 and October through February, 9 to 4:30.

Car Travel: Parking is hard to find along the Mall. You can find private parking garages north of the Mall in the Downtown area, where you'll have to pay to leave your car. If you're willing to walk, limited free parking is available on Ohio Drive SW near the Jefferson Memorial and East Potomac Park.

HELP, THERE'S A PROTEST ON THE MALL!

Since the 1890s, protesters have gathered on the Mall to make their opinions known. If you're not in a rallying mood, you don't have to let First Amendment activities prevent you from visiting the Smithsonian museums or enjoying a visit to the Mall.

■ **Use the back door:** All of the Smithsonian museums have entrances on Constitution or Independence Avenues, which do not border the Mall's lawn. Use these doors to gain admission without crossing the Mall itself.

■ **Know you're protected:** The Mall is a national park, just like Yosemite or Yellowstone. The National Park Service has a responsibility to visitors to make sure they can safely view park attractions. To this end, demonstrators are often required to keep main streets open.

■ **Avoid the crowds:** Even the biggest rallies don't cover the entire National Mall. If the crowd is by the Capitol, head west to visit the Lincoln Memorial. If protestors are gathered around the Washington Monument, visit the Jefferson Memorial on the opposite side of the Tidal Basin. There's plenty to see.

THE WHITE HOUSE AREA
AND FOGGY BOTTOM

Sightseeing
★★★★★
Dining
★★★
Lodging
★★
Shopping
★
Nightlife
★★

Foggy Bottom includes some of D.C.'s most iconic attractions, the top being the White House, the home of every U.S. president but George Washington. Visitors may have a tough time deciding what to see first: the numerous war memorials on the National Mall, the Tidal Basin, or some of Washington's better, if smaller, museums. Adding to the variety, you will find the Kennedy Center along the Potomac River and George Washington University's campus. Surprisingly, the area has a strong residential character as well, and is home to some of D.C.'s oldest houses.

WHITE HOUSE AREA WALK

Seeing everything this neighborhood has to offer could easily occupy the greater part of a day, so prioritize and be prepared to walk. Beginning at the White House, visitors can explore the neighborhood, either by checking out the monuments on the Mall or by heading west toward the government buildings. When the sun is shining, the monuments are particularly enticing, whereas tours of some of the government buildings are available in almost any weather. Many sites require advance reservations and few are kid-friendly, but history and art buffs should not miss these hidden gems.

Whether you choose to focus on monuments or government buildings, the **John F. Kennedy Center for the Performing Arts** offers spectacular evening performances. Within this thriving cultural center and memorial to the late president, six different theaters present music, dance, opera, and dramatic arts from around the country and the world. If you arrive

A statue of Andrew Jackson during the Battle of New Orleans presides over Lafayette Square

at the Kennedy Center by 6 pm, you can catch one of the free performances offered daily on its Millennium Stage.

CORE WHITE HOUSE AREA

Arriving at either the Farragut West or McPherson Square Metro stop, take a short walk to the trees and flower beds of **Lafayette Square**, an intimate oasis amid the bustle of Downtown Washington. The park was named for the Marquis de Lafayette, the young French nobleman who came to America to fight in the Revolution. His **statue** is in the southeast corner of the park, not far from the large **statue of Andrew Jackson**, the oldest equestrian statue in D.C.

Every president since Madison has visited nearby **St. John's Episcopal Church** constructed in 1816. The **Decatur House**, just west of the square, was the first private residence on Lafayette Square, and now houses the National Center for White House History and a museum shop. The only existing slave quarters in Washington remain on display in the two-story dependency in the rear of the property.

Looking south through the park's gardens, the **White House** beckons. White House tours should be scheduled well in advance. For up-to-date information on tours, visit the National Park Service website (⊕ *nps. gov/whho/planyourvisit/white-house-tours.htm*) or stop at the **White House Visitor Center,** in the Department of Commerce building on Pennsylvania Avenue between 14th and 15th streets NW.

Two imposing buildings flank the White House: the **Treasury Building** to the east and the Eisenhower Executive Office Building to the west. Robert Mills, the architect responsible for the Washington Monument and the Patent Office (now the Smithsonian American Art Museum),

GETTING ORIENTED

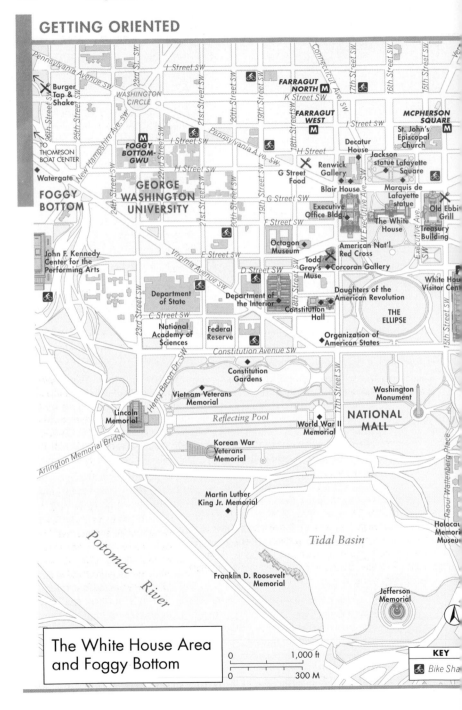

The White House Area and Foggy Bottom

| 0 | 1,000 ft |
| 0 | 300 M |

KEY

Bike Sha

GREAT EXPERIENCES IN THE WHITE HOUSE AREA

Corcoran Gallery of Art: The great 19th-century American painters were inspired by the sublime majesty of the American West. See the most-definitive works—Albert Bierstadt's *Mount Corcoran* and Frederick Church's *Niagara*.

Department of State Diplomatic Reception Rooms: One of D.C.'s best-kept secrets, this suite of rooms is filled with museum-quality art and historical treasures inspired by the country's founding years. You must reserve well in advance.

John F. Kennedy Center for the Performing Arts: See a free performance by anyone from the Joffrey Ballet to the National Symphony Orchestra here on the Millennium Stage, daily at 6 pm.

Thompson's Boat Center: Take in Washington's marble monuments, lush Roosevelt Island, and the Virginia coastline with a canoe ride down the Potomac.

Touring the White House: Check the White House website for updates on White House tours.

GETTING HERE

The White House can be reached by the Red Line's Farragut North stop or the Blue and Orange lines' McPherson Square and Farragut West stops. Foggy Bottom has its own Metro stop, also on the Blue and Orange lines. A free shuttle runs from the station to the Kennedy Center. Many of the other attractions are a considerable distance from the nearest subway stop. If you don't relish long walks or if time is limited, check the map to see if you need to make alternate travel arrangements to visit specific sights.

PLANNING YOUR TIME

Touring the area around the White House could easily take a day or even two. If you enjoy history, you may be most interested in the buildings in the Lafayette Square Historic District, **DAR Museum**, and **State Department**. If it's art you crave, head to the **Corcoran** galleries instead. Save the **Kennedy Center** for the evening.

QUICK BITES

Burger Tap & Shake and District Commons. This favorite serves burgers, hand-cut fries, and craft beers. For full-service dining, try its sister spot, District Commons, next door. ✉ 2200 Pennsylvania Ave. NW, Foggy Bottom ☎ 202/587-6258 ⊕ www.burgertapshake.com.

G Street Food. This popular spot serves breakfast and lunch options inspired by street food from across the globe. ✉ 1706 G St. NW, White House area ☎ 202/408–7474 ⊕ www.gstreetfood.com ⊙ Closed weekends.

Todd Gray's Muse at the Corcoran. This casual bistro on the museums' first floor serves coffee and pastries, locally sourced salads, and sandwiches. ✉ 500 17th St. NW, White House area ☎ 202/639–1786 ⊕ www.toddgraysmuse. com ⊙ Closed Mon. and Tues. No dinner.

designed Treasury's Greek Revival architecture and the grand colonnade that stretches down 15th Street. The building's southern facade has a **statue of Alexander Hamilton**, the department's first secretary. The granite edifice of the Eisenhower Building looks like a wedding cake styled after the Louvre.

CITY VIEW

For a different view of the city, don't miss the view from the roof of the Kennedy Center. There's also a café and restaurant there.

Built as a headquarters of the State, War, and Navy departments, it now houses offices for the vice president and other members of the executive branch. The building was the site of both the first presidential press conference in 1950 and the first televised press conference five years later.

As you go past the Executive Office Building, note the green canopy marking the entrance to **Blair House**, built in 1824. Known as "The President's Guest House," visiting heads of state use this residence as their temporary home. During the restoration of the White House, President Truman and his family stayed here, and it's believed that he fired General MacArthur while in the Lee Dining Room. Farther along Pennsylvania Avenue, the **Renwick Gallery**, the third oldest Smithsonian building and an extension of the American Art Museum, exhibits American crafts and decorative arts.

Seventeenth Street leads to the recently renamed Corcoran Contemporary, National Gallery of Art. The Beaux Arts building, which is in transition after being acquired by the National Gallery, will now focus mainly on contemporary works. One block west, at 18th Street, the **Octagon Museum** exhibits portray life in the city at the birth of the nation's new capital.

You could detour here to the left, cut across the Ellipse and see the White House and its perfect south lawn and vegetable garden from the south side. On the southern end stand the **Boy Scouts Memorial** and a weather-beaten **gatehouse**, once on Capitol Hill. By the southeast corner of the White House lawn, the **Tecumseh Sherman Monument** depicts the Civil War general mounted on his steed, surrounded by four sentries.

Down 17th Street, you can step into the **Daughters of the American Revolution (DAR)** headquarters. A tour lets you peek into a few of the 31 period rooms—each decorated in a style unique to one state and one time period—and the Beaux Arts auditorium now used as a genealogy library. The museum on the first floor hosts changing exhibitions.

Continuing south on 17th Street, you will come to the headquarters of the **Organization of American States**, which is made up of nations from North, South, and Central America. A patio adorned with a pre-Columbian-style fountain and lush tropical plants is a good place to rest when Washington's summer heat is at its most oppressive.

A MONUMENTAL STROLL
To see some of Washington's famous monuments, carefully cross Constitution Avenue to reach the tranquility of the **National Mall**, home of D.C.'s Monumental Core. Heading east, you can't miss the **Washington**

Punctuating the skyline like an exclamation point, the Washington Monument can be seen from 30 miles away.

Monument. The huge obelisk built in memory of George Washington dominates the skyline. The monument's pyramid-shape top and supporting structure has been under repair due to a 5.8-magnitude earthquake in 2011 and remains closed but should reopen soon.

To the west, stop at the **World War II Memorial** and continue along the **Reflecting Pool,** with the imposing **Lincoln Memorial** dominating the view ahead of you. On either side are the **Korean War** and **Vietnam Veterans memorials** and **Constitution Gardens.** If you can, make time to visit the **Tidal Basin,** home to the **Roosevelt** and **Jefferson** memorials, and the city's newest memorial, honoring **Martin Luther King Jr.** Each spring, usually between late March and early April, the cherry trees around the Tidal Basin burst into pink-and-white blooms. The city celebrates the beauty of this gift from Japan with a two-week **Cherry Blossom Festival.**

GOVERNMENT BUILDINGS

If you choose to forgo the monuments, take Constitution Avenue to the west. The headquarters of many government departments and national organizations reside along the blocks between E Street and Constitution Avenue west of the Ellipse. Several offer tours or exhibits for the public, but always check whether advance reservations are required, and bring photo ID.

Virginia Avenue takes you off Constitution Avenue and up past the **Department of the Interior,** which contains a museum with exhibits based on the work of its branches, such as the Bureau of Land Management, the National Park Service, and the U.S. Geological Survey. Reservations are required for the Department of the Interior's murals tour, depicting American history and landscapes. Created during the Great Depression,

DID YOU KNOW?

The best views of the cherry blossoms along the Tidal Basin are from the water. You can rent a paddleboat for a romantic drift or some family fun.

President Franklin D. Roosevelt's New Deal funded these murals. Turn left on C Street to the **Federal Reserve Building,** which displays special art exhibitions that are only worth visiting if you're fascinated with the subject or want to see the inside of the Fed; reserve in advance. Set back from the Fed, you'll find the **National Academy of Sciences.** It offers two galleries of science-related art. Robert Berks's sculpture of Albert Einstein outside the building has broader appeal and is a shady resting spot; the creator of the theory of relativity looks—dare we say?—cuddly.

You must reserve a tour at the **State Department** three months in advance, but it's worth the effort. A docent takes you to the top floor's **Department of State's Diplomatic Reception Rooms**—usually reserved for heads of state and special honorees. The great halls and gathering spaces are furnished with American decorative arts and antiques from the 18th and 19th centuries. These valuable furnishings are not museum pieces, but are actually used for entertaining dignitaries. Away from the White House and federal buildings, northern Foggy Bottom is the home of **George Washington University.** The university has no separate campus, but occupies many of the modern buildings and 19th-century houses between 19th and 24th streets south of Pennsylvania Avenue.

Near the Kennedy Center along the water, the **Watergate** made history on the night of June 17, 1972, but the apartment-office complex doesn't look so scandalous in person. Famous—and infamous—residents have included Attorney General John Mitchell and presidential secretary Rose Mary Woods of Nixon White House fame, as well as such D.C. insiders as Jacob Javits, Ruth Bader Ginsberg, Bob and Elizabeth Dole, Monica Lewinsky, and Condoleezza Rice.

If looking at the Potomac makes you yearn to get out on the water, the **Thompson's Boat Center** at the end of Virginia Avenue rents canoes, sailboats, and kayaks in the warmer months. Bike rentals are also available.

WHITE HOUSE AREA WITH KIDS

After touring the **White House,** you can take an additional look at White House life at the **White House Visitor Center,** where videos and photos capture first families. Unlike the actual White House, kids can roam around here and sit on the furniture.

At the **Daughters of the American Revolution Museum** kids ages five to seven can discover what life was like as a colonial child when they take part in the twice-monthly Colonial Adventure program.

Kids love the waterfalls, fountain jets, and interacting with statues at the Franklin D. Roosevelt Memorial on the west side of the Tidal Basin.

In summer, give kids a break from touring the monuments with an afternoon boat ride on the **Tidal Basin.** If you're feeling a bit more intrepid, you can rent canoes from **Thompson's Boat Center** and paddle along the Potomac.

CAPITOL HILL AND NORTHEAST D.C.

Sightseeing
★★★★
Dining
★★★
Lodging
★★★
Shopping
★★★
Nightlife
★★★★

The people who live and work on "the Hill" do so in the shadow of the edifice that lends the neighborhood its name: the gleaming white Capitol. This is where political deals and decisions are made. Beyond these grand buildings lies a vibrant and diverse group of neighborhoods with charming residential blocks lined with Victorian row houses and a fine assortment of restaurants and bars where senators, members of Congress, and lobbyists come to unwind or to continue their deal making. D.C.'s favorite market and newest sporting attraction are also here. A little farther afield, the rapidly developing H Street Corridor to the north and east offers hip and edgy shopping, dining, and nightlife.

CAPITOL HILL WALK

Capitol Hill's exact boundaries are changing. Most say the Hill is bordered to the west, north, and south by the Capitol, H Street NE, and I Street SE, respectively. Thanks to a bounty of successful building projects, the trendy neighborhood now extends east to the Anacostia River, or so say the real estate speculators. Simultaneously, Capitol Hill's historic-preservation movement has restored dozens of 19th-century houses, renewing a city that in recent decades has only known constant boom.

There's a lot to see here, but you can explore the streets in a couple of hours—if you're able to resist stopping at one of the many watering holes that dot the neighborhoods. A good place to start is **Union Station,** easily accessible on the Metro Red Line. The Beaux Arts station, modeled after a Roman bath, dominates the northwest corner of Capitol Hill. Although currently in restoration following the 2011 earthquake, the city's main train station still offers a colorful marketplace, with many shops and restaurants. In the station's front plaza sits a steely-eyed Christopher Columbus at the base of a column on the **Columbus Memorial Fountain,** designed by Lorado Taft.

Next door, the **National Postal Museum** will delight philatelists. The Smithsonian takes a playful approach to stamp collecting and the history of the U.S. Postal Service with its interactive exhibits that inhabit the lower level of the historic City Post Office Building. On the other side of Union Station, the atrium of the **Thurgood Marshall Federal Judiciary Building** is worth a quick peek. Designed by architect Edward Larabee Barnes, the enclosed garden sports bamboo five stories tall.

Following Delaware Avenue south, you come right up to the Capitol, the point from which the city is divided into quadrants: northwest, southwest, northeast, and southeast. North Capitol Street, which runs north from the Capitol, separates northeast from northwest; East Capitol Street separates northeast and southeast; South Capitol Street separates southwest and southeast; and the Mall (Independence Avenue on the south and Constitution Avenue on the north) separates northwest from southwest.

The massive **U.S. Capitol** sits majestically in a 58-acre park at the east end of the Mall, and is the foremost reason to visit Capitol Hill. The free tour (⊕ *tours.visitthecapitol.gov*) takes you through the impressive rotunda, Statuary Hall, and Old Senate Chamber. To see your legislators at work, however, you need to arrange in advance for free gallery passes. Contact your senator or representative's office. If you're a visitor from outside the United States, contact your embassy. The **Capitol Visitor Center,** located underneath the Capitol, provides guided tours, rotating exhibits, and a 13-minute orientation film. Enter on the east side of the building. The imposing buildings to the north and south of the Capitol house the offices of senators (north) and representatives (south).

Originally designed by Frederick Law Olmstead, the landscape architect responsible for Central Park in New York, the grounds around the Capitol provide visitors with seasonal displays of thousands of flowers in circular patterns. In front of the Capitol, three monuments flank a reflecting pool. In the center the **Ulysses S. Grant Memorial** is one of the largest sculpture groups in the city. To the south stands the **James A. Garfield Monument,** and to the north a **Peace Monument** commemorating sailors who died in the Civil War. Rest and reflect at the northwest corner of the shaded grounds in a hexagonal redbrick structure called **the Summerhouse.** Across Constitution Avenue a monolithic carillon forms the **Robert A. Taft Memorial,** dedicated to the longtime Republican senator and son of the 27th president.

Across from the Garfield Memorial, the **United States Botanic Garden** is the oldest botanic garden in North America. After touring the conservatory, be sure to wander through the rose, butterfly, water, and regional gardens of the **National Garden.** Another lovely landmark, the **Bartholdi Fountain,** is just in front of the Botanic Garden. The lovely assemblage

GETTING ORIENTED

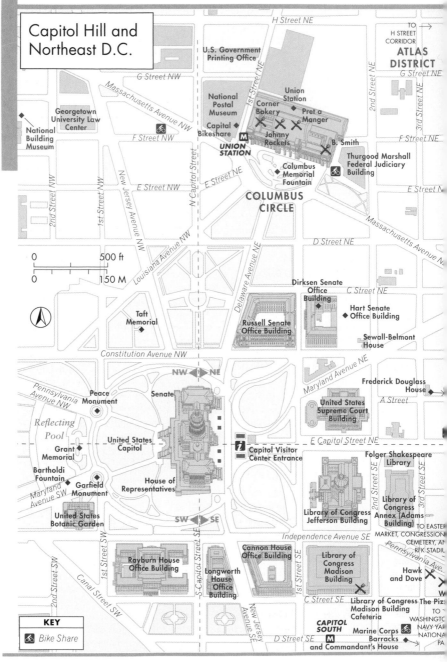

Capitol Hill and Northeast D.C.

H Street NE

TO →
H STREET
CORRIDOR

**ATLAS
DISTRICT**

U.S. Government
Printing Office

G Street NW

G Street NE

Massachusetts Avenue NW

National
Postal
Museum

Union
Station

Corner
Bakery

Pret a
Manger

Georgetown
University Law
Center

Capital
Bikeshare

2nd Street NE

3rd Street NE

National
Building
Museum

F Street NW

Johnny
Rockets

B. Smith

F Street NE

**UNION
STATION**

New Jersey Avenue NW

1st Street NE

E Street NW

N Capitol Street

E Street NE

Columbus
Memorial
Fountain

Thurgood Marshall
Federal Judiciary
Building

E Street N

**COLUMBUS
CIRCLE**

2nd Street NW

1st Street NW

Massachusetts Avenue N

D Street NE

0   500 ft

0   150 M

Louisiana Avenue NW

Delaware Avenue NE

Dirksen Senate
Office
Building

C Street NE

Hart Senate
Office Building

Taft
Memorial

Russell Senate
Office Building

Sewall-Belmont
House

Constitution Avenue NW

Maryland Avenue NE

Frederick Douglass
House

NW   NE

Pennsylvania
Avenue NW

Peace
Monument

Senate

United States
Supreme Court
Building

A Street

*Reflecting
Pool*

United States
Capitol

Capitol Visitor
Center Entrance

E Capitol Street NE

Grant
Memorial

Folger Shakespeare
Library

Bartholdi
Fountain

Maryland
Avenue SW

Garfield
Monument

House of
Representatives

Library of Congress
Jefferson Building

2nd Street SE

3rd Street SE

Library of
Congress
Annex (Adams
Building)

United States
Botanic Garden

SW   SE

TO EASTER
MARKET, CONGRESSION
CEMETERY, AN
RFK STADIL

Independence Avenue SE

2nd Street SW

1st Street SW

S Capitol Street SE

Rayburn House
Office Building

Cannon House
Office Building

Library of
Congress
Madison
Building

Pennsylvania Ave.

Hawk
and Dove

Canal Street SW

Longworth
House
Office
Building

New Jersey
Avenue SE

C Street SE

Library of Congress The Piz
Madison Building
Cafeteria

TO
WASHINGTO
NAVY YAR
NATIONA
PA

**CAPITOL
SOUTH**

Marine Corps
Barracks
and Commandant's House

W

D Street SE

KEY

Bike Share

GREAT EXPERIENCES ON CAPITOL HILL AND NORTHEAST D.C.

Barracks Row: Founded in 1801, it's one of the oldest neighborhoods in D.C. and was central to the defense of the city during the War of 1812 and Civil War. The commercial corridor boasts bars, shops, restaurants, and access to two landmarks, the Navy Yard and Washington Nationals Stadium.

The Capitol: See where democracy is put into action. Start your tour at the Visitors Center, then walk among marble American heroes and gape at the soaring Rotunda.

Eastern Market: One of D.C.'s most beloved weekend destinations is the place to pick up fresh produce, baked goods, and locally made crafts.

The Library of Congress: Contemplate George Washington's drafts of the Constitution and other historic documents, the lavishly sculpted Great Hall, and the splendor of the gilded Main Reading Room.

The Supreme Court: Round out your firsthand look at the three branches of government by watching the justices hear precedent-setting arguments.

United States Botanic Garden: Wrinkle your nose at the corpse flower, explore the jungle, gawk at the orchids, or stroll the paths of the new National Garden.

GETTING HERE

From the Red Line's Union Station, you can walk to most destinations on Capitol Hill. From the Blue and Orange lines, the Capitol South stop is close to the Capitol and Library of Congress, and the Eastern Market stop leads to the market and the Marine Corps Barracks. Bus nos. 31, 32, 36, and Circulator buses run from Friendship Heights through Georgetown and Downtown to Independence Avenue, the Capitol, and Eastern Market. A streetcar links Union Station with H Street's nightlife. Limited street parking is available.

PLANNING YOUR TIME

Touring Capitol Hill should take you about three hours, allowing for about an hour each at the Capitol, the **Botanic Garden**, and the **Library of Congress**.

If you want to see **Congress** in session, contact your legislator (or, if you are visiting from abroad, your country's embassy) in advance, and bear in mind that the House and the Senate are usually not in session in August.

Supreme Court cases are usually heard October through April, Monday through Wednesday, two weeks out of each month.

QUICK BITES

Library of Congress's Madison Building Cafeteria. Steps from the Capitol, this newly remodeled space on the sixth floor has a varied menu and floor-to-ceiling windows offering panoramic views of Washington. ⊠ *Madison Building, Library of Congress, Independence Ave. SE, between 1st and 2nd sts., Capitol Hill* ☎ *202/707–8300* ⊕ *www.loc.gov* ⊙ *Closed weekends.*

We, the Pizza. Top Chef's Spike Mendelsohn flips specialty pies and slices with creative ingredients. Eat in or take out. ⊠ *305 Pennsylvania Ave. SE, Capitol Hill* ☎ *202/544–4008* ⊕ *www.wethepizza.com* ⊙ *Closed Sun.*

Bustling Union Station is a great place to grab a bite and people-watch.

of aquatic monsters, sea nymphs, tritons, and lighted globes, all representing the elements of water and light, was created by Frederic-Auguste Bartholdi, sculptor of the Statue of Liberty.

Continue east on Independence Avenue, then north on 1st Street, where the Jefferson Building of the Library of Congress and the U.S. Supreme Court sit side by side. The **Library of Congress** has so many books, recordings, maps, manuscripts, and photographs that it actually takes three buildings to house it all. The **Jefferson Building** is the only part open to the public, and free tours highlight the **Great Hall,** Jefferson's book collection, the **Minerva Mosaic,** and an actual Gutenberg Bible, dating from around 1455. It is one of only three completed copies in existence. Peek into the **Main Reading Room,** and wander through changing exhibitions related to the library's holdings. The **Supreme Court Building** contains two floors of worthwhile exhibits, lectures, a film starring Chief Justice John Roberts, a gift shop, and a small cafeteria.

Behind the Library of Congress, the **Folger Shakespeare Library** holds an enormous collection of works by and about Shakespeare and his times, as well as a reproduced 16th-century theater and gallery that are open to visitors. North of the Folger on 2nd Street, the **Sewall-Belmont House** was the headquarters of the historic National Woman's Party and contains exhibits and artifacts from the suffrage and women's rights movements. Tours are by appointment only.

SOUTH AND EAST OF THE CAPITOL
Away from the Capitol, you'll find some enticing attractions, including one of D.C.'s oldest communities and a thriving market. This area is well served by the Metro, though you can get around on foot.

East of 2nd Street, the neighborhood changes dramatically from large-scale government buildings to 19th-century town houses. Among them is the first Washington home of the abolitionist and writer **Frederick Douglass,** at 1411 W St. SE, which you can visit by appointment.

Follow Pennsylvania Avenue south between 2nd and 4th streets to the main commercial thoroughfare. Restaurants, bars, and coffee shops frequented by those who live and work on the Hill line these blocks. Reaching Seward Square, take C Street one block to **Eastern Market** on the corner of 7th Street; it has been a feature of D.C. life since 1873. The main building, gutted by fire in 2007, houses an array of farmers, flower vendors, and other merchants who sell their fresh produce and crafts to locals and tourists alike. Open all week, the market really buzzes on weekends. Seventh Street takes you back to Pennsylvania Avenue, the Eastern Market Metro station, and to the historic **Barracks Row** neighborhood. Built along 8th Street after 1798, Barracks Row was the first commercial center in Washington, D.C. Rebuilt in 1901, this neighborhood housed a diverse population of newly arrived immigrants even before the Civil War. On the east side of the street visitors will find the barracks and, opposite, a variety of shops and restaurants. The **Marine Corps Barracks and Commandant's House,** the nation's oldest continuously active marine installation, is the home of the U.S. Marine Band. On Friday evenings May through August the **Marine Band** (the "President's Own") and the **Drum and Bugle Corps** (the "Commandant's Own") present hour-long ceremonies on the parade deck. You can reserve a seat at ⊕ *www.marines.mil,* but there is usually plenty of room.

Right at the end of 8th Street, on the bank of the Anacostia River, you will find the 115-acre **Washington Navy Yard,** the U.S. Navy's oldest outpost onshore. The **Navy Museum and Art Gallery** chronicles the history of the U.S. Navy and exhibits Navy-related paintings, sketches, and drawings. The Navy Yard visitor's entrance is at 11th and O streets SE. Inside the gates, large-scale weaponry dates back to when this complex was chiefly a Naval Gun Factory. From the Navy Yard, walk outside the gate to see the decommissioned Navy destroyer USS *Barry,* which is open for touring.

The waterfront development along the Anacostia River is shaping up to be a red-hot destination for residents and visitors alike. The retailers, eateries, bars, and loft apartments straddle parts of the new Anacostia Riverwalk Trail, a scenic boardwalk for pedestrians and cyclists. The Bluejacket Brewery, a farmers' market, and the Trapeze School of DC, add to the festive atmosphere. Eventually, this trail will stretch from the Maine Avenue Fish Market to Nationals Park, RFK Stadium, and the National Arboretum.

From the Navy Yard, walk west on the boardwalk to the new **Nationals Park,** home of the Washington Nationals. The park offers interactive tours on nongame days and throughout the off-season. From here it's just a short walk to the Navy Yard Metro station.

A 24-foot-high canopy walk at the U.S. Botanic Garden offers views of the lush jungle canopy.

NORTHEAST D.C.

On the outskirts of Capitol Hill gritty neighborhoods are experiencing gentrification at different rates. Although there are sights worth exploring, the long walk from the Capitol makes driving or taking public transportation preferable—such as the new streetcar link that runs eastward from Union Station along H Street.

The **H Street Corridor,** also known as the **Atlas District,** after the Atlas Performing Arts Center, is a diverse, edgy, and evolving stretch of nightlife between 3rd and 14th streets NE. A rapidly gentrifying neighborhood, restaurants and bars open monthly, and a younger crowd moves in with each new venue. You will find a mix of the original, the hip, and the unexpected. In September the annual H Street Music Festival celebrates the developing arts, entertainment, and fashion scene.

Following E Street east to 17th Street NE, the **Congressional Cemetery,** the first national cemetery created by the government, was established in 1807 "for all denomination of people." You can take a self-guided walking tour of the premises to find burial sites for J. Edgar Hoover, John Philip Sousa, and other notables. Due east from the Capitol on East Capitol Street, **RFK Stadium** is the home of the D.C. United soccer team.

Farther to the north, the National Shrine of the Immaculate Conception and Franciscan Monastery are open for tours of the buildings and tranquil gardens. Get there by car, or take bus no. 80 from Union Station, or the Metro to Brookland station. Although there is no food service at the shrine, the brand new Monroe Street Market offers a variety of restaurants, art studios, and shops from 7th to 12th Street NE.

CAPITOL HILL WITH KIDS

Capitol Hill offers plenty for kids to do. After they've had their fill of history, they can commune with nature, hit a home run, and sample sweet treats.

There are lots of locally made toys and games to see and touch at **Eastern Market.** Street performers entertain while kids indulge in blueberry pancakes with ice cream at the **Market Lunch** counter.

At the **United States Botanic Garden,** kids can become Junior Botanists and receive a free adventure pack with cool tools to use during their visit and afterwards at home, as well as access to a secret website. There's also a family guide available.

Catch a game at **Nationals Park** or take a tour on a nongame day. You'll see the Nationals dugout, the clubhouse, and press box, plus you can throw a pitch in the bullpen and test out the batting cages.

Tour the **Navy Yard** and **USS Barry** to see historic military weaponry and a battleship deployed during American wars.

Or take a tour with **DC Ducks:** During the 1½-hour ride in an amphibious vehicle over land and water, a wise-quacking captain mixes historical anecdotes with trivia.

DOWNTOWN

Sightseeing
★★★★

Dining
★★★★

Lodging
★★★★

Shopping
★★★

Nightlife
★★★★

Downtown D.C. is where government, commerce, and entertainment meet. The streets are wide, the buildings are tall (as they get in Washington), and D.C. feels like a big city (almost). This extensive area encompasses some distinct districts, packed with historic and cultural attractions, with still more in the pipeline. Downtown is compact; you can see the main sights in an hour and a half, not counting time spent inside museums. Travel light, however, for you'll have your bag screened before entering almost everywhere.

DOWNTOWN WALK

Downtown can be divided into several sections, each with its own personality. The wedge-shape area south of Pennsylvania Avenue, north of Constitution Avenue, and east of 15th Street is the **Federal Triangle,** the neighborhood's serious side with its imposing gray buildings and all-government mentality. **Penn Quarter,** Downtown's party side, makes up the area directly to the north of Pennsylvania Avenue. Here restaurants and bars mix with popular museums and a thriving theater district. **Chinatown** gives the neighborhood an international flair, while immediately to the east **Judiciary Square** acts like a stern older uncle frowning about all the goings-on.

FEDERAL TRIANGLE AND JUDICIARY SQUARE
Begin at **Metro Center,** the core of D.C.'s Metro system and its busiest station. From here take 12th Street south to **Federal Triangle,** just a short walk away. Constructed between 1929 and 1938, this mass of government buildings consolidated government workers in one place. The neighborhood was formerly known as Murder Bay for its notorious collection of rooming houses, taverns, tattoo parlors, and brothels.

When city planners moved in, they chose a uniform classical architectural style for the new buildings. As you pass by, give a nod to the **John A. Wilson Building, Internal Revenue Service Building, Department of Justice,** and Apex Building, which houses the **Federal Trade Commission.** These buildings are not open to the public.

Ahead of you, the **Ronald Reagan Building and International Trade Center** houses the most secure food court you will ever see. You need to show a photo ID and go through a security checkpoint. The Capitol Steps perform their political comedy sketches here on Friday and Saturday nights. The Old Post Office Pavilion, saved from demolition in 1973, will be under construction in 2014, as the Trump family transforms it into a luxury hotel. The observation deck in the clock tower will remain open to the public. Though not as tall as the Washington Monument, the Old Post Office's clock tower affords a great view of the city; plus, it is usually not crowded, and it is free. The windows are bigger, and—unlike those at the monument—they are open, allowing cool breezes to waft through.

Nearby, the **Department of Commerce** once housed the National Aquarium in its basement, but it is now closed, with many of its creatures transported to Baltimore's National Aquarium. Slightly hidden across the street a delightfully shady oasis, **Pershing Park,** home of the Reserve Officers Memorial, provides a pleasant area with picnic tables and a pond. Diagonally across the street, **Freedom Plaza,** named in honor of Martin Luther King Jr., has been home to many protests, from King's own "Resurrection City" of the Poor People's March to the more recent Occupy D.C. Movement. The site's stone is inlaid with a map from L'Enfant's original 1791 plan for the Federal City. To compare L'Enfant's vision with today's reality, stand in the middle of the map's Pennsylvania Avenue and look west. L'Enfant had planned an unbroken vista from the Capitol to the White House, but the Treasury Building, begun in 1836, ruined the view. Turning to the east, you can see the U.S. Capitol sitting on the former Jenkins Hill.

Follow Pennsylvania Avenue, the nation's symbolic Main Street, known for inaugural and other parades and civic demonstrations, toward the Capitol. On your left you'll see the **J. Edgar Hoover Federal Bureau of Investigation Building,** which is not open to the public. On the right, the **National Archives** preserves the original Declaration of Independence, the Constitution, and the Bill of Rights. Besides displaying these hallowed documents in an eerie, vaultlike environment, the Archives house a lesser-known, yet vibrant line-up of events, documentaries, and exhibits illuminating American history. The seven-level **Newseum** consists of 15 galleries showcasing 500 years of journalism history with dramatic multimedia displays. The spectacular stone-and-glass edifice next door is the Canadian Embassy.

Fourth Street leads to Judiciary Square, where city and federal courthouses thrive, as well as the **National Law Enforcement Officers Memorial.** To the west, the engaging **Marian Koshland Science Museum** explores the scientific issues that make the news. Across F street is the **National Building Museum,** known as much for its impressive interior hall as for its

GETTING ORIENTED

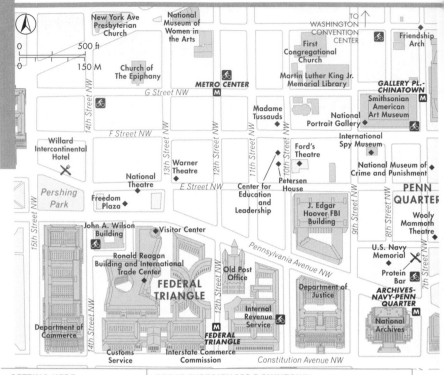

GETTING HERE

Take the Metro to Federal Triangle or Archives–Navy Memorial to visit the government buildings along Pennsylvania Avenue. The Gallery Place–Chinatown stop gives direct access to the Verizon Center, Chinatown, and the American Art and Spy museums. Judiciary Square has its own stop, and Metro Center is the best choice for the National Theatre and Penn Quarter. Bus routes crisscross the area as well. Limited street parking is available on nights and weekends away from the main Chinatown and Verizon Center area.

GREAT EXPERIENCES DOWNTOWN

International Spy Museum: Indulge your inner James Bond with a look at 007's Aston Martin from *Goldfinger*—along with more serious toys used by the CIA, FBI, and KGB.

The National Archives: After seeing the Declaration of Independence, Constitution, and Bill of Rights, lose yourself in the treasures of the Public Vault.

National Portrait Gallery and Smithsonian American Art Museum: These masterful museums have something for everyone.

Newseum: See parts of the Berlin Wall, and play the role of a journalist. Most Sunday mornings, you can observe a live taping of ABC's *This Week*, and the roof deck is a pleasure in good weather.

Theater District: Performances ranging from Shakespeare to contemporary dramas and musicals are mounted in Penn Quarter, Washington's answer to Broadway.

Downtown

Tony Cheng's Mongolian
H Street

Surratt Boarding House

CHINATOWN

Old Adas Israel Synagogue

Verizon Center

G Street NW

National Building Museum

Shakespeare Theatre

F Street NW

National Law Enforcement Officers Memorial

JUDICIARY SQUARE

Marian Koshland Science Museum

E Street NW

JUDICIARY SQUARE

D Street NW

DOWNTOWN EAST

C Street NW

Newseum

Federal Trade Commission

Canadian Embassy

Pennsylvania Avenue NW

U. S. Capitol

KEY

🚲 Bike Share

PLANNING YOUR TIME

Downtown is densely packed with major attractions—far too many to see in one day. You'll need at least an hour inside each attraction, so pick the two that appeal most and stroll past the rest. Art lovers might focus on the **National Portrait Gallery** and **Smithsonian American Art Museum**; history buffs might limit themselves to touring the **National Archives** and the **National Building Museum**; families with kids may prefer the **International Spy Museum**; and media junkies will want to visit the **Newseum** and the **Marian Koshland Science Museum**, which looks at the real story behind science topics that are widely reported.

SAFETY

Downtown's blocks of government and office buildings still become a bit of a ghost town when the working day is done, but a revitalized Penn Quarter remains energized late into the evenings, especially when there are events at the Verizon Center or at one or more of Downtown's major theaters.

QUICK BITES

Food Courts. There is a food court in Penn Quarter called The Shops at National Place (✉ 1331 Pennsylvania Ave. NW ☎ 202/662-1250). Other food courts are in Federal Triangle at the Ronald Reagan Building (✉ 1300 Pennsylvania Ave. NW ☎ 202/312-1300); on the lower level of Union Station (✉ 50 Mass. Ave. NE ⊕ www.unionstationdc.com); and in the Union Market near Gallaudet University (✉ 1309 5th St. NE ⊕ www.unionmarketdr.com). The J Street Food Court is on the George Washington University campus in Marvin Center (✉ 2121 I St. NW ☎ 202/994-1000); the International Square Food Court is in the White House Area business district (✉ 1875 I St. NW); and Hoya Court is in Georgetown University's Leavey Center (✉ 37th and O St. NW ⊕ dining. georgetown.edu).

Tony Cheng Mongolian Restaurant. Two restaurants in one that feature a Mongolian barbecue downstairs and a traditional Chinese menu upstairs. Dim sum and hot pots are served daily. ✉ 619 H St. NW, Chinatown ☎ 202/371-8669 ⊕ www.tonychengrestaurant.com.

Many people visit the Old Post Office Pavilion for the views from the old clock tower, but at lunchtime the international restaurants in the food court are also a big draw.

exhibits on architecture and the building arts. The **Old Adas Israel Synagogue** on 3rd Street is the oldest synagogue in D.C.

A couple of blocks to the west, new galleries, restaurants, and other cultural hot spots have taken over much of the real estate. Look out for the **Shakespeare Theatre Company's** performing arts center, **Sidney Harman Hall.** The area surrounding the **Verizon Center** sports arena has cinemas, restaurants, and shops. Expect crowds on weekend evenings as they gather around street performers. From here, you're only a block away from the Gallery Place/Chinatown Metro stop; continue north on 7th Street to Chinatown.

CHINATOWN AND PENN QUARTER

Chinatown begins just north of the Verizon Center. This compact neighborhood is marked by the ornate, 75-foot Friendship Arch at 7th and H streets and Chinese characters on storefronts such as Ann Taylor Loft and Starbucks. Nearly every Cantonese, Szechuan, Hunan, and Mongolian restaurant has a roast duck hanging in the window, and the shops here sell Chinese food, arts and crafts, and newspapers. Nearby, **Martin Luther King Jr. Memorial Library** is the only D.C. building designed by the illustrious modernist architect Ludwig Mies van der Rohe. From here detour west on G Street and north on 13th Street to see the **National Museum of Women in the Arts** and its showcase of works by female artists from the Renaissance to the present (it has the only Frida Kahlo in the city), and don't miss its new and changing outdoor sculpture installation by women artists alongside the building on New York Avenue.

South of Chinatown, below G Street, **Penn Quarter** begins. This neighborhood continues to expand and remains one of the hottest addresses in town for nightlife and culture. The **National Portrait Gallery** and the **Smithsonian American Art Museum** are the main cultural draws. The fun and interactive **International Spy Museum** across the street displays the largest collection of spy artifacts in the world, and the interactive Crime and Punishment Museum definitely makes CSI fans happy.

A block west along E Street brings you out to Washington's theater district, home to the venerable **Ford's Theatre,** the **Warner Theatre,** which has its own walk of fame on the sidewalk out front, and the **National Theatre.** Meanwhile, nearby on 7th and D streets, the **Woolly Mammoth Theatre Company** offers younger adults a hip theatrical alternative.

Tours of **Ford's Theatre,** the **Center for Education and Leadership,** and the **Petersen House** take you back to the night of Lincoln's assassination and explore the lasting legacy of his presidency. John Wilkes Booth and his coconspirators plotted the dirty deed at **Suratt Boarding House** a few blocks away at 604 H Street NW.

DOWNTOWN WITH KIDS

If you happen to time your visit with a monthly KidSpy workshop at the **International Spy Museum,** your junior James Bonds and young Nancy Drews can assume a new identity complete with disguise, go on a spy mission, meet real spies, and more. This is a great museum for tweens, but younger kids may not get it.

Teens will relish the creepy interactive exhibits at the **Crime and Punishment Museum.**

The **National Building Museum** takes building blocks to new heights as kids can strap on a tool belt and design their own homes or even cities.

At the **National Archives** kids can gawk at the Declaration of Independence, Constitution, and Bill of Rights; suddenly school history isn't so abstract.

The **Newseum** lets kids experience the stories behind the headlines, and they can even "broadcast" the news in front of the camera.

Both the **National Portrait Gallery** and **Smithsonian American Art Museum** have something for everyone, from presidential portraits to art made from aluminum foil, bottle caps, and even television sets.

GEORGETOWN

Sightseeing
★★★

Dining
★★★★★

Lodging
★★★★

Shopping
★★★★★

Nightlife
★★★★★

At first glance, Washington's oldest and wealthiest neighborhood may look genteel and staid, but don't be fooled: this is a lively part of town. Georgetown is D.C.'s top high-end shopping destination, with everything from eclectic antiques and housewares to shoes and upscale jeans. At night, particularly on weekends, revelers along M Street and Wisconsin Avenue eat, drink, and make merry. Perfect for strolling, this neighborhood's historic, tree-lined streets and waterfront parks offer wonderful views of the Potomac. Although the coveted brick homes north of M Street are the province of Washington's high society, the rest of the neighborhood offers ample entertainment for everyone.

GEORGETOWN WALK

Georgetown can be thought of in four sections: the marketplace along **M Street,** the **university,** the **historic residential** neighborhoods, and the **waterfront.** The most crowded stretches are along M Street and Wisconsin Avenue. The quietest strolls are through Georgetown University's campus. The neighborhood can be comfortably explored in an afternoon, though you may want to linger here. The waterfront with its C&O Canal, a sylvan spot for a bike ride, a morning jog, or a pleasant paddle, as well as the riverfront restaurants and parks at Washington Harbour on the Potomac, offer an array of possibilities.

M Street is a fitting introduction to the area that is known for its high-end clothing boutiques and fancy furniture shops, now squeezing cheek-by-jowl with chain stores such as J. Crew, H&M, and Zara. You might

Georgetown is known for its great window-shopping, as well as for being a notoriously difficult place to park.

see a crowd lining up to buy **Georgetown Cupcakes**, the site of the reality show *DC Cupcakes*. Slightly out of place amid the modern shops and cafés, the 18th-century **Old Stone House** and garden on M Street are thought to be the oldest in the city.

RESIDENTIAL GEORGETOWN AND GU

Leaving the throngs behind for now, 31st Street takes you north into the heart of residential Georgetown, where impossibly small cottages stand side by side with rambling mansions. At Q Street, **Tudor Place** was once the home of Thomas Peter, son of Georgetown's first mayor, and his wife, Martha Custis, Martha Washington's granddaughter. A house tour lets you see many of Martha Washington's Mount Vernon possessions, as well as a 1919 Pierce Arrow roadster.

Farther up 31st Street, the 10 acres of formal gardens and English parkland that make up **Dumbarton Oaks** can rightfully claim to be one of the loveliest spots in Washington, D.C. To the east, **Montrose Park** entertains kids, dogs, and picnickers with wide lawns, tennis courts, and a playground. The funerary obelisks, crosses, and gravestones of **Oak Hill Cemetery** mark the final resting place for actor, playwright, and diplomat John H. Payne, and William Corcoran, founder of the Corcoran Gallery of Art. A short detour east on Q Street, **Dumbarton House** (no relation to Dumbarton Oaks) is a distinctive example of Federal-era architecture and furnishings.

Circling back, Wisconsin Avenue leads downhill past a variety of small boutiques and cafés toward the intersection with M Street. Instead of following it the whole way, make a right on O Street, where you will find **St. John's Church,** one of the oldest churches in the city. Thirty-third

GETTING ORIENTED

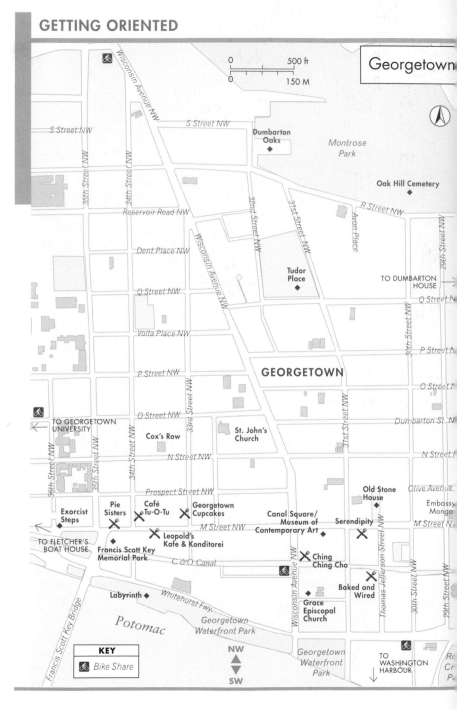

Georgetown

0   500 ft

0   150 M

KEY

🚲 Bike Share

NW
▲
▼
SW

GREAT EXPERIENCES IN GEORGETOWN

C&O Canal: Walk or bike along the path here, which offers bucolic scenery from the heart of Georgetown across Maryland.

Dumbarton Oaks: Stroll through the 10 acres of formal gardens—Washington's loveliest oasis.

M Street: Indulge in some serious designer retail therapy (or just window-shopping). Reward your willpower or great find with a great meal afterward—all on the same street.

Tudor Place: Step into Georgetown's past with a visit to the grand home of the Custis-Peter family. On view are antiques from George and Martha Washington's home at Mount Vernon and a 1919 Pierce Arrow roadster.

Washington Harbour and Waterfront Park: Come on a warm evening to enjoy sunset drinks while overlooking the Watergate, Kennedy Center, and Potomac River. Board a sightseeing cruise at the dock.

GETTING HERE

There's no Metro stop in Georgetown, so you have to take a bus or taxi or walk to this part of Washington. It's about a 20-minute walk from Dupont Circle and the Foggy Bottom Metro stations. Perhaps the best transportation deal in Georgetown is the Circulator. For a buck you can ride from Union Station along Massachusetts Avenue and K Street to the heart of Georgetown. Or try the Georgetown Circulator route, which connects M Street to the Dupont Circle and Rosslyn Metro stops. The Circulator runs daily at varying hours (⊕ www.dccirculator.com).

Other options include the G2 Georgetown University Bus, which goes west from Dupont Circle along P Street, and Friendship Heights bus nos. 31, 32, and 36 , which go south down Wisconsin Avenue and west down Pennsylvania Avenue toward Georgetown. From the Foggy Bottom Metro stop catch bus no. 38B to M Street.

PLANNING YOUR TIME

You can easily spend a pleasant day in Georgetown, partly because some sights (**Tudor Place, Dumbarton Oaks, Oak Hill Cemetery,** and **Dumbarton House**) are somewhat removed from the others and partly because the street scene, with its shops and people-watching, invites you to linger.

Georgetown is almost always crowded at night. Driving and parking are difficult, so the wise take a bus or taxi.

QUICK BITES

Ching Ching Cha. Step into this Chinese teahouse where tranquility reigns. In addition to tea, lunch and dinner may be ordered from a menu with light, healthful meals. ⊠ *1063 Wisconsin Ave. NW, Georgetown* ☎ *202/333–8288* ⊕ *www.chingchingcha.com.*

DGS Delicatessen. A modern take on a traditional deli, DGS pickles, cures, and smokes its food in-house. Take out or dine in. ⊠ *1317 Connecticut Ave. NW, Dupont Circle* ☎ *202/293–4400* ⊕ *www.dgsdelicatessen.com.*

Glen's Garden Market. Specialty food, beer and other beverages at this grocer/bar showcase products from the Mid-Atlantic region. ⊠ *2001 S St. NW, Dupont Circle* ☎ *202/588–5698* ⊕ *www.glensgardenmarket.com.*

In the 19th century mules pulled boats loaded with 100 tons of coal along the C&O Canal towpath.

Street brings you down to N Street to see some of the finest Federal-era architecture in D.C. **Cox's Row** is a group of five Federal houses, between nos. 3339 and 3327 N Street, named after Colonel John Cox, a former mayor of Georgetown who built them in 1817.

N street gives way to **Georgetown University.** Founded in 1789, it is the oldest Jesuit school in the country. The imposing, Victorian Healy Hall at its entrance was named for Patrick Healy, the president of George-town University in 1873, who was the biracial son of a slave and a white Irish slave-owner.

Turn left at 36th Street to return to M Street, perhaps via the undeni-ably spooky 75 steps that featured prominently in the horror movie *The Exorcist.* Find them past the old brick streetcar barn at No. 3600. Down on the western end of M Street, the small **Francis Scott Key Memorial Park** honors the Washington attorney who penned the national anthem dur-ing the War of 1812. This is a good spot for a picnic; for supplies, cross the street for sandwiches at Cafe Tu-o-Tu and pick up cupcakes at Pie Sisters. Or, you might be tempted to seek out **Leopold's Kafe & Konditorei** at the end of Cady's Alley and linger on its shady terrace. Flanking the southern edge of the park is the **C&O Canal,** which links the Potomac with the Ohio River. A sandy red path along the bank makes for a scenic walk or bike ride—look out for great blue herons and turtles lounging in the sun. Two miles west of the Key Bridge along the canal towpath, **Fletcher's Boat House** rents kayaks, canoes, and bikes. You can also follow the canal east through the heart of Georgetown, running parallel with M Street.

CLOSE UP

A History of Georgetown

The area that would come to be known as George (after George II), then George Towne, and finally Georgetown, was part of Maryland when it was settled in the early 1700s by Scottish immigrants, many of whom were attracted by the region's tolerant religious climate.

Georgetown's position—at the farthest point up the Potomac that's accessible by ship—made it an ideal transit and inspection point for farmers who grew tobacco in Maryland's interior. In 1789 the state granted the town a charter, but two years later Georgetown—along with Alexandria, its counterpart in Virginia—was included by George Washington in the Territory of Columbia, site of the new capital.

While Washington struggled, Georgetown thrived. Wealthy traders built their mansions on the hills overlooking the river; merchants and the working class lived in modest homes closer to the water's edge.

In 1810 a third of Georgetown's population was African-American—both free people and slaves. The Mt. Zion United Methodist Church on 29th Street is the oldest organized black congregation in the city, and when the church stood at 27th and P streets it was a stop on the Underground Railroad (the original building burned down in the mid-1800s).

Georgetown's rich history and success instilled in all its residents a feeling of pride that persists today. When Georgetowners thought the capital was dragging them down, they asked to be given back to Maryland, the way Alexandria was given back to Virginia in 1845.

Tobacco's star eventually fell, and Georgetown became a milling center, using waterpower from the Potomac. When the Chesapeake & Ohio (C&O) Canal was completed in 1850, the city intensified its milling operations and became the eastern end of a waterway that stretched 184 miles to the west.

The C&O took up some of the slack when Georgetown's harbor began to fill with silt and the port lost business to Alexandria and Baltimore, but the canal never became the success that George Washington had envisioned.

In the years that followed, Georgetown was a malodorous industrial district, a far cry from the fashionable spot it is today. Clustered near the water were a foundry, a fish market, paper and cotton mills, and a power station for the city's streetcar system.

Georgetown still had its Georgian, Federal, and Victorian homes, though, and when the New Deal and World War II brought a flood of newcomers to Washington, Georgetown's tree-shaded streets and handsome brick houses were rediscovered. Pushed out in the process were many of Georgetown's renters, including many of its black residents.

In modern times some of Washington's most famous residents have called Georgetown home, including former *Washington Post* executive editor Ben Bradlee, political pundit George Stephanopoulos, Secretaries of State John Kerry and Madeleine Albright, Senator John Warner and his wife at the time, Elizabeth Taylor, and *New York Times* op-ed doyenne Maureen Dowd, who lives in a townhouse where President Kennedy lived as a senator.

M STREET AND THE WATERFRONT

Whether you follow the canal or M Street as you head east back through Georgetown, you will eventually come to Washington Harbour. On the way, you may want to explore the busy area around the intersection of M Street and Wisconsin Avenue. The small **Museum of Contemporary Art,** a converted 1850s warehouse, is located in **Canal Square.** A short detour down Wisconsin Avenue will take you to **Grace Episcopal Church,** the church of choice for many 19th-century residents. You might want to make another short detour east to Thomas Jefferson Street for a stop for homemade tea and cakes at the fun and funky **Baked and Wired.** Then head south on 31st Street toward the Potomac to take a rest on a bench under the trees in the **Georgetown Waterfront Park.**

Following the Potomac east to K Street between 30th and 31st streets you will find **Washington Harbour,** a riverfront development specializing in restaurants and bars with scenic views of the river, the Watergate complex, and the Kennedy Center. Boat trips to Mount Vernon, the National Harbor, and Alexandria leave from here, offering a waterfront perspective of the city's monuments.

By night the hungry, thirsty and the ready-to-party pound the pavement on this side of D.C. with its assortment of Vietnamese, Thai, Middle Eastern, and Ethiopian restaurants as well as a variety of grubby pubs. After hours, college students and recent graduates overrun the bars, but a few lounges do cater to a more mature, upscale crowd.

WE HAVE A SITUATION

West of Wisconsin Avenue on M Street, the Shops at Georgetown Park occupies the site selected in the 1960s by the White House as the Situation Room with the first hotline to Moscow. Today's Situation Room is in the basement of the White House's West Wing; the staff of senior officers monitors and deals with world and U.S. crises.

GEORGETOWN WITH KIDS

In nice weather the **Waterfront Park** and **C&O Canal** offer pleasant walks and picnic opportunities. **Tudor House** hosts family-friendly events, such as tea parties and craft-making. Take the family to **Dumbarton Oaks,** where kids can stretch their legs, admire the flowers, and cavort with nature. North of M Street at 27th you'll find the **Rose Park** "Tot Lot," complete with climbing frames and sandpit. **Montrose Park** to the north also has a playground.

Serendipity, at 3150 M Street NW, is an old-fashioned ice-cream parlor famed for its frozen hot chocolate.

2

DUPONT CIRCLE AND LOGAN CIRCLE

Sightseeing
★★★★

Dining
★★★★★

Lodging
★★★★

Shopping
★★★★

Nightlife
★★★★

Dupont Circle, named for Civil War hero Admiral Samuel F. Dupont, is the grand hub of D.C., literally. This traffic circle is essentially the intersection of the main thoroughfares of Connecticut, New Hampshire, and Massachusetts avenues. More important though, the area around the circle is a vibrant center for urban and cultural life in the District.

Along with wealthy tenants and basement-dwelling twentysomethings, museums, art galleries, and embassies call this upscale neighborhood home. Offbeat shops, specialty bookstores, coffeehouses, and varied restaurants help the area stay funky and urban.

The Logan Circle neighborhood runs to the east along P Street and stretches north along the 14th Street Corridor, where sidewalk cafés, a handful of sights, and two theaters—Source DC and Studio—draw a lively nightlife crowd.

Add to the mix stores and clubs catering to the neighborhood's gay community and this area becomes a big draw for nearly everyone. Perhaps that's why the fountain at the center of the Dupont traffic island is such a great spot for people-watching.

DUPONT CIRCLE WALK

Two hours should be enough to walk the main sights here, longer if you want to linger in some of the neighborhood's fascinating small museums and enticing cafés.

Take the Metro to the dramatic Dupont Circle Q Street exit and find yourself in the heart of D.C.'s most eclectic neighborhood. If you arrive on a Sunday morning, you will emerge into the year-round **Fresh Farm Market** at the corner of Q and 20th streets. The large island in the middle of the traffic circle a few paces down Connecticut Avenue is a lively urban park, vibrant with skateboarders, chess players, and street performers, all congregating around a marble fountain created by Daniel

GETTING ORIENTED

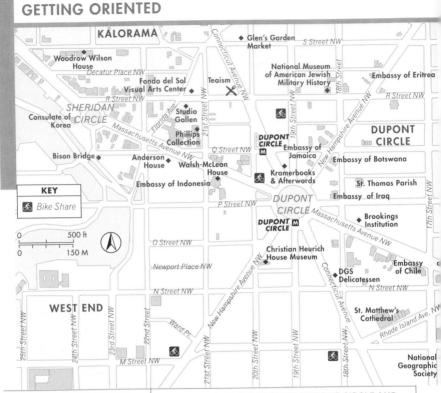

QUICK BITES

Kramerbooks & Afterwords Cafe. At this indie bookstore and café you can relax over a light meal, snack, or a drink after browsing. Wednesday through Saturday, live music entertains evening visitors. Open 24 hours on weekends. ✉ *1517 Connecticut Ave. NW, Dupont Circle* ☎ *202/387–1400* ⊕ *www.kramers.com.*

Teaism. Several dozen varieties of tea, and a selection of seafood and vegetarian entrées in bento boxes provide a light lunch or dinner. ✉ *2009 R St. NW, Dupont Circle* ☎ *202/667–3827* ⊕ *www.teaism.com.*

GREAT EXPERIENCES AROUND DUPONT CIRCLE AND LOGAN CIRCLE

Dupont Circle: Grab a cup of coffee and a *CityPaper* and take in the always-buzzing scene around the fountain.

Logan Circle: Take in a contemporary play at the Studio Theatre, then stay out late in the restaurants and bars on 14th and P streets.

National Geographic Society: See *National Geographic* magazine come to life in rotating exhibits at the society's Explorers Hall.

Phillips Collection: Admire masterpieces such as Renoir's *Luncheon of the Boating Party* and Degas's *Dancers at the Barre* at the country's first museum of modern art.

Woodrow Wilson House: Glimpse the life of the 28th American President, who lived here during his retirement, surrounded by all the modern luxuries of the early 1900s.

Dupont Circle and Logan Circle

A GOOD WALK: KALORAMA

To see the embassies and luxurious homes that make up the Kalorama neighborhood, begin your walk at the corner of S and 23rd streets.

Head north up 23rd, keeping an eye out for the emergency call boxes now turned into public art.

At the corner of Kalorama Road, head west, but don't miss the Tudor-style mansion at 2221 Kalorama Road, now home to the French ambassador.

Turn right on Kalorama Circle, where you can look down at Rock Creek Park and into Adams Morgan. Kalorama means "beautiful view" in Greek, and this is the sight that inspired the name.

From here you can retrace your steps, or take Kalorama Circle back to Kalorama Road, turn right, and make a left on Wyoming to bring you back to 23rd.

GETTING HERE

Dupont Circle has its own stop on the Metro's Red Line. Exit on Q Street for the Phillips Collection, Anderson House, and Kalorama attractions. Take the Connecticut Avenue exit for the National Geographic Society, Christian Heurich House museum, or shopping between Dupont Circle and Farragut North. Follow P Street to the east for Logan Circle. On-street parking in residential areas is becoming increasingly difficult to find, especially on weekend evenings.

PLANNING YOUR TIME

Visiting the Dupont Circle area takes at least half a day, although you can find things to keep you busy all day and into the evening. You'll likely spend the most time at the **Phillips Collection, Anderson House,** and **Woodrow Wilson House.** The hours will also fly if you linger over lunch or indulge in serious browsing in area shops.

Chester French. On sunny days the surrounding benches are pleasant spots for people-watching, newspaper reading, or relaxing with a cup of coffee and a snack. Also nearby is the bookstore **Kramerbooks & Afterwords,** which has a popular café, open daily and throughout the night on Friday and Saturday.

NORTHWEST OF DUPONT CIRCLE

Head up the main north–south artery of Connecticut Avenue, lined with shops, restaurants, and cafés that are busy day and night. Turning left onto R Street you'll pass number 2131, an understated white-painted town house, home to FDR and Eleanor Roosevelt between 1916 and 1920. Detour a block south on 21st Street to find the **Phillips Collection,** founded as the first permanent museum of modern art in the country, with a collection including works by Renoir, Degas, van Gogh, Picasso, Cassatt, Klee, and Matisse.

SEE AND BE SCENE

Dupont's gay scene is concentrated mainly on 17th Street. A variety of gay-friendly, lively, and offbeat bars and restaurants stretch between P and R streets, many with outdoor seating. JR's Bar & Grill and Cobalt are favorites. D.I.K. Bar is the place to be on the Tuesday before Halloween for the annual High Heel Drag Race down 17th Street. At the informal block party, elaborately costumed drag queens strut their stuff along the route from Church to Queen streets and then race to the finish line.

Along R Street lies a variety of art galleries. Nestled among them is the nonprofit **Fondo Del Sol Visual Arts Center,** devoted to the cultural heritage of Latin America and the Caribbean. Detour east on R Street for the **National Museum of American Jewish Military History,** which displays weapons, uniforms, medals, recruitment posters, and other military memorabilia related to American Jews serving in the U.S. military. This neighborhood also includes an Italianate mansion built in 1901 at **15 Dupont Circle.** President Calvin Coolidge and his wife lived here in 1927 while the White House was undergoing a renovation. Coolidge welcomed many dignitaries as houseguests there, including Charles Lindbergh after his transatlantic flight.

At the west end of R Street, **Sheridan Circle** and Massachusetts Avenue are home to a cluster of embassies in striking villas. North on Massachusetts Avenue, S Street edges into the Kalorama district. The **Woodrow Wilson House** shows the former president's home pretty much as he left it. On display are his personal possessions, such as hats and canes, and many gifts from foreign dignitaries.

Just south of Sheridan Circle the **Bison Bridge** is guarded by four bronze statues of the shaggy mammals. Nearby, the **Anderson House** was bequeathed by Larz and Isabel Anderson to the Society of the Cincinnati, an exclusive club of the descendants of Revolutionary War officers. Next door, the **Walsh-McLean House** was once home to the last private owner of the Hope Diamond (now in the National Museum of Natural History). Head back to Connecticut Avenue for tea, lunch, or a snack before continuing on.

SOUTHEAST OF DUPONT CIRCLE

Past Dupont Circle, heading down Massachusetts Avenue toward Scott Circle, you will pass the **Brookings Institution** and the Johns Hopkins University D.C. campus buildings. The **Christian Heurich House Museum,** once known as the Brewmaster's Castle, was the home of a German-born beer magnate and is nearby on New Hampshire Avenue. **Scott Circle** is decorated with statues of General Winfield Scott, Daniel Webster, and S. C. F. Hahnemann. If you walk to the south side of the circle and look down 16th Street, a familiar view of the White House awaits, but six blocks away. Nearby, down 17th Street, the **National Geographic Society** brings its magazines to life with interactive exhibits, photo galleries, and live shows.

A few sights lie clustered on or near M Street south of Scott Circle, including two noteworthy religious institutions: the **Metropolitan African Methodist Episcopal Church,** one of the most influential African-American churches in the city, and the Renaissance-style **St. Matthew's Cathedral,** the seat of Washington's Roman Catholic diocese, and where President Kennedy's funeral Mass was held.

LOGAN CIRCLE

The epicenter of this neighborhood, sometimes called MidCity, is at the intersection of P and 14th streets. Bars and restaurants buzz by day and spill out onto the sidewalks at night. In the early 2000s, gentrification took hold and brought to life a neighborhood damaged by the upheavals of the 1960s. Though revitalized, visitors should take a moment to notice the layers of history.

Logan Circle itself can be found to the east along P Street, a circle of brooding redbrick Victorian mansions built between 1875 and 1900, and the surrounding streets where many prominent African-Americans once lived. One block south of the circle on Vermont Avenue, the **Mary McLeod Bethune Council House** features exhibits on the achievements of African-American women. Around the corner on 14th, you'll come across the highly regarded **Studio Theater,** a number of contemporary art galleries, more boutiques, and music venues all part of 14th Street's thriving arts scene that continues to U Street.

DUPONT CIRCLE WITH KIDS

Dupont Circle isn't overflowing with activities for kids. But if you're there on a Sunday morning for the **farmers' market** on the corner of Q and 20th streets, you may be able to get them excited about fruits and vegetables. If not, the homemade ice cream and cookies will do the trick.

Stead Park is at 16th, and P Street has a lighted basketball court and a playground. Kalorama's quiet **Mitchell Park** at 1801 23rd Street has a grassy hill, tennis courts, and two playgrounds.

ADAMS MORGAN

Sightseeing
★

Dining
★★★★

Lodging
★

Shopping
★★★

Nightlife
★★★★

To the urban and hip, Adams Morgan is like a beacon in an otherwise stuffy landscape. D.C. may have a reputation for being staid and traditional, but drab suits, classical tastes, and bland food make no appearance here. Adams Morgan takes its name from two elementary schools that came together in 1958 after desegregation. It remains an ethnically diverse neighborhood with a United Nations of cuisines, offbeat shops, and funky bars and clubs.

Adams Morgan and its neighboring Columbia Heights comprise the city's Latin Quarter. The area wakes up as the sun goes down, and young Washingtonians in their weekend best congregate along the sidewalks, crowding the doors of this week's hot bar or nightclub. Typical tourist attractions are sparse, but the scene on a Saturday night has its own appeal. If you're here on the second Saturday in September, sample the vibrant neighborhood culture at the Adams Morgan Day Festival.

ADAMS MORGAN WALK

This walk centers around the heart of Adams Morgan on 18th Street and its intersection with Columbia Road, where the dining and nightlife scene stretches for several blocks of narrow streets. You can easily see Adams Morgan in an hour or two, so you may want to combine it with a trip to Dupont Circle or U Street, perhaps winding up here in the evening when this neighborhood gets hopping.

If you arrive from Dupont Circle, you'll walk north up 18th Street. As soon as you reach a stretch of restaurants, cafés, shops, and bars, you have reached Adams Morgan proper. The neighborhood's restaurant corridor lies on 18th Street south of Columbia Road and the parts of Columbia Road and Calvert Street directly adjacent. The city's most diverse eats are served along these few blocks—a succession of

Salvadoran *pupusas* (stuffed torti-llas), Ethiopian *injera* (a yeast-risen flatbread), French ratatouille, and West African *moi moi* (black-eyed pea cakes).

Adams Morgan's bar and club scene caters mostly to a young crowd in their twenties and thirties. The popular clubs often have lines out the door. If a drink is what you need, try **Bourbon** for a huge selection of wine, microbrews, 150 kinds of whiskey, and an outdoor patio, or the **Reef** with its colorful fish tanks and rooftop bar. **Madam's Organ** is a neighborhood institution, with live music every night, and **Habana Village** is one of the best places in the city for Cuban cuisine, salsa dancing, and Latin music.

LOOK UP

As you walk around Adams Morgan, note the many colorful and striking murals. Champorama Mural is one of the best; it is located in a tiny park just off 18th Street on the corner of Kalorama Road and Champlain Street. Among others, Toulouse-Lautrec is on 18th near Belmont Street. Find more on Columbia Road, including the oldest remaining mural in the neighborhood at 17th Street.

In the shops on 18th Street you can find used records, books, collectibles such as Jonathan Adler ceramics and Bakelite telephones, handmade jewelry, and a breathtaking number of doorknobs. Adopt some neighborhood swagger with treasures found in consignment and vintage clothing boutiques. Nearby is the funky **District of Columbia Arts Center,** a combination art gallery and performance space.

Columbia Road to the east between 16th and 18th is the area's Latin Quarter, as bilingual as it gets in Washington. At tables stretched along the street, sidewalk vendors hawk their goods. Continue walking northeast from Adams Morgan toward the Columbia Heights Metro station, where on Saturday morning two first-rate markets spring up—one in Mount Pleasant (at 17th Street and Lamont) and the other in Columbia Heights (at 14th Street and Park Road). Stands stimulate the senses with their produce, flowers, and fresh bread, not to mention exotic delicacies.

Columbia Heights' burgeoning development led big-box retailers like Target and Marshalls to set up shop in a center called DC USA. Accessible by Metro and Circulator buses, Columbia Heights was recently deemed "the hip strip" for its festive Civic Plaza, popular eateries, and Gala Hispanic Theatre.

At the corner of 16th and Columbia, **All Souls' Unitarian Church** was a cornerstone of the civil rights movement and community activism during the 20th century. As you head south on 16th, the **Mexican Cultural Institute** promotes Mexican art, culture, and science. The **Meridian and White-Meyer Houses** hold periodic art exhibits with an international flavor. On the opposite side of 16th Street, **Meridian Hill Park,** also known as Malcolm X Park, was once considered a possible location for the White House. Stop off here for shade and city views, and don't miss the statues of Joan of Arc and Dante. On Sunday afternoon, a drum circle gathers.

GETTING ORIENTED

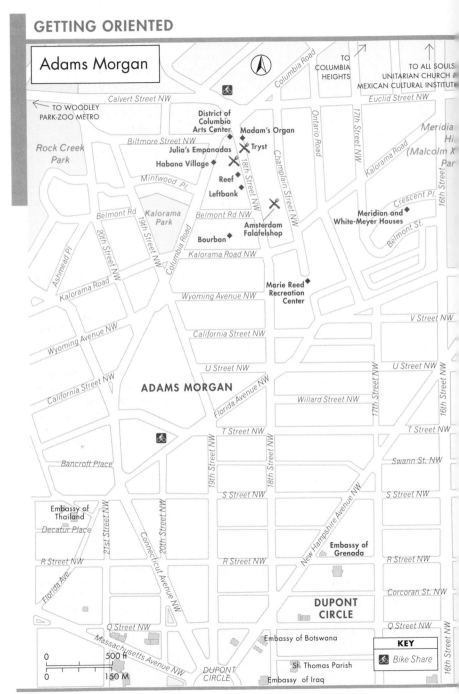

Adams Morgan

TO WOODLEY
PARK-ZOO METRO

Rock Creek
Park

Calvert Street NW

District of
Columbia
Arts Center

Biltmore Street NW

Julia's Empanadas

Habana Village ◆

Mintwood Pl.

Reef ◆

Leftbank ◆

Madam's Organ

✕ Tryst

Belmont Rd   Kalorama
Park

Belmont Rd NW

Bourbon ◆

Amsterdam
Falafelshop

Kalorama Road NW

Wyoming Avenue NW

Marie Reed
Recreation
Center

California Street NW

Columbia Road

TO
COLUMBIA
HEIGHTS

TO ALL SOULS
UNITARIAN CHURCH &
MEXICAN CULTURAL INSTITUTE

Euclid Street NW

Ontario Road

17th Street NW

Champlain Street NW

Kalorama Road

Crescent Pl.

Meridian and ◆
White-Meyer Houses

Belmont St.

Meridia
Hi
(Malcolm X
Par

16th Street

V Street NW

Ashmead Pl.

Kalorama Road

20th Street NW

19th Street NW

Wyoming Avenue NW

California Street NW

ADAMS MORGAN

U Street NW

Florida Avenue NW

Willard Street NW

T Street NW

Bancroft Place

19th Street NW

18th Street NW

T Street NW

S Street NW

U Street NW

17th Street NW

16th Street NW

U Street NW

T Street NW

Swann St. NW

S Street NW

Embassy of
Thailand

Decatur Place

R Street NW

Florida Ave.

21st Street NW

Connecticut Avenue NW

20th Street NW

New Hampshire Avenue NW

R Street NW

Embassy of
Grenada

R Street NW

Corcoran St. NW

**DUPONT
CIRCLE**

Q Street NW

16th Street NW

Q Street NW

Massachusetts Avenue NW

DUPONT
CIRCLE

Embassy of Botswana

St. Thomas Parish

Embassy of Iraq

0   500 ft
0   150 M

KEY
🚲 Bike Share

GREAT EXPERIENCES IN ADAMS MORGAN

Eat ethnic food: Adams Morgan rivals U Street with its plentiful and delicious Ethiopian restaurants. If you'd rather dine using utensils, you can choose among Japanese, Brazilian, Salvadorian, Mexican, Indian, and other ethnic cuisines.

Hang out like a local: The residents of Adams Morgan make an art of relaxing. Follow their lead and settle into one of Tryst's overstuffed armchairs with a laptop or a copy of the New Republic and a coffee, or kill hours browsing the "rare and medium-rare" selections at Idle Time Books.

Move to the beat: Every evening from 3 to 9 pm and on Sunday afternoon, drummers from all walks of life form the Drum Circle in Meridian Hill Park, hashing out the beats while some dance and others simply sit back and watch.

Stay out all night: If you want to party on until the break of dawn, this is the place to do it. Don't miss the live music at Madam's Organ, the salsa dancing at Habana Village, and the cool kids making the scene at the Black Squirrel or Bourbon.

GETTING HERE

Adams Morgan has two Metro stops that are a pleasant 10-minute walk away. From the Woodley Park/Zoo Metro station take a short walk south on Connecticut, then turn left on Calvert Street, and cross over Rock Creek Park on the Duke Ellington Bridge. If you get off at the Dupont Circle Metro stop walk east, turning left on 18th Street.

The heart of Adams Morgan is at the intersection of Columbia Road and 18th Street. Don't even dream about finding parking here on weekend evenings.

If you take the Metro, remember that stations close at midnight, or 3 am on Friday and Saturday nights. If you're not ready to turn in by then, you'll need to hail a cab.

PLANNING YOUR TIME

Window-shopping around Adams Morgan and surrounding environs can occupy the better part of an afternoon, and if you take advantage of the restaurants and nightlife here, there's no telling when your head will hit the pillow.

The few tourist attractions in this area are not time-intensive, but they can be a long walk from restaurants.

QUICK BITES

Amsterdam Falafel. At this favorite for bargain lunches or late night eats, garnish your falafel with a choice of 21 toppings. ⊠ 2425 18th St. NW, Adams Morgan ☎ 202/234-1969 ⊕ www.falafelshop.com

Julia's Empanadas. Try these handmade empanadas (including the fruit-filled variety) served in a paper bag to go, so you can walk to a nearby park. Plus, there's free Wi-Fi. ⊠ 2452 18th St. NW, Adams Morgan ☎ 202/328-6232 ⊕ www.juliasempanadas.com.

Tryst Coffeehouse-Bar-Lounge. Stop in for breakfast, lunch, hot chocolate or something stronger after hours—as late as 4 am on weekends. Old couches and chairs make you linger longer. There's live jazz Monday to Wednesday evenings. ⊠ 2459 18th St. NW, Adams Morgan ☎ 202/232-5500 ⊕ www.trystdc.com.

U STREET CORRIDOR

Sightseeing
★★

Dining
★★★★

Lodging
★

Shopping
★★★★

Nightlife
★★★★★

Home-style Ethiopian food, offbeat boutiques, and live music are fueling the revival of the U Street area. Just a few years back, this neighborhood was surviving on memories of its heyday as a center of black culture and jazz music in the first half of the 20th century.

The neighborhood was especially vibrant from the 1920s to the 1950s, when it was home to jazz genius Duke Ellington, social activist Mary McLeod Bethune, and poets Langston Hughes and Georgia Douglas Johnson. The area's nightclubs hosted Louis Armstrong, Cab Calloway, and Sarah Vaughn. In the 1950s Supreme Court Justice Thurgood Marshall, then still a lawyer, organized the landmark *Brown v. Board of Education* case at the 12th Street YMCA. Now this diverse neighborhood has experienced a lively resurgence of culture, nightlife, and renovation of many historic buildings—and the crowds are back.

U STREET CORRIDOR WALK

You'll need a couple of hours to explore U Street fully, especially if you want to stop in the African-American Civil War Museum. For maps, shopping, and dining information, stop in the Greater U Street Neighborhood and Visitor Center next to Ben's Chili Bowl, and don't stray too far off the main drag, especially at night.

Begin at the 10th Street exit of the U Street/Cardozo Metro station and emerge right at the **African-American Civil War Memorial,** which honors the black soldiers who fought in the Union Army. For more on that story, walk two blocks west to the **African-American Civil War Museum,** which tells the tale of Africans in America from the slave trade through the civil rights movement with numerous photos and documents. Don't miss the **Duke Ellington Mural** on the western side of the building.

Once the hub of black cultural life, with first-run movies and live performances, the **Lincoln Theater** now functions as an event venue. The historic 12th Street YMCA has become the **Thurgood Marshall Center,**

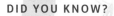

GETTING ORIENTED

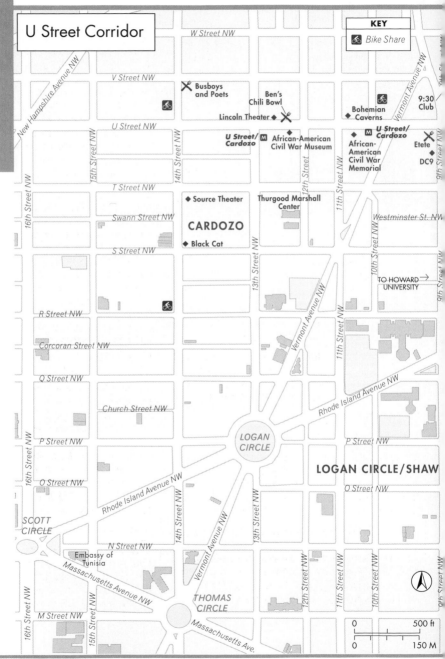

U Street Corridor

KEY
🚲 Bike Share

W Street NW

V Street NW

Busboys and Poets

Ben's Chili Bowl

Lincoln Theater ◆

Bohemian Caverns ◆

9:30 Club

U Street NW

U Street/ Cardozo Ⓜ

African-American Civil War Museum

Ⓜ U Street/ Cardozo

African-American Civil War Memorial ◆

Etete

DC9 ◆

T Street NW

◆ Source Theater

Thurgood Marshall Center

Westminster St. NW

Swann Street NW

CARDOZO

S Street NW

◆ Black Cat

TO HOWARD → UNIVERSITY

R Street NW

Corcoran Street NW

Q Street NW

Church Street NW

LOGAN CIRCLE

P Street NW

P Street NW

LOGAN CIRCLE/SHAW

O Street NW

O Street NW

Rhode Island Avenue NW

SCOTT CIRCLE

N Street NW

Embassy of Tunisia

Massachusetts Avenue NW

THOMAS CIRCLE

Massachusetts Ave.

M Street NW

New Hampshire Avenue NW
16th Street NW
15th Street NW
14th Street NW
13th Street NW
12th Street
11th Street NW
10th Street NW
9th Street NW
Vermont Avenue NW
Rhode Island Avenue NW

0   500 ft
0   150 M

GREAT EXPERIENCES ON U STREET CORRIDOR

African-American Civil War Memorial and Museum: Learn about the lives of slaves and freedmen, and discover whether your ancestors fought in black regiments during the Civil War.

Ben's Chili Bowl: This D.C. institution has perfected its recipe over the last 50 years and satisfies meat eaters and vegetarians alike.

Boutiques: Whether you're after funky footwear or flashy housewares, hit the shops on U and 14th streets for trendy finds.

Ethiopian food: Nothing brings you closer to your meal than eating with your hands. Use the spongy injera bread to scoop up delectable dishes from East Africa.

Jazz and live music: Music greats like Duke Ellington made this neighborhood famous back in the 1920s. Relive the glory years at a jazz performance at Bohemian Caverns or HR 57, or rock out to today's music at the 9:30 Club or Black Cat.

GETTING HERE

The Green Line Metro stops at 13th and U, in the middle of the main business district. To get to the African-American Civil War Memorial, get out at the 10th Street exit. Limited parking can be found on the residential streets north and south of U Street, but as the area gets more popular, spots are getting harder to find on weekend nights.

The area is within walking distance from Dupont Circle and Adams Morgan, but at night you are better off on the bus or in a cab, especially if you are alone. Bus nos. 90 and 92 travel from Woodley Park through Adams Morgan to 14th and U, while bus nos. 52, 53, and 54 travel north from several downtown Metro stops up 14th Street (check ⊕ *www.wmata. com* for information).

PLANNING YOUR TIME

You'll need half a day at most to see U Street's attractions and visit its boutiques. You can also fill an evening with dinner on U Street, a show at the **9:30 Club** or **Bohemian Caverns** or at the newly opened Lincoln Theatre and drinks afterward. If you're not driving, allow plenty of time for public transportation.

QUICK BITES

Ben's Chili Bowl. This D.C. landmark now has a visitors center, but still serves chili any which way imaginable. Try the chili half-smoke, a spicy hot dog with mustard, onions, and, of course, chili. There's also "Ben's Next Door" with an upscale menu, cocktails, and live music. ✉ *1213 U St NW, U St. Corridor* ☎ *202/667-0909* ⊕ *www. benschilibowl.com.*

Busboys and Poets. Step into this bookstore–cum–restaurant that serves up a menu of sandwiches, pizzas, burgers, and poems. Named in honor of poet Langston Hughes, this gathering spot hosts readings, open-mike nights, and live music. ✉ *2021 14th St. NW, U St. Corridor* ☎ *202/387-7638* ⊕ *www. busboysandpoets.com.*

Safety

The blocks between 10th and 16th streets are well-lit and busy, but the area gets grittier to the north and east. Use your street sense, especially at night, when it's a good idea to take a cab.

a community center that houses a museum on the history of African Americans in the U Street/Shaw neighborhood. Duke Ellington fans can find his former homes at 1805 and 1813 13th Street.

Although the neighborhood was nearly destroyed in the rioting that followed the 1968 assassination of Martin Luther King Jr., U Street has reclaimed some of its former musical vibe. **Bohemian Caverns** combines a restaurant with an underground music venue and upstairs club that has hosted jazz greats since 1926. On V Street, the **9:30 Club** attracts big-name rock bands and lesser-known indie artists to one of the East Coast's coolest concert halls. South on 14th Street, the **Black Cat** rocks out with independent and alternative bands from the city and around the world. **DC9** hosts an eclectic mix of local and national bands and DJs. Find it on the corner of 9th and U.

A longtime center for African-American life in the District, U Street is now home to many of the city's African immigrants, who have brought their culinary traditions to the neighborhood. Standout restaurants in D.C.'s unofficial Little Ethiopia, such as **Etete,** tempt diners with spongy injera bread and hearty meat and vegetarian dishes. Although trendy multicultural dining is in abundance here, the city's humble roots remain strong. The granddaddy of Washington diners, **Ben's Chili Bowl,** has been serving chili, chili dogs, chili burgers, and half-smokes (spicy sausages served in a hot-dog bun) since 1958. A sign inside used to let you know that only Bill Cosby eats at Ben's for free, until November 2008, when the Obama family was added to the list.

U Street's shopping scene has garnered attention in recent years as well. Most of the boutiques are clustered on U Street between 14th and 16th streets. Pop in and out of the little shops to find cutting-edge footwear, Asian furnishings, playful housewares, and eclectic or vintage clothing. Fourteenth Street has some rich pickings as well, and you could happily detour all the way south to **Logan Circle,** past the **Source Theater.** To the east of the commercial district lies the historically black college Howard University, which now educates a diverse student body. Notable graduates include authors Zora Neale Hurston and Toni Morrison, opera singer Jessye Norman, and the political adviser and Nobel Peace Prize-winner Ralph Bunche.

U STREET CORRIDOR WITH KIDS

U Street really comes into its own at night, but tweens and teens can have a good time here during the day. Kids of any age can have a great lunch at Ben's Chili Bowl, and they're warmly welcomed in Etete as well. Teens like browsing the eclectic shops on U Street and down 14th Street and lunching at the original Busboys and Poets, named in honor of poet Langston Hughes.

2

UPPER NORTHWEST

Sightseeing
★★★★
Dining
★★
Lodging
★★
Shopping
★★★★
Nightlife
★

The upper northwest corner of D.C. is predominantly residential and in many places practically suburban. However, there are several good reasons to visit the leafy streets, including the National Zoo and National Cathedral. If the weather is fine, spend an afternoon strolling through Hillwood Gardens or tromping through Rock Creek Park's many acres. You'll have to travel some distance to see multiple attractions in one day, but many sights are accessible on foot from local Metro stops.

UPPER NORTHWEST WALK

Upper Northwest is not a neighborhood; it is a geographic grouping of several neighborhoods, including Cleveland Park, Woodley Park, Tenleytown, Foxhall, and Friendship Heights. The majority of attractions lie on or near Connecticut Avenue north of Woodley Park or on Massachusetts Avenue north of Georgetown. The **Kreeger Museum** is the exception, with its location in Foxhall, northwest of Georgetown. This area divides into three walks. Either focus on the zoo and surrounding area, or head up to the cluster of museums and landmarks around Cleveland Park and Massachusetts Avenue. Alternatively, Rock Creek Park offers shady walks and activities for kids, or hit the shops at the edge of D.C. If you plan to see a lot of the area in one day, use the bus or Metro or drive.

ZOO AND SURROUNDINGS

The **National Zoo** is a reason in itself to head uptown. Although recent attention has focused on giant pandas Tian Tian and Mei Xiang as well as the new baby Bao Bao, the Smithsonian's free zoological park is also home to red pandas, clouded leopards, and Japanese giant salamanders

GETTING ORIENTED

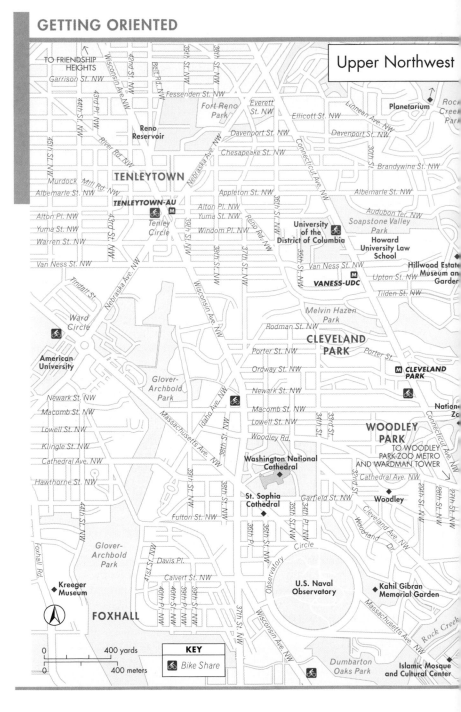

Upper Northwest

TO FRIENDSHIP HEIGHTS

Garrison St. NW

Wisconsin Ave. NW

42nd St. NW

Belt Rd. NW

39th St. NW

38th St. NW

Fessenden St. NW

43rd Pl. NW

44th St. NW

45th St. NW

River Rd. NW

Fort Reno Park

Everett St. NW

Ellicott St. NW

Linnean Ave. NW

Planetarium

Rock Creek Park

Reno Reservoir

Davenport St. NW

Davenport St. NW

30th St.

Chesapeake St. NW

Brandywine St. NW

Murdock Mill Rd. NW

Nebraska Ave. NW

TENLEYTOWN

Albemarle St. NW

Appleton St. NW

Albemarle St. NW

TENLEYTOWN-AU

Alton Pl. NW

36th St. NW

Audubon Ter. NW

Alton Pl. NW

Yuma St. NW

Soapstone Valley Park

Yuma St. NW

43rd St. NW

Tenley Circle

Windom Pl. NW

Reno Rd. NW

University of the District of Columbia

Howard University Law School

Warren St. NW

39th St. NW

38th St. NW

37th St. NW

35th St. NW

Van Ness St. NW

Van Ness St. NW

Hillwood Estate Museum and Garden

VANESS-UDC

Upton St. NW

Tindall St.

Nebraska Ave. NW

Wisconsin Ave. NW

Tilden St. NW

Ward Circle

Melvin Hazen Park

Rodman St. NW

CLEVELAND PARK

American University

Porter St. NW

Porter St.

Glover-Archbold Park

Ordway St. NW

CLEVELAND PARK

Newark St. NW

Massachusetts Ave. NW

Idaho Ave. NW

Newark St. NW

Macomb St. NW

Macomb St. NW

34th St.

33rd St.

Nation Zo

Lowell St. NW

Lowell St. NW

WOODLEY PARK

Klingle St. NW

38th St. NW

Woodley Rd.

TO WOODLEY PARK-ZOO METRO AND WARDMAN TOWER

Cathedral Ave. NW

Washington National Cathedral

32nd St.

Cathedral Ave. NW

Hawthorne St. NW

39th St. NW

38th St. NW

St. Sophia Cathedral

Garfield St. NW

Woodley

29th St. NW

27th St. NW

Glover-Archbold Park

Fulton St. NW

36th St. NW

35th St. NW

34th Pl. NW

Cleveland Ave. NW

Woodland Dr.

Foxhall Rd.

Davis Pl.

41st St. NW

Calvert St. NW

40th St. NW

40th Pl. NW

39th St. NW

36th Pl. NW

Circle

Kreeger Museum

40th Pl. NW

39th Pl. NW

Observatory

U.S. Naval Observatory

Kahil Gibran Memorial Garden

FOXHALL

37th St. NW

Wisconsin Ave. NW

Massachusetts Ave. NW

Rock Creek

0 400 yards

0 400 meters

Dumbarton Oaks Park

Islamic Mosque and Cultural Center

KEY

🚲 Bike Share

GREAT EXPERIENCES IN UPPER NORTHWEST

House museums: The Hillwood Estate, Museum and Gardens showcase cereal heiress Marjorie Merriweather Post's collection of Imperial Russian art and Fabergé eggs, and 25 gorgeous acres of formal French and Japanese gardens. Chagalls, Picassos, and Monets inside contrast with the architecture at the modernist Kreeger Museum.

National Zoo: Visit the giant pandas, elephants, lions, and other members of the animal kingdom while you enjoy a stroll outdoors.

Shopping in Friendship Heights: The city's most glamorous shopping lines Wisconsin Avenue at the Maryland border. Want to actually buy something? Plenty of stores cater to shoppers on a budget, too.

U.S. Naval Observatory: View the heavens through one of the world's most powerful telescopes (on Monday evening with a reservation).

Washington National Cathedral: Look for the Darth Vader gargoyle on the soaring towers of this landmark, then relax among the rosebushes in the Bishop's Garden. Concerts are held here, too.

GETTING HERE

Connecticut Avenue attractions, such as the zoo, are accessible from the Red Line Metro stops between Woodley Park/Zoo and Van Ness. The Friendship Heights Bus travels north from Georgetown along Wisconsin Avenue and takes you to the National Cathedral

Parking can be tricky along Massachusetts Avenue. It is more practical for good walkers to hoof it up the street or take bus no. N2, N3, N4, or N6 between Dupont Circle and Friendship Heights. For more-outlying sights, driving or cabbing it may be the best way to visit.

PLANNING YOUR TIME

The amount of time you spend at the zoo is up to you; animal enthusiasts could easily spend a full day here. You may want to plan your trip around daily programs, such as the elephant-training session or the small-mammal feeding. For the optimal experience, see the animals when they are most active—in the early morning and late afternoon.

For other itineraries, be sure to leave room in your schedule for travel between sights and, if you have a car, for parking. To maximize your time, call ahead to inquire whether on-site parking is available and when the next tour will begin.

QUICK BITES

If you've got the time, skip lunch at the zoo's eateries and head north or south on Connecticut to find a wealth of dining options. The streets immediately surrounding the Woodley Park and Cleveland Park Metro stations are chock-ablock with restaurants, bakeries, and ice-cream stores.

Hillwood Estate's Japanese garden provides a tranquil spot for quiet contemplation.

as well as the traditional lions, tigers, and bears. The zoo makes for a picturesque stroll on warm days, but be prepared for some hills to climb and crowds on sunny weekends.

South of the zoo lies **Woodley Park,** a residential neighborhood filled with stately apartment buildings. The stretch of Connecticut Avenue between Calvert and Woodley Road is notable for its popular array of restaurants and the **Wardman Tower,** a cross-shape tower built in 1928 as a luxury apartment building. Once known for its famous residents, it's now part of the Marriott Wardman Park Hotel. **Woodley,** a Georgian mansion that served as the summer home of four presidents, lies on Cathedral Avenue between 29th and 31st streets. At Woodley Park/Zoo Metro, the Red Line takes you back downtown.

CLEVELAND PARK AND MASSACHUSETTS AVENUE

These attractions are more scattered, so allow a bit more time, and plan to drive or take the bus or Metro.

A 20-minute walk uphill from the Van Ness Red Line stop or an easy drive or cab ride away, the **Hillwood Estate, Museum and Gardens** displays cereal heiress Marjorie

GETTING TO THE ZOO

If you're just going to the zoo, leave the Metro at Cleveland Park instead of Woodley Park/Zoo for a shorter downhill walk. At the end of your visit, return downhill to the Metro via Woodley Park/Zoo. If the zoo doesn't wipe you out, tag on a trip to Adams Morgan, easily accessible on foot from the Woodley Park/Zoo Metro stop.

Merriweather Post's collection of 18th- and 19th-century French and

Russian decorative art. The grounds and gardens equal the art collection in beauty and size. Also in this area, **Howard University Law School** is famed for its African-American graduates, such as Oliver Hill, Thurgood Marshall, and Charles Hamilton Houston.

Farther south you could combine several attractions on Massachusetts Avenue. The **Islamic Mosque and Cultural Center**, with its 162-foot-high minaret, is the oldest Islamic house of worship in D.C. The **Khalil Gibran Memorial Garden** combines Western and Arab symbols in remembrance of the Lebanese-born poet. Opposite the garden, the **U.S. Naval Observatory** makes a stand for science. Continuing north, the Greek Orthodox **St. Sophia Cathedral** is noted for the handsome mosaic work on the interior of its dome. Dominating the skyline, the **Washington National Cathedral** is the sixth-largest cathedral in the world. Its Gothic décor features fanciful gargoyles, including one shaped like Darth Vader. In 2011 the Cathedral sustained damage caused by an earthquake but continues to host services and offer tours, including a tour and tea in the **Pilgrim Observation Gallery.**

ROCK CREEK PARK, FOXHALL, AND OUTER D.C.

Although the 1,800 acres of **Rock Creek Park** span much of Washington and into Maryland, two of the main driving entrances are in Upper Northwest. Take Tilden Road to get to the Peirce Mill and Military Road to reach the nature center and planetarium.

Tucked away in the Foxhall neighborhood, the **Kreeger Museum** showcases the small but impressive collections of paintings, sculpture, and African art collected by wealthy businessman David Kreeger. Tour the hall where he entertained famous musicians and the dining room decorated entirely with Monets. Advance reservations required except on Friday and Saturday.

At the Maryland border, the intersection of Wisconsin and Western avenues forms **Friendship Heights**. This shopping-mall district is the place to pick up the latest finds at Tiffany, Jimmy Choo, Louis Vuitton, and Neiman Marcus. TJ Maxx and Loehmann's provide designer deals. Catch sight of Top Chef's Bryan Voltaggio at his new restaurant Range in Chevy Chase Pavilion.

UPPER NORTHWEST WITH KIDS

At the **National Zoo** the Kids Farm and Pizza Garden keep kids busy learning how to take care of animals and where food comes from. **Rock Creek Nature Center and Planetarium** (✉ *5300 Glover Rd. NW* ⊙ *Closed Mon. and Tues.*) offers daily guided nature walks and a variety of hands-on experiences for kids in the **Discovery Room**. They can look inside beehives, create rainstorms, and crawl inside a volcano. Fish and amphibian feeding time is 4 pm. The **planetarium** has weekend shows for kids.

At the **National Cathedral,** kids can see gargoyles pulling just about every face imaginable. The **Children's Chapel** is designed to the scale of a six-year-old child, and the Space Window contains a piece of rock from the moon.

MUSEUMS

Updated by
Catherine
Sharpe

The internationally renowned collections of the Smithsonian—140 million objects, specimens, and artworks displayed in the world's largest museum complex—make Washington one of the great museum cities. The holdings of the 19 Smithsonian museums range from a 65-million-year-old *Tyrannosaurus rex* skeleton to masterpieces by Da Vinci and Picasso, the Hope Diamond, the original "Star-Spangled Banner," and the space shuttle *Discovery*—and all are on view for free. Add in the legendary art treasures of the National Gallery, Portrait Gallery, the Phillips Collection, and Dumbarton Oaks, and Washington, D.C. becomes a true feast for the eyes.

PLANNING

HITTING THE HIGHLIGHTS

Stand in awe as you read the Declaration of Independence, Constitution, Bill of Rights, and 1297 Magna Carta, all of which are displayed at the National Archives. Be amazed by the history of air and space travel as you look up and see the 1903 Wright Brothers' Flyer and then hold your breath while watching astronauts repair the International Space Station in a mesmerizing IMAX movie at the National Air and Space Museum. Behold the masterpieces of Monet and Botticelli at the National Gallery of Art. Imagine yourself as Thomas Jefferson composing documents at his "writing box," or as Judy Garland playing Dorothy in the Wizard of Oz, when she clicked her ruby slippers three times—both are on display at the National Museum of American History.

Thought-provoking modern art is on view at the constantly changing Hirshhorn Museum, where an Alexander Calder mobile might hover

over a multimedia installation by one of today's hottest talents, or you can simply contemplate color or spend a few meditative moments in the Phillips Collection's intimate Rothko Room or Laib Wax Room. At the National Building Museum you can design and build your own monument, city or structure, then delve into investigative reporting and the history of journalism at the captivating and high-tech Newseum.

VISITING THE SMITHSONIAN

Most of the 19 Smithsonian museums are open between 10 and 5:30 more than 360 days a year, and all are free, though there may be charges for some special exhibits. During the spring and summer, many of the museums offer extended hours and close at 7:30. To get oriented, start with a visit to the Smithsonian building—aka the "Castle," for its towers-and-turrets architecture—which has information on all the museums.

SPECIAL EVENTS

Smithsonian museums regularly host an incredible spectrum of special events, from evenings of jazz and dance nights to food and wine tastings, films, lectures, and events for families and kids. A full schedule is available at ⊕ *www.si.edu/events*. Popular events include live jazz on Friday evenings in summer from 5 to 8:30 at the National Gallery of Art sculpture garden and Take Five performances every third Thursday from 5 to 7 at the Smithsonian American Art Museum. The National Museum of the American Indian often holds weekend festivals that showcase the history and culture of native peoples from the around the world, complete with workshops, film screenings, hands-on activities for all ages, craft shows, and cooking demonstrations.

MUSEUMS WITH KIDS

At the Museum of Natural History children can see live tarantulas, explore butterfly gardens, take in an IMAX movie, or even brave a sleepover. They'll conduct lively experiments at Spark!Lab or get hands-on at Q?RIUS. Whether they're three or 13 years old, they're bound to find dozens of awesome artifacts from important events in American history at the Museum of American History. At the National Air and Space Museum they can almost touch the stars and be awed by famous spaceships, fighter planes, and even the Space Shuttle *Discovery*. Budding artists can create their own masterpieces during free art workshops at the National Gallery and the Sackler Gallery of Art's ImaginAsia. Two-to-six-year-olds can build towers, explore a playhouse and pretend to be a dump truck driver at the National Building Museum's Building

---

BEST GIFT SHOPS

National Air and Space Museum. This is the largest of all the Smithsonian museum stores.

National Building Museum. With shelves filled with Pantone crockery, Nano Blocks, and slickly photographed tomes on architecture, design lovers and modernists will be in heaven.

National Gallery of Art. Here you can find one of the country's largest selections of books on art and art history, along with posters, prints, stationery, and gifts.

Zone. Youngsters will be dancing in the aisles, traveling back in time or exploring new worlds during Tot-Rock concerts, puppet shows, storytelling sessions, and other family-friendly performances at Discovery Theater in the Ripley Center next to the Smithsonian Castle. At the Spy Museum, kids can try to outsmart a villain from the James Bond movies and check out some of the cool gadgets used by Bond and his nemeses.

MUSEUMS WITH LATE HOURS

Smithsonian American Art Museum, daily until 7:30 pm.

Museum of Crime and Punishment, daily until 7 pm, Friday and Saturday until 8 pm.

National Portrait Gallery, daily until 7 pm.

Phillips Collection, Thursday until 8:30 pm.

THE MALL

The Freer and Sackler galleries. *See the highlighted listing in this chapter.*

Hirshhorn Museum and Sculpture Garden. *See the highlighted listing in this chapter.*

Fodor's Choice
★

The Mall. America's "town green"—that might be the best short description of this fabled strip of Washington, D.C., the heart of almost every visitor's trip to Washington. The Mall is a picnicking park, a jogging path, and an outdoor stage for festivals and fireworks. People come here from around the globe to tour the illustrious Smithsonian Institution museums, celebrate special events, or rally to make the world a better place. And because the taxpayers foot the bill for the majestic museums here, they're all free to the public.

Visitors often confuse the Mall with the National Mall. The Mall is the expanse of lawn between 3rd and 14th streets, while the National Mall is the park that spans from the Capitol to the Potomac, including the Mall, the monuments, and the Tidal Basin. To reach the monuments, head west from the Mall or south from the White House and be prepared for a long walk.

With 12 museums spread out along 11 city blocks, you just can't expect to see everything in one day. To avoid mental and physical exhaustion, try to devote at least two days to the Mall and prioritize.

If you want a day devoted to history and culture, start at the National Archives, Bureau of Engraving & Printing or Holocaust Museum (all of which allow you to make advance reservations); and then grab lunch at the Ronald Reagan International Building's Food Court. You can spend the afternoon at either the American History Museum or at the Museum of the American Indian at the other end of the Mall.

If you want a day filled with spectacular paintings and sculptures, begin at the National Gallery of Art. There's also a sculpture garden directly across the Mall at the Hirshhorn, which has an excellent collection of avant-garde art in its indoor galleries. If you prefer international artifacts, head to the Freer Gallery of Art, Sackler Gallery or National Museum of African Art.

THE FREER AND SACKLER GALLERIES

✉ *Freer: 12th St. and Jefferson Dr. SW; Sackler: 1050 Independence Ave. SW, The Mall* ☎ *202/633–1000* ⊕ *www.asia.si.edu* ✉ *Free* ☽ *Daily 10–5:30* Ⓜ *Smithsonian.*

3

TIPS

■ The Freer and Sackler galleries are home to the largest Asian art research library in the United States, open to the public five days a week without an appointment.

■ Free highlight tours are held daily, except on Wednesday and federal holidays. There is often a variety of other free tours as well; ask at the information desks.

■ The museums regularly host films, concerts, talks, and other events. Visit the website to see what's on. Enhance your visit, or take the galleries home with you, with free iPad apps featuring the Peacock Room and select exhibitions.

■ In the family-oriented ImaginAsia workshops, held most weekends at the Sackler Gallery, children ages six to 14 and their adult companions create art ranging from origami to Chinese mirrors.

The Smithsonian Institution has two museums of Asian art: the Freer Gallery of Art, which opened to the public in 1923, and the Arthur M. Sackler Gallery, which welcomed its first visitors in 1987. Both are physically connected by an underground passageway, and ideologically linked through the study, exhibition, and sheer love of Asian art. In addition, the Freer Gallery contains an important collection of 19th-century American art, punctuated by James McNeil Whistler's Peacock Room.

Highlights

Marvel at the collections of Imperial Chinese decorative arts, including exquisite porcelain, gorgeous jade carvings and intricately painted silk scrolls.

Behold the *bodhisattva*: a 12th-century Japanese sculpture of a Buddhist approaching Nirvana.

Ogle the undulating curves of the 10th-century Indian bronze sculptures of the dancing god Shiva and his wife, the goddess Parvati.

Be amazed in the Peacock Room, a jewel box of a space designed by James McNeill Whistler, with its gold murals on peacock-blue walls, and a peacock-feather-pattern gold leaf ceiling. At noon on the 3rd Thursday of every month, the floor-to-ceiling shutters are opened, bathing the room in glittering natural light. The museum is home to the world's largest collection of Whistler paintings.

Admire the manuscripts of 15th-century Persian love poetry, in exquisite calligraphy accompanied with intricate gold and silver painted decoration.

Discover the voice of contemporary Asian artists through cutting-edge immersive installations in the Sackler Gallery.

HIRSHHORN MUSEUM AND SCULPTURE GARDEN

✉ *Independence Ave. and 7th St. SW, The Mall* ☎ *202/633-2829* ⊕ *www.hirshhorn.si.edu* ▥ *Free* ⊙ *Museum daily 10–5:30, sculpture garden daily 7:30 am–dusk* Ⓜ *Smithsonian or L'Enfant Plaza (Maryland Ave. exit).*

TIPS

■ The sculpture garden makes an inspiring spot for a picnic.

■ Docents lead impromptu 45-minute highlight tours daily at 12:30 and on weekends at 3:30.

■ Have a question? Seek out the museum's Interpretive Guides, who wear question-mark badges.

■ Teens should check out the ArtLab, a design studio where they can experiment with new technology and learn digital-media techniques.

■ About three times a year, to coincide with a major installation, the museum hosts Hirshhorn After Hours events: parties that last until midnight and feature performance art, live music, dancing, and gallery talks.

■ The museum regularly screens premieres of independent films.

Conceived as the nation's museum of modern and contemporary art, the Hirshhorn is home to nearly 12,000 works by masters who include Pablo Picasso, Piet Mondrian, and Willem de Kooning, as well as contemporary superstars Olafur Eliasson, Damien Hirst and Salvatore Scarpitta. The art is displayed in a circular 1974 poured-concrete building, designed by Gordon Bunshaft, that was initially dubbed the "Doughnut on the Mall." Most of the collection was bequeathed by the museum's founder, Joseph H. Hirshhorn, a Latvian immigrant who made his fortune in uranium mines.

Highlights

The sculpture collection has masterpieces by Henry Moore, Alberto Giacometti and Constantin Brancusi. Outside, a 32-foot-tall yellow cartoon brush-stroke sculpture by pop-art iconographer Roy Lichtenstein has become a local landmark.

Inside, the newly renovated third level is the place to see dramatic postwar art from the museum's permanent collection, displayed thematically, with works by artists such as Joseph Cornell, Anish Kapoor, Louise Bourgeois, and Sol LeWitt.

The second level houses rotating exhibits devoted to particular artists or themes. In celebration of the Hirshhorn's 40th anniversary, "Days of Endless Time," an exhibition of moving-image artwork, will be on display through February 2015.

The lower level houses thematic installations featuring works from the permanent collection, as well as the Black Box, a space for moving image installations by international artists.

If you're with kids, start out at the National Air and Space Museum, a must-see just for the "wow" factor alone. Grab lunch at the museum's food court or at a hot dog cart outside. If your young bunch can handle two museums in a day, cross the lawn to the Natural History Museum. This itinerary works well for science buffs, too.

For a day devoted to the best of the best of the Mall—in other words, the best of the Smithsonian—start at the Air and Space Museum, then skip to the side-by-side Natural History and American History museums. Picnic on the Mall or hit the museum cafeterias so as not to waste a moment.

Remember that while many of the structures on the Mall present their finest face toward the great lawn, they all have entrances on Constitution or Independence avenues, which do not border the Mall's lawn. Use these doors to gain admission without crossing the Mall itself.

Planning: Since 9/11, security has increased and visitors will need to go through screenings and bag checks, which can create long lines during peak tourist season. Most of the museums on the Mall open daily at 10 and close at 5:30, except during the spring and summer when most extend their closing times to 7:30.

The Mall is accessible by public transportation. There are several nearby Metro stations: on the Blue and Orange lines, the Federal Triangle stop is convenient to the Natural History and American History museums, and the Smithsonian stop is close to the Holocaust Memorial Museum and Sackler Gallery. On the Yellow and Green lines, Archives/Navy Memorial takes you to the National Gallery of Art. The L'Enfant Plaza stop, accessible from the Blue, Orange, Yellow, and Green lines, is the best exit for the Hirshhorn and Air and Space Museum.

Martz/Gray Line (⊕ *www.graylinedc.com/tours*) offers two transportation options: an Express Shuttle bus between Union Station and Arlington National Cemetery, which stops at most major attractions on the Mall as well as key monuments on the National Mall; and Big Bus Tours with four routes and 60 stops including Mall museums, National Mall monuments, the National Zoo, White House, and Washington National Cathedral, which let you hop on and off their double-decker buses. Old Town Trolley Tours (⊕ *www.oldtowntrolleytours.com*) also has a 20-stop route along the Mall and downtown that allows you to get on and off their charming orange and green trolleys. You can purchase a one- or two-day pass and even track the location of your trolley and closest stop with the company's online GPS tracking tool.

There's metered parking along the Mall; you can pay with a credit card or via the mobile app. And there are parking garages north of the Mall in the Downtown area, where you pay a daily rate. If you're willing to walk, limited free parking is available on Ohio Drive SW near the Jefferson Memorial and East Potomac Park. ⊠ *The Mall.*

National Archives. *See the highlighted listing in this chapter.*

National Gallery of Art, East Building. The East Building opened in 1978 in response to the changing needs of the National Gallery, especially to house a growing collection of modern art. It's currently undergoing a three-year renovation that will add an additional 12,260 square feet of exhibit space and an outdoor sculpture terrace overlooking Pennsylvania Avenue. For the most up to date information on the project, refer to the gallery's website, ⊕ *www.nga.gov/renovation.*

Even though the East Building galleries are closed, you can still admire its unique structure—the trapezoidal shape of the site prompted architect I. M. Pei's dramatic approach: two interlocking spaces shaped like triangles provide room for galleries, auditoriums, and administrative offices. Despite its severe angularity, Pei's building is inviting. The ax-blade-like southwest corner has been darkened and polished smooth by thousands of hands irresistibly drawn to it. Inside, the sunlit atrium is dominated by a colorful 76-foot-long Alexander Calder mobile, the perfect introduction to galleries that will again with filled with masterworks of modern and contemporary art when the renovation project is completed. ⊠ *Constitution Ave., between 3rd and 4th sts. NW, The Mall* 🕾 *202/737–4215* ⊕ *www.nga.gov* 🕾 *Free* ☉ *Mon.–Sat. 10–5, Sun. 11–6* Ⓜ *Archives/Navy Memorial.*

National Gallery of Art, West Building. *See the highlighted listings in this chapter.*

National Museum of American History. *See the highlighted listings in this chapter.*

National Museum of Natural History. *See the highlighted listing in this chapter.*

National Museum of the American Indian. *See the highlighted listing in this chapter.*

Smithsonian Castle Information Center. The original home of the Smithsonian Institution is an excellent first stop on The Mall to help you get your bearings and plan your exploration of the museums. Built of red sandstone, this Medieval Revival style building, better known as the Castle, was designed by James Renwick Jr., the architect of St. Patrick's Cathedral in New York City. Although British scientist and founder James Smithson never visited America, his will stipulated that, should his nephew, Henry James Hungerford, die without an heir, Smithson's entire fortune would go to the United States, "to found at Washington, under the name of the Smithsonian Institution, an establishment for the increase and diffusion of knowledge." The museums on the Mall are the Smithsonian's most visible example of this ideal, but the organization also sponsors traveling exhibitions and maintains research posts in outside-the-Beltway locales, such as the Chesapeake Bay and the tropics of Panama.

A 10-minute video gives an overview of the Smithsonian museums and the National Zoo, and the exhibition *The Smithsonian Institution:*

America's Treasure Chest features objects representing all the museums that reveal the breadth and depth of the Smithsonian's collections. The Castle also has smaller temporary exhibitions, a good café, brochures in several languages, and a museum store. Kids appreciate the historic carousel at the north entrance; at the south entrance you'll find the manicured Haupt Garden and copper-domed kiosk called the Dillon Ripley Center, which houses the Discovery Theater. ■ **TIP→ The center opens at 8:30 am, 1½ hours before the other museums, so you can plan your day without wasting sightseeing time.** ✉ *1000 Jefferson Dr. SW, The Mall* ☎ *202/633–1000* ⊕ *www.si.edu* 🎫 *Free* ⊙ *Daily 8:30–5:30* Ⓜ *Smithsonian.*

FAMILY   **Smithsonian National Museum of African Art.** This unique underground building houses stunning galleries, a library, photographic archives, and educational facilities. The rotating exhibits illuminate African visual arts, including sculpture, textiles, photography, archaeology, and modern art. Long-term installations explore the sculpture of sub-Saharan Africa, the art of Benin, the pottery of Central Africa, the archaeology of the ancient Nubian city of Kerma, and artistry of everyday objects. The museum's educational programs for both children and adults include films with contemporary perspectives on African life, storytelling programs, and festivals including Community Day. The hands-on workshops, such as traditional basket-weaving, bring Africa's oral and cultural traditions to life. Workshops and demonstrations by African and African-American artists offer a chance to meet and talk to practicing artists. The well-stocked museum shop sells collectibles, pottery, art, jewelry, books, and maps. ✉ *950 Independence Ave. SW, The Mall* ☎ *202/633–4600* ⊕ *africa.si.edu* 🎫 *Free* ⊙ *Daily 10–5:30* Ⓜ *Smithsonian.*

United States Holocaust Memorial Museum. *See the highlighted listing in this chapter.*

WHITE HOUSE AREA

Art Museum of the Americas. Changing exhibits highlight modern and contemporary Latin American and Caribbean artists in this small gallery, part of the Organization of American States (OAS). The collection has 2,000 objects reflecting the diversity of expression found in the region. A public garden connects the Art Museum and the OAS building. ✉ *201 18th St. NW, White House area* ☎ *202/370–0147* ⊕ *www.amamuseum. org* 🎫 *Free* ⊙ *Tues.–Sun. 10–5* Ⓜ *Farragut West.*

Corcoran Gallery of Art. In April 2014, Washington's oldest privately owned art museum entered into a collaboration with the National Gallery of Art and George Washington University. As of this writing, the National Gallery will acquire most of the art held by the formerly independent museum, while some of the pieces will be donated to museums around the country. The Corcoran's art—considered by many art historians to be one of the greatest collections of 18th-, 19th- and 20th-century European and American masterpieces—includes paintings by Degas, Gilbert Stuart, John Copley, Rembrandt Peale, Mary Cassatt,

Continued on page 108

NATIONAL AIR AND SPACE MUSEUM

(above) Neil Armstrong and Buzz Aldrin's spacesuits.
(left) You can see into the cockpit of the Airbus A320

The country's second most-visited museum, attracting 9 million people annually to its vast and diverse collection of historic aircraft and spacecraft, is the perfect place to amaze the kids with giant rocket ships, relive the glory days of fighter jets, and even learn to fly. Its 22 galleries tell the story of humanity's quest for flight—from the Wright brothers' experiments with gliders to space exploration.

PLANNING YOUR TIME

If you only have short time take the free ninety-minute docent-led tour of the museum's highlights, which leaves daily at 10:30 and 1 from the Welcome Center.

To get the most from the museum, plan your must-sees in advance and allow plenty of time—at least two hours—to take everything in. The museum has three basic types of exhibits: aircraft and spacecraft; galleries of history and science; and experiences, such as IMAX films and hands-on workshops. An ideal visit would include a mix of these.

Before your visit, buy timed tickets online up to two weeks in advance for the popular IMAX films and planetarium shows to bypass the long lines and sold-out screenings.

When you arrive at the museum, consult the guides at the welcome desk; they can help you fine-tune your plan. If you didn't buy tickets for IMAX online, buy them now.

If you're traveling with kids, arrive early to avoid lines and pick up a kids' guide with games and activities at the welcome desk. Ask for the daily schedule of science demonstrations and (Thursday–Saturday only) Story Times for kids ages 2 to 8. If it's a clear day, visit the Public Observatory for daytime telescopic viewing and a chat with an astronomer. Strollers are allowed through security; there is a family bathroom on the first floor near the food court and a baby changing station near the Early Flight gallery.

If you just can't get enough, the Steven F. Udvar-Hazy Center, a companion museum near Dulles International Airport, features two massive hangars filled with hundreds more aircraft, spacecraft, aviation artifacts and a hangar where you can see restoration work in progress.

✉ Independence Ave. and 6th St. SW, The Mall ☎ 202/633–1000, 866/868–7774 movie information, 202/633–5285 TDD ⊕ www.airandspace.si.edu ✉ Free, IMAX or Planetarium $9, IMAX feature film $15 flight simulators $7–$8 ☻ Daily 10–5:30, Mar 28–Sept 5 open most days to 7:30

MUSEUM HIGHLIGHTS

AIRCRAFT AND SPACECRAFT

On entering the museum, you'll see that the **Milestones of Flight** gallery is undergoing restoration. The expanded exhibit will feature new digital displays that, combined with artifacts and models, will dramatically showcase the world's air and space innovations.

Albatros D.va

Make like Buzz Lightyear and head to infinity and beyond with a walk through the **Skylab Orbital Workshop**, the largest component of America's first space station in the **Space Race** gallery. Also on display are an arsenal of rockets and missiles, from the giant **V-2 rocket** to the devastatingly accurate **Tomahawk Cruise missile**. The **Apollo Lunar Module** is also a must-see in **Exploring the Moon.**

HISTORY AND SCIENCE

Even those who don't like history flock to the fascinating **Wright Brothers** gallery to see the first machine to achieve piloted flight, the **1903 Wright Flyer** and the Barron Hilton **Pioneers of Flight** gallery with Amelia Earhart's Lockheed Vega.

For history buffs, the **Great War in the Air, World War II,** and **Sea-Air Operations** galleries are essential, with legendary fighter planes such as the **Supermarine Spitfire**.

In the history of space exploration, **Apollo to the Moon** is packed with artifacts from moon missions.

Is there life on Mars? Find out in the science-oriented **Explore the Universe, Looking at Earth,** and **Moving Beyond Earth** galleries.

IMAX AND PLANETARIUM SHOWS

Lift off with an **IMAX** film. You'll feel like you've left the ground with the swooping aerial scenes in **To Fly!** or **Hidden Universe 3D**. Or take a trip into deep space with Hubble 3D. In the **Albert Einstein Planetarium,** you can watch the classic tour of the nighttime sky as well as shows like **Dark Universe.**

HANDS-ON

Test your top gun skills at one of the popular **Flight Simulators** where you'll get full-on fighter plane experience—barrel rolls and all.

TOURING TIPS

Avoid the Crowds: Between April and September (and on holiday weekends) the museum is slammed with visitors; it is least crowded September to March. It's always a good idea to come before noon to beat the rush.

Where to Eat: A huge food court offers McDonald's, Boston Market, and Donato's Pizzeria, and is the most simple and practical eating option around.

Souvenirs: The three-story museum store is the largest in all the Smithsonian museums, and one of the best. Along with souvenirs, books, and collectors' items, it also displays a model of the *USS Enterprise*, used in the filming of the first *Star Trek* television series. If you have kids, don't start your tour here or you may never leave!

Flight Simulators: Tickets can be purchased at the IMAX box office or in the **Flight Simulators** gallery.

Soviet SS-20 nuclear missile.

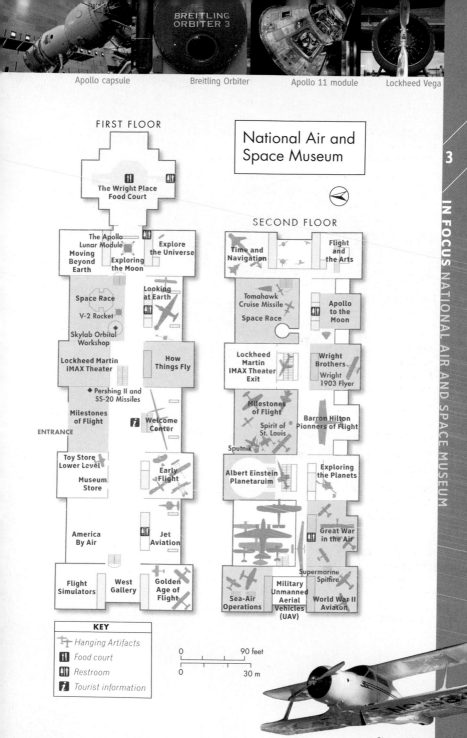

Apollo capsule Breitling Orbiter Apollo 11 module Lockheed Vega

Staggerwing

NASM TALKS TO FODOR'S

The original 1903 Wright Flyer.

Boeing F4B-4

Gen. John R. Daily (USMC, Ret.), director of the National Air and Space Museum, talks to Coral Davenport about what interests him at the Air and Space Museum.

BE AMAZED
"I would like visitors to take away a better understanding of the importance of air, aviation, and space in the leadership role of this country and technology. Also, an education in the four forces of flight—gravity, lift, thrust, and drag. **How Things Fly** is a physics lab designed to be understandable for kids, but I've watched so many adults be amazed as they learn the basics of the physics of flight in that gallery."

FLY THROUGH THE AGES
"The history is extremely important—but of them all, the **Wright Brothers** gallery is probably the most important. Also, the **Golden Age of Flight** gallery, about the period when aviation was young, and people were doing crazy things—wing walking, barnstorming. The **World War II** galleries are also a big draw. I think a lot of parents and grandparents most closely relate to those galleries. They bring their families and tell stories about what it was like flying air raids over Germany."

MAKING CONNECTIONS
"This is a personal museum. There are attachments between individuals and artifacts. Sometimes families come in because Dad wants to look at his old airplane. But the designers have put together rich cross-cultural exhibits—showing the historic, but also the cultural and social impacts of aviation. They show what people were wearing, how developments in aviation led to fads and movements. It's hard to tie it all together sometimes but this museum helps people make those connections."

FAVORITE PLANE
"The **Boeing F4B-4** in **Sea-Air Operations** is my favorite plane—my father flew that exact plane the year I was born. It's a pre-World War II airplane. When you compare that to the **X-15** or the **Bell X-1**, you see the tremendous leap that aviation took in the middle of the century, as a result of World War II."

1960s flight attendant uniform

NATIONAL AIR AND SPACE MUSEUM
STEVEN F. UDVAR-HAZY CENTER

For more giant jets and spaceships, you won't want to miss the museum's **Udvar-Hazy Center** at Washington Dulles International Airport in northern Virginia. The center showcases the museum's growing collection of historic air- and spacecraft, which is much too large to fit into the building on the Mall.

Unlike the museum on the Mall, the Udvar-Hazy Center focuses on one thing: planes and rockets. This focus makes the center more appealing for families with kids too young to take in detailed historic narratives. It is also much less crowded than the Mall museum.

The giant three-level Boeing Aviation Hangar is devoted to historic aircraft, such as the **Lockheed SR-71 Blackbird**, the fastest jet in the world; the sassy-looking **DeHavilland Chipmunk**, a prototype aerobatic airplane; the sleek, supersonic **Concorde**, and the **Enola Gay,** which in 1945 dropped the atomic bomb on Hiroshima, Japan.

You can see the Space Shuttle **Discovery,** as well as satellites, space stations, and space missile launchers in the James S. McDonnell Space Hangar. In the Mary Baker Engen Restoration Hangar, you can watch specialists repair and restore historic aircraft, such as the Curtiss SB2C-5 Helldiver that just went on display.

TOURING TIPS

Getting Here: You'll need a car as there is no nearby Metro or bus stop. The drive takes about 30–40 minutes from D.C. Take I-66 West to Route 28 North (Exit 53B); drive 5 miles and exit at the Air and Space Museum Parkway, follow signs to the museum. Parking is $15.

Airport Shuttle: You can combine a morning visit with an afternoon departure flight from nearby Dulles Airport. There are 15-minute shuttles every hour between the airport and museum for $1. A taxi ride costs about $15.

When you arrive: Head to the welcome desk for a map to guide you around the museum. Allow at least an hour to tour and another 45 minutes to see an **IMAX** film.

With Kids: Pick up museum guides with games and activities for kids ages 9 and up at the welcome desk and ask which Discovery Stations are at the museum that day.

Where to Eat: There is a McDonald's and McCafe.

✉ 14390 Air and Space Museum Parkway, Chantilly, VA
☎ 202/633-1000, 866/868-7774 movie information, 202/633-5285 TDD ⊕ www.airandspace.si.edu ✉ Free, IMAX feature film $15, Planetarium $9, flight simulators $7–$8
⊙ Daily 10–5:30

NATIONAL ARCHIVES

✉ *Constitution Ave., between 7th and 9th sts., The Mall* ☎ *866/272-6272, 877/444-6777 for tours and reservations* ⊕ *www.archives.gov* 🎫 *Free; $1.50 convenience fee for online reservations* ⊙ *Daily 10-5:30; tours weekdays at 9:45 am with reservation* Ⓜ *Archives/Navy Memorial.*

TIPS

■ Reservations to visit the Archives are highly recommended, unless you want to wait up to an hour to get in. Reservations for guided tours, or a self-guided visit, should be made at least six weeks in advance. March, April, May and the weekends around Thanksgiving and Christmas are the busiest. Expect to spend at least two hours here.

■ The archives research entrance on Pennsylvania Avenue is open to anyone. Archivists can help family genealogists track down birth, death, military, and census records, immigrant ships' passenger lists, letters, maps, or anything else you're looking for.

Monument, museum, and the nation's memory, the Archives, headquartered in a grand marble edifice on Constitution Avenue, preserves more than 10 billion paper records dating back to 1774 and billions of recent electronic records. The National Archives and Records Administration is charged with preserving and archiving the most important U.S. government records at its records centers nationwide and in presidential libraries.

Highlights

Charters of Freedom—The Declaration of Independence, the Constitution, and the Bill of Rights—are the star attractions and are housed in the Archives' cathedral-like rotunda, each on a marble platform, encased in bulletproof glass.

On display at the entrance to the new David M. Rubenstein Gallery is the 1297 Magna Carta, the document of English common law whose language inspired the Constitution. This sets the stage for the "Records of Rights" exhibit in this interactive gallery that traces the civil rights struggles of African Americans, women and immigrants. Themed display areas include "Bending Towards Justice," "Remembering the Ladies," and "Yearning to Breathe Free" with thought-provoking photographs, historical documents and videos. Highlights include a YMCA English guide for new citizens from the 1920's, the discharge papers of a slave who fought in the Revolutionary War to gain his freedom; the legislative mark-up copy of the 1964 Civil Rights Act; and letters to the President from children questioning the morality of segregation.

Watch films of flying saucers, used as evidence in congressional UFO hearings, listen to the Nuremberg trials or Congress debating Prohibition—selections from the Archives' 500,000 film and audio recordings.

NATIONAL GALLERY OF ART, WEST BUILDING

✉ *4th St. and Constitution Ave. NW, The Mall*
☎ *202/737–4215* ⊕ *www.nga.gov* ▣ *Free* ⊙ *Mon.–Sat. 10–5, Sun. 11–6* Ⓜ *Archives/Navy Memorial.*

3

TIPS

■ There are free docent-led tours daily, and a recorded tour of highlights of the permanent collection is available free of charge on the main floor adjacent to the rotunda. For a cheat-sheet tour, pick up the laminated "What to See in One Hour" (it's also available on the website), which pinpoints 12 must-see masterworks.

■ The gallery has a full calendar of free concerts, films, lectures, and other events. Among the most popular is the summer "Jazz in the Garden" series, held Friday evenings in the sculpture garden. Take a break at one of the museum's cafés, or at the sculpture garden's Pavilion Cafe, open year-round.

■ Events for children include storytelling that integrates the art; hands-on studio sessions and Teen Studio Saturdays, led by curators combining instruction and studio experimentation. Some welcome walk-ins and others require advance registration; check the website (wwww.nga.gov) for details.

The two buildings of the National Gallery hold one of the world's foremost collections of paintings, sculptures, and graphics, from the 13th to the 21st centuries. Opened in 1941, the domed museum was a gift to the nation from treasury secretary Andrew Mellon. The rotunda, with 24 marble columns surrounding a fountain topped with a statue of Mercury, sets the stage for the masterpieces on display in more than 100 galleries.

Highlights

The only painting by Leonardo da Vinci on display in the Americas, *Ginevra de' Benci* is the centerpiece of the collection's survey of Italian Renaissance paintings and sculpture; it also includes Raphael's *Alba Madonna* and Sandro Botticelli's *Adoration of the Magi.*

The masters of painting light, Rembrandt van Rijn and Johannes Vermeer, anchor the magnificent collection of Dutch and Flemish works.

Nineteenth-century French Galleries house gorgeous French Impressionist masterworks by such superstars as Vincent Van Gogh, Paul Cezanne, Claude Monet, Auguste Renoir, and Edgar Degas. The gallery is organized into groupings that showcase the bold innovations that occured during the era of impressionism and post-impressionism.

The Sculpture Garden

Walk beneath flowering trees in the sculpture garden, on the Mall between 7th and 9th streets. Walkways take you through sculptures from the museum's permanent collection, including Roy Lichtenstein's playful *House I*, Miró's *Personnage Gothique, Oiseau-Eclair,* and the newest addition, Marc Chagall's *Orphée,* a 17 feet by 10 feet mosaic made of thousands of colored glass and stone pieces. The central fountain is converted to an outdoor skating rink in winter.

NATIONAL MUSEUM OF AMERICAN HISTORY

✉ *Constitution Ave. and 14th St. NW, The Mall* ☎ *202/633–1000* ⊕ *www.americanhistory.si.edu* 🎟 *Free* ⊙ *Daily 10–5:30 with occasional extended hrs to 7:30 pm; check website* Ⓜ *Smithsonian or Federal Triangle.*

TIPS

■ Pick up a map at the information desk on the first floor or the welcome center on the second floor.

■ During the high season and on holidays, expect waits of up to 20 minutes for the Star-Spangled Banner and the First Ladies' gallery.

■ The Stars and Stripes Café on the lower level offers a salad bar and sandwiches; the Constitution Café on the first floor serves coffee, ice cream, and snacks.

■ The main museum store is on the first floor; another is on the third floor.

The 3 million artifacts and archival collections in the country's largest American history museum explore America's cultural, political, and scientific past, with holdings as diverse and iconic as Abraham Lincoln's top hat, Thomas Edison's lightbulbs, Julia Child's entire kitchen, and Judy Garland's ruby slippers from *The Wizard of Oz.*

Highlights

The centerpiece of the Star-Spangled Banner gallery is the banner that in 1814 was hoisted to show that Fort McHenry had survived 25 hours of British rocket attacks, inspiring Francis Scott Key to write the lyrics that became the national anthem.

For political and military history, visit the American Presidency, Gunboat Philadelphia, and Price of Freedom: Americans at War galleries.

"American Stories" showcases historic and cultural touchstones of American history through more than 100 objects from the museum's vast holdings: a walking stick used by Benjamin Franklin, a sunstone capital from a Mormon temple, Lincoln's gold pocket watch, Archie Bunker's chair, Muhammad Ali's boxing gloves, a fragment of Plymouth rock, and a Jim Henson puppet.

What's more, this is the only museum in the world with an active program of using historical musical instruments for live performances; the Smithsonian Chamber Music Society holds regular concerts.

NATIONAL MUSEUM OF THE AMERICAN INDIAN

✉ *4th St. and Independence Ave. SW, The Mall* ☎ *202/633-1000* ⊕ *www.americanindian.si.edu* 🎫 *Free* ⊙ *Daily 10–5:30* Ⓜ *L'Enfant Plaza.*

3

TIPS

■ Visit between 10 and 2 on a sunny day to see the central atrium awash in rainbows created by the light refracted through prisms in the ceiling aligned with Earth's cardinal points.

■ From roasted venison and Peruvian seviche to pork pibil tacos and quinoa salad, the museum's Mitsitam Native Foods Café offers a modern perspective on foods that have been grown, raised, and harvested in North and South America for thousands of years.

■ Free tours are offered daily, and the museum's 6,000-square-foot family-friendly imagiNATIONS Activity Center includes hands-on activities throughout the year, including an interactive quiz show modeled after Jeopardy! and an igloo-building exercise.

The Smithsonian's newest museum, opened in 2004, stands apart visually and conceptually from the other cultural institutions on the Mall. The undulating exterior, clad in pinkish-gold limestone from Minnesota, evokes natural rock formations shaped by wind and water. Inside, four floors of galleries cover 10,000 years of history of the thousands of native tribes of the Western Hemisphere. However, only 5% of the museum's holdings are on display at any one time, and they are arranged to showcase specific tribes and themes, rather than a chronological history. Some visitors find this approach confusing, but touring with one of the Native American guides can help bring the history and legends to life.

Highlights

Live music, dance, theater, and storytelling are central to experiencing this museum. Tribal groups stage performances in the two theaters and sun-lighted ceremonial atrium.

The *Our Universe* exhibit tells the unique creation legends of eight different tribes, with carvings, costumes, and videos of tribal storytellers. The stories rotate to give exposure to the different tribes of the Americas.

Central to the native story is the transformation that convulsed the tribes of America in 1492, the year of first contact with Europeans. The exhibits focusing on the native world before and after "first contact" are among the most compelling.

NATIONAL MUSEUM OF NATURAL HISTORY

✉ *Constitution Ave. and 10th St. NW, The Mall* ☎ *202/633–1000* ⊕ *www. mnh.si.edu* 🎫 *Free, IMAX $9, Butterfly Pavilion $6 (free Tues.)* ⏰ *Daily 10–5:30 (until 7:30 May–Sept.); Discovery Room Tues.–Fri. noon–2:30, weekends 10:30–3:30* Ⓜ *Smithsonian or Federal Triangle.*

TIPS

■ The IMAX theater shows two- and three-dimensional natural history films throughout the day. Buy advance tickets at the box office when you arrive, then tour the museum.

■ The Butterfly Pavilion makes a great photo op. Timed tickets sell out fast—buy them in advance online or when you arrive. The pavilion is free on Tuesday, but still requires a timed ticket.

■ The Discovery Room has hands-on activities and workshops for kids.

■ The museum's three restaurants received a 3-star certification from the Green Restaurant Association; they serve local, all-natural, organic, sustainable fare on compostable flatware.

This is one of the world's great natural history museums, with 18 exhibition halls featuring dinosaur fossils, glittering gems, and creepy-crawly insects. More than 126 million specimens attract more than 7 million visitors annually.

Highlights

Discover Q?RIUS, a hands-on space featuring 6,000 natural- and human-made objects, on-site experts, and an array of digital tools that focus on the natural world.

Walk among hundreds of brilliantly colored, live butterflies in the Butterfly Pavilion, which requires a separate admission. For a different kind of entomological experience, check out giant millipedes and furry tarantulas in the O. Orkin Insect Zoo.

See perfectly preserved giant squids, a jaw-dropping whale replica, and the vivid ecosystem of a coral reef in the Sant Ocean Hall, where tours are offered weekends at 11 and 2. The Ocean Explorer Theater simulates a dive into the depths of the sea.

The newest addition to the museum's collection of 46 million fossils is the Wankel T. rex found in Montana in 1988. One of the most complete T. rex skeletons ever discovered, it will form the centerpiece of the 25,000-square-foot dinosaur hall that's scheduled for completion in 2019. Currently, select dinosaurs and fossils are on display in other parts of the museum, but in 2015 the much-anticipated "The Last American Dinosaurs: Discovering a Lost World" opens.

Drool over the National Gem Collection in the *Janet Annenberg Hooker Hall of Geology, Gems and Minerals,* including Marie Antoinette's earrings, the 77-carat Cindy Chao Royal Butterfly Brooch, and the Hope Diamond—a 45.52-carat blue gem donated by Harry Winston in 1958.

UNITED STATES HOLOCAUST MEMORIAL MUSEUM

✉ *100 Raoul Wallenberg Pl. SW or 14th St. SW, The Mall* ☎ *202/488-0400, 800/400-9373 for tickets* ⊕ *www. ushmm.org* ✉ *Free; $1/ticket service fee for advance online reservations* ⊙ *Daily 10–5:20* Ⓜ *Smithsonian.*

TIPS

■ Like the history it covers, the museum can be disturbing; it's not recommended for children under 11, although Daniel's Story, in a ground-floor exhibit not requiring tickets, is designed for children ages eight and up. Ask for the Family Guide that accompanies the exhibits for children.

■ Plan to spend two to three hours here.

■ Check at the desk for any special programs scheduled that day.

■ Timed-entry passes (distributed on a first-come, first-served basis at the 14th Street entrance starting at 10 or available in advance through the museum's website with a $1/ticket service fee) are necessary for the permanent exhibition March through August. Allow extra time to enter the building in spring and summer, when long lines can form. September through February, no passes are required.

This museum asks visitors to consider how the Holocaust was made possible by the choices of individuals, institutions and governments, and what lessons they hold for us today. The permanent exhibition tells the stories of the millions of Jews, Gypsies, Jehovah's Witnesses, homosexuals, political prisoners, the mentally ill, and others killed by the Nazis between 1933 and 1945. The exhibitions are detailed and graphic; the experiences memorable and powerful.

Highlights

The presentation is as extraordinary as the subject matter: upon arrival, you are issued an "identity card" containing biographical information on a real person from the Holocaust. As you move through the museum, you read sequential updates on your card.

Hitler's rise to power and the spread of European anti-Semitism are thoroughly documented in the museum's early exhibits, with films of Nazi rallies, posters, newspaper articles, and recordings of Hitler's speeches immersing you in the world that led to the Holocaust.

You are confronted with the truths of the Holocaust in the exhibit *The Final Solution*, which details the Nazis' murder of six million Jews. Exhibits include film footage of scientific experiments done on Jews, artifacts such as a freight car like those used to transport Jews from Warsaw to concentration camps, and crematoria implements. There are films and audio recordings of Holocaust survivors telling their harrowing stories.

After this powerful experience, the adjacent Hall of Remembrance, filled with candles and hand-painted tiles dedicated to children who died in the Holocaust, provides a much-needed space for quiet reflection.

and John Singer Sargent; photography by Richard Avedon and William Eggleston; and postwar art by Cy Twombly, Lee Bontecou, Andy Warhol, and Ellsworth Kelly. Modern and contemporary art will be displayed on the 2nd floor under the name Corcoran Contemporary, National Gallery of Art. Also in this marble Beaux Arts building will be a Corcoran Legacy Gallery, showcasing works that reflect the historical significance of the museum. As part of this partnership, George Washington University will manage not only the building, but also the highly reputed Corcoran School of Art + Design. Check the website for the latest news on this collaboration. ⊠ *500 17th St. NW, White House area* ☏ *202/639–1700* ⊕ *www.corcoran.org* ⌨ *Free* ☼ *Call or check website for hours* Ⓜ *Farragut West or Farragut North.*

FAMILY **Daughters of the American Revolution Museum (DAR).** The Beaux Arts-style Memorial Continental Hall was the site of the DAR's annual congress until the larger Constitution Hall was built, and now serves as its headquarters. An entrance on D Street leads to the museum, where the 30,000-item collection includes fine examples of colonial and Federal furniture, textiles, quilts, silver, china, porcelain, stoneware, earthenware, and glass. Thirty-one period rooms are decorated in styles representative of various U.S. states, ranging from an 1850 California adobe parlor to a New Hampshire attic filled with 18th- and 19th-century toys. Two galleries—one featuring changing exhibitions—hold decorative arts. Docent tours of the period rooms are available weekdays 10–2:30 and Saturday 9–4:30. On exhibit through August 2015 is "Eye on Elegance: Early Quilts of Virginia and Maryland." The museum hosts a lunch lecture series and Family Saturdays; check the website for dates. ⊠ *1776 D St. NW, White House area* ☏ *202/628–1776* ⊕ *www. dar.org* ⌨ *Free* ☼ *Weekdays 9:30–4, Sat. 9–5* Ⓜ *Farragut West.*

CAPITOL HILL, NORTHEAST D.C., AND ANACOSTIA

CAPITOL HILL

Folger Shakespeare Library. The collection of works by and about Shakespeare and his times is second to none, and though the reading rooms are open only to academic researchers, the white-marble Art Deco building, decorated with sculpted scenes from the Bard's plays, is well worth a look. Inside is a reproduction of a 16th-century inn-yard theater—the site for performances of Shakesperean plays, chamber music, readings, lectures, and family programs—and a gallery, designed in the manner of an Elizabethan Great Hall, that holds rotating exhibits from the library's collection. One of the Folger's Shakespeare First Folios is always on view and may be thumbed through digitally in the Great Hall. A manicured Elizabethan garden on the grounds is open to the public, and the gift shop contains many collectibles featuring the Bard and English theater. The building was designed by architect Paul Philippe Cret and dedicated in 1932. Henry Clay Folger, the library's founder, was Standard Oil's president and chairman of the board. ⊠ *201 E. Capitol St. SE, Capitol Hill* ☏ *202/544–4600* ⊕ *www.folger.edu* ⌨ *Free* ☼ *Mon.–Sat. 10–5, Sun. noon–5* Ⓜ *Capitol South.*

Sewall-Belmont House & Museum. Standing strong on Capitol Hill for more than 200 years, this house witnessed the construction of the U.S. Capitol and Supreme Court, and its early occupants participated in the formation of Congress. In 1929, the National Woman's Party (NWP) purchased the house, and it soon evolved into a center for feminist education and social change. For more than sixty years, the trailblazing NWP utilized its strategic location, steps from the U.S. Capitol and its Congressional offices, to lobby for women's political, social and economic equality. Today, an expansive collection of artifacts from the suffrage and equal rights campaigns brings the story of the Women's Rights movement to life. The innovative tactics and strategies these women devised became the blueprint for women's progress throughout the 20th century. ✉ *144 Constitution Ave. NE, Capitol Hill* ☎ *202/546–1210* ⊕ *www.sewallbelmont.org* 🎫 *$8* ⊙ *Thurs.–Sat. tours at 11, 1 and 3* Ⓜ *Union Station.*

FAMILY **Smithsonian National Postal Museum.** The National Museum of Natural History has the Hope Diamond, but the National Postal Museum has the envelope wrapping used to mail the gem to the Smithsonian—part of a collection that consists of more than 6 million stamps. Exhibits, underscoring the important part the mail has played in America's development, include horse-drawn mail coaches, railroad mail cars, airmail planes, and a collection of philatelic rarities. Learn about stamp collecting and tour Systems at Work, an exhibit that demonstrates how mail has gone from the mailbox to its destination for the past 200 years, featuring a high-def film highlighting amazing technologies. The Mail Call exhibit shows the history of the military postal system from the Revolutionary War to today, including a video entitled "Missing You—Letters from Wartime." The William Gross Stamp Gallery, the largest of its kind in the world, has an additional 20,000 objects never before on public display, showing how closely stamps have intertwined with American history. The museum is housed in the old Washington City Post Office, designed by Daniel Burnham and completed in 1914. Nostalgic odes to the noble mail carrier are inscribed on the exterior of the marble building; one of them, "The Letter," eulogizes the "Messenger of sympathy and love / Servant of parted friends / Consoler of the lonely / Bond of the scattered family / Enlarger of the common life." ✉ *2 Massachusetts Ave. NE, Capitol Hill* ☎ *202/633–5555* ⊕ *www.postalmuseum.si.edu* 🎫 *Free* ⊙ *Daily 10–5:30; tours at 11 and 1 from info desk* Ⓜ *Union Station.*

NORTHEAST D.C.

FAMILY **Washington Navy Yard.** A 115-acre historic district with its own street system, the Washington Navy Yard is the Navy's oldest outpost on shore. Established in 1799 as a shipbuilding facility, the district was burned by the Americans during the War of 1812 to keep the British from capturing the base and the four Navy ships docked there. Rebuilt and converted to weapons production by the mid-19th century, the Navy Yard became integral to the defense of Washington during the Civil War, and the Lincoln assassination conspirators were held there. Charles Lindbergh landed at the Navy Yard after his famous transatlantic flight.

The Navy Yard gradually fell into disuse, until the 1960s when it was revived as a thriving administrative and cultural center. It currently houses the **National Museum of the US Navy** (⇨ *See separate listing*), which includes the **Cold War Gallery**. Outside the base, at 8th and I Street, you can see the impressive **Home of the Commandants**, a mansion housing the commandant of the Marines Corps, and the historic Marine Barracks. ■**TIP**➡ **Every Friday May through August, the U.S. Marine Band hosts a parade of music and marching starting at 8:45 pm. It's best to make reservations in advance to secure a seat for this summer concert (**⊕ **www.barracks.marines.mil).**

The west side of the Yard is flanked by a waterfront promenade, the **Anacostia Riverwalk,** which is open to pedestrian traffic Tuesday through Sunday.

On weekdays, enter the Navy Yard on 11th and O Street; on weekends, you enter on 6th and M Street. Visitors 18 and older must show valid government-issued identification (a driver's license or passport). Access and ID requirements are subject to change; check the website for latest information. The Metro stations are several blocks from the entrance to Navy Yard, so prepare to walk some distance. The $1 per fare DC Circulator "Union Station to Navy Yard" route runs every day except Sunday. Personal vehicles are permitted into the Navy Yard on weekends (use the 6th and M Street entrance), and there is metered public parking under the Southeast Freeway on 8th Street. Restaurants and shopping are nearby at Barracks Row and The Yard. ⊠ *O and 11th St. SE, Southeast* ⊕ *www.history.navy.mil* 🚇 *Free* ☉ *Weekdays 9–5, weekends 10–5* Ⓜ *Eastern Market or Navy Yard.*

National Museum of the US Navy. The Navy Museum, in Building 76 of the Navy Yard, chronicles the history of the U.S. Navy from the Revolution to the present. Exhibits range from the fully rigged foremast of the USS *Constitution* (better known as *Old Ironsides*) to a U.S. Navy Corsair fighter plane dangling from the ceiling. All around are models of fighting ships, a real Vietnam-era Swift boat, working periscopes, displays on battles, and portraits of the sailors who fought them. In front of the museum is a collection of guns, cannons, and missiles, and the decommissioned U.S. Navy destroyer USS *Barry* floats a short distance away on Riverwalk by the Anacostia River. The **Navy Art Collection,** including many works by Navy artists, is also housed in the museum. A new addition to the Navy Museum is the **Cold War Gallery** with exhibits that explore the Navy's response to the threat of Soviet military power and communist ideology. ⚠ **At the time of writing access to the museum is extremely limited and will be for the foreseeable future and all visitors must have a DOD Common Access Card (CAC) or military ID. This may change, but it's important to call before visiting to check on the current situation.** ⊠ *Navy Yard, 805 Kidder Breese St. SE, entrance at 11th and O St. SE, Southeast* ✛ *Enter through the visitor's gate at 11th and O St. SE (weekdays) or 6th and M St. SE (weekends) and show a valid photo ID; you'll receive a pass and map of the surroundings* 🕾 *202/433–3815 for museum, 202/433–4882 for USS Barry* ⊕ *www.history.navy.mil* 🚇 *Free* ☉ *Museum: weekdays 9–5, weekends 10–5; USS Barry: Mar.–Oct., Thurs. and Fri. 9–5, Sat. 10–5. Hrs, access* *and ID requirements are subject to change; call or check website before visiting* Ⓜ *Eastern Market.*

ANACOSTIA

Frederick Douglass National Historic Site. Cedar Hill, the Anacostia home of abolitionist Frederick Douglass, was the first Black National Historic Site that Congress designated. Douglass, a former slave who escaped to freedom and delivered rousing abolitionist speeches at home and abroad, resided here from 1877 until his death in 1895. The house has a wonderful view of Washington across the Anacostia River and contains many of Douglass's personal belongings. The home has been meticulously restored to its original grandeur; you can view Douglass' hundreds of books displayed on his custom-built bookshelves, and Limoges china on the Douglass family dining table. A short film on Douglass' life is shown at a nearby visitor center. Entry to the home requires participation in a 30-minute ranger-led tour, for which you must arrive 20 minutes in advance; reserve by phone or online. ✉ *1411 W St. SE, Anacostia* ☎ *202/426–5961, 202/444–6777 for museum tours* ⊕ *www.nps.gov/frdo; www.recreation.gov for online ticket reservations* ⌂ *House $1.50, Garden and Visitors Center free* ♥ *Nov.–Mar., daily 9–4:30; Apr.–Oct., daily 9–5; check website for tour times* Ⓜ *Anacostia.*

> **CAPITAL FACTS**
>
> The federal government bought Ford's Theatre in 1866 for $100,000 and converted it into office space. It was remodeled as a Lincoln museum in 1932 and was restored to its 1865 appearance in 1968.

DOWNTOWN

FAMILY

Fodor's Choice

★

Ford's Theatre National Historic Site. The events that took place here on the night of April 14, 1865, shocked the nation. During a performance of *Our American Cousin,* John Wilkes Booth entered the state box at Ford's Theatre and shot Abraham Lincoln in the back of the head. The stricken president was carried across the street to the house of tailor William Petersen. Charles Augustus Leale, a 23-year-old surgeon, was the first man to attend the president. To let Lincoln know that someone was nearby, Leale held his hand throughout the night. Lincoln died the next morning. The theater and Petersen's house are now the anchors of an ambitious block-long, Lincoln-centered cultural campus commemorating the president. The theater, which stages performances year-round, is restored to look as it did when Lincoln attended, including the presidential box draped with flags as it was on the night he was shot. The portrait of George Washington on the box is the same one over which Lincoln sat; its frame has a nick made by Wilkes's spur as he leapt from the box to the stage. In the restored **Petersen House** you can see the room where Lincoln died and the parlor where his wife, Mary Todd, waited in anguish through the night.

The centerpiece of the **Center for Education and Leadership** is a jaw-dropping, three-story tower of 6,800 books written about Lincoln. In the center, visitors take a step back in time, to April 15, 1865, entering a 19th-century street scene where they find a reproduction of Lincoln's funeral train car and see its route to Springfield, Illinois. Visitors also learn about the manhunt for John Wilkes Booth and his co-conspirators' trial. Exhibits also explore the fate of Lincoln's family after his death, explain the milestones of reconstruction, and describe Lincoln's legacy and his enduring impact on U.S. and world leaders. A visit ends with a multiscreened video wall that shows how Lincoln's ideas resonate today.

Visits to Ford's Theatre National Historic Site require a free, timed-entry ticket. Same-day tickets are available at the theater box office beginning at 8:30 am on a first-come, first-served basis. You can also reserve tickets in advance through Ticketmaster (⊕ *www.ticketmaster. com*) with a $2.50 fee per ticket. During the spring of 2015, Ford's will honor Lincoln's legacy with "Ford's 150: Remembering the Lincoln Assassination" with a special theater productions, round-the-clock vigils, panel discussions, and an exhibition of artifacts connected with the assassination that are being returned to Ford's for the first time since 1865. Check the website for details. ⊠ *511 10th St. NW, Downtown* ☎ *202/426–6924* ⊕ *www.fords.org* ⊠ *Free, except for performances* ⊙ *Daily 9–5; theater closed during rehearsals and matinees, generally Thurs. and weekends* Ⓜ *Metro Center or Gallery Pl./Chinatown.*

International Spy Museum. *See the highlighted listing in this chapter.*

Madame Tussauds. A branch of the famous London-based waxworks franchise focuses on U.S. presidential history. You can see and pose for pictures (some for a small fee) with uncanny likenesses of the Founding Fathers or any of the presidents, including Barack Obama and his wife, or sit inside the Oval Office, painstakingly re-created in wax. The Civil Rights room features Martin Luther King Jr. and Rosa Parks. There are cultural icons, sports figures, and a behind-the-scenes exhibit where experts demonstrate wax sculpting. The Glamour Room is populated with waxen re-creations of George Clooney, Beyonce, Angelina Jolie, and Brad Pitt, among others. ■TIP→ Purchase tickets online for the best daily discount. ⊠ *1025 F St. NW, Downtown* ☎ *202/942–7300, 866/823–9565 to confirm hrs* ⊕ *www.madametussaudsdc. com* ⊠ *$21.50* ⊙ *Apr.–Sept., Sun.–Fri. 10–6, Sat. 10–8; Oct.–Mar., Mon.–Thurs. noon–6, Fri.–Sun. 10–6* Ⓜ *Metro Center or Gallery Pl./ Chinatown.*

Marian Koshland Science Museum. Part of the National Academy of Sciences, this small but engaging museum invites older kids and adults to interact with current scientific issues in a thought-provoking setting. Visitors have the opportunity to use science to solve problems and engage in conversation. In "Earth Lab: Degrees of Change" you'll examine the energy sector and employ strategies to lower carbon dioxide emissions to a level that will significantly reduce the impact of climate change. "The Life Lab" takes a look at decisions you make throughout your life and explores how the brain develops. There's a driving simulator, a 3-D look inside the brain, plus exhibits on the science of healthy eating through the life span. In the newest exhibit, "The Idea Lab," you'll explore the concept of resilience in your life and community. Map risk and resilience, play a disaster simulation game and create

INTERNATIONAL SPY MUSEUM

✉ 800 F St. NW, Downtown
☎ 202/393-7798 ⊕ www.
spymuseum.org 🎫 Permanent
exhibition $20.95, Opera-
tion Spy $14.95 ⊙ Daily 9–7
(hrs vary; check website
before visiting) Ⓜ *Gallery Pl./*
Chinatown.

3

TIPS

■ Advance tickets (purchased at the museum or on its website) are highly recommended. All tickets are date and time specific. Tickets are most likely available (and your visit less crowded) on Tuesday, Wednesday, and Thursday or daily after 2 pm. Allow about two hours for a visit.

■ This is a great museum for kids age 10 and up; younger ones might not get it. At the popular monthly KidSpy workshop for kids ages 10–14, participants can assume a cover identity and disguise, make a portable lie detector, crack a cipher, check out surveillance electronics, and more.

■ The museum regularly hosts films, events, and lectures by espionage experts. A GPS-guided walking tour, Spy in the City, takes "agents" 12 years and older on a mission outside the museum walls.

It's believed that there are more spies in Washington than in any other city in the world, making it a fitting home for this museum, which displays the world's largest collection of spy artifacts. Museum advisers include top cryptologists; masters of disguise; and former CIA, FBI, and KGB operatives. Exhibits range from the coded letters of Revolutionary War überspy Benedict Arnold and the KGB's lipstick pistol, to high tech 21st-century espionage toys, showcased with theatrical panache in a five-building complex (one, the Warder-Atlas Building, housed Washington's Communist party in the '40s).

Highlights

"The Secret History of History" takes you through the espionage behind the headlines, from Moses's use of spies in Canaan to the birth of the KGB.

"Exquisitely Evil: 50 Years of Bond Villains" is a heavy mix of flash and fun as you come face-to-face with villains from dozens of Bond films. More than 100 artifacts are exhibited, from the steel teeth worn by actor Richard Kiel as "Jaws" in 1979's *Moonraker* to Raoul Silva's laptop in *Skyfall*. Historical documents and videos demonstrate the threat of nuclear weapons, terrorism, and cyber attacks through time. And—of course—Bond's famous Aston Martin is on display.

"Operation Spy," a one-hour immersive experience, drops you into a high-stakes intelligence mission.

an emergency plan. ■TIP➔ Though the interactive exhibits are fun and educational, they are aimed at ages 12 and up. ✉ *525 E St. NW, Downtown* ☎ *202/334–1201* ⊕ *www. koshland-dc.org* ✉ *$7* ⊙ *Wed.– Mon. 10–6* Ⓜ *Gallery Pl./Chinatown or Judiciary Sq.*

National Building Museum. *See the highlighted listing in this chapter.*

National Museum of Crime and Punishment. America's history of crime and the judicial system are explored in

WORD OF MOUTH

"I checked out the National Building Museum. Since it's away from the Mall, it's not crowded at all, and has some interesting displays and an awesome museum shop. If you're interested in how D.C. and the various monuments were built (including the politics that were played), stop by." —Pisces

exhibits that demonstrate tactics used by law enforcement, the work of forensic scientists and crime scene investigators, and the consequences for committing a crime. Exhibits range from a medieval torture chamber to the getaway car used by bank robbers Bonnie and Clyde. With more than 100 interactives, you can put your hands in pillory stocks, take a lie detector test, enter a jail cell, and experience a simulated crime-scene investigation. From pirates, witches, and Wild West outlaws, to white-collar criminals, serial killers, and computer hackers, many displays involve reading, are at times grim, and are better for older children. Created in partnership with *America's Most Wanted* host John Walsh, the lower level of the museum includes a behind-the-scenes look at the program.

The museum recommends purchasing advance, discounted tickets on the website: tickets are spaced hourly with a specific date and time. ✉ *575 7th St. NW, Downtown* ☎ *202/393–1099* ⊕ *www.crimemuseum. org* ✉ *$21.95, audio tour $5, forensic lab $8, top detective challenge $10* ⊙ *Late Aug.–mid-Mar., Sun.–Thurs. 10–7, Fri. and Sat. 10–8; mid-Mar.–late Aug., Mon.–Thurs. 9–7, Fri. and Sat. 9–8, Sun. 10–7* Ⓜ *Gallery Pl./Chinatown.*

National Museum of Women in the Arts. Founded in 1987, this is the only major museum in the world solely dedicated to recognizing women's creative contributions. The Museum brings to light remarkable women artists of the past, while promoting the best women artists working today. In addition to traveling exhibitions, the museum holds a collection of 4,500 artworks including paintings, drawings, sculpture, prints, and photographs by Frida Kahlo, Camille Claudel, Mary Cassatt, Alma Thomas, Judy Chicago, Magdalena Abakanowicz, Nan Goldin, Louise Dahl-Wolfe, Helen Frankenthaler, and Élisabeth Vigée-Lebrun. The museum oversees the New York Avenue Sculpture Project, the first outdoor sculpture corridor in Washington, featuring changing installations by women artists. The beautifully restored 1907 Renaissance Revival building was designed by Waddy B. Wood. ✉ *1250 New York Ave. NW, Downtown* ☎ *202/783–5000* ⊕ *www.nmwa.org* ✉ *$10* ⊙ *Mon.–Sat. 10–5, Sun. noon–5* Ⓜ *Metro Center.*

National Portrait Gallery. *See the highlighted listing in this chapter.*

Newseum. *See the highlighted listing in this chapter.*

NATIONAL BUILDING MUSEUM

✉ *401 F St. NW, between 4th and 5th sts., Downtown* ☎ *202/272-2448* ⊕ *www. nbm.org* ⊠ *Free; Building Zone and temporary exhibits $8* ⊘ *Mon.–Sat. 10–5, Sun. 11–5 (Building Zone closes at 4)* Ⓜ *Judiciary Sq. or Gallery Pl./Chinatown.*

TIPS

■ Free historic building tours are offered daily at 11:30, 12:30, and 1:30. Or, you can take a self-guided smartphone audio tour that starts at the information desk.

■ Interactive Discovery Cart programs for children ages five and up are offered on weekends at 11:45 and 1:45.

■ Before entering the building, walk down its F Street side. The terra-cotta frieze by Caspar Buberl between the first and second floors depicts soldiers marching and sailing in an endless procession around the building. The architect, U.S. Army Corps of Engineers' General Montgomery C. Meigs, lost his eldest son in the Civil War, and, though the frieze depicts Union troops, he intended it as a memorial to all who were killed in the bloody war.

■ Find the café in the museum's Great Hall, and don't miss the highly regarded shop.

Architecture, design, landscaping, and urban planning are the themes of this museum, the nation's premier cultural organization devoted to the built environment. The open interior of the mammoth redbrick edifice is one of the city's great spaces, and has been the site of many presidential inaugural balls. The eight central Corinthian columns are among the largest in the world, rising to a height of 75 feet. Although they resemble Siena marble, each is made of 70,000 bricks that have been covered with plaster and painted. For years, the annual *Christmas in Washington* TV special has been filmed in this breathtaking hall.

Highlights

The long-term exhibition "House & Home" features a kaleidoscopic array of photographs, objects, models, and films that takes visitors on a tour of houses both surprising and familiar, through past and present, exploring American domestic life and residential architecture.

In "PLAY WORK BUILD," children and adults alike are encouraged to let their imaginations run wild with building blocks—small, big, and virtual.

Among the most popular permanent exhibits is the Building Zone, where kids ages two to six can get a hands-on introduction to building by constructing a tower, exploring a kid-size playhouse, or playing with bulldozers and construction trucks.

There is also a constant series of temporary exhibits. On exhibit through May 25, 2015 is "Cool & Collected: Recent Acquisitions," featuring the work of local sculptor Raymond Kaskey, among other new objects in the museum's collection. "Designing for Disaster," through August 2, 2015, demonstrates plans for disaster-resilient communities.

Smithsonian American Art Museum. *See the highlighted listing in this chapter.*

GEORGETOWN

Dumbarton Oaks. Career diplomat Robert Woods Bliss and his wife, Mildred, bought the property in 1920 and tamed the sprawling grounds into acres of splendid gardens designed mainly by Beatrix Farrand. In 1940, the Blisses gave the estate to Harvard University as a study center, library, museum, and garden. The museum holds a world-renowned collection of Byzantine and pre-Columbian art. Both collections are small but choice, reflecting the enormous skill and creativity developed at roughly the same time in two very different parts of the world. The Byzantine collection includes beautiful examples of both religious and secular items executed in mosaic, metal, enamel, stone, textile, and ivory. Pre-Columbian works—artifacts and textiles from Mexico and Central and South America by peoples such as the Aztec, Maya, Inca, and Olmec—are arranged in an enclosed glass pavilion designed by Philip Johnson.

Normally on public view are the lavishly decorated music room (which hosted representatives from the U.S., Great Britain, China, and the Soviet Union to lay the groundwork for the United Nations in 1944), special changing exhibits, and selections from Mrs. Bliss's collection. On weekends, visitors can see the Rare Book Reading Room and docents are on hand to share the history of the room and its furnishings and artwork. The gardens are especially glorious during the spring when the peonies are in full bloom. ⊠ *1703 32nd St. NW, Georgetown* ☎ *202/339–6401, 202/339–6409 for tours* ⊕ *www.doaks.org* ✉ *Free, Gardens $8* ☉ *Museum Tues.–Sun. 2–5, Garden Tues.–Sun. 2–6; historic rooms tour Sat. at 3, garden tours Tues., Wed., Thurs. and Sat. at 2:10* Ⓜ *Dupont Circle.*

Old Stone House. Washington's oldest surviving building, this fieldstone house in the heart of Georgetown was built in 1765 by a cabinetmaker named Christopher Layman. It was used as both a residence and place of business by a succession of occupants until 1953 when it was purchased by the National Park Service. Over the next seven years, the park service conducted an extensive restoration that has preserved the building's Revolutionary-war era architecture and design. Five of the house's rooms are furnished with the simple, sturdy artifacts—plain tables, spinning wheels, and so forth—of 18th-century middle-class life. You can take a self-guided tour of the house and its lovely English-style gardens. ⊠ *3051 M St. NW, Georgetown* ☎ *202/895–6070* ⊕ *www. nps.gov/olst* ✉ *Free* ☉ *Wed.–Sun. noon–5; garden during daylight hrs* Ⓜ *Foggy Bottom.*

Tudor Place. Stop at Q Street between 31st and 32nd streets; look through the trees to the north, to the top of a sloping lawn, and you can see the neoclassical Tudor Place, designed by Capitol architect Dr. William Thornton and completed in 1816. On the house tour you can see the largest collection of George and Martha Washington items on public display outside Mt. Vernon, Francis Scott Key's law partner's

NATIONAL PORTRAIT GALLERY

✉ *8th and F sts. NW,
Downtown* ☎ *202/633–8300*
⊕ *www.npg.si.edu* ✉ *Free*
◷ *Daily 11:30–7* Ⓜ *Gallery
Pl./Chinatown.*

TIPS

■ The Portrait Gallery and American Art Museum are two different museums in the same building—the art complements the portraits, setting up a dialogue between the two.

■ The elegant courtyard has a café and is frequently the site of performances and special events. At the "Portrait Connection" computer kiosks, you can search a database of the gallery's collections.

■ There are free docent-led tours most weekdays at 11:45, 1, and 2:15, and most weekends at 11:45, 1:30, and 3:15. Check the website to confirm times. At the Lunder Conservation Center on the third and fourth floors, you can watch conservators restoring works.

■ Inspire art appreciation in children through NPG's Open Studio on Friday from 1:30 to 4:30, Portrait Story Days on weekends, and Family Days with art scavenger hunts. All are free; no registration required.

The intersection of art, biography, and history is illustrated here through hundreds of images of men and women who have shaped U.S. history. There are prints, paintings, photos, and multimedia sculptures of subjects from George Washington to Madonna.

Highlights

This museum shares the National Historic landmark building Old Patent Office with the Smithsonian American Art Museum. Built between 1836 and 1863, and praised by Walt Whitman as the "noblest of Washington buildings," this marble edifice is considered one of the country's finest examples of Greek Revival architecture.

The museum has the only complete collection of presidential portraits outside the White House, starting with Gilbert Stuart's iconic "Lansdowne" portrait of George Washington. Interesting perspectives include the plaster cast of Abraham Lincoln's head and hands and political cartoonist Pat Oliphant's sculpture of George H. W. Bush bowling.

The American Origins exhibit chronicles the first contact between Europeans and Native Americans, the Founding Fathers, and historic figures through the Industrial Age. Subjects include Benjamin Franklin (the painting, by Joseph Duplessis, is the basis for Franklin's likeness on the $100 bill), Native American diplomat Pocahontas, and Thomas Edison in his workshop.

From a sculpture of 20th-century icon Gertrude Stein and portraits of World War II generals Eisenhower and Patton to Andy Warhol's *Time Magazine* cover of Michael Jackson and the painting of Bill and Melinda Gates by Jon Friedman, the third-floor gallery, Twentieth-Century Americans, offers a vibrant tour of the people who shaped the country and culture of today.

NEWSEUM

✉ *555 Pennsylvania Ave. NW, Downtown* ☎ *888/639-7386* ⊕ *www.newseum. org* 🎟 *$22.95* ⊙ *Daily 9–5* Ⓜ *Archives/Navy Memorial or Judiciary Square.*

TIPS

■ ABC's This Week is filmed here nearly every Sunday morning; watch it live from the giant screen in the atrium.

■ Tickets for the Newseum are valid for two consecutive days.

■ Celebrity chef Wolfgang Puck designed the menu for the food court, as well as for the restaurant The Source, adjoining the museum.

■ The best way to tour the museum is to view the orientation film on the concourse level then take the elevator to the top floor and work your way down.

■ The top-floor terrace offers one of the best views of the Capitol.

The setting, in a dramatic glass-and-silver structure on Pennsylvania Avenue, smack between the White House and the Capitol, is a fitting location for a museum devoted to the First Amendment and the role of free press in democracy. Visitors enter the 90-foot-high media-saturated atrium, overlooked by a giant breaking-news screen and a helicopter suspended overhead. From there, 15 galleries display 500 years of news history, including exhibits on the First Amendment; global news; the rise of multimedia; and how radio, TV, and the Internet transformed worldwide news. The FBI exhibit has more than 200 artifacts, including the Unabomber's cabin, Patty Hearst's coat and gun, and photos, news clippings and interactive displays on the relationship between the FBI and the news media. The space and exhibits are high-tech, multimedia, and often shamelessly fun, though there also are heart-rending images of 9/11 and the Journalists Memorial, honoring journalists killed while reporting the news.

Highlights

The largest piece of the Berlin wall outside Germany, including a guard tower, is permanently installed in an exhibit explaining how a free press was a key contributor to the fall of the wall.

Fifteen state-of-the art theaters, including an eye-popping "4-D" theater and another with a 90-foot-long screen, show features, news, sports, and documentaries throughout the day.

In the Interactive Newsroom you can play the role of journalist, try your hand at investigative reporting to solve an animal breakout at the zoo, or, step behind a camera to capture the most compelling photograph of a river rescue.

Evocative press photos are on display at the Pulitzer Prize Photographs gallery.

SMITHSONIAN AMERICAN ART MUSEUM

✉ *8th and G sts. NW, Downtown* ☎ *202/633-7970*
⊕ *www.americanart.si.edu*
▧ *Free* ⊙ *Daily 11:30-7:30*
Ⓜ *Gallery Pl./Chinatown.*

3

TIPS

■ At any given time, much of the museum's holdings are in storage, but you can view more than 3,000 artworks in its Luce Foundation Center, a study center and visible storage space on the third and fourth floors.

■ Free Wi-Fi is available in the museum's Kogod Courtyard, enclosed by an elegant glass canopy designed by world-renowned architect Norman Foster.

■ The museum regularly holds lectures, films, and evenings of live jazz in its auditorium and courtyard.

■ The Courtyard Café has casual dining, drinks, and views of interior landscaping.

■ Free docent-led tours are available every day at 12:30 and 2.

From Georgia O'Keeffe's stunning *Yellow Calla* painting to Michael Crocker's *Elvis Presley Face Jug #4*, the American Art Museum features one of the world's biggest and most inclusive collections of American art spanning more than three centuries. Over the past few years, the museum has broadened its collection to include modern and contemporary art. Among the artists represented are Robert Indiana, Edward Hopper, Roy Lichtenstein, Robert Rauschenberg, and David Hockney. The museum shares a National Historic Landmark building with the National Portrait Gallery.

Highlights

On the first floor, you'll see selected works from Lee Friedlander's *The American Monument* series, masterpieces by Winslow Homer and James McNeill Whistler and striking pieces by Andrew Wyeth and Isamu Noguchi, among others.

The collection galleries on the second floor link artworks to major moments in America's past, from the American Colonies and the founding of the new republic, to western expansion and discovery, to the Civil War and late 19th-century America, to early modernism.

The museum has the largest collection of New Deal art and the finest collection of American impressionist paintings, including the light filled canvasses of Mary Cassatt and Childe Hassam and the sophisticated Gilded Age portraits by John Singer Sargent.

The museum's third floor features modern and contemporary paintings and sculpture and the Watch This! gallery where you can see a selection of works from the museum's media art and film collection.

desk, and spurs belonging to soldiers who were executed as spies in the Civil War. You can only visit the house by guided tour (given hourly; last tour at 3), but before and afterward you can wander freely, with map or smartphone audiotour through the formal garden, full of roses and boxwoods, many planted in the early 19th century. ■ **TIP**→ **Looking for a special group activity? Make reservations for Tudor Place History Teas, which include a guided tour of the house, free time in the garden, and full tea service with pastries, sandwiches, fruit, dessert, and tea. Or, request Box Lunches for a picnic in the garden.** ✉ *1644 31st St. NW, Georgetown* ☎ *202/965–0400* ⊕ *www.tudorplace.org* ✐ *$10; garden only, $3* ☉ *Feb.–Dec., Tues.–Sat. 10–4, Sun. noon–4* Ⓜ *Dupont Circle.*

DUPONT CIRCLE

Anderson House. A palatial home that's a surprise even to many long-time Washingtonians, Anderson House isn't an embassy, though it does have a link to that world. Larz Anderson, a U.S. diplomat from 1891 to 1913 and his wife Isabel, an author and benefactress, traveled the world during their postings in England, Italy and Belgium, and in Larz's position as Ambassador to Japan. They filled their residence, which was completed for them in 1905, with an extensive collection of fine and decorative art. Guided tours of the first and second floors, gorgeously furnished with the Andersons' eclectic collection of furniture, tapestries, paintings, sculpture, historic artifacts, and Asian art, reveal much about life in Gilded Age Washington. Anderson House is the headquarters of the Society of the Cincinnati, a nonprofit and hereditary organization that promotes appreciation for the American Revolution, and also includes an exhibition gallery and research library. ✉ *2118 Massachusetts Ave. NW, Dupont Circle* ☎ *202/785–2040* ⊕ *www. societyofthecincinnati.org* ✐ *Free* ☉ *Tues.–Sat. 1–4* Ⓜ *Dupont Circle.*

Heurich House Museum. This opulent Romanesque Revival mansion, also known as the Brewmaster's Castle, was the home of Christian Heurich, a German immigrant who made his fortune in the beer business. Heurich's brewery was in Foggy Bottom, where the Kennedy Center stands today. During the late 19th cenutry, he was the second largest landowner and the largest private employer in the city. The building, a National Register of Historic Places landmark, is considered one of the most intact Victorian houses in the country, and all the furnishings were owned and used by the Heurichs. The interior is an eclectic gathering of plaster detailing, carved wooden doors, and painted ceilings. The downstairs Breakfast Room, which also served as Heurich's *bierstube* (or beer hall), is decorated like a Ratskeller and adorned with German sayings such as "A good drink makes old people young." Heurich must have taken proverbs seriously. He drank beer daily, had three wives, and lived to be 102. ✉ *1307 New Hampshire Ave. NW, Dupont Circle* ☎ *202/429–1894* ⊕ *www.heurichhouse.org* ✐ *$5* ☉ *Tours Thurs.–Sat. at 11:30, 1, and 2:30* Ⓜ *Dupont Circle.*

FAMILY **National Geographic Museum.** Founded in 1888, the National Geographic Society is best known for its magazine, and entering this welcoming 13,000-square-foot exhibition space feels like stepping into its pages.

The small museum has child-friendly interactives and is home to a rotating display of objects from the society's permanent collections—cultural, historical, and scientific—as well as traveling exhibitions. It also has weekend showings in its 3-D movie theater. The M Street Lobby photography exhibit, as well as the outdoor photo display around the perimeter of the museum, are free. ⊠ *17th and M sts. NW, Dupont Circle* ☎ *202/857–7588, 202/857–7689 for group tours* ⊕ *events. nationalgeographic.com/events/national-geographic-museum/* ⊠ *$11, 3-D movies $7* ⊙ *Daily 10–6 (hrs vary)* Ⓜ *Farragut North.*

Phillips Collection. *See the highlighted listing in this chapter.*

Textile Museum. This 46,000-sq-ft. museum, which recently opened on the campus of George Washington University, showcases weavings, carpets, and tapestries that date from 3000 BC to the present. Rotating exhibits are taken from a permanent collection of 19,000 historic and ethnographic items that include Coptic and pre-Columbian textiles, Kashmir embroidery, and Turkmen tribal rugs. Also within this impressive building are the Arthur D. Jenkins Library for the Textile Arts and the Textile Museum Shop, packed with handmade textiles from around the world, books, and clothing accessories. ⊠ *701 21st St. NW, Foggy Bottom* ☎ *202/667–0441* ⊕ *www.textilemuseum.org* ⊠ *Suggested donation $8* Ⓜ *Dupont Circle.*

Woodrow Wilson House. President Wilson and his second wife, Edith Bolling Wilson, retired in 1921 to this Georgian Revival house designed by Washington architect Waddy B. Wood. (Wood also designed the Department of the Interior and the National Museum of Women in the Arts.) It was on this quiet street where Wilson lived out the last few years of his life.

Toward the end of his second term, President Wilson suffered a stroke. Edith made sure he was comfortable in their home; she had a bed constructed that had the same dimensions as the large Lincoln bed Wilson had slept in while in the White House. She also had the house's trunk lift (a sort of dumb waiter for luggage) converted to an Otis elevator so the partially paralyzed president could move from floor to floor. When the streetcars stopped running in 1962, the elevator stopped working; it had received its electricity directly from the streetcar line. It has since been restored and is available for visitors with accessibility needs.

Wilson died in 1924—Edith survived him by 37 years—and bequeathed the house and its contents to the National Trust for Historic Preservation. Tours of the home provide a wonderful glimpse into the lives of this couple and the dignitaries who visited them here. You'll be able to view such items as Wilson's clothing, his collection of canes, a Gobelins wall-sized tapestry that was a gift from the people of France, a mosaic from Pope Benedict XV, a baseball signed by King George V, the pen used by Wilson to sign the declaration of war that launched U.S. into World War I, and the shell casing from the first shot fired by U.S. forces in the war. The house also contains memorabilia related to the history of the short-lived but influential League of Nations, including the colorful flag Wilson hoped would be adopted by that organization. ⊠ *2340 S St.*

PHILLIPS COLLECTION

✉ *1600 21st St. NW, Dupont Circle* ☎ *202/387–2151* ⊕ *www.phillipscollection. org* ✒ *Free for permanent collection weekdays; admission varies weekends and for special exhibitions* ⊗ *Tues., Wed., Fri., and Sat. 10–5, Thurs. 10–8:30, Sun. 11–6* Ⓜ *Dupont Circle.*

TIPS

■ On Thursday, The Phillips is open until 8:30 pm. and on the first Thursday of the month, Phillips after 5 ($12) combines live music, gallery talks, food, and a cash bar. Reservations are advised.

■ Music at The Phillips, a tradition since 1941, is a concert series held on Sunday at 4 from October through May. Tickets are $30 and include museum admission that day. Reservations are recommended.

■ Take a break in Tryst at the Phillips café, overlooking the museum courtyard.

■ Spotlight Talks, 15 minutes long and focusing on one work, are offered Tuesday to Friday at noon. Tours are also offered at noon on weekends: an introduction to the collection on Saturday and special exhibitions on Sunday. Tours are unreserved and included in admission.

■ Download the Phillips's free app (using the museum's free Wi-Fi) to learn more about the works in the galleries.

The first museum of modern art in the country, the masterpiece-filled Phillips Collection is unique in origin and content. It opened in 1921 in the Georgian Revival mansion of collector Duncan Phillips, who wanted to showcase his art in a museum that would stand as a memorial to his father and brother. Having no interest in a painting's market value or its faddishness, Phillips searched for pieces that impressed him as outstanding products of a particular artist's unique vision. At the heart of the collection are impressionist and modern masterpieces by Pierre-Auguste Renoir, Vincent van Gogh, Paul Cézanne, Edgar Degas, Pablo Picasso, Paul Klee, Pierre Bonnard, and Henri Matisse. By combining works of different nationalities and periods in displays that change frequently, the Phillips makes for a museumgoing experience that is as intimate as it is inspiring. The domestic scale and personal atmosphere encourage visual conversations among the works.

Highlights

The collection's most famous piece is Renoir's Impressionist work, *Luncheon of the Boating Party*. Other works include Degas's *Dancers at the Barre* and Van Gogh's *Entrance to the Public Garden at Arles*.

The chapel-like Rothko Room emerged when modern master Mark Rothko said he preferred to exhibit in intimately scaled rooms; Phillips designed the gallery specifically for him.

Jacob Lawrence's epic *Migration Series* portrays the mass movement of African Americans from the rural South to the industrial North beginning in World War I.

NW, Dupont Circle ☎ *202/387–4062* ⊕ *www.woodrowwilsonhouse. org* ✉ *$10* ◷ *Tues.–Sun. 10–4* Ⓜ *Dupont Circle.*

UPPER NORTHWEST

Hillwood Estate, Museum and Gardens. Long before the age of Paris Hilton, cereal heiress Marjorie Merriweather Post was the most celebrated socialite of the 20th century, famous for her fabulous wealth and beauty, as well as her passion for collecting art and creating some of the world's most lavish homes. Of these, the 25-acre Hillwood Estate, which Merriweather

> ### CAPITAL FACTS
>
> Until the Clintons bought a house here, Wilson was the only president who stayed in D.C. after leaving the White House. He's still the only president buried in the city, inside the National Cathedral.

Post bought in 1955, is the only one now open to the public. The 36-room Georgian mansion, where she regularly hosted presidents, diplomats, and royalty, is sumptuously appointed, with a formal Louis XVI drawing room, private movie theater and ballroom, and magnificent libraries filled with portraits of the glamorous hostess, her family and acquaintances, as well as works from her rich art collection. She was especially fascinated with Russian art, and her collection of Russian icons, tapestries, gold and silver work, and Fabergé eggs is considered to be the largest and most significant outside of Russia. She devoted equal attention to her gardens: you can wander through 13 acres of them. You should allow two to three hours to take in the estate, gardens, and museum shop. Reservations are recommended on spring weekends for tours and lunch or tea in the café. The estate is best reached by taxi or car (free parking is available on the grounds). It's a 20- to 30-minute walk from the Metro. ✉ *4155 Linnean Ave. NW, Upper Northwest* ☎ *202/686–5807, 202/686–8500* ⊕ *www.hillwoodmuseum.org* ✉ *$15* ◷ *Select Sundays, Tues.–Sat. 10–5* Ⓜ *Van Ness/UDC.*

Kreeger Museum. The cool white domes and elegant lines of this postmodern landmark stand in stark contrast to the traditional feel of the rest of the Foxhall Road neighborhood. Designed in 1963 by iconic architect Philip Johnson, the building was once the home of GEICO insurance executive David Lloyd Kreeger and his wife Carmen. Music is a central theme of the art and the space: the Kreegers wanted a showpiece residence that would also function as a gallery and recital hall. The art collection includes works by Renoir, Degas, Cézanne, and Munch, African artifacts, and outstanding examples of Asian art. The domed rooms also have wonderful acoustics, and serve as an excellent performance venue for the classical concerts that are regularly performed here. Information about upcoming performances is available on the museum's website. The museum is not reachable by Metro; you need to take a car or taxi to get here. ✉ *2401 Foxhall Rd. NW, Upper Northwest* ☎ *202/338–3552* ⊕ *www.kreegermuseum.org* ✉ *$10* ◷ *Tues.–Thurs. tours at 10:30 and 1:30 by reservation only; Fri. and Sat. 10–4, with* *optional tours (no reservation needed) Fri. at 10:30 and 1:30 and Sat. at 10:30, noon and 2* ⓧ *Closed Sun., Mon., and Aug.*

President Lincoln's Cottage. In June 1862 President Lincoln moved from the White House to this Gothic Revival cottage on the grounds of the Soldiers' Home to escape the oppressive heat of Washington and to grieve for the loss of his son Willie. Lincoln and his wife Mary lived in the cottage until November of that year, and because they found it to be a welcome respite from wartime tensions, they returned again during the summers of 1863 and 1864. Lincoln ultimately spent a quarter of his presidency at this quiet retreat; he was here just one day before he was assassinated. Considered the most significant historic site of President Lincoln's presidency outside the White House and now a National Trust historic site, it was here that the president developed the Emancipation Proclamation. A reproduction of the walnut-paneled desk on which he wrote this historic document can be seen in the Cottage. (The original desk is in the Lincoln Bedroom of the White House.)

Check in at the Robert H. Smith Visitor Education Center—where there's a gift shop, small museum and introductory film—for the one-hour tours. On the Signature Tour, given hourly Monday through Saturday 10–3 and Sunday 11–3, you'll discover what many of Lincoln's visitors in the 1860s experienced. The Emancipation Tour, available Tuesday and Saturday at 3, takes you inside Lincoln's mind as he anguished over the Civil War and emancipation. ■TIP➜ **Only 20 spots are available per tour and weekends often sell out, so it's best to make reservations via the website or E-Tix.**

Although the museum is reachable by Metro and bus no. H8, it's much easier to drive or take a cab. Visitors may also picnic on the cottage grounds, which have been landscaped to look as they did when Lincoln lived here. ■TIP➜ **As you go up the hill toward the Cottage, there's a panoramic view of the city, including the Capitol Dome. The 251-acre Soldier's Home sits atop the third tallest point in D.C.** ⊠ *Armed Forces Retirement Home, 140 Rock Creek Church Rd. and Upshur St. NW, Columbia Heights* ☎ *202/829–0436, 800/514–3849 for E-Tix* ⊕ *www. lincolncottage.org* 🎫 *$15* ⓧ *Mon.–Sat. 9:30–4:30, Sun. 10:30–4:30* Ⓜ *Georgia Ave./Petworth.*

4

MONUMENTS AND MEMORIALS

Updated by
Catherine
Sharpe

Washington is a monumental city. In the middle of traffic circles, on tiny slivers of park, and at street corners and intersections, you'll find statues, plaques, and simple blocks of marble honoring the generals, artists, and statesmen who helped shape the nation. Of these tributes, the greatest and grandest are clustered west of the Mall on ground reclaimed from the marshy flats of the Potomac—which also happens to be the location of Washington's most striking display of cherry trees.

These memorials now look like part of the landscape, but their beginnings were often controversial. From the Lincoln Memorial to the Martin Luther King Jr. Memorial, they sparked sometimes-fierce debate over how and why America should enshrine its history. Now, they are icons of unquestionable significance.

Visit the memorials on the Mall and Tidal Basin at night for fewer crowds and cooler air. Although you won't get the views, the lighting is particularly beautiful on the Lincoln and Jefferson memorials. Inside the Lincoln, lights and shadows play across his face, making him appear even more thoughtful.

Across the Potomac, Arlington National Cemetery has a power all its own. Though it pays tribute to great Americans, including John F. Kennedy and his brothers, what's most striking about the cemetery is its "sea of stones"—the thousands upon thousands of graves holding men and women who served in the U.S. military.

ASK A RANGER

You may think of park rangers as denizens of the woods, but they're a conspicuous presence at Washington's memorials—look for the olive-green and gray uniforms. Rangers lead talks about each memorial run by the Park Service (every hour on the hour, from 10 to 9) unless they are short-staffed, which does happen. They are an invaluable source of information; don't hesitate to ask questions of them. Kids can get Junior Park Ranger activity booklets from the ranger booths at the Lincoln, Roosevelt, Vietnam,

World War II, and King memorials. The National Park Service also has two wonderful programs: "Walk with a Ranger" is a 1½- to 2-hour daily walk to the monuments and memorials, often with a theme. They start at 2 pm (meet at Lincoln Memorial) and 7 pm (meet at World War II Memorial); "Run with a Ranger," on the 2nd and 4th Saturdays of every month March through November, is a 3- to 4-mile ranger-led themed run that includes short lectures at key monuments and statues.

4

PLANNING

PLANNING YOUR TIME

It takes about four or five hours to tour the monuments west of the Mall, with time to relax on a park bench and grab a snack from a vendor or one of the snack bars east of the Washington Monument, near the Lincoln Memorial

If you're visiting during the first two weeks in April, take extra time around the Tidal Basin and the Washington Monument to marvel at the cherry blossoms. Mid-April through November, you might want to spend an hour on a paddleboat in the Tidal Basin. In summer, consider taking a Martz Gray Line bus and travel between the monuments in air-conditioned comfort.

Across the Potomac, Arlington National Cemetery merits a couple of hours on its own.

TOURS

Washington Walks (⊕ *www.washingtonwalks.com*) has tours with witty commentary that cover most of the major monuments and memorials. They operate April through October, and each two-hour tour costs $15. **DC by Foot** (⊕ *www.dcbyfoot.com*) offers free (guides work for tips) walking tours of the memorials. Tours meet at the southwest corner of 15th Street and Constitution Avenue NW (closest to the Washington Monument) at 10 and 7 most days, but check the website for details. **Bike and Roll Washington DC** (⊕ *www.bikethesites.com*) conducts tours on wheels from mid-March to mid-November. The cost is $40–$45 and includes bike rental, helmet, bottled water, and snack.

MONUMENTAL SOUVENIRS

At **Arlington National Cemetery** there are gift shops at the Welcome Center, the Women in Military Service for America Memorial, and the Arlington House. The National Park Service contracts with a private company that operates gift shops and bookstores at or near the **FDR**

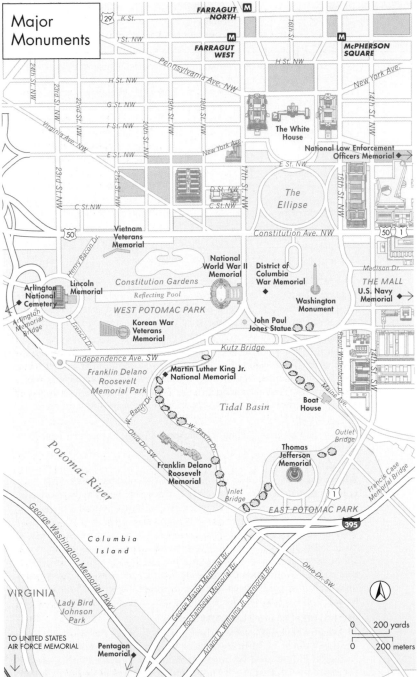

Major Monuments

Memorial (the largest), **Jefferson Memorial, Lincoln Memorial, Martin Luther King Jr. Memorial,** and the **Washington Monument.** The books are different at each shop, but the souvenirs tend to be the same.

THE MALL

District of Columbia War Memorial. Despite its location and age, visitors often overlook this memorial on the National Mall that President Herbert Hoover dedicated in 1931. Unlike the neighboring memorials on the Mall, this relatively small structure isn't a national memorial. The 47-foot-high circular domed, columned temple is dedicated to the 499 men and women (military and civilian) from Washington, D.C., who died in the Great War. Unofficially referred to as the World War I memorial, the marble structure was in disrepair and hidden by trees for decades. Through the American Recovery and Reinvestment Act of 2009, the memorial was restored to its original grandeur and is now maintained by the National Park Service. On November 10, 2011, the memorial, which had the John Phillip Sousa band playing at its original dedication, was rededicated as local musicians from the Duke Ellington School of the Arts performed. ⊠ *Independence Ave. SW, north side, between World War II Memorial and Lincoln Memorial, The Mall* ☎ *202/426–6841* ⊕ *www.nps.gov/ nacc* ⊙ *24 hrs* Ⓜ *Foggy Bottom.*

> ### WORD OF MOUTH
>
> "The memorials on the National Mall are a must for me, but the Mall is very long—walking from the Capitol to the Lincoln Memorial can take quite a while. I know there are tours of the memorials available, so you might look into those." —jent103
>
> "Metro stations do not access the "memorials" section of the National Mall, so plan on hoofing it." —furledleader

DOWNTOWN

United States Navy Memorial. Although Pierre L'Enfant included a Navy Memorial in his plans for Washington, D.C., it wasn't until 1987 that one was built. The main attraction here is a 100-foot-diameter granite map of the world, known as the Granite Sea. It's surrounded by fountains, benches, and six ship masts. The *Lone Sailor,* a 7-foot-tall statue, stands on the map in the Pacific Ocean between the United States and Japan. The Naval Heritage Center, next to the memorial in the Market Square East Building, displays videos and exhibits of uniforms, medals, and other aspects of Navy life. If you've served in the Navy, you can enter your record of service into the Navy Log here. The theater shows a rotating series of Navy-related movies throughout the day. Bronze relief panels on the Pennsylvania Avenue side of the memorial depict 26 scenes commemorating events in the nation's naval history and honoring naval communities. ■TIP➔ The panels are at a perfect height for children to look at and touch; challenge your child to find these items: a helicopter, a seagull, a U.S. flag, a sailor with binoculars, a dog, penguins, and seals. If you look carefully at the flagpole nearest

FRANKLIN DELANO ROOSEVELT MEMORIAL

✉ *400 W. Basin Dr. SW, West side of Tidal Basin, The Mall* ☎ *202/426–6841* ⊕ *www.nps. gov/fdrm* ✂ *Free* ⊙ *24 hrs; staffed daily 9:30 am–11:30 pm* Ⓜ *Smithsonian.*

TIPS

■ If you come with a toddler, head straight to the third room. Though youngsters can't sit on Roosevelt's lap, they can pet Fala, Roosevelt's Scottish terrier. The tips of Fala's ears and his nose shine from all the attention.

■ Allow about 30 minutes at this memorial. Take your time walking through the most expansive presidential memorial in Washington and read the lines from FDR's speeches.

■ This was the first memorial designed to be wheelchair accessible. Several pillars with Braille lettering and tactile images help the visually impaired.

■ This memorial presents great opportunities for family photographs. You can strike a pose while petting Fala, joining the men in the breadline, or listening to Roosevelt's fireside chat.

■ At night the lighting over the waterfalls creates interesting shadows, and there's less noise from airplanes overhead.

This 7.5-acre memorial to the 32nd president includes waterfalls and reflecting pools, four outdoor gallery rooms—one for each of Roosevelt's presidential terms (1933 to 1945)—and 10 bronze sculptures. The granite megaliths connecting the galleries are engraved with some of Roosevelt's famous statements, including, "The only thing we have to fear is fear itself."

Highlights

Congress established the Franklin Delano Roosevelt Memorial Commission in 1955, and invited prospective designers to look to "the character and work of Roosevelt to give us the theme of a memorial." Several decades passed before Lawrence Halprin's design for a "walking environmental experience" was selected. It incorporates work by artists Leonard Baskin, Neil Estern, Robert Graham, Thomas Hardy, and George Segal, and master stone carver John Benson.

The statue of a wheelchair-bound Roosevelt near the entrance of the memorial was added in 2001. Originally, the memorial showed little evidence of Roosevelt's polio, which he contracted at age 39. He used a wheelchair for the last 24 years of his life, but kept his disability largely hidden from public view. The statue was added after years of debate about whether to portray Roosevelt realistically or to honor his desire not to display his disability.

You're encouraged to touch the handprints and Braille along the columns in the second room, which represent the working hands of the American people.

A bronze statue of First Lady Eleanor Roosevelt stands in front of the United Nations symbol in the fourth room. She was a vocal spokesperson for human rights and one of the most influential women of her time.

KOREAN WAR VETERANS MEMORIAL

✉ *Daniel French Dr. SW and Independence Ave. SW, West end, The Mall* ☎ *202/426-6841* ⊕ *www.nps.gov/kwvm* 💳 *Free* ⊘ *24 hrs; staffed daily 9:30 am–11:30 pm* Ⓜ *Foggy Bottom.*

TIPS

■ Allow about 10 or 15 minutes at this memorial.

■ A sign at the entrance to the memorial indicates the time of the next park ranger-led interpretive talk.

■ You can get service information on the soldiers who died in the Korean War from the touch-screen computer at the memorial information booth. Further information about veterans and casualties is available at www.korean-war.org.

■ It may be tempting for kids to trek through the field with the statues, but it's not allowed. They can strike a pose next to the wall and see their reflection added to those of the 19 soldiers.

■ Visit the shop in the nearby Lincoln Memorial for books and souvenirs relating to the Korean War.

This memorial to the 1.5 million United States men and women who served in the Korean War (1950–53) highlights the high cost of freedom. Nearly 37,000 Americans were killed on the Korean peninsula, 8,000 were missing in action, and more than 103,000 were wounded. The privately funded memorial was dedicated on July 27, 1995, on the 42nd anniversary of the Korean War Armistice. Compare this memorial to the more intimate Vietnam Veterans Memorial and the grandiose World War II Memorial.

Highlights

In the *Field of Service*, 19 oversize stainless steel soldiers toil through a rugged triangular terrain toward an American flag; look beneath the helmets to see their weary faces. The reflection in the polished black granite wall to their right doubles their number to 38, symbolic of the 38th parallel, the latitude established as the border between North and South Korea in 1953, as well as the 38 months of the war.

Unlike many memorials, this one contains few words, but what's here is poignant. The 164-foot-long granite wall etched with the faces of 2,400 unnamed servicemen and servicewomen says simply, "Freedom is not free." The plaque at the base of the flagpole reads, "Our nation honors her sons and daughters who answered the call to defend a country they never knew and a people they never met." The only other words are the names of 22 countries that volunteered forces or medical support, including Great Britain, France, Greece, and Turkey.

The adjacent circular Pool of Remembrance honors all who were killed, captured, wounded, or missing in action; it's a quiet spot for contemplation.

LINCOLN MEMORIAL

✉ *23rd St. SW and Indepen-dence Ave. SW, West end, The Mall* ☎ *202/426–6841* ⊕ *www.nps.gov/linc* ✉ *Free* ☽ *24 hrs; staffed daily 9:30 am–11:30 pm* Ⓜ *Foggy Bottom.*

TIPS

■ The power of pennies? On the lower level of the memorial is a small museum financed with pennies collected by schoolchildren.

■ Lincoln's face and hands look especially lifelike because they're based on castings done while he was president. Those who know sign language might recognize that the left hand is shaped like an A and the right like an L. It's unlikely this was inten-tional, but the sculptor, Daniel Chester French, did have a deaf son.

■ Marchers flock to the Lincoln every year, drawing attention to various causes.

■ Lincoln's famous Emancipa-tion Proclamation, which set the stage for ending slavery, is occasionally on display at the National Archives (EConstitu-tion Ave., between 7th and 9th sts.).

■ See where Lincoln was shot (on April 14, 1865) at Ford's Theatre (E511 10th St. NW).

Many consider the Lincoln Memorial the most inspir-ing monument in Washington, but that hasn't always been the case: early detractors thought it inappropriate that a president known for his humility should be hon-ored with what some felt amounts to a grandiose Greek temple. The memorial was intended to be a symbol of national unity, but over time it has come to represent social justice and civil rights.

Highlights

Daniel Chester French's statue of the seated president gazes out over the Reflecting Pool. The 19-foot-high sculpture is made of 28 pieces of Georgia marble.

The surrounding white Colorado-marble memorial was designed by Henry Bacon and completed in 1922. The 36 Doric columns represent the 36 states in the Union at the time of Lincoln's death; their names appear on the frieze above the columns. Over the frieze are the names of the 48 states in existence when the memorial was dedicated. Alaska and Hawaii are represented with an inscription on the terrace leading up to the memorial. At night the memorial is illuminated, creating a striking play of light and shadow across Lincoln's face.

Two of Lincoln's great speeches—the second inaugural address and the Gettysburg Address—are carved on the north and south walls. Above each is a Jules Guerin mural: the south wall has an angel of truth freeing a slave; the unity of North and South is opposite.

The memorial's powerful symbolism makes it a popu-lar gathering place: In its shadow Americans marched for integrated schools in 1958, rallied for an end to the Vietnam War in 1967, and laid wreaths in a ceremony honoring the Iranian hostages in 1979. It may be best known, though, as the site of Martin Luther King Jr.'s "I Have a Dream" speech.

MARTIN LUTHER KING, JR.

✉ *1964 Independence Ave. SW, The Mall* ☎ *202/426-6841* ⊕ *www.nps.gov/ mlkm* ✉ *Free* ⊙ *24 hrs; staffed daily 9:30 am–11:30* Ⓜ *Smithsonian.*

TIPS

■ Allow about 20 to 30 minutes at this memorial, which was designed as a place for reflection.

■ Cross West Basin Drive to visit the Park Ranger station and gift shop, which sells books on MLK for all ages and a variety of keepsakes.

■ Where are the words "I have a dream?" You won't find them set in stone. You also won't see any mention of King's race or religion in the quotes.

■ Walk over to the Lincoln Memorial, where you can stand on the same step where King delivered his "I Have a Dream" speech. A plaque marks the spot.

■ Contrary to popular belief, King wasn't the first African-American with a memorial in D.C. That honor belongs to Mary McLeod Bethune, founder of the National Council of Negro Women and an informal adviser to FDR. Bethune is depicted in a 17-foot-tall bronze statue (ELincoln Park, East Capitol and 12th sts. NE). King is, however, the first African-American to be placed in Area 1 of the National Mall.

A "King" now stands tall among the presidents on the National Mall. At the dedication on October 16, 2011, President Barack Obama said, "This is a day that would not be denied." The memorial opened 15 years after Congress approved it in 1996 and 82 years after the famed civil rights leader was born in 1929.

Highlights

Located strategically between the Lincoln and Jefferson memorials and adjacent to the FDR Memorial, the crescent-shape King Memorial sits on a 4-acre site on the curved bank of the Tidal Basin.

There are two main ways to enter the memorial. From West Basin Drive, walk through a center walkway cut out of a huge boulder, the Mountain of Despair. From the Tidal Basin entrance, a 28-foot tall granite boulder shows King looking out toward Jefferson. The symbolism of the mountain and stone are explained by King's words: "With this faith, we will be able to hew out of the mountain of despair a stone of hope." The centerpiece stone was carved by Chinese sculptor Lei Yixin; his design was chosen from more than 900 entries in an international competition. Fittingly, Yixin first read about King's "I Have a Dream" speech at age 10 while visiting the Lincoln Memorial.

The themes of democracy, justice, hope, and love are reflected through quotes on the south and north walls and on the Stone of Hope. The quotes reflect speeches, sermons, and writings penned by King from 1955 through 1968. Waterfalls in the memorial reflect King's use of the biblical quote, "Let justice roll down like waters and righteousness like a mighty stream."

NATIONAL WORLD WAR II MEMORIAL

⊠ *17th St. SW and Home Front Dr. SW, between Independence Ave. SW and Constitution Ave. NW, The Mall* ☎ *202/426–6841* ⊕ *www.nps.gov/nwwm* 🎟 *Free* ☉ *24 hrs; staffed daily 9:30 am–11:30 pm* Ⓜ *Smithsonian.*

TIPS

■ Look for veterans. A visit to this memorial becomes even more inspiring when you have what might be the last opportunities to talk with the men and women who fought in World War II and are part of what former NBC news anchor Tom Brokaw called "The Greatest Generation."

■ Computers at the National Park Service kiosk behind the Pacific side of the memorial contain information about soldiers who lost their lives in the war.

■ Ask your children to look carefully at the bas-reliefs for a dog and a radio as large as today's big-screen televisions. Then try to find Kilroy, the cartoonlike character who appears to be looking over a ledge (Hint: He's in two places). The image and the phrase "Kilroy was here" were popular graffiti left by U.S. soldiers during the war.

This symmetrically designed monument honors the 16 million Americans who served in the armed forces, the more than 400,000 who died, and all who supported the war effort at home.

Highlights

An imposing circle of 56 granite pillars, each bearing a bronze wreath, represents the U.S. and its territories of 1941–45. Four bronze eagles, a bronze garland, and two 43-foot-tall arches inscribed with "Atlantic" and "Pacific" surround the large circular plaza. The roar of the water comes from the Rainbow Pool, here since the 1920s and renovated to form the centerpiece of the memorial. There are also two fountains and two waterfalls.

The Field of Stars, a wall of 4,000 gold stars, commemorates the more than 400,000 Americans who lost their lives in the war.

Although the parklike setting and the place of honor between the Washington Monument and the Lincoln Memorial may seem appropriate, some people were critical when the site for the memorial was announced, because they felt it would interrupt the landscape between the two landmarks and because it uses some of the open space that had been the site of demonstrations and protests.

Bas-relief panels tell the story of how World War II affected Americans by depicting women in the military, V-J Day, medics, the bond drive, and more activities of the time. The 24 panels are divided evenly between the Atlantic front and the Pacific front.

THOMAS JEFFERSON MEMORIAL

✉ *Tidal Basin, south bank, off Ohio Dr. SW, The Mall* ☎ *202/426-6841* ⊕ *www.nps. gov/thje* 🎟 *Free* ⏱ *24 hrs; staffed daily 9:30 am–11:30 pm* Ⓜ *Smithsonian.*

4

TIPS

■ Check out the view of the White House from the memorial's steps—it's one of the best.

■ Jefferson was the second president to live in the White House, but the first full-term occupant.

■ Park ranger programs are offered throughout the day, and you can ask questions of the ranger on duty.

■ Learn more about Jefferson by visiting the exhibit called Light and Liberty on the memorial's lower level. It chronicles highlights of Jefferson's life and has a timeline of world history during his lifetime.

■ Allow 15 minutes to walk here from the Metro. The memorial is the southernmost of Washington's major monuments and memorials, and it's a full four blocks and a trip around the Tidal Basin from the nearest Metro stop, Smithsonian.

■ Limited free parking is available under the 14th Street Bridge, off Ohio Drive near where it intersects with East Basin Drive.

In the 1930s Congress decided that Thomas Jefferson deserved a monument positioned as prominently as those honoring Washington and Lincoln. Workers scooped and moved tons of the river bottom to create dry land for the spot directly south of the White House where the monument was built. Jefferson had always admired the Pantheon in Rome, so the memorial's architect, John Russell Pope, drew on it for inspiration. His finished work was dedicated on April 13, 1943, the bicentennial of Jefferson's birth.

Highlights

Early critics weren't kind to the memorial—rumor has it that it was nicknamed "Jefferson's muffin" for its domed shape. The design was called outdated and too similar to that of the Lincoln Memorial. Indeed, both statues of Jefferson and Lincoln are 19 feet, just 6 inches shorter than the statue of Freedom atop the Capitol.

The bronze statue of Jefferson, standing on a 6-foot granite pedestal, looms larger than life. It wasn't always made of bronze. The first version was made of plaster, because bronze was too expensive and was needed for the war. The statue you see today was erected in 1947.

You can get a taste of Jefferson's keen intellect from his writings about freedom and government inscribed on the marble walls surrounding his statue.

Many people may be surprised to learn that Jefferson didn't list being president as one of his greatest accomplishments. When he appraised his own life, Jefferson wanted to be remembered as "Author of the Declaration of American Independence, of the Statute of Virginia for religious freedom, and Father of the University of Virginia."

VIETNAM VETERANS MEMORIAL

✉ *Constitution Gardens, 23rd St. NW and Constitution Ave. NW, The Mall* ☎ *202/426–6841* ⊕ *www.nps.gov/vive* 🎫 *Free* ☉ *24 hrs; staffed daily 9:30 am–11:30 pm* Ⓜ *Foggy Bottom.*

TIPS

■ Names on the wall are ordered by date of death. To find a name, consult the alphabetical lists found at either end of the wall. You can get assistance locating a name at the white kiosk with the brown roof near the entrance. At the wall, rangers and volunteers wearing yellow caps can look up the names and supply you with paper and pencils for making rubbings. Every name on the memorial is preceded (on the west wall) or followed (on the east wall) by a symbol designating status. A diamond indicates "killed, body recovered." A plus sign (found by a small percentage of names) indicates "killed, body not recovered." If you're visiting with older children or teens, be prepared for questions about war and death. Sometimes children think all 58,282 soldiers are buried at the monument. They aren't, of course, but the wall is as evocative as any cemetery.

"The Wall," as it's commonly called, is one of the most visited sites in Washington. The names of more than 58,000 Americans who died in the Vietnam War are etched in its black granite panels, creating a somber, dignified, and powerful memorial. It was conceived by Jan Scruggs, a former infantry corporal who served in Vietnam, and designed by Maya Lin, then a 21-year-old architecture student at Yale.

Highlights

Thousands of offerings are left at the wall each year: many people leave flowers, others leave personal objects such as the clothing of soldiers or letters of thanks from schoolchildren. The National Park Service collects and stores the items. In 2003, President George W. Bush signed a law authorizing the Vietnam Veterans Memorial Fund to build an education center at The Wall that will display some of the offerings, as well as the faces of those lost to the war. Fundraising is underway and the project is expected to break ground in 2016.

The statues near the wall came about in response to controversies surrounding the memorial. In 1984 Frederick Hart's statue of three soldiers and a flagpole was erected south of the wall, with the goal of winning over veterans who saw the memorial as a "black gash of shame." A plaque was added in 2004 to honor veterans who died after the war as a direct result of injuries suffered in Vietnam, but who fall outside Department of Defense guidelines for remembrance at the wall.

The Vietnam Women's Memorial was dedicated on Veterans Day 1993. Glenna Goodacre's bronze sculpture depicts two women caring for a wounded soldier while a third woman kneels nearby; eight trees around the plaza commemorate the eight women in the military who died in Vietnam.

WASHINGTON MONUMENT

✉ *15th St. NW, between Constitution Ave. NW and Independence Ave. SW, The Mall* ☎ *202/426–6841, 877/444–6777 for advance tickets* ⊕ *www.nps.gov/ wamo; www.recreation.gov for advance tickets* 🎟 *Free; $1.50 service fee per advance ticket* ☉ *Memorial Day–Labor Day, daily 9 am–10 pm (last tour at 9:45 pm); Sept.–May, daily 9 am–5 pm (last tour at 4:45)* Ⓜ *Smithsonian.*

TIPS

■ The steps of the Lincoln Memorial provide a glorious view of this beloved landmark.

■ All visitors ages two and older require a free, timed ticket to go inside the monument and ride the elevator to the top. A limited number of tickets are distributed each day at 8:30 am, at the marble lodge on 15th Street. In spring and summer, lines are likely to start hours before the monument opens and tickets will run out. Your best bet is to reserve tickets as far in advance as possible. You can do this online or by calling the toll-free reservation line. There's a $1.50 service charge per ticket. Tickets can be picked up on the day of your tour from the will call window at the monument lodge.

■ Maps below viewing-station windows point out some of Washington's major buildings, but you might want to bring a more detailed map (available at the monument's bookstore).

The 555-foot, 5-inch Washington Monument punctuates the capital like a huge exclamation point. And it is now reopened after a three-year project to repair the damage caused in 2011 by a rare but powerful earthquake.

The monument was part of Pierre L'Enfant's plan for Washington, but his intended location proved to be marshy, so it was moved 100 yards southeast to firmer ground (a stone marker now indicates L'Enfant's original site). Construction began in 1848 and continued, with interruptions, until 1884. Upon its completion, the monument was the world's tallest structure and weighed more than 81,000 tons.

Highlights

Six years into construction, members of the anti-Catholic Know-Nothing Party stole and smashed a block of marble donated by Pope Pius IX. This action, combined with funding shortages and the onset of the Civil War, brought construction to a halt. After the war, building finally resumed, and though the new marble came from the same Maryland quarry as the old, it was taken from a different stratum with a slightly different shade.

193 memorial stones from countries, individuals, and societies around the world were inserted into the interior walls of the monument.

An elevator whizzes to the top of the monument in 70 seconds—a trip that in 1888 took 12 minutes via steam-powered elevator. From the observation deck you can see most of the District of Columbia, as well as parts of Maryland and Virginia—but not as far as Bristol, Virginia, the epicenter of the 2011 earthquake. After taking in the views, walk a few steps down to the museum with exhibits on the history of the monument and for the two-minute elevator descent. Park rangers are on hand to share anecdotes and answer questions.

the entrance to the Heritage Center, you'll see a time capsule, scheduled to be opened in 2093. ⊠ *701 Pennsylvania Ave. NW, Downtown* ☎ *202/737-2300* ⊕ *www.navymemorial.org* ⌧ *Free* ⊙ *24 hrs; Naval Heritage Center daily 9:30–5* Ⓜ *Archives/Navy Memorial.*

PENN QUARTER

National Law Enforcement Officers Memorial. These 3-foot-high walls bear the names of 20,267 American police officers killed in the line of duty since 1791. On the third line of panel 13W are the names of six officers killed by William Bonney, better known as Billy the Kid. J. D. Tippit, the Dallas policeman killed by Lee Harvey Oswald, is honored on the ninth line of panel 63E. Other names include the 72 officers who died due to the events of 9/11. Directories there allow you to look up officers by name, date of death, state, and department. Call to arrange for a free tour. A National Law Enforcement Museum is in the works, scheduled for completion in 2016; until then, a small visitor center (⊠ *400 7th St. NW*) has a computer for looking up names, a display on the history of law enforcement, and a small gift shop. ⊠ *400 block of E St. NW, Penn Quarter* ☎ *202/737-3400* ⊕ *www.lawmemorial.org* ⌧ *Free* ⊙ *Weekdays 9–5, Sat. 10–5, Sun. noon–5* Ⓜ *Judiciary Square.*

SUBURBAN VIRGINIA

ARLINGTON

Pentagon Memorial. Washington's own "9/11 memorial" honors the 184 people who perished when the hijacked American Airlines Flight 77 crashed into the northwest side of the Pentagon. Benches engraved with the victims' names are arranged in order by date of birth and where they were when they died. The names of the victims who were inside the Pentagon are arranged so that visitors reading their names face the Pentagon, and names of the victims on the plane are arranged so that visitors reading their names face skyward. Designed by Julie Beckman and Keith Kaseman, the memorial opened to the public on September 11, 2008, the seventh anniversary of the attacks. Volunteer docents periodically stand near the entrance and answer questions. There is no public parking, with the exception of five stalls for handicap-permitted vehicles. ⊠ *1 Rotary Rd., Pentagon, Arlington, Virginia* ☎ *301/740–3388* ⊕ *www.pentagonmemorial.org* ⌧ *Free* ⊙ *24 hrs; restroom facilities 7 am–10 pm* Ⓜ *Pentagon.*

United States Air Force Memorial. Three steel spires slice through the sky representing flight, the precision of the "bomb burst" maneuver performed by the Air Force Thunderbirds, and the core values of the Air Force: integrity, service, and excellence. At the base is a statue of the honor guard, a glass wall engraved with the missing man formation, and granite walls inscribed with Air Force values and accomplishments. ⊠ *1 Air Force Memorial Dr., off Columbia Pike, Arlington, Virginia* ☎ *703/979–0674* ⊕ *www.airforcememorial.org* ⌧ *Free* ⊙ *Apr.–Sept., daily 8 am–11 pm; Oct.–Mar., daily 8 am–9 pm. Gift shop weekdays 9–4* Ⓜ *Pentagon City or Pentagon.*

ARLINGTON, THE NATION'S CEMETERY

The most famous, most visited cemetery in the country is the final resting place for close to 400,000 Americans, from unknown soldiers to John F. Kennedy. With its tombs, monuments, and "sea of stones," Arlington is a place of ritual and remembrance, where even the most cynical observer of Washington politics may find a lump in his throat or a tear in his eye.

EXPERIENCING THE SEA OF STONES

In 1864, a 200-acre plot directly across the Potomac from Washington, part of the former plantation home of Robert E. Lee, was designated America's national cemetery. Today, the cemetery covers 624 acres.

Today, Arlington's major monuments and memorials are impressive, but the most striking experience is simply looking out over the thousands upon thousands of headstones aligned across the cemetery's hills.

Most of those buried here served in the military—from reinterred Revolutionary War soldiers to troops killed in Iraq and Afghanistan. As you walk through the cemetery, you're likely to hear a trumpet playing taps or the report of a gun salute. An average of 27 funerals a day are held here, Monday through Friday. There currently are nearly 400,000 graves in Arlington; it's projected that the cemetery will be filled by 2060.

FINDING A GRAVE

At the Welcome Center, staff members and computers can help you find the location of a specific grave. You need to provide the deceased's full name and, if possible, the branch of service and year of death.

WHO GETS BURIED WHERE

With few exceptions, interment at Arlington is limited to active-duty members of the armed forces, veterans, and their spouses and minor children. In Arlington's early years as a cemetery, burial location was determined by rank (as well as, initially, by race), with separate sections for enlisted soldiers and officers. Beginning in 1947, this distinction was abandoned. Grave sites are assigned on the day before burial; when possible, requests are honored to be buried near the graves of family members.

ABOUT THE HEADSTONES

Following the Civil War, Arlington's first graves were marked by simple white-washed boards. When these decayed, they were replaced by cast-iron markers covered with zinc to prevent rusting. Only one iron marker remains, for the grave of Captain Daniel Keys (Section 13, Lot 13615, Grid G-29/30).

In 1873, Congress voted in the use of marble headstones, which continues to be the practice today. The government provides the standard-issue stones free of charge. Next of kin may supply their own headstones, though these can only be used if space is available in one of the sections where individualized stones already exist.

THE SAME, BUT DIFFERENT

Regulation headstones can be engraved with one of 54 symbols indicating religious affiliation. In section 60, the headstones of soldiers killed in Afghanistan and Iraq reflect the multicultural makeup of 21st-century America. Along with a variety of crosses and the Star of David, you see the nine-pointed star of the Baha'i; a tepee and three feathers representing the Native American faiths; the Muslim crescent and star; and other signs of faith. (Or lack of it. Atheism is represented by a stylized atom.)

Opposite: Sea of Stones; Upper left: Burial ceremony; Bottom left: A soldier placing flags for Memorial Day. Right: Coast Guard headstone.

PLANNING YOUR VISIT TO ARLINGTON

ARLINGTON BASICS

Getting Here: You can reach Arlington on the Metro, by foot over Arlington Memorial Bridge (southwest of the Lincoln Memorial), or by car—there's a large parking lot by the Visitors Center on Memorial Drive. Also, the Martz Gray Line bus (☎ *800/862–1400* ⊕ *www.graylinedc.com*) and Old Town Trolley (☎ *202/832–9800* ⊕ *www.old towntrolley.com*) both have Arlington National Cemetery stops in their loops.

🕘 Apr.–Sept., daily 8–7; Oct.–Mar., daily 8–5.

💲Cemetery free, parking $1.75 per hr for the first three hours, $2.50 per hr thereafter. Martz Gray Line $45. Tourmobile Arlington Tour $7.50, Old Town Trolley $35.

☎ *877/907–8585* for general information and to locate a grave.

⊕ *www.arlingtoncemetery.mil*

✗No food or drink is allowed at the cemetery. There are water fountains in the Welcome Center, and from fall through spring a water fountain operates near the amphitheater at the Tomb of the Unknowns. You can also purchase bottled water at the Women's Memorial.

TOURING OPTIONS

Your first stop at the cemetery should be the Welcome Center, where you can pick up a free brochure with a detailed map. Once there you have a choice: tour by bus or walk.

Arlington by Bus. Martz Gray Line tour buses leave every 15 to 25 minutes from just outside the Welcome Center April through September, daily 8:30–6:30, and October through March, daily 8:30–4:30. The 40-minute tour includes stops at the Kennedy grave sites, the Tomb of the Unknowns, and Arlington House. Your bus driver will provide basic facts about the cemetery.

Arlington on Foot. Walking the cemetery requires some stamina, but it allows you to take in the thousands of graves at your own pace. On the facing page is a walking tour that includes the major points of interest. Audio tours are available in the Welcome Center.

Above: 3rd Infantry Honor Guard

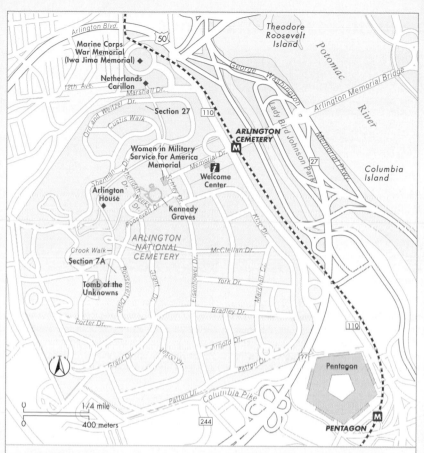

A WALKING TOUR

■ Head west from the Welcome Center on Roosevelt Drive and turn right on Weeks Drive to reach the **Kennedy graves**; just to the west is **Arlington House**. (¼ mile)

■ Take Crook Walk south, following the signs, to the **Tomb of the Unknowns**; a few steps from the tomb is **Section 7A**, where many distinguished veterans are buried. (³⁄10 mile)

■ To visit the graves of soldiers killed in Afghanistan and Iraq, take Roosevelt Drive past Section 7 and turn right on McClellan Drive, turn right when you get to Eisenhower Drive, then go left onto York Drive. The graves will be on your right. (⁶⁄10 mile)

■ Walk north along Eisenhower Drive, which becomes Schley Drive; turn right onto Custis Walk, which brings you to **Section 27**, where 3,800 former slaves are buried. (¾ mile)

■ Leave the cemetery through the Ord and Weitzel Gate, cross Marshall Drive carefully, and walk to the 50-bell **Netherlands Carillon**, where there's a good vista of Washington. To the north is the **United States Marine Corps War Memorial**, better known as the **Iwo Jima Memorial**. (¼ mile)

ARLINGTON'S MAIN ATTRACTIONS

The Kennedy Graves

Once while taking in the view of Washington from Arlington National Cemetery, President John F. Kennedy commented, "I could stay here forever." Seeing Kennedy's grave is a top priority for most visitors. He's buried beneath an eternal flame, next to graves of two of his children who died in infancy, and of his wife, Jacqueline Kennedy Onassis. Across from them is a low wall engraved with quotations from Kennedy's inaugural address. Nearby, marked by simple white crosses, are the graves of Robert F. Kennedy and Ted Kennedy.

The gas-fueled flame at the head of John F. Kennedy's grave was lit by Jacqueline Kennedy during his funeral. A continuously flashing electric spark reignites the gas if the flame is extinguished by rain, wind, or any other cause.

Many visitors ask where Kennedy's son John F. Kennedy Jr. is buried. His ashes were scattered in the Atlantic Ocean, near the location where his plane went down in 1999.

Arlington House

Long before Arlington was a cemetery, it was part of the 1,100-acre estate of George Washington Parke Custis, a grandchild of Martha and (by marriage) George Washington. Custis built Arlington House between 1802 and 1818. After his death, the property went to his daughter, Mary Anna Randolph Custis, who wed Robert E. Lee in 1831. The couple made Arlington House their home for the next 30 years.

In 1861 Lee turned down the position of commander of the Union forces and left Arlington House, never to return. Union troops turned the house into an Army headquarters, and 200 acres were set aside as a national cemetery. By the end of the Civil War headstones dotted the estate's hills.

The house looks much as it did in the 19th century and a quick tour takes you past objects once owned by the Custises, the Lees, and the Washingtons. The views from Arlington House remain spectacular. ☎ 703/235-1530 ⊕ www.nps.gov/arho ⊡ Free ⊙ Daily 9:30–4:30.

Robert E. Lee

Tomb of the Unknowns

The first burial at the Tomb of the Unknowns, one of the cemetery's most imposing monuments, took place on November 11, 1921. In what was part of a world-wide trend to honor the dead after the unparalleled devastation of World War I, an unidentified soldier was interred under the large white-marble sarcophagus. Unknown servicemen killed in World War II and Korea joined him in 1958.

The Memorial Amphitheater west of the tomb is used for ceremonies on Veterans Day, Memorial Day, and Easter. Decorations awarded to the unknowns are displayed in an indoor trophy room.

One of the most striking activities at Arlington is the precision and pageantry of the changing of the guard at the Tomb of the Unknowns. From April through September, soldiers from the Army's U.S. Third Infantry (known as the Old Guard) change guard every half hour during the day. For the rest of the year, and at night all year long, the guard changes every hour.

The Iwo Jima Memorial

Ask the tour bus driver at Arlington where the Iwo Jima is, and you might get back the quip "very far away." The memorial commonly called the Iwo Jima is officially named the United States Marine Corps War Memorial, and it's actually located just north of the cemetery. Its bronze sculpture is based on one of the most famous photos in American military history, Joe Rosenthal's February 23, 1945, shot of five marines and a navy corpsman raising a flag atop Mt. Suribachi on the Japanese island of Iwo Jima. By executive order, a real flag flies 24 hours a day from the 78-foot-high memorial. ☎ 703/289–2500

On Tuesday evening at 7 PM from early June to mid-August there's a Marine Corps sunset parade on the grounds of the Iwo Jima Memorial. On parade nights a free shuttle bus runs from the Arlington Cemetery visitors' parking lot.

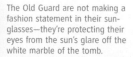

The Old Guard are not making a fashion statement in their sunglasses—they're protecting their eyes from the sun's glare off the white marble of the tomb.

DID YOU KNOW?

Each year on July 4, the National Symphony Orchestra goes out with a bang, ending its performance with Tchaikovsky's "1812 Overture" and using real cannons (with blanks)!

OFFICIAL WASHINGTON

Updated by
Catherine
Sharpe

Given the heightened security concerns of present-day Washington, it might come as a surprise to learn that most government institutions continue to welcome the general public. The Founding Fathers' mandate of a free and open government lives on—just with metal detectors and bag searches. Though security checks are no one's idea of fun, most people find them a small price to pay for the opportunity to get a firsthand look at the government in action. Being in the famous halls of the Capitol or the Supreme Court is a heady experience. It's one part celebrity sighting and one part the world's best civics lesson.

Although the Capitol, White House, and Supreme Court get the lion's share of the attention, other government institutions hold their own, sometimes-quirky appeal. Art enthusiasts can gaze in wonder at the works on display at the Red Cross headquarters and the Interior Department, while military buffs can retrace the footsteps of four- and five-star generals in the seemingly endless hallways of the Pentagon.

If you're fascinated by finance, you'll want to plan ahead for visits to the Federal Reserve and the Department of Treasury. You need to sign up three months in advance for a tour of the Department of State, but your advance work will be rewarded with a visit to the plush Diplomatic Reception Rooms, where few sightseers tread.

PLANNING

WHEN TO PLAN AHEAD

You can visit many of Washington's government offices, but you have to do some advance planning in many cases. Here's a rundown of how far in advance you need to make arrangements.

SITE	TIME IN ADVANCE
Capitol Tour	Morning of visit–3 months
Congressional session	2 weeks–2 months
Supreme Court	Morning of visit
American Red Cross	1 week
Department of Interior	2–4 weeks
Department of State	3 months
Federal Reserve	2 weeks
Pentagon	2 weeks–3 months
Treasury Building	1–2 months
White House	3 weeks–6 months

NO ADVANCE PLANNING REQUIRED

Two of the most impressive places in Washington don't require advance reservations. The **Library of Congress** and the **Washington National Cathedral** are architectural and artistic treasures.

The cathedral was dubbed at its creation a "House of Prayer for All People," and does indeed draw people from all over the world seeking comfort and reflection. Statues of George Washington and Abraham Lincoln make it clear that this is a place where church and state are welcome to coexist. With its murals, paintings, sculptures and statues, and, of course, millions of books and manuscripts, the Library of Congress is truly impressive. Even if you're not a bookworm, the free docent-led tour is one of the best things going in the city.

CAPITOL VISITOR CENTER

One of the most visited attractions, the **Capitol Visitor Center** is the starting point for tours of the Capitol and where you'll discover a plethora of historical treasures, including a table used by Abraham Lincoln during his 1865 inaugural address. Crowds in spring and summer can number in the thousands, so plan for at least three hours here. The five-football-fields-size underground complex is a destination in itself, with the model of the statue of *Freedom*, a 530-seat dining room that serves the famous Senate bean soup, and exhibits on the Capitol. Tours of the Capitol run Monday through Saturday from 8:50 to 3:20. Allow extra time to go through security.

To visit the Capitol, you'll need to either reserve tickets online at ⊕ *www.visitthecapitol.gov* or contact your representative or senator.

OFFICIAL WASHINGTON WITH KIDS

Before visiting the Capitol, have a discussion with your kids about Congress's role in the government and the Capitol's place in history. Then during the tour, encourage them to move up front to see and hear better.

Kids can email the president at ✎ *president@whitehouse.gov* or send a letter to the White House. The president and first lady even have their own zip code: 20500.

Kids get a kick out of seeing currency printed at the **Bureau of Engraving and Printing.** At the gift shop they can buy bags of shredded bills and get a postcard-size rendering of a dollar with their face in the place of George Washington's.

WHITE HOUSE EVENTS

DECEMBER AT THE WHITE HOUSE

The White House is decorated for Christmas during December every year. Even before you enter the State Dining Room, you can smell the gingerbread. The White House gingerbread-house tradition began during the Nixon administration, and has been continued ever since.

Since 1961 the Christmas tree in the Blue Room (another stands in the East Room) has reflected themes. In 1974 the Fords' Christmas tree ornaments emphasized thrift and recycling. In 1991 the Bushes' tree featured needlepoint figurines. Holiday cards created by military children, as well as ornaments with patches, medals, and badges representing all branches of the military adorned the Obamas' 2011 Christmas tree.

■TIP→ December is far and away the most difficult time of year to secure a tour. The White House is able to accommodate fewer than 10% of the tour requests it receives.

EASTER EGG ROLL

Kids have been rolling Easter eggs at the White House since at least 1878. Over the years the Egg Rolls have evolved into elaborate affairs with bands and bunnies. The event is held the Monday after Easter, from 8 am to 7 pm on the South Lawn of the White House. Tickets are distributed via an online lottery system. Each group has to include at least one child 13 years old or under and no more than two adults.

For the most up-to-date information on the Easter Egg Roll, call the White House 24-hour information line at ☎ *202/456–7041.*

PLANNING A VISIT

You can request a free tour of The White House anywhere from three weeks to six months prior to your visit; spaces are very limited so the earlier the better. Citizens of the U.S. must submit tour requests through their representative or senator. Each member of Congress has his or her own procedures and requirements for tour requests. You can find their contact information online at ⊕ *www.house.gov* and ⊕ *www.senate. gov.* Don't be reluctant to contact your Congress member—they and their staff have lots of experience handling such requests. Some will even invite you to meet with them and talk about your interests and concerns. If you aren't an American, contact your country's embassy to see if they can help you get a tour.

THE MALL

FAMILY **Bureau of Engraving and Printing.** Paper money has been printed here since 1914, when the bureau relocated from the redbrick-towered Auditors Building at the corner of 14th Street and Independence Avenue. In addition to paper currency, military certificates and presidential invitations are printed here, too. You can only enter the bureau on tours, which last about 40 minutes. March through August, free same-day timed-entry

Continued on page 161

SEX! POWER! MONEY!
★ ★ ★
SCANDALOUS WASHINGTON

Newt Gingrich's 2012 presidential bid ended with disclosures that he had had an affair with his now-third wife, Callista (pictured with him above), while still married to his second, plus the "Tiffanygate" shadow cast by his $500,000 loan from the jeweler.

Every "gotcha!" headline since President Nixon's burglars at the Watergate has been affixed with a "-gate," but Washington's memory of kickbacks, sleaze, and dirty deeds goes back centuries further. Before there was Monica, there was Marilyn; before Marilyn, there was Carrie and Peggy and Nan. Most people are familiar with Whitewater, but what of the Star Route and Teapot Dome? The history of the United States is thick with plots, scams, and bad behavior. Herewith, selections from Washington's long and democratic history of scandal.

SEX!

Petticoat Tales

Margaret "Peggy" Eaton

Ooh la la, whispered Washington's society matrons, when President Andrew Jackson's war secretary John Henry Eaton fell for Margaret "Peggy" Timberlake, a young widow he had known for years. Pretty, charming Peggy had a fast reputation for 1829, and soon rumors flew about the circumstances of her husband's death, the paternity of her two children, and Eaton. It was all idle gossip—until Eaton married her, after which the other Cabinet wives shunned her, and the social stir of insult and offense all but shut down business at the White House for *two years.* In 1831, the Cabinet resigned en masse and Jackson was finally able to get some work done. As for Peggy? After Eaton's death, she sparked another scandal, by marrying her granddaughter's 19-year-old dance instructor. *(Location: Peggy Eaton is buried in Oak Hill Cemetery, 3001 R St. NW)*

Fanne Fox

Naked Ambition

In 1974, Wilbur Mills spent his days chairing the House Ways and Means Committee—and his nights with a stripper known as "Fanne Fox, the Argentine Firecracker." A typical Capitol romance, until his car was stopped one night by police, and his lady friend leapt from the car and into the Tidal Basin, leaving a drunken Mills to his fate. Surprisingly, Mills' political career survived—until he appeared later that year, drunk, onstage with Fox at a Boston burlesque. *(Location: Tidal Basin)*

Hail to the Cheat

Warren Harding

President Bill Clinton was hardly the first and likely not the worst of the White House philanderers. That dubious honor may go to President Warren Harding, a legendary Lothario who is purported to have carried on with paramours Carrie Phillips and Nan Britton (among others) in some unlikely places, including a White House closet. (When his wife Florence came by, a Secret Service agent warned him with a discreet knock on the door.) Relative propriety in the 1920's press meant that any blue dresses remained unreported, but Harding may have left behind a more incriminating piece of evidence—an illegitimate daughter, Elizabeth Ann. *(Location: White House)*

POWER!

Reporters Bob Woodward, left, and Carl Bernstein, whose reporting of the Watergate scandal won them a Pulitzer Prize, sit in the newsroom of the *Washington Post* on May 7, 1973.

He Really Bugs Me

The Big Kahuna of Washington scandals had humble beginnings, in the discovery of a taped-open door at the Watergate Hotel one night in June of 1972. The door led to burglars, on a mission to bug the Democratic National Committee, and the burglars led through the Republican party machine straight to the White House and President Richard "Tricky Dick" Nixon. Two young reporters, Bob Woodward and Carl Bernstein, uncovered the most impossible-seeming story of the century, and their secret meetings with anonymous leaker "Deep Throat" (W. Mark Felt) are the stuff of legend. One of many fond memories of the moment when Washington lost America's trust. Nixon's immortal, and untruthful, declaration, "I am not a crook." *(Location: Watergate Hotel, Virginia Ave., near 27th St. NW)*

Taxman to Axman

When Treasury Secretary William Richardson hired contractor-cum-bounty hunter John Sanborn in 1872 to help the IRS collect taxes, the idea was simple. Sanborn chased down tax cheats, and was allowed to keep half of the take for his trouble. But when he ran out of tax evaders and went after honest companies, Richardson turned a blind eye—in exchange for his own cut

From Ronald with Love

Oliver North

Two wrongs *can* make a right: a right-wing guerilla organization, that is. President Ronald Reagan likened Nicaragua's Contras to the Founding Fathers. Too bad funding the insurgent group was illegal. So was a secret deal the White House made to sell arms to Iran. When it was discovered in 1986 that the cash from Iran had been funneled to the Contras, the Gipper had some explaining to do. Luckily for him, National Security Council aide Oliver North had a shredder, and he wasn't afraid to use it. North's secretary, Fawn Hall, took care of the rest by smuggling out remaining suspect documents in her boots and skirt. *(Location: Old Executive Office Building, 17th & F Streets NW)*

MONEY!

Teapot Dome scandal cartoon by Clifford Kennedy Berryman

A Cozy Deal

It may seem old hat today—access to public resources awarded in a no-bid contract to cronies of someone in the president's inner circle—but in 1922 it was front-page news. Interior Secretary Albert Fall had authority over the Teapot Dome strategic oil reserve transferred from the Department of the Navy to Interior, and once he was in charge, he leased the land to Mammoth Oil. The deal was technically legal—what *wasn't* was the $404,000 kickback he got for arranging it. Fall nearly succeeded in keeping his stake quiet, until he raised suspicions by having the office of the lead Senate investigator ransacked. *(Location: Department of Interior, 1849 C St. NW)*

Secretary of Shame

In 1872, the House of Representatives was so determined to remove War Secretary William Belknap that it voted to impeach him, even after he had already resigned. The high-living general was caught having awarded a lucrative military trading post appointment in exchange for kickbacks; the quarterly bribes he took came to ten times his official salary. The House's venom waxed poetic: legislators voted unanimously that the Secretary was "basely prostituting his high office to his lust for private gain." Belknap resigned in disgrace—and tears—and committed suicide in 1890. *(Location: House of Representatives)*

Sex, Laws and Videotape

One of the more titillating modern-day scandals in our nation's capital connects a fake sheikh, a former *Playboy* model turned Italian princess, and a congressman.

John Jenrette (D-South Carolina) was one of six U.S. lawmakers brought down by the FBI's 1980 investigation of influence peddling, also known as ABSCAM. Jenrette served 13 months in federal prison after he was busted for accepting $50,000 in bribes from an agent posing as an Arab sheikh. Elements of the investigation and arrests were woven into the plot of the Oscar-nominated film *American Hustle.*

Jenrette's wife at the time, Rita, leveraged ABSCAM notoriety into an entertainment career and posed twice for *Playboy* magazine in the 1908s. Rita and John divorced in 1981, and in May 2009 she married an Italian prince—news that didn't become public until December 2013—and now lives in Rome.

tour passes are issued starting at 8 am (plan on being in line no later than 7 am) at the Raoul Wallenberg Place SW ticket booth. For the rest of the year, tickets are not required and visitors simply wait in line—up to two hours in spring and summer, longer if a tour bus unloads just as you arrive; waits will likely be short in the off-peak months, September through February. You also can arrange a tour through your U.S. senator or representative. ⊠ *14th and C sts. SW, The Mall* ☎ *202/874-2330, 866/874-2330 for tour info* ⊕ *moneyfactory.gov* ⊠ *Free* ☉ *Sept.–Feb., tours weekdays every 15 mins 9–10:45 and 12:30–2, visitor center weekdays 8:30–3:30; Mar.– Aug., tours weekdays every 15 mins 9–10:45, 12:30–3:45 and 5–6, visitor center weekdays 8:30–6:30* Ⓜ *Smithsonian.*

> **CAPITAL FACTS**
>
> ■ The Bureau of Engraving and Printing turns out some $38 million worth of currency a day.
>
> ■ The largest room in the State Department has a specially loomed carpet so heavy and large it had to be airlifted in by helicopter.

THE WHITE HOUSE AREA

American Red Cross. The national headquarters for the American Red Cross, a National Historic Landmark since 1965, is composed of four buildings. Guided tours show off the oldest, a neoclassical structure of blinding-white marble built in 1917 to commemorate women who cared for the wounded on both sides during the Civil War. Three stained-glass windows designed by Louis Comfort Tiffany illustrate the values of the Red Cross: faith, hope, love, and charity. Other holdings included on the 60-minute tour include an original Norman Rockwell painting, sculptures, and two signature quilts. Weather permitting, the tour includes a visit to the courtyard. Reservations are required for the free tour; schedule via email (⟨ *tours@redcross.org*) or phone. ⊠ *430 17th St. NW, White House area* ☎ *202/303-4233* ⊕ *www.redcross. org* ⊠ *Free* ☉ *Tours only, Wed. and Fri. at 10 and 2* Ⓜ *Farragut West.*

Department of the Interior. The outside of the building is plain, but inside a wealth of art reflects the department's work. Heroic oil paintings of dam construction, gold panning, and cattle drives line the hallways. Exhibits in the **Department of the Interior Museum** outline the work of the Bureau of Land Management, the U.S. Geological Survey, the Bureau of Indian Affairs, the National Park Service, and other department branches. The museum is currently closed for renovations, and public programs are offered in other parts of the main building once or twice a month. On Tuesday and Thursday at 2, you can view more than 75 of the museum's dramatic murals created in the 1940s by photographer Ansel Adams and other artists such as Maynard Dixon and John Steuart Curry. Reservations are required for the Murals Tour; call at least two weeks in advance. The Indian Craft Shop across the hall from the museum sells Native American pottery, dolls, carvings, jewelry, baskets, and books. ⊠ *1849 C St. NW, White House area* ☎ *202/208-4743*

⊕ *www.doi.gov/interiormuseum* ⊠ *Free* ⊙ *Weekdays 8:30–4:30; craft shop also 3rd Sat. 10–4* Ⓜ *Farragut West.*

Treasury Building. Once used to store currency, this is the largest Greek Revival edifice in Washington. Robert Mills, the architect responsible for the Washington Monument and the Patent Office (now the Smithsonian American Art Museum), designed the grand colonnade that stretches down 15th Street. After the death of President Lincoln, the Andrew Johnson Suite was used as the executive office by the new president while Mrs. Lincoln moved out of the White House. Other vestiges of the building's earlier days are the two-story marble Cash Room and the gilded west dome. One-hour tours arranged through your congressperson are available most Saturdays at 9, 9:45, 10:30, and 11:15; participants must be U.S. citizens or legal residents. ⊠ *15th St. and Pennsylvania Ave. NW, White House area* ☎ *202/622–2000* ⊕ *www.treasury.gov/about/history/Pages/tours.aspx* Ⓜ *McPherson Sq. or Metro Center.*

The White House. America's most famous house was designed in 1792 by the Irishman James Hoban. It was known officially as the Executive Mansion until 1902, when President Theodore Roosevelt rechristened it the White House, long its informal name. The house has undergone many structural changes: Andrew Jackson installed running water, James Garfield put in the first elevator, and Harry Truman had the entire structure gutted and restored, adding a second-story porch to the south portico.

■TIP→ **To see the White House you need to contact your U.S. representative or senator (or embassy if you aren't a U.S. citizen). Requests can be made up to six months in advance (especially for spring, summer or December tour requests) and no less than 21 days in advance. You'll be asked for the names, birth dates and Social Security numbers of everyone in your group. On the morning of your tour, call the White House Visitors Office information line for any updates; tours are subject to last-minute cancellations. Arrive 15 minutes early. Your group will be asked to line up in alphabetical order. Everyone 18 years and older must present government-issued photo ID and no purses, backpacks or bags are allowed on the tour (and no storage lockers are provided so leave them in your hotel room). Photography is prohibited and there are no public restrooms. The security process will probably last as long as the tour itself, 20–25 minutes.**

The self-guided tour includes rooms on the ground floor, but the State Floor has the highlights. The East Room is the largest room in the White House, the site of ceremonies and press conferences; this is also where Theodore Roosevelt's children roller-skated and one of Abraham Lincoln's sons harnessed a pet goat to a chair and went for a ride. The portrait of George Washington that Dolley Madison saved from torch-carrying British soldiers in 1814 hangs in the room, and the White House Christmas tree stands here every winter. The only president to get married in the White House, Grover Cleveland, was wed in the Blue Room. The second daughter of President Cleveland and First Lady Frances, Esther, holds the distinction of being the only child born

The White House

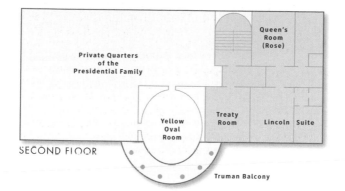

SECOND FLOOR

- Private Quarters of the Presidential Family
- Queen's Room (Rose)
- Yellow Oval Room
- Treaty Room
- Lincoln Suite
- Truman Balcony

5

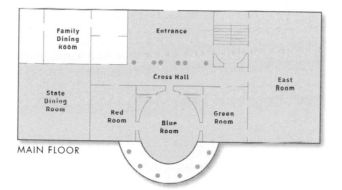

MAIN FLOOR

- Family Dining Room
- Entrance
- State Dining Room
- Cross Hall
- East Room
- Red Room
- Blue Room
- Green Room

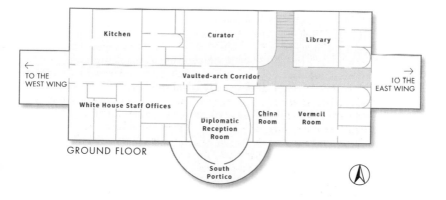

GROUND FLOOR

- Kitchen
- Curator
- Library
- TO THE WEST WING
- Vaulted-arch Corridor
- TO THE EAST WING
- White House Staff Offices
- Diplomatic Reception Room
- China Room
- Vermeil Room
- South Portico

in the White House. The Red Room, decorated in early-19th-century American Empire style, has been a favorite of first ladies. Mary Todd Lincoln had her coffee and read the morning paper here. In 1961, First Lady Jacqueline Kennedy undertook an extensive restoration of the White House to preserve and showcase the historical and architectural significance of the home and its contents. The East Garden, which now bears her name, honors her contributions.

Your tour of the White House will be enhanced by visiting the newly refurbished White House Visitor Center at 1450 Pennsylvania Avenue NW, featuring new displays, photos and a 30-minute video on the White House. ⌂ *1600 Pennsylvania Ave. NW, White House area* ☎ *202/208–1631, 202/456–7041 for 24-hr info line* ⊕ *www.whitehouse.gov* ▧ *Free* ☉ *Visitor Center: daily 7:30–4. Self-guided tours, with advance reservations: Tues.–Thurs. 7:30–11, Fri. 7:30–noon, Sat. 7:30–1* Ⓜ *Federal Triangle, Metro Center, or McPherson Sq.*

FOGGY BOTTOM

Department of State. U.S. foreign policy is administered by battalions of brainy analysts in the huge Department of State building (often referred to as the State Department). All are presided over by the secretary of state, who is fourth in line for the presidency (after the vice president, speaker of the House, and president pro tempore of the Senate). On the top floor are the opulent Diplomatic Reception Rooms, decorated like the great halls of Europe and the rooms of wealthy colonial American plantations. Furnishings include a Philadelphia highboy, a Paul Revere bowl, and the desk on which the Treaty of Paris, which ended the Revolutionary War, was signed in 1783. ■ TIP→ To visit the reception rooms, register online for a tour three months in advance. The tours are recommended for visitors 13 years and older. ⌂ *2201 C St. NW, Foggy Bottom* ☎ *202/647–3241* ⊕ *www.state.gov/m/drr* ▧ *Free* ☉ *Tours weekdays at 9:30, 10:30, and 2:45* Ⓜ *Foggy Bottom.*

Federal Reserve Building. This imposing marble edifice, its bronze entryway topped by a massive eagle, was designed by Folger Library architect Paul Cret. Its appearance seems to say, "Your money's safe with us." Even so, there's no money here, as the Fed's mission is to set interest rates and keep the economy on track. The stately facade belies a friendlier interior, with a varied collection of art and three special art exhibitions every year. Tours of the building are available for groups of 10 or more, all aged 18 years or more; they must be booked at least two weeks in advance. ⌂ *20th St. and Constitution Ave. NW, Foggy Bottom* ☎ *202/452–3324 to arrange group tours* ⊕ *www.federalreserve.gov/ finearts* ▧ *Free* ☉ *Weekdays 10–3:30 during art exhibitions* Ⓜ *Foggy Bottom.*

CAPITOL HILL

Historic Congressional Cemetery. Established in 1807 "for all denomination of people," this cemetery is the final resting place for such notables as U.S. Capitol architect William Thornton, Marine Corps march composer John Philip Sousa, Civil War photographer Mathew Brady, FBI director J. Edgar Hoover, and many members of Congress. Air Force veteran and gay rights activist Leonard Matlovich is also buried here under a tombstone that reads, "When I was in the military, they gave me a medal for killing two men and a discharge for loving one." The cemetery is about a 20-minute walk from the Capitol. You can take your own self-guided tour year-round during daylight hours; pick up a map at the gatehouse or download one from the cemetery website. On Saturday April through October, you can join one of the free docent-led tours at 11. Additionally, on the third Saturday of the month at 1 pm, there are Civil War themed tours. Narrated cell-phone tours are available by dialing ☎ 202/747–3474. ✉ 1801 E St. SE, Capitol Hill ☎ 202/543–0539 ⊕ www.congressionalcemetery.org ⊙ Daily dawn–dusk; office weekdays 9–5 Ⓜ Stadium Armory or Potomac Ave.

> **DID YOU KNOW?**
>
> In the 2007 movie *National Treasure: Book of Secrets*, the main character played by Nicholas Cage walks through stacks of books in a public area at the Library of Congress. In reality, you can't just take books off the shelves, but you can read books at the library. Go to Room LM140 of the Madison Building with a driver's license or passport and complete a form to get registered to use the library.

Library of Congress. The largest library in the world has more than 155 million items on approximately 838 miles of bookshelves. Only 35 million of its holdings are books—the library also has 3.4 million recordings, 13.6 million photographs, 5.4 million maps, 6.5 million pieces of sheet music, and 68 million manuscripts. Also here is the Congressional Research Service, which, as the name implies, works on special projects for senators and representatives.

Built in 1897, the copper-domed **Thomas Jefferson Building** is the oldest of the three buildings that make up the library. Like many other structures in Washington, the library was criticized by some as being too florid, but others praised it as the "book palace of the American people," noting that it "out-Europed Europe" in its architectural splendor. The dome, topped with the gilt "Flame of Knowledge," is certainly decorative, with busts of Dante, Goethe, Nathaniel Hawthorne, and other great writers perched above its entryway. The *Court of Neptune*, Roland Hinton Perry's fountain at the base of the front steps, rivals some of Rome's best.

The Jefferson Building opens into the Great Hall, richly adorned with mosaics, paintings, and curving marble stairways. The grand, octagonal Main Reading Room, its central desk surrounded by mahogany readers' tables under a 160-foot-high domed ceiling, inspires researchers and readers alike. Computer terminals have replaced card catalogs, but books are still retrieved and dispersed the same way: readers (16 years or older) hand request slips to librarians and wait patiently for their materials to be delivered. Researchers aren't allowed in the stacks, and only members of Congress and other special borrowers can check books out. Items from the library's collection—which includes one of

CLOSE UP

Inside the Sausage Factory: How Laws are Made

Amid the grand halls of the Capitol building, members of Congress and their aides are busy crafting the laws of our land. It's not a pretty process; as congressional commentators have quipped, laws are like sausages—it's best not to know how they're made. But for iron stomachs, here's a brief tour through Washington's sausage factory.

THE IDEA STAGE

Most laws begin as proposals that any of Congress's 535 members may offer in the form of bills. Many are trivial, such as renaming post-office branches. Others are vital, like funding the federal government. Once introduced, all proposals move to a relevant congressional committee.

CONGRESSIONAL COMMITTEES AND COMMITTEE HEARINGS

Although thousands of proposals are introduced each year, almost all die in committee. Congress never has enough time to entertain each bill, so committee leaders prioritize. Some bills are dismissed for ideological reasons. Others simply lack urgency. Efforts to rein in fuel costs, for instance, are popular when gas prices are high. Lobbying and special interest money are other major factors influencing the content and even success or failure of individual bills.

For bills that advance, merits and drawbacks are debated in committee hearings. These hearings—staged in the congressional office buildings adjacent to the Capitol—are usually open to the public; check ⊕ *www. house.gov* and ⊕ *www.senate.gov* under the "committee" headings for schedules. Committee members then vote on whether to move bills to the chamber floor.

PASSING THE HOUSE, SENATE, AND WHITE HOUSE

A bill approved by committee still faces three formidable tests before becoming a law: it must pass the full House, the full Senate, and usually the White House.

Each legislative chamber has different rules for approving bills. In the House, proposals that clear a committee and have the blessing of House leaders need only a simple majority. In the Senate, legislation can be delayed by filibustering—a time-honored process of talking nonstop on the Senate floor—until a majority votes to end the delay. If the House and Senate pass different versions of the same proposal, then those differences are reconciled in a joint conference committee before returning to the respective floors for another round of voting.

A bill passed by both the House and Senate then proceeds to the White House. The president can either sign it—in which case it becomes law—or veto it, in which case it returns to Congress. Lawmakers can override a veto, but two-thirds of each chamber must support the override to transform a vetoed bill into law. When President George W. Bush twice vetoed a popular children's health care proposal, House supporters couldn't rally the two-thirds majority to override it. The bill enjoyed President Obama's support and became law after he took office.

It's complicated. But then, no one studying sausage ever said it's easy to decipher the ingredients.

5

only three perfect Gutenberg Bibles in the world—are on display in the Jefferson Building's second-floor Southwest Gallery and Pavilion. Information about current and upcoming exhibitions, which can include oral-history projects, presidential papers, photographs, and the like, is available by phone or online. ■ TIP➜ To even begin to come to grips with the scope and grandeur of the library, one of the free hourly tours is highly recommended. Well-informed docents provide fascinating information about the library's history and holdings; they can decode the dozens of quirky allegorical sculptures and paintings throughout the building. ⊠ *Jefferson Bldg., 1st St. and Independence Ave. SE, Capitol Hill* ☎ *202/707–9779* ⊕ *www.loc.gov* ✉ *Free* ☉ *Mon.–Sat. 8:30–4:30; reading room hrs may run later. Tours Mon.–Sat. at 10:30, 11:30, 1:30, and 2:30* Ⓜ *Capitol South.*

The Supreme Court. *See the highlighted listing in this chapter.*

DOWNTOWN

Ronald Reagan Building and International Trade Center. At over 3 million square feet, this is the largest federal building in Washington, and the only structure for use by both government and private entities. A blend of classical and modern architecture, it is also officially the World Trade Center, Washington, D.C. The Reagan Building hosts a number of special events and exhibitions throughout the year, in addition to its permanent art collection including a 3-ton, 9-by-3-foot section of the Berlin Wall and dramatic sculptural pieces. You'll also be able to see the plans for the Dwight D. Eisenhower Memorial (slated for completion in 2016 on Capitol Hill); as well as the "Make it in America" and "Woodrow Wilson Presidential Memorial" exhibits. Free guided tours of the Reagan Building are offered Monday, Wednesday, and Friday at 11. There's a food court on the lower level, and a theatrical group, the Capitol Steps, performs works of political satire in the Amphitheater on Friday and Saturday nights at 7:30. During the summer months, check out Live!, a free concert series, on Woodrow Wilson Plaza, performed daily from noon to 1:30. A farmers' market, with demonstrations by local chefs, takes over the plaza on Friday during the spring and summer. ⊠ *1300 Pennsylvania Ave. NW, Downtown* ☎ *202/312–1300* ⊕ *www.itcdc.com* ✉ *Free* ☉ *Tours Mon., Wed., and Fri. at 11* Ⓜ *Federal Triangle.*

UPPER NORTHWEST

Fodor's Choice
★

Washington National Cathedral. Construction of the sixth-largest cathedral in the world began in 1907, and what is officially known as the Cathedral Church of St. Peter and St. Paul was finished and consecrated in 1990. Like its 14th-century Gothic counterparts, the stunning National Cathedral has a nave, flying buttresses, transepts, and vaults that were built stone by stone. The cathedral is Episcopalian, but it's the site of frequent ecumenical and interfaith services. State funerals for presidents Eisenhower, Reagan, and Ford were held here, and the tomb of Woodrow Wilson, the only president buried in Washington, is on the

Continued on page 177

ON THE HILL, UNDER THE DOME: EXPERIENCING THE CAPITOL

In Washington, the Capitol literally stands above it all: by law, no other building in the city can reach the height of the dome's peak.

Beneath its magnificent dome, the day-to-day business of American democracy takes place: senators and representatives debate, coax, and cajole, and ultimately determine the law of the land.

For many visitors, the Capitol is the most exhilarating experience Washington has to offer. It wins them over with a three-pronged appeal:

■ It's the city's most impressive work of architecture.

■ It has on display documents, art, and artifacts from 400 years of American history.

■ Its legislative chambers are open to the public. You can actually see your lawmakers at work, shaping the history of tomorrow.

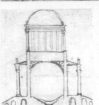

(Clockwise from top left) Moving into the new Capitol circa 1800; 19th–century print by R. Brandard; Thornton sketch circa 1797; the Capitol before the dome.

1792 - 1807 A Man with a Plan

William Thornton, a physician and amateur architect from the West Indies, wins the competition to design the Capitol. His plan, with its central rotunda and dome, draws inspiration from Rome's Pantheon. On September 18, 1793, George Washington lays the Capitol's cornerstone. In November 1800, Congress moves from Philadelphia to take up residence in the first completed section, the boxlike area between the central rotunda and today's north wing. In 1807, the House wing is completed, just to the south of the rotunda; a covered wooden walkway joins the two wings.

1814 - 1826 Washington Burns

In 1814, British troops march on Washington and set fire to the Capitol, the White House, and other government buildings. The wooden walkway is destroyed and the two wings gutted, but the walls remain standing after a violent rainstorm douses the flames. Fearful that Congress might leave Washington, residents fund a temporary "Brick Capitol" on the spot where the Supreme Court is today. By 1826, reconstruction is completed under the guidance of architects Benjamin Henry Latrobe and Charles Bulfinch; a low dome is made of wood sheathed in copper.

1850s - 1880s Domed if You Do

North and south wings are added through the 1850s and '60s to accommodate the growing government of a growing country. To maintain scale with the enlarged building, work begins in 1885 on a taller, cast-iron dome. President Lincoln would be criticized for continuing the expensive project during the Civil War, but he calls the construction "a sign we intend the Union shall go on."

(Clockwise from top left) The east front circa 1861; today the Capitol is a tourist mecca with its own visitor center; *Freedom* statue.

Expanding the Capitol

1960s - Today

The east front is extended 33½ feet, creating 100 additional offices. In 1983 preservationists fight to keep the west front, the last remaining section of the Capitol's original facade, from being extended; in a compromise the facade's crumbling sandstone blocks are replaced with stronger limestone. In 2000 the ground is broken on the subterranean Capitol Visitor Center, to be located beneath the grounds to the building's east side. The extensive facility, three-fourths the size of the Capitol itself, was finally completed on December 2, 2008 to the tune of $621 million.

Freedom atop the Capitol Dome

The twin-shelled Capitol dome, a marvel of 19th-century engineering, rises 285 feet above the ground and weighs 4,500 tons. It can expand and contract as much as 4 inches in a day, depending on the outside temperature.

The allegorical figure on top of the dome is *Freedom*. Sculpted in 1857 by Thomas Crawford, *Freedom* was cast with help from Philip Reid, a slave. Crawford had first planned for the 19½-foot-tall bronze statue to wear the cloth liberty cap of a freed Roman slave, but Southern lawmakers, led by Jefferson Davis, objected. An "American" headdress composed of a star-encircled helmet surmounted with an eagle's head and feathers was substituted. A light just below the statue burns whenever Congress is in session.

Before the visitor center opened, the best way to see the details on the *Freedom* statue atop the Capitol dome was with a good set of binoculars. Now, you can see the original plaster model of this classical female figure up close. Her right hand rests on a sheathed sword, while her left carries a victory wreath and a shield of the United States with 13 stripes. She also wears a brooch with "U.S." on her chest.

THE CAPITOL VISITOR CENTER

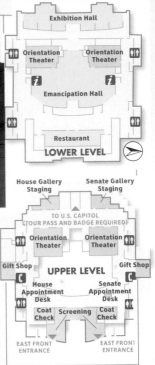

Exhibition Hall

Orientation Theater | Orientation Theater

Emancipation Hall

Restaurant

LOWER LEVEL

House Gallery Staging | Senate Gallery Staging

TO U.S. CAPITOL
(TOUR PASS AND BADGE REQUIRED)

Orientation Theater | Orientation Theater

Gift Shop | **UPPER LEVEL** | Gift Shop

House Appointment Desk | Senate Appointment Desk

Coat Check | Screening | Coat Check

EAST FRONT ENTRANCE | EAST FRONT ENTRANCE

The enormous and sunlit Capitol Visitor Center (CVC) is the start for all Capitol tours, and brings a new depth to the Capitol experience with orientation theaters, an interactive museum, and live video feeds from the House and Senate. It also provides weary travelers with welcome creature comforts, including a 530-seat restaurant.

DESIGN

At 580,000 square feet, the visitor center is approximately three-quarters the size of the 775,000-square-foot Capitol. The center's belowground location preserves the historic landscape and views designed by Frederick Law Olmsted in 1874. Inside, skylights provide natural light and views of the majestic Capitol dome. The center opened in December 2008, three years late and $356 million over budget.

EMANCIPATION HALL

The center's largest space is a gorgeous sunlit atrium called Emancipation Hall in honor of the slaves who helped to build the Capitol in the 1800s. The plaster model of the *Freedom* statue, which tops the Capitol's dome, anchors the hall. Part of the Capitol's National Statuary Hall collection is also on display here.

MUSEUM

Other attractions include exhibits about the Capitol, historical artifacts, and documents. A marble wall displays historic speeches and decisions by Congress, like President John F. Kennedy's famous 1961 "Man on the Moon" speech and a letter Thomas Jefferson wrote to Congress in 1803 urging the funding of the Lewis and Clark Expedition.

KIDS AT THE CVC

The Capitol Visitor Center is a great place for families with children who may be too young or too wiggly for a tour of the Capitol. In the Exhibition Hall, the 11-foot tall touchable model of the Capitol, touch screen computers, and architectural replicas welcome hands-on exploration.

Challenge younger kids to find statues of a person carrying a spear, a helmet, a book, and a baby.

Tweens can look for statues of the person who invented television, a king, a physician, and a representative who said, "I cannot vote for war."

PLANNING YOUR CAPITOL DAY

LOGISTICS

To tour the Capitol, you can book free, advance passes at ⊕ *www.visitthecapitol.gov* or through your representative's or senator's offices. In addition, a limited number of same-day passes are available at the Public Walk-Up line on the lower level of the visitor center. Tours run every 15 minutes; the first tour begins at 8:50 and the last at 3:20, Monday through Saturday. The center is closed on Sunday

Plan on two to four hours to tour the Capitol and see the visitor center. You should arrive at least 30 minutes before your scheduled tour to allow time to pass through security. Tours, which include a viewing of the orientation film *Out of Many, One,* last about one hour.

If you can't get a pass to tour the Capitol, the Capitol Visitor Center is still worth a visit. You can also take one of the free guided tours that do not require reservations.

To get passes to the chambers of the House and Senate, contact your representative's or senator's office. Many will also arrange for a staff member to give you a tour of the Capitol or set you up with a time for a Capitol Guide Service tour. When they're in session, some members even have time set aside to meet with constituents. You can link to the e-mail of your representative at ⊕ *www.house.gov* and of your senators at ⊕ *www.senate.gov.*

SECURITY

Expect at least a 30-minute wait going through security when you enter the Capitol Visitor Center. Bags can be no larger than 14 inches wide, 13 inches high, and 4 inches deep. View the list of prohibited items on ⊕ *www.visitthecapitol.gov.* (There are no facilities for storing prohibited belongings.) For more information, call ☎ *202/226–8000, 202/224–4049 TTY.*

BEAN SOUP AND MORE

A favorite with legislators, the Senate bean soup has been served every day for more than 100 years in the exclusive Senate Dining Room. It's available to the general public in the restaurant of the CVC (⊙ Open 7:30 AM–4 PM) on a rotating basis. You can also try making your own with the recipe on the Senate's Web site (⊕ www.senate.gov).

GETTING HERE— WITHOUT GETTING VOTED IN

The Union Station, Capitol South and Federal Center, SW Metro stops are all within walking distance of the Capitol. Follow the people wearing business suits— chances are they're headed your way. Street parking is extremely limited, but Union Station to the north of the Capitol has a public garage and there is some metered street parking along the Mall to the west of the Capitol.

TOURING THE CAPITOL

National Statuary Hall

Your 30- to 40-minute tour conducted by the Capitol Guide Service includes stops at the Rotunda, followed by the National Statuary Hall, the Hall of Columns, the old Supreme Court Chamber, the crypt (where there are exhibits on the history of the Capitol), and the gift shop. Note that you *don't* see the Senate or House chambers on the tour. (Turn the page to learn about visiting the chambers.) The highlights of the tour are the first two stops. . . .

THE ROTUNDA

You start off here, under the Capitol's dome. Look up and you'll see *Apotheosis of Washington*, a fresco painted in 1865 by Constantino Brumidi. The figures in the inner circle represent the 13 original states; those in the outer ring symbolize arts, sciences, and industry. Further down, around the Rotunda's rim, a frieze depicts 400 years of American history. The work was started by Brumidi in 1877 and continued by another Italian, Filippo Costaggini. American Allyn Cox added the final touches in 1953.

NATIONAL STATUARY HALL

South of the Rotunda is Statuary Hall, which was once the chamber of the House of Representatives. When the House moved out, Congress invited each state to send statues of two great deceased residents for placement in the hall. Because the weight of the statues threatened to make the floor cave in, and to keep the room from being cluttered, more than half of the sculptures have ended up in other spots in the Capitol. Ask your guide for help finding your state's statues.

ARTIST OF THE CAPITOL

Constantino Brumidi (1805-80) devoted his last 25 years to frescoing the Capitol; his work dominates the Rotunda and the Western Corridor. While painting the section depicting William Penn's treaty with the Indians for the Rotunda's frieze *(pictured above)*, a 74-year-old Brumidi slipped from the 58-foot scaffold, hanging on until help arrived. He would continue work for another four months, before succumbing to kidney failure.

TRY THIS

Because of Statuary Hall's perfectly elliptical ceiling, a whisper uttered along the wall can be heard at the point directly opposite on the other side of the room. Try it when you're there—if it's not noisy, the trick should work.

ONE BIG HAWAIIAN

With a solid granite base weighing six tons, Hawaii's Kamehameha I in Statuary Hall is among the heaviest objects in the collection. On Kamehameha Day (June 11, a state holiday in Hawai'i), the statue is draped with leis.

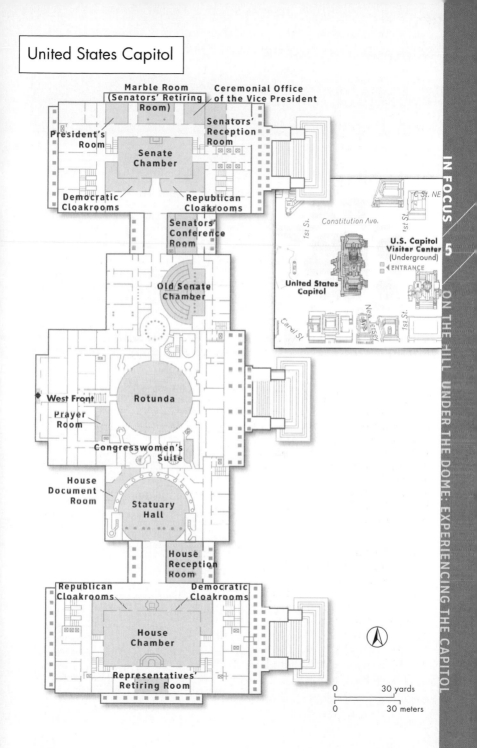

United States Capitol

Marble Room
(Senators' Retiring
Room)

Ceremonial Office
of the Vice President

President's
Room

Senators'
Reception
Room

Senate
Chamber

Democratic
Cloakrooms

Republican
Cloakrooms

Senators'
Conference
Room

Old Senate
Chamber

West Front

Rotunda

Prayer
Room

Congresswomen's
Suite

House
Document
Room

Statuary
Hall

House
Reception
Room

Republican
Cloakrooms

Democratic
Cloakrooms

House
Chamber

Representatives'
Retiring Room

C St. NE

1st St.

Constitution Ave.

1st St.

U.S. Capitol
Visitor Center
(Underground)

ENTRANCE

United States
Capitol

New Jersey Ave.

Canal St.

1st St.

0   30 yards

0   30 meters

GOING TO THE FLOOR

A tour of the Capitol is impressive, but the best part of a visit for many people is witnessing the legislators in action. Free gallery passes into the House and Senate chambers have to be obtained from your representative's or senator's office. They aren't hard to come by, but getting them takes some planning ahead. Once you have a pass, it's good for any time the chambers are open to public, for as long as the current Congress is sitting. Senate chambers are closed when the Senate is not in session, but the House is open.

Judiciary Committee

HOUSE CHAMBER

The larger of two chambers may look familiar: it's here that the president delivers the annual State of the Union. When you visit, you sit in the same balcony from which the First Family and guests watch the address.

Look carefully at the panels above the platform where the Speaker of the House sits. They're blue (rather than green like the rest of the panels in the room), and when the House conducts a vote, they light up with the names of the representatives and their votes in green and red.

House session

SENATE CHAMBER

With 100 members elected to six-year terms, the Senate is the smaller and ostensibly more dignified of Congress's two houses. Desks of the senators are arranged in an arc, with Republicans and Democrats divided by the center aisle. The vice president of the United States is officially the "president of the Senate," charged with presiding over the Senate's procedures. Usually, though, the senior member of the majority party oversees day-to-day operations, and is addressed as "Mr. President" or "Madam President."

SWEET SPOT IN THE SENATE

In the sixth desk from the right in the back row of the Senate chamber, a drawer has been filled with candy since 1968. Whoever occupies the desk maintains the stash.

THE SUPREME COURT

*✉ 1 1st St. NE, Capitol Hill
☎ 202/479-3030 ⊕ www.
supremecourt.gov ☑ Free
⊙ Weekdays 9-4:30; court in
session Oct.-June Ⓜ Union
Station or Capitol South.*

5

TIPS

■ The Washington Post carries a daily listing of what cases the court will hear. The court displays its calendar of cases a month in advance on its website; click on "Oral Arguments."

■ You can't bring your overcoat or electronics such as cameras and cell phones into the courtroom, but you can store them in a coin-operated locker.

■ When court isn't in session, you can hear lectures about the court, typically given every hour on the half hour from 9:30 to 3:30. On the ground floor you can also find revolving exhibits, a video about the court, a gift shop, an information desk, and a larger-than-life statue of John Marshall, the longest-serving chief justice in Supreme Court history.

■ Rumor has it that some lawyers visit the statue of John Marshall to rub the toe of his shoe for good luck on their way to arguing before the court.

It wasn't until 1935 that the Supreme Court got its own building: a white-marble temple with twin rows of Corinthian columns designed by Cass Gilbert. Before then, the justices had been moved around to various rooms in the Capitol; for a while they even met in a tavern. William Howard Taft, the only man to serve as both president and chief justice, was instrumental in getting the court a home of its own, though he died before the building was completed. Today you can sit in the gallery and see the court in action. Even when court isn't in session, there are still things to see.

Highlights

The court convenes on the first Monday in October and hears cases until April (though court is in session through June). There are usually two arguments a day at 10 and 11 in the morning, Monday through Wednesday, in two-week intervals.

On mornings when court is in session, two lines form for people wanting to attend. The "three-to-five-minute" line shuttles you through, giving you a quick impression of the court at work. The full-session line gets you in for the whole show. If you want to see a full session, it's best to be in line by at least 8:30. For the most contentious cases, viewers have been known to queue up days before. In May and June the court takes to the bench Monday morning at 10 to release orders and opinions. Sessions usually last 15 to 30 minutes and are open to the public.

How does a hardworking Supreme Court justice unwind? Maybe on the building's basketball court, known as "the highest court in the land." It's not open to the public, but try to imagine Antonin Scalia and Ruth Bader Ginsburg trading elbows in the lane.

nave's south side. ■TIP➔ The view of the city from the Pilgrim Observation Gallery is exceptional. Enjoy English tea in the gallery most Tuesdays and Wednesdays after a one-hour cathedral tour.

The English-style **Bishop's Garden** provides a counterpoint to the cathedral towers with boxwoods, ivy, tea roses, yew trees, and arches, bas-reliefs, and stonework from European ruins.

WORD OF MOUTH

"The Pentagon tour is surprisingly convenient, since the Pentagon has its own Metro stop. The security is tight, but quick and efficient." —KatieL

The cathedral's **Flower Mart** is held annually on the first Friday and Saturday in May and is one of Washington's premiere festivals. Each year, one Washington embassy is honored and festivalgoers are treated to the culture, traditions, food, and art of the selected country, though lobster rolls are traditionally on offer on the Friday evening of the festival. This is one of only two times during the year that you can climb the 333 steps to the cathedral's tower.

In 2011, the cathedral sustained earthquake damage (the same quake caused extensive damage to the Washington Monument). Using limestone from the quarry that supplied material for the building of the cathedral, stone carvers continue repairs. Restoration work is expected to continue through 2016, but the cathedral remains open during the process. ⊠ *Wisconsin and Massachusetts aves. NW, Upper Northwest* ☎ *202/537-6200, 202/537-6207 for tour info* ⊕ *www. nationalcathedral.org* 🔊 *Suggested tour donation $10* ⊙ *Weekdays 10–5:30, Sat. 10–4:30, Sun. 8–5 (for services). Tours (every 30 mins): weekdays 10–11:15 and 1–3:30, Sat. 10–11:15 and 1–3, Sun. 1–2:30. Gardens daily dawn–dusk* Ⓜ *Cleveland Park or Tenleytown–AU, then take any 30-series bus.*

SUBURBAN VIRGINIA

Pentagon. The headquarters of the United States Department of Defense is the largest low-rise office building in the world. Approximately 24,000 military and civilian workers arrive daily. Astonishingly, the mammoth structure, completed in 1943, took less than two years to construct.

Following the September 2001 crash of hijacked American Airlines Flight 77 into the northwest side of the building, the damaged area was removed in just over a month and repaired in a year. In this same area is the America's Heroes Memorial and Chapel, which pays tribute to the civilians and military members killed in the attack. In 2008, the two-acre Pentagon Memorial, with its 184 benches commemorating the lives lost in 2001, was dedicated. Tours of the Pentagon are free; reserve online through the Pentagon Tour Office at least two weeks, but no more than three months, in advance. ⊠ *I–395 at Columbia Pike, and Rte. 27, Arlington, Virginia* ☎ *703/697-1776* ⊕ *pentagontours. osd.mil* ⊙ *Tours weekdays 9–3 by reservation. Pentagon Memorial 24 hrs* Ⓜ *Pentagon.*

WHERE TO EAT

Updated by
Elana Schor

Washington has long benefited from a constant infusion of different cultures, making it a stellar culinary host for visitors and transplants from around the world, but recent years have made the fifth or sixth banana of American haute cuisine into a foodie town in its own right. You can find almost any cuisine here, from Salvadoran to Ethiopian, despite D.C.'s lack of true ethnic neighborhoods. But now you can also sample cooking from some of the country's hottest new chefs and sip craft cocktails that could be mistaken for Manhattan's. Just follow your nose.

Although most neighborhoods lack a unified culinary flavor, make no mistake: D.C. is a city of distinctive areas, each with its own style. Chinatown, for example, is known for chic small plates of various origins. You'll find Japanese noodle shops next to Mexican taquerias and Indian bistros. These spots wax and wane on the popularity scale with each passing season; it's worth taking a stroll down the street to see what's new. Downtown, you'll find many of the city's blue-chip law firms and deluxe, expense-account restaurants, as well as stylish lounges, brewpubs, and upscale eateries that have sprung up to serve the crowds that attend games at the Verizon Center.

Wherever you venture forth in the city, there are a few trends worth noting: artisanal cocktails, charcuterie-and-cheese plates, and back-to-basics New American cuisine are in vogue. You'll find tapas-style portions pervasive, whether you're at a Greek, Asian, or American restaurant. High-end restaurants in town also have begun to add bar menus with smaller plates that are much less expensive than their entrées, but created with the same finesse.

Though Italian, French, and fusion spots continue to open at a ferocious pace, Washingtonians are always hungry to try something new, whether it's Chinese smoked lobster, fiery Indian curry, or crunchy and addictive Vietnamese spring rolls.

PLANNING

RESERVATIONS
Plan ahead if you're determined to snag a sought-after reservation. Some renowned restaurants are booked weeks in advance. But you can get lucky at the last minute if you're flexible—and friendly. Most restaurants keep a few tables open for walk-ins and VIPs. Show up for dinner early (5:30 pm) or late (after 10 pm) and politely inquire about any last-minute vacancies or cancellations. If you're calling a few days ahead of time, ask if you can be put on a waiting list. Occasionally, an eatery may ask you to call the day before your scheduled meal to reconfirm: don't forget, or you could lose out.

HOURS
Washington has less of an around-the-clock mentality than other big cities, with many big-name restaurants shutting down between lunch and dinner and closing their kitchens by 11 pm. Weekend evenings spent Downtown can also be a hassle for those seeking quick bites, because many popular chain eateries cater to office workers and shut down on Friday at 6 pm. For a midnight supper, the best bets are Dupont Circle and the U Street Corridor, while families looking for late lunches should head north from the Mall to find kitchens that stay open between mealtimes.

WHAT TO WEAR
As unfair as it seems, the way you look can influence how you're treated—and where you're seated. Generally speaking, jeans and a button-down shirt will suffice at most table-service restaurants in the $–$$ range. Some pricier restaurants require jackets, and some insist on ties. In reviews, we mention dress only where men are required to wear a jacket or a jacket and tie. But even when there's no formal dress code, we recommend wearing jackets and ties in $$$ and $$$$ restaurants. If you have doubts, call the restaurant and ask.

PRICES
If you're watching your budget, be sure to ask the price of daily specials recited by the waiter or captain. The charge for specials at some restaurants is noticeably out of line with the other prices on the menu. Beware of the $10 bottle of water; ask for tap water instead. And always review your bill.

If you eat early or late you may be able to take advantage of prix-fixe deals not offered at peak hours. Most upscale restaurants offer great lunch deals with special menus at cut-rate prices designed to give customers a true taste of the place.

Credit cards are widely accepted, but many restaurants (particularly smaller ones Downtown) accept only cash. If you plan to use a credit card, it's a good idea to double-check its acceptability when making reservations or before sitting down to eat.

6

UPPER NORTHWEST
casual neighborhood joints

ADAMS MORGAN AND U STREET CORRIDOR
ethnic eats and quirky bars

GEORGETOWN
mix of white-tablecloth and no-tablecloth eateries

DUPONT CIRCLE
upscale, stylish restaurants with lively bar scene

CHINATOWN
tapas-style restaurants with eclectic cuisine

FOGGY BOTTOM
cheap cafés popular with students

DOWNTOWN
revitalized arts district with upscale eateries

CAPITOL HILL
pub grub and cafés aplenty for harried staffers

Florida Ave.

U St.

16th St.

Columbia Rd.

Vermont Ave.

Sheridan Circle

Massachusetts Ave.

Florida Ave.

New Hampshire Ave.

Dupont Circle

Logan Circle

Rhode Island Ave.

Rock Creek

Scott Circle

Thomas Circle

M St.

M St.

Connecticut Ave.

K St.

15th St.

14th St.

New York Ave.

Whitehurst Fwy.

Washington Circle

Pennsylvania Ave.

23rd St.

Theodore Roosevelt Island

Virginia Ave.

Constitution Ave.

THE MALL

Independence Ave.

Reflecting Pool

THE MONUMENTS

Arlington Memorial Br.

Columbia Island

Tidal Basin

Francis Case Memorial Br.

Washington Canal

VIRGINIA

Potomac River

| 0 | 500 yards |
| 0 | 500 meter |

WHAT IT COSTS				
	$	$$	$$$	$$$$
AT DINNER	under $17	$18–$25	$26–$35	over $35

Prices in the reviews are the average cost of a main course at dinner or, if dinner is not served, at lunch.

TIPPING AND TAXES

In most restaurants, tip the waiter 16%–20%. (To figure the amount quickly, just double the sales tax noted on the check—it's 10% of your bill.) Tip at least $1 per drink at the bar and $1 for each coat checked. Never tip the maître d' unless you're out to impress your guests or expect to pay another visit soon.

If you're dining with a group, make sure not to overtip: review your check to see if a gratuity has been added, as many restaurants automatically tack on an 18% tip for groups of six or more.

DINING WITH KIDS

Though it's unusual to see children in the dining rooms of D.C.'s most elite restaurants, eating with youngsters in the nation's capital does not have to mean culinary exile. Many of the restaurants reviewed here are excellent choices for families and are marked with a ☺ symbol.

SMOKING

Smoking is banned in all restaurants and bars, with the exception of a few spaces that have enclosed and ventilated rooms—usually for cigar aficionados.

RESTAURANT REVIEWS

Listed alphabetically within neighborhood. Use the coordinate at the end of the review (✛ 2:B2) to locate a property on the Where to Eat and Stay map.

THE WHITE HOUSE AREA AND FOGGY BOTTOM

The history-steeped Foggy Bottom area boasts architectural landmarks like the Watergate Hotel. Around George Washington University there's cheaper, college-friendly fare like burrito joints and coffee shops. Nearby, the Kennedy Center draws a more mature crowd with tastes that have evolved past burgers and nachos.

$$$$
MODERN
AMERICAN
Fodor'sChoice
★

✕ **Blue Duck Tavern.** Many chefs are fond of artisanal and local ingredients. Chef Sebastien Archambault is so committed to the cause that fixings are often strewn across marble counters in the restaurant's show kitchen. By now diners have gotten used to watching pastry chefs churn ice cream to be served minutes later in glass ice buckets, but sweets—and watching for the town's biggest political names to claim their favorite tables—aren't the only pleasures. The kitchen, located in the Park Hyatt Hotel, wows with Modern American riffs like 12-hour suckling pig in jus, an oven-roasted marrowbone with creamy insides, and rightly famous "triple" steak fries, thrice-doused in dreamy duck fat.

BEST BETS FOR WASHINGTON, D.C., DINING

With thousands of restaurants to choose from, how will you decide where to eat? Fodor's writers and editors have selected their favorite restaurants by price, cuisine, and experience in the lists here. You can also search by neighborhood for excellent eating experiences—just peruse the following pages.

Fodor's Choice ★

2941 Restaurant, $$$, p. 214
Blue Duck Tavern, $$$$, p. 185
Central Michel Richard, $$$, p. 194
Fiola, $$$$, p. 195
Hank's Oyster Bar, $$, p. 204
Inn at Little Washington, $$$$, p. 215
Komi, $$$$, p. 204
Nora, $$$$, p. 205
Rasika, $$, p. 200
Ray's to the Third, $, p. 215
Rose's Luxury, $$$, p. 191
Sweetgreen, $, p. 206
Taylor Gourmet, $, p. 212
Zaytinya, $$, p. 200

Best by Price

$

Ben's Chili Bowl, p. 209
Good Stuff Eatery, p. 190
Ray's to the Third, p. 215
Rocklands, p. 203
Sweetgreen, p. 206
Taylor Gourmet, p. 212
Teaism, p. 198

$$

Bistrot du Coin, p. 203
Etete, p. 210
Granville Moore's Brickyard, p. 190
Hank's Oyster Bar, p. 204
Jaleo, p. 199
Kushi, p. 199
Matchbox, p. 199
Zaytinya, p. 200

$$$

2941 Restaurant, p. 214
Art and Soul, p. 189
Central Michel Richard, p. 194
Estadio, p. 207
Rose's Luxury, p. 191

$$$$

1789 Restaurant, p. 201
Blue Duck Tavern, p. 185
Charlie Palmer Steak, p. 190
CityZen, p. 194
Fiola, p. 195
Inn at Little Washington, p. 215
Komi, p. 204
Nora, p. 205
Obelisk, p. 205

Best by Cuisine

AFRICAN

Etete, $$, p. 210
Ethiopic, $, p. 190

AMERICAN

2941 Restaurant, $$$, p. 214
Blue Duck Tavern, $$$$, p. 185
Cashion's Eat Place, $$$, p. 207
Inn at Little Washington, $$$$, p. 215
Ted's Bulletin, $, p. 192

ASIAN (VARIOUS)

Full Kee, $, p. 198
Kushi, $$, p. 199
Teaism, $, p. 198

BELGIAN

Belga Café, $$$, p. 189
Brasserie Beck, $$$, p. 193
Granville Moore's Brickyard, $$, p. 190
Marcel's, $$$$, p. 188

ECLECTIC

Ardeo, $$$, p. 213
Komi, $$$$, p. 204

FRENCH

Bistro Bis, $$$, p. 189
Bistro Français, $$$, p. 201
Central Michel Richard, $$$, p. 194

GREEK/TURKISH

Cava Mezze, $$, p. 189
Zaytinya, $$, p. 200

INDIAN

Rasika, $$, p. 200

ITALIAN

Bibiana Osteria and Enoteca, $$, p. 193
Cafe Milano, $$$$, p. 202
Fiola, $$$$, p. 195
Obelisk, $$$$, p. 205

JAPANESE

Kaz Sushi Bistro, $$, p. 196

Kushi, $$, p. 199

Sushi-Ko, $$, p. 203

LATIN AMERICAN

Ceiba, $$, p. 194

PIZZA

2 Amys, $$, p. 212

Matchbox, $$, p. 199

Pizzeria Paradiso, $$, p. 206

Seventh Hill, $, p. 192

SEAFOOD

Black Salt, $$$, p. 213

Hank's Oyster Bar, $$, p. 204

Johnny's Half Shell, $$$, p. 191

Pearl Dive Oyster Palace, $$$, p. 211

SOUTHERN

Georgia Brown's, $$$, p. 195

Hill Country, $$, p. 199

Oohhs & Aahhs, $$, p. 211

SPANISH

Estadio, $$$, p. 207

Jaleo, $$, p. 199

Taberna del Alabardero, $$$, p. 197

STEAK

Cafe Milano, $$$$, p. 202

The Capital Grille, $$$$, p. 194

Charlie Palmer Steak, $$$$, p. 190

The Palm, $$$$, p. 205

Best by Experience

BEST BRUNCH

Belga Café, $$$, p. 189

Birch & Barley, $$, p. 206

Black Salt, $$$, p. 213

Georgia Brown's, $$$, p. 195

BEST FOR BUSINESS

The Capital Grille, $$$$, p. 194

Charlie Palmer Steak, $$$$, p. 190

The Palm, $$$$, p. 205

BEST HOTEL DINING

Blue Duck Tavern, $$$$, p. 185

CityZen, $$$$, p. 194

Poste Moderne Brasserie, $$$, p. 200

BEST POLITICO-WATCHING

Cafe Milano, $$$$, p. 202

Charlie Palmer Steak, $$$$, p. 190

BEST WITH KIDS

Ben's Chili Bowl, $, p. 209

Five Guys, $, p. 202

Good Stuff Eatery, $, p. 190

Kramerbooks & Afterwords, $$, p. 204

The Market Lunch, $, p. 191

Rocklands, $, p. 203

CAPITAL CLASSICS

1789 Restaurant, $$$$, p. 201

Ben's Chili Bowl, $, p. 209

Occidental Grill, $$$$, p. 196

GOOD FOR GROUPS

Hill Country, $$, p. 199

Zaytinya, $$, p. 200

GREAT VIEWS

2941 Restaurant, $$$, p. 214

Charlie Palmer Steak, $$$$, p. 190

MOST ROMANTIC

1905, $$, p. 208

Birch & Barley, $$, p. 206

Ethiopic, $, p. 190

Komi, $$$$, p. 204

PRETHEATER

Jaleo, $$, p. 199

Rasika, $$, p. 200

QUIET MEAL

Equinox, $$$, p. 195

Obelisk, $$$$, p. 205

Taberna del Alabardero, $$$, p. 197

SPECIAL OCCASION

2941 Restaurant, $$$, p. 214

CityZen, $$$$, p. 194

TRENDY

Marvin, $$, p. 210

Rasika, $$, p. 200

Westend Bistro, $$$, p. 188

Zaytinya, $$, p. 200

WINE BARS

Bistrot Lepic, $$$, p. 213

Sonoma, $$, p. 192

Vidalia, $$$$, p. 206

6

The dining room is stylish, done up with Shaker furniture and quilts. $ *Average main: $38* ✉ *1201 24th St. NW, Foggy Bottom* ☎ *202/419–6755* ⊕ *www.blueducktavern.com* ✍ *Reservations essential* ۞ *No lunch* Ⓜ *Foggy Bottom/GWU* ✤ *1:D5.*

$$

MODERN
AMERICAN
FAMILY

✗ **Founding Farmers.** Inside this ultramodern take on the old-school farmhouse, affordable eco-chic is the mantra. Local farms provide most of the fresh vegetables in the salads and sustainable practices are used to catch every type of fish on the menu. The sheer number of offerings can make for a disorienting experience, with 16 options for pastas and flatbreads alone, but its combination of affordability and reliability is unmatched in the neighborhood. ■**TIP➔ Visitors with early museum call times are well-served by the 7 am breakfast.** Vegans will be particularly pleased with the array of meat- and egg-free options, and teetotalers are advised to try some of the staff's award-winning throwback sodas, such as the daily rickey or lemon-lime ginger. $ *Average main: $18* ✉ *1924 Pennsylvania Ave. NW, Foggy Bottom* ☎ *202/822–8783* ⊕ *www.wearefoundingfarmers.com* ✍ *Reservations essential* Ⓜ *Foggy Bottom/GWU* ✤ *1:E6.*

$$$$

BELGIAN

✗ **Marcel's.** Chef Robert Wiedmaier trained in the Netherlands and Belgium, and in this, his first solo venture, his French-inspired Belgian cooking focuses on well-designed presentations for the plate. Don't miss the mussels, if they're available, and take advantage of the perfectly seared diver scallops served with delicate Japanese citrus sauce or sage beurre blanc, depending on the season. The duck breast is a marvel, its succulent dark meat coated in flavorful jus. In season, be sure to order the fig tart with citrus crème anglaise and honey-cinnamon ice cream. Prices range from $85 for four courses to $145 for seven, with à la carte ordering available. $ *Average main: $115* ✉ *2401 Pennsylvania Ave. NW, Foggy Bottom* ☎ *202/296–1166* ⊕ *www.marcelsdc.com* ✍ *Reservations essential* ۞ *No lunch* Ⓜ *Foggy Bottom/GWU* ✤ *1:D5.*

$$$

MODERN
AMERICAN

✗ **Westend Bistro.** Eric Ripert, the chef of New York City's award-winning restaurant Le Bernardin, quietly removed his name from this upscale boîte in the Ritz-Carlton Hotel a few years ago, but new chef Devin Bozkaya is working hard to keep wowing the swells of Foggy Bottom. Portions of swanky comfort food, such as macaroni-and-cheese and fish burgers with saffron aioli, have grown larger since the handover, but be warned that the handmade cocktails are now a skyscraping $15. $ *Average main: $29* ✉ *1190 22nd St. NW, Foggy Bottom* ☎ *202/974–5566* ⊕ *www.westendbistrodc.com* ✍ *Reservations essential* ۞ *No lunch weekends* Ⓜ *Foggy Bottom/GWU* ✤ *1:E5.*

CAPITOL HILL

"The Hill," as locals know it, was once an enclave of congressional boardinghouses in the shadow of the Capitol building but is now D.C.'s largest historic district, with an eclectic mix of restaurants. Around the Capitol South Metro station, government offices end and neighborhood dining begins. Here, along tree-lined streets, you'll find local bars and restaurants that cater to lunch and happy-hour crowds during the week and residents on weekends.

Neighborhood establishments and all-American pubs line historic Barracks Row (✉ *8th St. SE*), with Eastern Market anchoring the homey House side of the Hill; the Senate end is given a more hustle-and-bustle vibe with the chain dining and upscale boîtes of Union Station.

$$$ MODERN AMERICAN

🍴 **Art and Soul.** Best known as Oprah's longtime personal chef, Art Smith is now serving the Washingtonian crowd at this funky Southern-fried spot, located in the Liaison Capitol Hill. Down-home cravings get an upscale twist in a chic kitchen where a three-course $25 "power lunch" draws movers and shakers but the bacon cornbread still bakes in a can. The bar makes no bones about its fancy provenance, offering few wines by the glass below $13 and a high-end Brazilian refresher with the Congress-ready moniker "The Quorum." [$] *Average main: $28* ✉ *415 New Jersey Ave. NW, Capitol Hill* ☎ *202/393–7777* 🌐 *www.artandsouldc.com* [M] *Union Station* ↕ *2:F3.*

$$$ EUROPEAN

🍴 **Belga Café.** You can go traditional with mussels and the crispiest of french fries or dabble in what the chef calls Euro-fusion at this sleek café done up with dark wood and exposed brick. Classic dishes such as Flemish beef stew made with dark Gulden Draak beer and pepper-crusted steak in cognac sauce are expertly turned out, along with newer takes such as endive salad with a sabayon made from the wheaty ale Hoegaarden. Speaking of quaffs, Belgium's love of them is reflected in the three-page ale list. Crowds at lunch and dinner—and especially for the überpopular waffle-centric brunch, so popular it's served for seven hours—sometimes mean you'll have to wait for a table, even with a reservation. [$] *Average main: $28* ✉ *514 8th St. SE, Capitol Hill* ☎ *202/544–0100* 🌐 *www.belgacafe.com* [M] *Eastern Market* ↕ *2:H6.*

$$$ FRENCH

🍴 **Bistro Bis.** A zinc bar, spacious brown-leather booths, and a glass-front display kitchen create great expectations at Bistro Bis, the second restaurant from Jeffrey Buben, owner of the much-acclaimed Vidalia. The seasonal menu seamlessly merges Modern American standards with French bistro classics. For a first course, be sure to try the steak tartare. Main-course hits include classic steak frites, trout with capers, and curried sea bass with pureed cauliflower. But don't be fooled by its daylong hours and convenient location—the mood is more meet-the-parents than family-friendly. [$] *Average main: $29* ✉ *Hotel George, 15 E St. NW, Capitol Hill* ☎ *202/661–2700* 🌐 *www.bistrobis.com* ✍ *Reservations essential* [M] *Union Station* ↕ *2:F3.*

$$ MEDITERRANEAN

🍴 **Cava Mezze.** This modern mecca for *mezes* (small plates for sharing) delivers delicious and chic Mediterranean without the whiz-bang conceits of its pricier small-plate cousins. The entire Greek catalogue is here for the taking, from fluffy *taramosalata* (salmon roe dip) with a touch of citrus to rich, melt-in-your-mouth spinach pie. There are few surprises on the menu, save for the gloriously salty halloumi cheese topped with mint, but the leather-lined room and gallant service make the traditional dishes feel new again. There are two other locations: in Rockville, Maryland, and the Clarendon neighborhood of Arlington, Virginia; both are accessible by public transportation. Quicker, more informal Cava Grill spinoffs serve the menu's greatest hits near the Bethesda and Columbia Heights Metro stops. [$] *Average main: $22*

6

✉ *527 8th St. SE, Capitol Hill* ☎ *202/543–9090* 🌐 *cavamezze.com* 🕒 *No lunch Mon.* [M] *Eastern Market* ⊕ *2:H6.*

$$$$ STEAKHOUSE 🍴 **Charlie Palmer Steak.** It's hard not to feel like a master of the universe when ensconced in this coolly elegant dining room in the imposing shadow of the Capitol. Oversize floral arrangements, tones of blue-gray, a dramatic glass-enclosed wine cellar, and quasi-Danish modern furniture form a backdrop to the contemporary cuisine. Dry-aged rib-eye, marinated hanger steak, and porterhouse steak with morel mushrooms are the meaty choices. But brown-butter-drenched tortelloni and poached lobster make a good showing, too, as do sides such as mashed Yukon Golds and Brussels sprouts with pancetta. The crème brûlée trio finishes things off nicely. [$] *Average main: $42* ✉ *101 Constitution Ave. NW, Capitol Hill* ☎ *202/547–8100* 🌐 *www.charliepalmer.com* 🕒 *Closed Sun. No lunch Sat.* [M] *Union Station* ⊕ *2:F4.*

$ AFRICAN 🍴 **Ethiopic.** The spongy rolls of sourdough *injera* bread (ubiquitous on Ethiopian plates) used in place of utensils can make traditional Ethiopian feel decidedly undelicate, but the bright surroundings and friendly service here make for a downright romantic experience. Venture off the well-beaten path of spicy lamb and lentils to try the spicy chickpea dumplings or fragrant simmered split peas, laden with garlic and served in a clay pot. For devoted meat lovers, the rosemary notes in the beef *tibs* (a type of hearty steak cut) and the chicken legs' rich red pepper sauce will crown a memorable, affordable meal. The full bar also serves potent Ethiopian beers. [$] *Average main: $14* ✉ *401 H St. NE, Capitol Hill* ☎ *202/675–2066* 🌐 *www.ethiopicrestaurant.com* 🕒 *Closed Mon. No lunch Tues.–Thurs.* [M] *Union Station* ⊕ *2:H2.*

$ BURGER FAMILY 🍴 **Good Stuff Eatery.** Fans of Bravo's *Top Chef* will first visit this brightly colored burgers-and-shakes shack hoping to spy charismatic TV chef Spike Mendelsohn, but they will return for the comfort-food favorites. The lines can be long, as it has quickly become a favorite lunch spot of congressional aides, but Spike's inventive beef dishes—including the "Blazin' Barn" Asian burger topped with Thai basil and pickled radish—are worth the wait. After placing your order cafeteria-style, remember to grab several of the fresh dipping sauces for the tasty thyme-and-rosemary-seasoned hand-cut skinny fries or Vidalia onion rings. Just as important, leave room for a toasted marshmallow or chocolate malted shake that's as thick as the ones you remember from childhood. [$] *Average main: $8* ✉ *303 Pennsylvania Ave. SE, Capitol Hill* ☎ *202/543–8222, 202/337–4663* 🌐 *www.goodstuffeatery.com* 🕒 *Closed Sun.* [M] *Eastern Market* ⊕ *2:H5.*

$$ BELGIAN 🍴 **Granville Moore's Brickyard.** This Belgian beer hall with a gourmet soul is worth a visit despite its location in D.C.'s Atlas District, an area that can be seedy after dark. Snag a seat at the bar or at one of the first-come, first-served tables, and linger over unfiltered artisanal brews that range from Chimay to the obscure, lip-smacking Brasserie des Rocs. The food is terrific, specifically the pots of steamed mussels served with crunchy, twice-fried frites paired with homemade dipping sauces. The bison burger and rotating cast of hearty salads, usually incorporating a meat or cheese, are indulgent without crossing the line into predictable pub grub. [$] *Average main: $18* ✉ *1238 H St. NE, Capitol Hill*

☎ 202/399–2546 🌐 *www.granvillemoores.com* ✍ *Reservations not accepted* ⏲ *No lunch Mon.–Thurs.* [M] *Union Station* ✥ *2:H2.*

$ AMERICAN 🍴 **Jimmy T's Place.** This D.C. institution is tucked in the first floor of an old row house only five blocks from the Capitol. Sassy waiters, talkative regulars, and this small diner's two boisterous owners, who run the grill, pack the place daily. Enjoy favorites such as grits, pumpkin pancakes, omelets, or the homey eggs Benedict, made with a toasted English muffin, a huge piece of ham, and lots of hollandaise sauce—but expect the unexpected in terms of clientele, and don't forget to play by the rules (i.e. no substitutions and as few questions for the staff as possible). [$] *Average main: $6* ✉ *501 E. Capitol St. SE, Capitol Hill* ☎ *202/546–3646* 💳 *No credit cards* ⏲ *Closed Mon. and Sat. No dinner* [M] *Capitol S* ✥ *2:H5.*

$$$ SOUTHERN 🍴 **Johnny's Half Shell.** On the Senate side of the Capitol, this eatery's Southern-tinged mid-Atlantic fare—pristine Kumamoto oysters, flavorful seafood stews, fried oyster po'boys, and a stellar pickled-onion-and-blue-cheese-topped "Baltimore" hot dog, only available at lunch—takes the cake for fine and speedy dining. Not surprisingly, the crowd is heavy on politicos drawn as much by the buzz as by the healthy-yet-savory grilled calamari salad. Members of Congress can often be found here on weekdays, downing a quick Gruyère-cheese omelet during breakfast in the company of top campaign contributors. [$] *Average main: $32* ✉ *400 N. Capitol St. NW, Capitol Hill* ☎ *202/737–0400* 🌐 *www.johnnyshalfshell.net* ⏲ *Closed Sun.* [M] *Union Station* ✥ *2:F3.*

6

$ AMERICAN FAMILY 🍴 **The Market Lunch.** For a perfect Saturday morning or afternoon on the Hill, take a walk around the Capitol, a stroll through Eastern Market, and then dig in to a hefty pile of blueberry buckwheat pancakes from this casual counter. Informal seating makes it ideal for kids (though be prepared to pay extra if they want real maple syrup). Favorites include eggs, grits, or pancakes in the morning and crab cakes, fried shrimp, or fish for lunch. Expect long lines and plan to be in line by noon on Saturday in order to ensure availability of every dish. **■ TIP→ Follow convention and order quickly, eat, and give up your seat for the next customer.** [$] *Average main: $14* ✉ *Eastern Market, 225 7th St. SE, Capitol Hill* ☎ *202/547–8444* 🌐 *www.easternmarket-dc.org/default.asp?contentID=46* ✍ *Reservations not accepted* 💳 *No credit cards* ⏲ *Closed Mon. No dinner; brunch Sat. only* [M] *Eastern Market* ✥ *2:H6.*

$$$ MODERN AMERICAN Fodor's Choice ★ 🍴 **Rose's Luxury.** The neon sign above one of the two interior bars at what its chef calls the city's "most exclusively unexclusive" kitchen reads "awesome"—the perfect adjective for cooking that's both welcoming and groundbreaking. The sausage-and-lychee salad, made for stirring tableside into a coconut cream and habanero accompaniment that is as delightful as it is shocking, became an instant classic as hours long lines formed outside this supremely stylish recreation of a hipster's dream dinner party. It may take careful planning and patience, but scoring a table here is the experiential equivalent of doughnuts topped with cheddar cheese: a worthy, witty home run. [$] *Average main: $32* ✉ *717 8th St. SE, Eastern Market* ☎ *202/580–8889* 🌐 *www.rosesluxury.com* ✍ *Reservations not accepted* ⏲ *No lunch* ✥ *2:H6.*

$ PIZZA 🍴 **Seventh Hill.** When this hand-tossed-pizza spot first opened, it seemed like a risky bet given the high bar set by capital favorites such as Matchbox and 2 Amys. But the breezy charm of this casual bistro quickly vaulted its pies to the top of the heap. Each is named for a nearby neighborhood—the zesty mating of basil and anchovies on the "SW Waterfront" pie is matched only by the creamy goat cheese of the "Eastern Market." Pizzas match well with the small cast of bottled beers available at this bright, Eurocentric spot with a welcoming vibe. Make sure to save room for the decadent hazelnut-chocolate dessert calzone. [$] *Average main: $16* ✉ *327 7th St. SE, Capitol Hill* ☎ *202/544–1911* 🌐 *www.montmartredc.com/seventhhill* ✍ *Reservations not accepted* ⏲ *Closed Mon.* [M] *Eastern Market* ✣ *2:H6.*

$$ WINE BAR 🍴 **Sonoma.** This chic multilevel wine bar has pours aplenty (in both tasting portions and full glasses) along with well-thought-out charcuterie boards piled with prosciutto and fluffy, grill-charred focaccia. There's more filling fare, too, like spinach gnocchi with goat cheese and pancetta. By day the crowd skews to Senate staffers enjoying the complimentary newspapers and Wi-Fi during breakfast, but by night the place becomes a hipster hub in the bar on the second level—think low tables and sofas—while a youngish crowd shares cheese plates and sips $4 Italian beers in the crowded street-level dining room. [$] *Average main: $20* ✉ *223 Pennsylvania Ave. SE, Capitol Hill* ☎ *202/544–8088* 🌐 *www.sonomadc.com* ⏲ *No brunch Sat.* [M] *Capitol S* ✣ *2:H5.*

$ DINER FAMILY 🍴 **Ted's Bulletin.** This cheeky homage to mid-20th-century diners is styled after a newspaper office, with menus printed in broadsheet format and specials mounted on the wall in mismatched plastic lettering. But one bite of the grilled cheese with tomato soup or the "Burgh" burger, served on Texas toast with coleslaw, french fries, and a runny egg, will convince you that the kitchen's skills are no joke. Kids will love the 16 clever milk shake flavors, and their parents will love the nine extra shakes that come with a kick of liquor added. (The Nutty Professor, made with hazelnut liqueur, is worth writing home about, as are the homemade Pop-Tarts.) [$] *Average main: $15* ✉ *505 8th St. SE, Capitol Hill* ☎ *202/544–8337* 🌐 *www.tedsbulletincapitolhill.com* [M] *Eastern Market* ✣ *2:H6.*

DOWNTOWN

Until recently, tourists who trekked north from the Mall hungry for something more than Smithsonian cafeteria food were stranded Downtown with little but high-end options. Now young Washingtonians are taking advantage of residential development and moving off Capitol Hill to Downtown, pulling trendy and affordable dining choices up north.

Chinatown and nearby Penn Quarter are the nerve center of the area, thanks to the Verizon Center and a row of popular clothing stores, but the crowds mean an inevitable wait for tables.

If you're in the mood to splurge without feeling like a stuffed shirt, perennials like Ceiba have a more relaxed vibe on weekends.

$$ MODERN HAWAIIAN 🍴 **The Arsenal at Bluejacket.** Most restaurants pair beers with food. Here you'll find the opposite: refined but hardy new American fare designed to complement the craft brews designed by suds expert Greg Engert. If you're not sure whether an herbal saison or the spicy fruit of a scotch ale would go best amid the sweet notes of duck cassoulet with red wine-glazed onions or the salty, crispy punch of a kale Caesar salad, don't be afraid to ask the gracious cast of servers. Never get too distracted that you forget to look up at the artful industrial décor at this symbol of revitalization in the Navy Yard area, and never get so attached to happy hour that you forget to return for the impeccable brunch, where Snickers donuts are all the rage. [$] *Average main: $24* ✉ *300 Tingey St. SE, Waterfront* ☎ *202/524–2862* 🌐 *bluejacketdc.com* ✍ *Reservations essential* 🕘 *No brunch Sat.* ✥ *2:F6.*

$ THAI 🍴 **Beau Thai.** This dream of a local haunt was founded by an experienced Thai chef and two American entrepreneurs inspired by her flair for spice. The drunken noodle is light yet flavorful, the green curry is complex, and the sesame-crusted tofu appetizer achieves that nirvana of bean curd: carnivores can't get enough of it—just like patrons can't get their fill of this chic dining room and its uptown counterpart in Mount Pleasant. [$] *Average main: $14* ✉ *1700 New Jersey Ave. NW, Shaw* ☎ *202/536–5636* 🌐 *www.beauthaidc.com.* ✥ *1:H3.*

$$ ITALIAN 🍴 **Bibiana Osteria and Enoteca.** You might call this the Italian version of the überpopular Indian spot Rasika, and you'd be correctly noting the modernist fingerprints of local impresario Ashok Bajaj. The 120-seat dining room, decorated in Bajaj's favored spare tones and metallic accents, specializes in hearty Florence-inspired cuisine dished out by uncommonly attentive and knowledgeable servers. In a city where Italian spots too often hit obvious notes such as brick-oven pizzas, celebrity customers such as Claire Danes can try presentations such as crispy duck breast with kumquats and blue crab served atop linguine colored jet-black by squid ink. The surroundings may be rich, but the ample portions and sensible offerings such as the $27 three-course lunch make for a recession-friendly splurge. [$] *Average main: $24* ✉ *1100 New York Ave. NW, entrance at 12th and H sts., Downtown* ☎ *202/216–9550* 🌐 *www.bibianadc.com* 🕘 *Closed Sun. No lunch Sat.* [M] *Metro Center* ✥ *2:C2.*

$$ INDIAN 🍴 **Bombay Club.** One block from the White House, the beautiful Bombay Club tries to re-create the refined aura of British private clubs in colonial India. Potted palms and a bright blue ceiling above white plaster moldings adorn the dining room. On the menu are unusual seafood specialties and a large number of vegetarian dishes, but the real standouts are the aromatic curries. The bar, furnished with rattan chairs and dark-wood paneling, serves hot hors d'oeuvres at cocktail hour. The attire tends toward upscale business-casual. [$] *Average main: $24* ✉ *815 Connecticut Ave. NW, Downtown* ☎ *202/659–3727* 🌐 *www.bombayclubdc.com* ✍ *Reservations essential* 🕘 *No lunch Sat.* [M] *Farragut W* ✥ *1:G6.*

$$$ BELGIAN 🍴 **Brasserie Beck.** Give in to sensory overload at this homage to the railway dining rooms that catered to the prewar European elite. Every detail of Beck's interior exudes luxury, from the vintage-accented clocks

6

that stand above mahogany booths to the exposed stainless-steel kitchen (rechristened the "epicurean solarium" by the architects). The food is just as rich as you'd expect: entrée-size salads with bacon and egg, *fruits de mer* platters laden with enough shellfish for a small army, and a dizzying lineup of artisanal beers. The production is impressive, and you'll remember the food fondly after returning home—but you might consider a fast the next day. [$] *Average main: $31* ✉ *1101 K St. NW, Downtown* ☎ *202/408–1717* 🌐 *www.brasseriebeck.com* [M] *McPherson Sq.* ⊕ *2:C1.*

$$$$ STEAKHOUSE 🍴 **The Capital Grille.** A few blocks from the U.S. Capitol, this New England–tinged steakhouse became a favorite among Republican congressmen during the heyday of fallen super-lobbyist Jack Abramoff. Politics aside, the cuisine, wine list, and surroundings are all top-shelf. Don't let the meat hanging in the window distract you from the fact that this restaurant has a lot more to offer than fine dry-aged porterhouse cuts and delicious cream-based potatoes. For instance, don't miss the panfried calamari with hot cherry peppers. [$] *Average main: $55* ✉ *601 Pennsylvania Ave. NW, Downtown* ☎ *202/737–6200* 🌐 *www.thecapitalgrille.com* 🕒 *No lunch Sun.* [M] *Archives/Navy Memorial* ⊕ *2:D4.*

$$ LATIN AMERICAN 🍴 **Ceiba.** At this popular pan-Latin restaurant you'll probably want to start with a mojito or a pisco sour cocktail, then taste the tuna tartare taquitos or *flauta* tortillas stuffed with spicy lamb. This is a menu meant for grazing, but the main courses, like ribeye with chimichurri sauce and *feijoada* (stew of beans and meat) made from pork shanks, still satisfy. Also stellar are desserts such as cinnamon-dusted churros to dip in Mexican hot chocolate. Island-theme murals, angular cream banquettes, an open kitchen, and vaulted ceilings set the scene. ■ **TIP→ For a more casual experience, try the early- and late-evening happy hours, when first-come, first-served seats are easy to snag in the lounge.** [$] *Average main: $25* ✉ *701 14th St. NW, Downtown* ☎ *202/393–3983* 🌐 *www.ceibarestaurant.com* 🕒 *Closed Sun. No lunch Sat.* [M] *Metro Center* ⊕ *2:B3.*

$$$ FRENCH Fodor's Choice ★ 🍴 **Central Michel Richard.** French powerhouse chef Michel Richard has set up camp Downtown with this semicasual bistro offering up Franco-American spin-offs like fried chicken, bacon-and-onion tart, and a ginger-flecked Ahi tuna burger. Light fixtures are subtly stamped with the word "Central." A jazzy portrait of Richard (think Andy Warhol) stares down from one wall. The mood is playful and low-key; cocktails and champagne flow. And there are even a few carryovers from Richard's dearly departed four-star flagship, Citronelle, such as "Michel's Chocolate Bar," the chef's sinful house-made riff on a Kit Kat wafer. [$] *Average main: $30* ✉ *1001 Pennsylvania Ave. NW, Downtown* ☎ *202/626–0015* 🌐 *www.centralmichelrichard.com* ✍ *Reservations essential* 🕒 *No lunch weekends* [M] *Archives/Navy Memorial* ⊕ *2:C3.*

$$$$ AMERICAN 🍴 **CityZen.** The Mandarin Oriental Hotel's rarefied dining room has fast become a destination for those serious about food. In a glowing space with soaring ceilings, chef Eric Ziebold, formerly of Napa Valley's famed French Laundry, creates luxe prix-fixe lineups from the finest ingredients. Unexpected little treasures abound, such as buttery miniature Parker House rolls. Main courses could include venison with

chestnut macaroons or crispy branzino with roasted olives, and desserts such as chocolate-marshmallow s'more soufflé seem spun out of air. To take full advantage of the dining experience, opt for the six-course chef's tasting menu, letting the kitchen know about allergies or aversions. [$] *Average main: $110* ✉ *Mandarin Oriental, 1330 Maryland Ave. SW, Downtown* ☎ *202/787–6148* 🌐 *www.mandarinoriental.com/washington/dining/cityzen* ⏲ *Closed Sun. and Mon. No lunch* [M] *Smithsonian* ✣ *2:B6.*

$$$ AMERICAN 🍴 **Equinox.** Locally born chef-owner Todd Gray looks to regional purveyors for hard-to-find heirloom and local foodstuffs at his low-key American eatery. The furnishings and the food are simple and elegant, and the fresh ingredients speak for themselves. Broccoli and fennel accompany silky salmon, heirloom carrots lend a fresh tang to rich bacon-wrapped monkfish, and nutty sunchokes complement the earthy flavors of Pennsylvania-raised lamb braised in beer. The five-course tasting menu is available with a splendidly curated series of vegan options, as well as wine pairings. [$] *Average main: $33* ✉ *818 Connecticut Ave. NW, Downtown* ☎ *202/331–8118* 🌐 *www.equinoxrestaurant.com* ⏲ *No lunch weekends* [M] *Farragut W* ✣ *2:A2.*

$$$$ MODERN ITALIAN Fodor's Choice ★ 🍴 **Fiola.** Washington foodies wept when Fabio Trabocchi took his Italian talents to the briefly beloved Fiamma in New York City, but he soon returned to the District to open this refined yet ultramodern Downtown kitchen. Trabocchi's flights of fancy, such as smoked caviar-topped tuna and other quasi-raw small plates known as *susci*, are just as delightful as his standard offerings—try the rich pappardelle with shortrib ragù or oysters with icy granita. Happy hour and lunch bring an affordable cast of small plates to go with the inventive cocktails and encyclopedic wine list, but date night is the best way to experience this gem. [$] *Average main: $44* ✉ *601 Pennsylvania Ave. NW, Penn Quarter* ☎ *202/628–2888* 🌐 *www.fioladc.com* ✍ *Reservations essential* ⏲ *Closed Sun. No lunch Sat.* [M] *Archives/Navy Memorial* ✣ *2:D4.*

$ ECLECTIC 🍴 **G Street Food.** Like Washington, D.C.'s layout and architecture, this upscale cafeteria takes a cue from Europe. The cosmopolitan menu echoes the best of the eclectic café scene worldwide; omelets range from a garlicky green asparagus and feta to Norwegian lox, and lunch ups the ante with a Korean-Mexican kimchi quesadilla and south Indian cauliflower salad. Lines here can look oppressive at midday, as government workers come flocking for falafel and fresh-cut fries, but stick around and you'll be rewarded with a midday meal that's smarter, and often more affordable, than the chain spots. A sister location, recently opened six blocks to the northwest, offers the same stellar menu. [$] *Average main: $10* ✉ *1706 G St. NW, Downtown* ☎ *202/408–7474* 🌐 *www.gstreetfood.com* ✍ *Reservations not accepted* ⏲ *Closed weekends. No dinner* [M] *Farragut W* ✣ *1:F6.*

$$$ SOUTHERN 🍴 **Georgia Brown's.** An elegant New South eatery and a favorite hangout of local politicians—First Lady Michelle Obama famously broke bread here with the mayor's wife and Second Lady Jill Biden—Georgia Brown's serves catfish two ways, either grilled in spicy jerk seasoning or fried in cornmeal; thick, rich she-crab soup spiked with sherry; and grilled salmon with mango relish. Fried green tomatoes are filled with

6

goat cheese, and a pecan pie is made with bourbon and imported Belgian dark chocolate. ■ TIP➡ The Sunday "jazz brunch" adds live music and a decadent chocolate fondue fountain to the mix, and the ample happy hour menu is available all afternoon on Saturday. The airy, curving dining room has white honeycomb windows and unusual ceiling ornaments of bronze ribbons. Ⓢ *Average main: $27* ✉ *950 15th St. NW, Downtown* ☎ *202/393–4499* ⊕ *www.gbrowns.com* Ⓜ *McPherson Sq.* ✛ *2:A2.*

$$
ECLECTIC

✕ **The Hamilton.** Words don't do justice to the remodeling of a former warehouselike Borders bookstore into this classy cavalcade of culinary hits bolstered by a below-ground live music hall where New Orleans trumpeteers and gospel singers perform into the night. Hungry for a sandwich? The oyster po'boy arrives crispy with a New Orleans–style tartar sauce. Prefer a salad? The salmon version takes a trip to the Mediterranean, with bulgur wheat and feta. And if dessert's your game, the salted caramel cheesecake goes for broke with caramel popcorn on top. The kitchen's ambitions were so big that it originally stayed open 24 hours a day; they've now scaled back the hours but will still work their tails off to please patrons. Ⓢ *Average main: $24* ✉ *600 14th St. NW, Downtown* ☎ *202/787–1000* ⊕ *www.thehamiltondc.com* ⚓ *Reservations essential* Ⓜ *Metro Center* ✛ *2:B3.*

$$
JAPANESE

✕ **Kaz Sushi Bistro.** Traditional Japanese cooking is combined with often-inspired improvisations ("freestyle Japanese cuisine," in the words of chef-owner Kaz Okochi) at this serene location. For a first-rate experience, sit at the sushi bar and ask for whatever is best—you're in good hands, but the unique arrangements on the regular menu, from tuna-with-almonds to salmon-and-mango, are just as memorable. It's not all raw here; the cast of small plates served warm might include fresh fish braised in soy or grilled tofu. Ⓢ *Average main: $25* ✉ *1915 I St. NW, Downtown* ☎ *202/530–5500* ⊕ *www.kazsushibistro.com* ☉ *Closed Sun. No lunch Sat.* Ⓜ *Farragut W* ✛ *1:F6.*

$$$$
AMERICAN

✕ **Occidental Grill.** One of the most venerable restaurants in the city is located adjacent to the hotel that once helped coin the phrase "lobbyist" for its lively ground-floor social scene. The kitchen's walls are covered with photos of politicians and other notables who have come here for the food and the attentive service. Toplining the menu are New American standards such as roasted rack of lamb, seared scallops and shortribs done "surf and turf"–style, and crab cakes. Brunch is particularly strong in the pastry department. Ⓢ *Average main: $38* ✉ *1475 Pennsylvania Ave. NW, Downtown* ☎ *202/783–1475* ⊕ *www. occidentaldc.com* ⚓ *Reservations essential* Ⓜ *Metro Center* ✛ *2:B3.*

$$
AMERICAN

✕ **Old Ebbitt Grill.** People flock here to drink at the several bars, which seem to go on for miles, and to enjoy well-prepared buffalo wings, hamburgers, and hearty sandwiches. A 150-year-old institution, the Old Ebbitt also has one of Washington's most well-known raw bars. Pasta is homemade, and the late-night menu runs the gamut from hummus to tacos until 1 am. Despite the crowds, the restaurant never feels cramped, thanks to its well-spaced, comfortable booths. Service can be slow at lunch; if you're in a hurry, try the café-style Ebbitt Express next door.

D.C. FOOD TRUCKS

The nation's capital loves celebrity chefs and pricey bistros, but its latest romance is both affordable and accessible: food trucks. The mobile food rush reached its peak several years ago when local brick-and-mortar restaurateurs attempted to fight the trucks' appeal by passing an ordinance to keep them from staying too long in one place. That battle continues, but visitors keen to try the best D.C. trucks can always take advantage of Twitter. Even nonmembers of the networking site are free to visit the trucks' pages to track their locations—and in many cases, check out menus to see whether chicken vindaloo or red velvet cupcakes are on the docket at these favorite spots.

Fojol Brothers (🌐 *twitter.com/fojolbros*) calls itself a "traveling culinary carnival"—and with good reason. The quartet of cooks behind its African-Indian fusion eats are fond of fake mustaches that complete their masquerade as chefs from mythical Benethopia and Merlindia. But there's nothing faux about the fragrant flavors of their buttered chicken, berbere lentils, and pumpkin stews.

Red Hook Lobster Pound (🌐 *twitter.com/lobstertruckdc*) is the Washington outpost of a popular Brooklyn, New York, spot that purveys rolls filled with überfresh shellfish from Maine (tossed with light mayo) and Connecticut (kissed by creamy butter) variations. Add a decadent chocolate whoopie pie for dessert, and try the equally good shrimp roll for $7 less.

Hula Girl (🌐 *twitter.com/hulagirltruck*) is a celebration of all things Hawaiian, from the salty and quirky tang of Spam musubi, the iconic fried meat wrapped in seafood, to the crunchy, refreshing sesame-tinged salad topped with fresh teriyaki steak.

[$] *Average main: $26* ✉ *675 15th St. NW, Downtown* ☎ *202/347–4800* 🌐 *www.ebbitt.com* [M] *Metro Center* ✣ *2:B3.*

$ FRENCH 🍴 **Paul.** This chic, quick café is the Parisian equivalent of Starbucks, but that doesn't mean Americans of all walks of life won't be blown away by the fluff of its cheese *gougères* puffs, the heft of its salty-sweet *croque monsieur* sandwich, and the delicate crunch of its almond-flour *macaron* cookies. Recently opened spinoffs in Farragut North, Foggy Bottom, and Georgetown have not sapped the appeal of the perfect pastry, so there can be lengthy waits during the lunch rush. But when you compare the prices and quality to other downtown lunch options after a morning of museum trekking, nothing comes close. [$] *Average main: $10* ✉ *801 Pennsylvania Ave. NW, Downtown* ☎ *202/524–4500* 🌐 *www.paul-usa.com* ✍ *Reservations not accepted* [M] *Archives* ✣ *2:D4.*

$$$ SPANISH 🍴 **Taberna del Alabardero.** A lovely formal dining room, skillful service, and sophisticated cooking make this restaurant one of Washington's perennial favorites despite its occasionally lamentable portions. Start with tapas: fried artichokes with traditional Iberian ham or scallops with mango. Proceed to onion soup with goat cheese and venture on to one of four authentic paellas and fine Spanish country dishes. Strawberries with crisped meringue are a light ending to this rich fare. The

plush interior and handsome bar make things romantic and help attract a well-heeled clientele. [$] *Average main: $35* ✉ *1776 I St. NW, at 18th St., Downtown* ☎ *202/429–2200* 🌐 *www.alabardero.com* 🕒 *Closed Sun. No lunch weekends* [M] *Farragut W* ✥ *1:F6.*

$ ASIAN FAMILY 🍴 **Teaism.** This informal teahouse stocks more than 50 imported teas (black, white, and green), but it also serves healthful and delicious Japanese, Indian, and Thai food as well as tea-friendly sweets like the locally famous chocolate salty oat cookies. You can mix small dishes—curry chicken salad, bright ginger-marinated cucumber—to create meals or snacks. There's also a grass-fed burger with Asian slaw or the winter-beating *ochazuke,* hot green tea poured over seasoned rice. The smaller Connecticut Avenue branch, closed on weekends, tucked neatly on a corner adjacent to Lafayette Park and the White House, is a perfect spot to grab lunch after touring the nation's power center. Another outpost, in Dupont Circle, caters to locals looking for a quick bite while tourists choose other brunch spots. Breakfast is served daily. [$] *Average main: $12* ✉ *400 8th St. NW, Downtown* ☎ *202/638–6010* 🌐 *www.teaism.com* [M] *Archives/Navy Memorial* ✥ *2:D3.*

$$$$ ASIAN FUSION 🍴 **Wolfgang Puck's The Source.** Iconic chef Puck's first foray into Washington, D.C., provides diners with two alternate experiences. The downstairs area is home to an intimate lounge where guests can try small plates like sweet-and-spicy shrimp dumplings or a standard crop of sushi rolls. Dim sum brunch is served here Saturday 11:30 am–3 pm. Upstairs the focus is on haute cuisine: think spicy clouds of raw tuna in delicate seaweed cones with a sprinkle of tiny fish roe, and suckling pig tender enough to fall off your fork. The service is so dedicated it borders on slavish. Don't miss the lacquered duck with rhubarb and the chocolate-chip cookies made in-house. [$] *Average main: $48* ✉ *575 Pennsylvania Ave. NW, Downtown* ☎ *202/637–6100* 🌐 *www.wolfgangpuck.com/restaurants/fine-dining/3941* ✍ *Reservations essential* 🕒 *Closed Sun.* [M] *Archives/Navy Memorial* ✥ *2:D4.*

CHINATOWN

$ CHINESE 🍴 **Full Kee.** Many locals swear by this standout from the slew of mediocre Chinese joints in the area. The style-free interior can be off-putting to some—reminiscent of the fluorescent-lit dives of Manhattan's Chinatown—but the cuisine is better than anything within the city limits. Addictive shrimp or scallops in garlic sauce cry out for a carry-out to enjoy again later, as do the wide assortment of Cantonese-style roasted meats. Tried-and-true dishes include the dumplings, crispy duck, eggplant with garlic sauce, and garlicky sautéed leek flower. [$] *Average main: $14* ✉ *509 H St. NW, Chinatown* ☎ *202/371–2233* 🌐 *www.fullkeedc.com* 💳 *No credit cards* [M] *Gallery Pl./Chinatown* ✥ *2:D2.*

$$ MODERN ITALIAN 🍴 **Graffiato.** Manhattan-trained Mike Isabella brought a rock-star cool to his stint on "Top Chef," and his venture down I–95 gave the same instant pizzazz to Washington's often-staid culinary scene. Everyone does wood-fired pizzas, but Graffiato (the Italian word for "scratched," an excellent description of its artful-grunge ambience) does a Jersey Shore pie inspired by Isabella's home state that piles pink cherry-pepper aioli onto fried calamari. Everyone does a beet salad, but here the typical goat cheese is tossed aside for funky hazelnut and chocolate flavors.

This TV name lives up to the hype—just don't expect to hear much over the Bon Jovi that keeps the party going during prime dinner hours. [$] *Average main: $25* ✉ *707 6th St. NW, Chinatown* ☎ *202/289–3600* 🌐 *www.graffiatodc.com* ✍ *Reservations essential* [M] *Gallery Pl./Chinatown* ⊕ *2:D2.*

$$ BARBECUE 🍴 **Hill Country.** Barbecue partisans, put down your forks! Few who stop by this bustling hive of smoky brisket and gooey ribs can deny that it does Texas meat right—right down to the pay-by-the-pound ethos that lets you sample one slice of lean beef and one scoop of gooey shoepeg corn pudding alongside a small, succulent game hen cooked over a can of beer, so tender it drips juice down your chin. But this family-friendly retreat cleans up into a social destination come happy hour and beyond, when $20 margarita pitchers reel in the twentysomethings and Wednesday becomes a rollicking country-western karaoke night. [$] *Average main: $18* ✉ *410 7th St. NW, Chinatown* ☎ *202/556–2050* 🌐 *www.hillcountrywdc.com* [M] *Archives/Navy Memorial* ⊕ *2:D3.*

$$ SPANISH 🍴 **Jaleo.** You are encouraged to make a meal of the long list of tapas at this lively Spanish bistro, although the five types of handcrafted paella are the stars of an ample entrée menu. Tapas highlights include the *gambas al ajillo* (sautéed garlic shrimp), tender piquillo peppers stuffed with goat cheese, and the grilled homemade chorizo, which also comes draped in velvety mashed potatoes. Adventurers are encouraged to sample the octopus. Cocktail specialties range from a sweet and fruity sangria to a half-dozen herbal riffs on the gin-and-tonic. Two spin-off locations, in Bethesda, Maryland, and Arlington, Virginia, are equally memorable. [$] *Average main: $22* ✉ *480 7th St. NW, Chinatown* ☎ *202/628–7949* 🌐 *www.jaleo.com* [M] *Gallery Pl./Chinatown* ⊕ *2:D3.*

$$ JAPANESE 🍴 **Kushi.** The boisterous chatter in this warehouse of a dining room may make for a less-than-calm dinner, but crowds are buzzing with good reason over their fresh sashimi and succulent grilled meats. For pleasing prices, the *izakaya* side of the restaurant turns out smoky wood-fired skewers of salmon, mushroom, duck sausage, and more. Smooth tuna tataki and a spicy snow-crab tempura roll rule the raw-fish menu, and rare Eastern liquors such as Choya Kokutu dark rum make for clever cocktails. Teens will get a kick out of this breath of chic air in the often staid D.C. dining scene, and the twenties crowd will appreciate the late-night hours. [$] *Average main: $22* ✉ *465 K St. NW, Chinatown* ☎ *202/682–3123* 🌐 *www.eatkushi.com* [M] *Gallery Pl./Chinatown* ⊕ *2:E1.*

$$ AMERICAN FAMILY 🍴 **Matchbox.** The miniburgers, served on toasted brioche buns with a huge mound of fried onion strings, get the most press, but the main clue to what to order at this convivial triple-decker bar-restaurant is the glowing wood-burning pizza oven. The personal pizzas are "New York–style," with a thin, crisp crust. You probably won't mistake them for the very best of New York, but the spicy "Fire and Smoke" pie does the Big Apple one better. Homey plates such as braised shortribs with pumpkin risotto add substance to the menu. There's a great lineup of draft beers and cocktails, plus a brunch anchored by a crowd-pleasing skillet of cinnamon rolls. Two other locations, in the hopping U St. Corridor and near Eastern Market, are architectural stunners. [$] *Average*

6

main: $25 ✉ *713 H St. NW, Chinatown* ☎ *202/289–4441* ⊕ *www. matchboxchinatown.com* Ⓜ *Gallery Pl./Chinatown* ✛ *2:D2.*

$$ ✕ **Oyamel.** The specialty at this Mexican stunner is *antojitos,* literally
MEXICAN translated as "little dishes from the streets." But the high ceilings, gracious service, and gorgeous Frida Kahlo–inspired interior are anything but street, and even the smallest of dishes is bigger than life when doused with chocolatey *mole poblano* sauce or piquant lime-cilantro dressing. Standouts include house-made margaritas topped with a clever salt foam, the Veracruz cod in a hearty olive-tomato confit, and grasshopper tacos—yes, those are bugs basted in tequila and chili sauce . . . and they're delightful. Museumgoers shouldn't miss the filling and fanciful lunch specials. Ⓢ *Average main: $21* ✉ *401 7th St. NW, Chinatown* ☎ *202/628–1005* ⊕ *www.oyamel.com* Ⓜ *Archives/Navy Memorial* ✛ *2:D3.*

$$$ ✕ **Poste Moderne Brasserie.** Inside trendy Hotel Monaco, Poste woos din-
MODERN ers with a towering skylighted space that until 1901 was the General
AMERICAN Post Office. Homing in on Modern American brasserie fare, chef Dennis Marron conjures up such satisfying dishes as beef Bourguignon and steak frites. In season, soft-shell crabs are not to be missed. For dessert there's the humbly named Peanut Butter Cup, a palate-pleasing chocolate-nut tart with salted peanut sauce. In warmer months the neoclassical courtyard is a serene spot for fruit-infused cocktails and brunch, with an ample build-your-own bloody mary bar that's a steal at $8. Year-round, the lively bar inside attracts scenesters with booths on raised platforms. Ⓢ *Average main: $30* ✉ *Hotel Monaco, 555 8th St. NW, Chinatown* ☎ *202/783–6060* ⊕ *www.postebrasserie.com* Ⓜ *Gallery Pl./Chinatown* ✛ *2:D3.*

$$ ✕ **Rasika.** Adventurous wine lists, stellar service, inventive presenta-
INDIAN tions that don't scrimp on the spice—this Indian kitchen would have
Fodor's Choice been a local legend even without the romantic yet supersleek décor that
★ drives date-night crowds to snap up reservations weeks in advance. The menu highlights unique tandooris and grills, from trout to chicken, and überpopular vegetarian dishes such as the fried spinach leaves with sweet yogurt sauce called *palak chaat.* For an easier time getting a table, try the prix-fixe pre-theater or lunch menu. For a less swanky but equally impressive experience, try chef Vikram Sunderam's sister restaurant across town. Ⓢ *Average main: $22* ✉ *633 D St. NW, Chinatown* ☎ *202/637–1222* ⊕ *www.rasikarestaurant.com* ☾ *Closed Sun. No lunch Sat.* Ⓜ *Archives/Navy Memorial* ✛ *2:D3.*

$$ ✕ **Zaytinya.** This sophisticated urban dining room with soaring ceilings
MIDDLE EASTERN is a local favorite for meeting friends or dining with a group. Zaytinya,
Fodor's Choice which means "olive oil" in Turkish, devotes practically its entire menu
★ to Turkish, Greek, and Lebanese small plates, known as *meze.* To get the full experience, make a meal of three or four of these, such as the popular beef-and-bulgur kibbeh fritters with finger-licking yogurt to dip in, or the hearty fattoush shepherd's salad in bright pomegranate dressing. ■ TIP➜ So many options make this a great choice for vegetarians and meat lovers alike. Reservations get snapped up quickly here, but those who practice their pouncing technique can be rewarded when a roomy bar table open up. Ⓢ *Average main: $21* ✉ *701 9th St.*

NW, Chinatown ☎ 202/638–0800 🌐 www.zaytinya.com ✍ Reservations essential [M] Gallery Pl./Chinatown ✣ 2:D2.

GEORGETOWN

Georgetown's picturesque Victorian streetscapes make it D.C.'s most famous neighborhood, with five-star restaurants in historic row houses and casual cafés sandwiched between large national chain stores.

At its beginnings in the mid-1700s, Georgetown was a Maryland tobacco port. Today the neighborhood is D.C.'s premier shopping district, as well as a tourist and architectural attraction. The neighborhood's restaurants range from upscale Italian to down-home barbecue. Residents' resistance to opening a Metro station in the area was once a touchy subject, but more frequent bus service on the DC Circulator from Dupont Circle has eased any sense of cultural xenophobia among the well-heeled locals.

Georgetown's main thoroughfares, M Street NW and Wisconsin Avenue NW, are always bustling with university students, professionals, and tourists. On a given day you may encounter political activists on the sidewalks, wedding parties posing for photos, and gossiping teens laden with shopping bags.

6

$$$$ AMERICAN 🍴 **1789 Restaurant.** This dining room with Early American paintings and a fireplace could easily be a room in the White House. But all the gentility of this 19th-century town-house restaurant is offset by the down-to-earth food on the menu, which changes daily. The soups, including the celery root topped with Maine lobster hash, are flavorful. Leg of lamb and pork loin, both raised nearby, are specialties, but even the less local seafood is marked with its origin so diners know where it comes from. Service is fluid and attentive. Try the carrot cake or butterscotch-tinged "monkey bread" brioche for a sweet finish. [$] *Average main: $42 ✉ 1226 36th St. NW, Georgetown ☎ 202/965–1789 🌐 www.1789restaurant.com ✍ Reservations essential 👔 Jacket required 🕒 No lunch ✣ 1:A5.*

$$ CAJUN 🍴 **Bayou.** New Orleans and Washington, D.C., might seem to have little in common, but both cities share a common love of carousing after hours and belt-stretching cuisine. The urban marriage is consummated beautifully at this two-level po'boy palace, where live bands every weekend turn the top floor into a mini–Bourbon Street. Down below, though, the food rules—such as a pork chop done right by its Andouille sausage accompaniment and a fried green tomato appetizer hearty enough to join the entrée menu. Daily specials, such as Wednesday gator night, round out the down-home picture. [$] *Average main: $23 ✉ 2519 Pennsylvania Ave. NW, Georgetown ☎ 202/223–6941 🌐 www.bayouonpenn.com/www 🕒 Closed Mon. ✣ 1:D5.*

$$$ FRENCH 🍴 **Bistro Français.** Washington's chefs head to Bistro Français for minute steak with parsley butter, sirloin sandwiches, and rotisserie chicken. Daily specials may include suprême of salmon with broccoli mousse and beurre blanc. In the less formal café, sandwiches and omelets are available in addition to entrées. The Bistro also has fixed-price lunches and early and late-night dinner specials that include an appetizer and

dessert, as well as a champagne brunch on weekends. ■TIP→ It stays open until 3 am on weekdays and 4 am on weekends. Ⓢ *Average main: $28* ✉ *3124 M St. NW, Georgetown* ☎ *202/338–3830* ⊕ *www. bistrofrancaisdc.com* ✛ *1:B5.*

$$$$
ITALIAN

✕ **Cafe Milano.** By night you're likely to rub shoulders with local socialites, professional sports stars, visiting celebrities, and the Euro-trendy crowd at Cafe Milano's cheek-by-jowl bar. Expect authentic, sophisticated Italian cooking and a pricey wine list. Specialties are caprese salad made with imported buffalo mozzarella, thin-crust pizzas anchored by San Marzano tomato sauce, sumptuous pasta dishes in pesto or fresh vegetable sauces, and the type of beautifully composed and dressed salads favored by ladies who lunch. Ⓢ *Average main: $40* ✉ *3251 Prospect St. NW, Georgetown* ☎ *202/333–6183* ⊕ *www.cafemilano.net* ✛ *1:A5.*

$
FAST FOOD
FAMILY

✕ **Five Guys.** One of the quirky traditions of this homegrown fast-food burger house is to note on the menu board where the potatoes for that day's fries come from, be it Maine, Idaho, or elsewhere. The place gets just about everything right: from the grilled hot dogs and hand-patted burger patties—most folks get a double—to the fresh hand-cut fries with the skin on and the high-quality toppings such as grilled onions and mushrooms. Add an eclectic option for vegetarians, who are welcome to cram as many toppings as they can onto a bun, and you've got a unique fast-food experience. There are a dozen locations around the D.C. metro area including Dupont Circle, Downtown, Columbia Heights, Arlington, and Bethesda. Ⓢ *Average main: $6* ✉ *1335 Wisconsin Ave. NW, Georgetown* ☎ *202/337–0400* ⊕ *www.fiveguys.com* ✛ *1:B4.*

$$
AUSTRIAN

✕ **Kafe Leopold.** Forget all the clichés about heavy Austrian fare served by waiters in lederhosen. Leopold is about as Euro-trendy as it gets, with an all-day coffee and drinks bar, an architecturally hip dining space, and a chic little patio complete with a minifountain. Food is pared-down Mitteleuropean: mushroom tart, crisp schnitzel paired with peppery greens, an endive salad with mustard dressing. In the middle of a design-obsessed alley just off of M Street, the café draws an artsy city crowd that's content to sit and watch the scene evolve, just as it's done in Europe. Brunch is a particularly popular setting for such people-watching manna, and the neat-as-a-pin breakfast is available daily until 4 pm. Ⓢ *Average main: $21* ✉ *3315 Cady's Alley NW, Georgetown* ☎ *202/965–6005* ⊕ *www.kafeleopolds.com* ⌧ *Reservations not accepted* ✛ *1:A5.*

$
VIETNAMESE

✕ **Miss Saigon.** Shades of mauve and green, black Art Deco accents, and potted palms decorate this Vietnamese gem in an often-overpriced and -overhyped neighborhood. Appearances count here, but on the plate and not in the clientele—and you'll be grateful for that when you tuck into the crisp spring rolls or refreshing salad of shredded green papaya, cucumber, and basil, topped with shrimp or chicken. Daily specials include imaginative preparations of the freshest seafood. In addition, "caramel"-cooked and grilled meats are standouts. Ⓢ *Average main: $17* ✉ *3057 M St. NW, Georgetown* ☎ *202/333–5545* ⊕ *www. ms-saigonus.com* Ⓜ *Foggy Bottom/GWU* ✛ *1:B5.*

$ ✗ **Rocklands.** This tiny branch of the popular local barbecue chain does
BARBECUE   mostly takeout business, but even when eaten with plastic silverware,
FAMILY   the baby back ribs and smoked half chicken are still as tender as adver-
tised. Disposable coolers are also sold here, perfect for filling up with
corn pudding and cucumber salad for a picnic by the waterfront. Those
who think that barbecue can never deliver a new taste will be humbled
by the Pearl, a portable $6.49 stack of macaroni-and-cheese, tender
pork, and baked beans that sounds excessive but hits the spot. Locations in Northern Virginia's Arlington and Alexandria neighborhoods
are equally reliable. $ Average main: $14 ⊠ 2418 Wisconsin Ave. NW,
Georgetown ☎ 202/333–2558 ⊕ www.rocklands.com ⊹ 1:A2.

$$ ✗ **Sushi-Ko.** At the city's self-touted first raw-fish restaurant, the cuts are
JAPANESE   always ocean-fresh, the cocktails fruity, and the presentations classic:
think blue crab topped with avocado and tuna crowned by jalapeño
and cilantro. Hot delicacies are reliable, such as duck breast cooked
in honey or melt-on-the-tongue fried tempura that has an especially
strong vegetable assortment. Dessert is not an afterthought, thanks
to bread pudding with green-tea mousse and other Japanese-inspired
turns. $ Average main: $22 ⊠ 5455 Wisconsin Ave. NW, Chevy Chase,
Maryland ☎ 301/961–1644 ⊕ www.sushikorestaurants.com ☉ No
lunch Sat.–Mon. Ⓜ Friendship Heights ⊹ 1:A2.

6

DUPONT CIRCLE AND LOGAN CIRCLE

Dupont Circle and Logan Circle defy the staid, conservative reputa-
tion of Washington, turning D.C. Technicolor in the evening hours.
The high-rent, liberal-minded neighborhoods have hip art galleries,
bookstores, and yoga studios that draw a mix of yuppies and activists.
If possible, make reservations for sit-down meals, and expect crowds,
especially on weekends.

DUPONT CIRCLE

$$ ✗ **Bistrot du Coin.** An instant hit in its Dupont Circle neighborhood,
FRENCH   this moderately priced French bistro with a monumental zinc bar is
noisy, crowded, and fun. The traditional bistro fare includes starter and
entrée portions of 10 different mussels preparations, rightly dubbed the
moules festival. Steaks, garnished with a pile of crisp fries, are the main
attraction, but you might also try the miniature ravioli or *magret de
canard* (a maple-infused duck breast with pepper-cream sauce). Wash
it down with house Beaujolais, Côtes du Rhône, or an Alsatian white.
$ Average main: $22 ⊠ 1738 Connecticut Ave. NW, Dupont Circle
☎ 202/234–6969 ⊕ www.bistrotducoin.com ☉ Brunch weekends from
11 am Ⓜ Dupont Circle ⊹ 1:E3.

$$ ✗ **DGS Delicatessen.** Your favorite Jewish grandma might be thrown for a
DELI   loop by this precocious reboot of her staple dishes—what, regular *kasha
varnishkes* were so boring, they had to throw Middle Eastern harissa
spices in with the buckwheat-pasta mix?—but she will be won over
by the traditional matzoh ball soup at this popular new comfort-food
outpost. Even when she's not in town, the younger set will get a kick
out of chef Barry Koslow's take on favorite New York deli items, like
the "loaded latke" potato pancake topped with jalapeño, for a bargain

price during happy hour. (One more touch Grandma will appreciate: the initials in the title hark back to a long-departed local Jewish chain, District Grocery Stores.) [$] *Average main: $19* ✉ *1317 Connecticut Ave. NW, Dupont Circle* ☎ *202/293–4400* 🌐 *www.dgsdelicatessen.com* [M] *Dupont Circle* ✥ *1:F4.*

$$ SEAFOOD Fodor's Choice ★

🍴 **Hank's Oyster Bar.** The watchword is "simplicity" at this chic take on the shellfish shacks of New England. A half-dozen oyster varieties are available daily on the half shell, both from the West Coast and local Virginia waters, alongside another handful of daily fish specials, from bouillabaisse to coffee-rubbed tuna, and a "meat-and-two" daily special for those who prefer turf to surf. Don't be shy about asking for seconds on the complimentary baking chocolate presented along with your check—the kitchen doesn't serve sweets, but it doesn't need to. There's another location in Capitol Hill, with a quirky bar that turns out classic ales and '90s one-hit-wonder inspired Vanilla Ice cocktails, plus a third outpost in Old Town Alexandria. [$] *Average main: $25* ✉ *1624 Q St. NW, Dupont Circle* ☎ *202/462–4265* 🌐 *www.hanksdc.com* ⏲ *No brunch weekdays; lunch Fri. only* [M] *Dupont Circle* ✥ *1:G4.*

$$$$ MODERN AMERICAN Fodor's Choice ★

🍴 **Komi.** Johnny Monis, the young, energetic chef-owner of this small, personal restaurant, offers one of the most adventurous dining experiences in the city. The multicourse prix-fixe ($135), which can run up to two-dozen small dishes at the chef's discretion, showcases contemporary fare with a distinct Mediterranean influence. ■ **TIP→ Reservations open 30 days in advance, with phones open from noon to 4 pm.** The menu famously changes daily, but buzzed-about plates include mascarpone-filled dates with sea salt and succulent spit-roasted goat with pita bread. It doesn't come cheap, and it always goes better with the $70 wine pairings, but do expect the four-hour ride of your foodie life in Monis's renowned hands. [$] *Average main: $135* ✉ *1509 17th St. NW, Dupont Circle* ☎ *202/332–9200* 🌐 *www.komirestaurant.com* ✍ *Reservations essential* ⏲ *Closed Sun. and Mon. No lunch* [M] *Dupont Circle* ✥ *1:G4.*

$$ CAFÉ FAMILY

🍴 **Kramerbooks & Afterwords.** This popular bookstore-cum-café is a favorite neighborhood breakfast spot. ■ **TIP→ It's also a late-night haunt on Friday and Saturday, when it's open around the clock.** There's a simple menu with a handful of special entrées, but many people drop in just for cappuccino and dessert. In keeping with that spirit, reservations are only available for large parties and carry a minimum order requirement. The "sharezies" menu of small plates, such as cured salmon and cornflake-crusted catfish, is a great bang for the buck at $23 for three. Catch a live music performance—everything from rock to the blues—here Wednesday through Saturday nights. [$] *Average main: $20* ✉ *1517 Connecticut Ave. NW, Dupont Circle* ☎ *202/387–3825* 🌐 *www.kramers.com/cafe.html* [M] *Dupont Circle* ✥ *1:F4.*

$$$$ THAI

🍴 **Little Serow.** Remember the last time a quirky new musical group or movie seemed to take over the world, racking up fans despite being more than a little, well, weird? This is that phenomenon in a restaurant. This basement hideout next-door to chef Johnny Monis's world-beating Komi gives the wunderkind chef a chance to cook Thai *his* way—which happens to be the northern Thais' way. The ingredients are spicy, the presentations sometimes off-putting (what is a snakehead fish?), and the waitresses can be sullen pixies, but for sheer moxie and skill, the food is the best in the city. Maybe the best anywhere south of New York. Just remember: No substitutions or special requests, and they mean it. [$] *Average main: $45* ✉ *1511 17th St. NW, Dupont Circle* 🌐 *www.littleserow.com* ✍ *Reservations not accepted* 🕓 *Closed Sun. and Mon. No lunch* [M] *Dupont Circle* ✥ *1:G4.*

$
ASIAN
🍴 **Nooshi.** When this noodle restaurant added an extensive sushi menu, it changed its name to Nooshi (noodles plus sushi). Always packed at midday by office workers seeking a quick bite or takeout, this attractive Pan-Asian noodle house has remarkably good Chinese, Japanese, Thai, Indonesian, Malaysian, and Vietnamese dishes. Try the tongue-searing spicy Phuket noodles; Nasi Goreng, an Indonesian fried rice with chicken satay; or the Vietnamese rice noodles with grilled chicken. [$] *Average main: $15* ✉ *1120 19th St. NW, Dupont Circle* ☎ *202/293–3138* 🌐 *www.nooshidc.com* 🕓 *No lunch Sun.* [M] *Farragut W* ✥ *1:F5.*

$$$$
AMERICAN
Fodor's Choice
★
🍴 **Nora.** Chef and founder Nora Pouillon helped pioneer the sustainable-food revolution with the first certified organic restaurant in the country, and her seasonal ingredients are out of this world. Settle into the sophisticated and attractive quilt-decorated dining room and start with the roasted beets with blood orange or a locally grown salad. Entrées such as grass-fed shortribs and seared salmon with chard emphasize the well-balanced, earthy ingredients. A four-course tasting menu is available, at a reduced price for vegetarians. [$] *Average main: $40* ✉ *2132 Florida Ave. NW, Dupont Circle* ☎ *202/462–5143* 🌐 *www.noras.com* ✍ *Reservations essential* 🕓 *Closed Sun. No lunch* [M] *Dupont Circle* ✥ *1:E3.*

$$$$
ITALIAN
🍴 **Obelisk.** You won't find the menu online or much buzz among locals, but this Italian stalwart has maintained a pull on special-occasion diners for nearly three decades thanks in large part to its under-the-radar reputation. The three-course prix-fixe, your only option, changes every day, combining traditional dishes with the innovations of founding chef Peter Pastan, also known for steering legendary pizzeria 2 Amys. Representative main courses are lamb with garlic and sage and handmade ravioli with unexpected fillings. The dining room is tiny, but the warm and attentive service makes this feel like a hidden gem. Diners always walk away pleased with their portion sizes, even given the high price tag. [$] *Average main: $75* ✉ *2029 P St. NW, Dupont Circle* ☎ *202/872–1180* ✍ *Reservations essential* 🕓 *Closed Sun. and Mon. No lunch* [M] *Dupont Circle* ✥ *1:E4.*

$$$$
STEAKHOUSE
🍴 **The Palm.** A favorite lunchtime hangout of power brokers, from politics to media, the Palm has walls papered with caricatures of the famous patrons who have dined there. Main attractions include gargantuan steaks and Nova Scotia lobsters, several kinds of potatoes, and New York cheesecake. One of the Palm's best-kept secrets is that it's also a terrific old-fashioned Italian restaurant—try the veal marsala—and a surprisingly affordable downtown business lunch option, with three courses for $25.90. [$] *Average main: $52* ✉ *1225 19th St. NW, Dupont*

Circle ☎ *202/293–9091* 🌐 *www.thepalm.com* ✍ *Reservations essential* ⏲ *No lunch weekends* [M] *Dupont Circle* ✣ *1:F5.*

$$ PIZZA FAMILY ✕ **Pizzeria Paradiso.** A trompe-l'oeil ceiling adds space and light to a simple interior at the ever-popular Pizzeria Paradiso, which has spinoff locations in Georgetown and suburban Alexandria, Virginia. The restaurant sticks to crowd-pleasing basics: pizzas, panini, salads, and desserts. Although the standard pizza is satisfying, you can enliven it with fresh buffalo mozzarella or unusual toppings such as potatoes, capers, and mussels. Gluten allergies are accommodated with special dough, available on request. Wines are well chosen and well priced. The intensely flavored gelato is a house specialty. [$] *Average main: $18* ✉ *2003 P St. NW, Dupont Circle* ☎ *202/223–1245* 🌐 *www.eatyourpizza.com* [M] *Dupont Circle* ✣ *1:E4.*

$ ECLECTIC Fodor's Choice ★ ✕ **Sweetgreen.** When three Georgetown University graduates carved out a closet-sized niche to sell freshly made salads and tart frozen yogurt in 2007, no one in the city batted an eye. Since then, their empire has expanded to 16 locations—and a popular annual music festival—while branching out into fresh juice and healthful, tasty "market sides" that use all local ingredients, such as spicy kale and balsamic roasted sweet potatoes. The guacamole salad, which brilliantly deposits every flavor of the Mexican dip onto mixed greens, remains a classic. But everything else about this franchise is breaking new ground. [$] *Average main: $10* ✉ *1512 Connecticut Ave. NW, Dupont Circle* ☎ *202/387–9338* 🌐 *www.sweetgreen.com* [M] *Dupont Circle* ✣ *1:E4.*

$$$ MODERN AMERICAN ✕ **Tabard Inn.** Fading portraits and overstuffed furniture make the lobby lounge look like an antiques store, but this hotel restaurant's culinary sensibilities are thoroughly modern. The menu, which changes daily, consistently offers interesting seafood and vegetarian options. An exemplary entrée is the broiled striped bass with mussels and chives, a hearty but elegant take on classic Continental flavors. A vegetarian option might be beet and goat cheese ravioli draped in fragrant brown butter. **■ TIP→ In good weather you can eat in the tranquil courtyard during first-come, first-served breakfast hours or the tantalizing brunch—just don't skip the homemade doughnuts.** [$] *Average main: $30* ✉ *Hotel Tabard Inn, 1739 N St. NW, Dupont Circle* ☎ *202/331–8528* 🌐 *www.tabardinn.com/restaurant* [M] *Dupont Circle* ✣ *1:F4.*

$$$$ SOUTHERN ✕ **Vidalia.** There's a lot more to Chef Jeffrey Buben's distinguished restaurant than the sweet Vidalia onion, which is a specialty in season. Inspired by the cooking and the ingredients of the South and the Chesapeake Bay region, Buben's version of New American cuisine revolves around the best seasonal fruits, vegetables, and seafood he can find. Try the seared foie gras with banana bread, the shrimp on yellow grits, or the sensational lemon chess pie. The sleek modern surroundings, including a wine bar, are equal to the food. [$] *Average main: $36* ✉ *1990 M St. NW, Dupont Circle* ☎ *202/659–1990* 🌐 *www.vidaliadc.com* ⏲ *Closed Sun. July and Aug. No lunch weekends* [M] *Dupont Circle* ✣ *1:F5.*

LOGAN CIRCLE

$$ AMERICAN ✕ **Birch & Barley.** In a city where culinary classicism is too often code for predictable steaks and pastas, this earth-toned kitchen is a welcome throwback to the age before zany fusion ingredients turned

dinner into science class. The six entrées, as well as rotating trios of flatbread and pasta, are odes to autumnal flavors that pair perfectly with the 555 (yes, that's not a typo) varieties of artisan beers on offer. Try the ricotta cavatelli topped by melt-in-your-mouth roasted pork or the succulent Brat burger with creamy Emmentaler and kick back for a leisurely, romantic repast. Just save room for the delightful desserts, particularly the house-made versions of childhood classics such as the Snickers bar and pudding pop. [$] *Average main: $24* ✉ *1337 14th St. NW, Logan Circle* ☎ *202/567–2576* 🌐 *www.birchandbarley.com* ✍ *Reservations essential* 🕒 *Closed Mon. Brunch Sun. only* [M] *U St./Cardozo* ✚ *1:H4.*

$$$ SPANISH 🍴 **Estadio.** The name of this polished palace means "stadium," and its gorgeously baroque-style interior, which surrounds a high-wire open kitchen, makes a perfect stage for energetic and flavorful new uses of top-notch ingredients. The menu, developed by chef Haidar Karoum and owner Mark Kuller during research jaunts through Spain, is a master class in tapas, with sherry-soused monkfish punched up by garlicky romesco sauce and tortilla española smoother than any served in Barcelona. The bar menu is equally inventive, though watch out for smaller-than-normal wine pours. Try a "slushito" to get a delightful alcoholic twist on the beloved Slurpee. For dessert, don't miss the sweet-and-salty manchego cheesecake with pistachio granola. [$] *Average main: $27* ✉ *1520 14th St. NW, Logan Circle* ☎ *202/319–1404* 🌐 *www.estadio-dc.com* ✍ *Reservations essential* [M] *U St./Cardozo* ✚ *1:H4.*

$$ ASIAN FUSION 🍴 **Masa 14.** This modern lounge blends Asian and Latin American flavors, with a menu of memorable small plates. The shrimp flatbread spotlights creamy Oaxaca cheese, and pork belly buns take on a taco flare thanks to pineapple-and-cilantro garnish. The cocktail list, head lined by nearly 100 varieties of tequila, is the star of the city's longest bar (65 feet). This collaboration between raw-fish guru Kaz Okochi and fusion impresario Richard Sandoval has a notably abridged sushi list—but with house music thumping and bartenders shaking fresh libations, few patrons end up missing yellowtail or uni. **■ TIP→ The prix-fixe all-you-can-eat-and-drink brunch is a rare find in any city, and a challenge worth taking at $35.** [$] *Average main: $22* ✉ *1825 14th St. NW, Logan Circle* ☎ *202/328–1414* 🌐 *www.masa14.com* 🕒 *No lunch; no brunch weekdays* [M] *U St./Cardozo* ✚ *1:H3.*

ADAMS MORGAN

In Adams Morgan legions of college kids descend on 18th Street for abundant drink specials and dance clubs. Quaint ethnic cafés (Ethiopian, French, Italian) are bustling during evening hours. But as the night wears on the crowds gravitate to greasy spoons and "jumbo slice" pizza joints. The next culinary frontier lies just east along Columbia Road, where the immigrant community dines on ethnic cuisine while young families flock to increasingly upscale bistros for refined takes on comfort-food favorites.

$$$ AMERICAN 🍴 **Cashion's Eat Place.** Walls are hung with family photos, and tables are jammed with regulars feasting on home-style cooking that stays

impressively modern in the tradition of founder Ann Cashion, a capital cuisine superstar who sold the spot to her longtime sous chef many years ago. The menu at this neighborhood favorite changes daily, but roast chicken, steak, and seafood are frequent choices. Side dishes, such as sweet potatoes roasted with fig-scented bourbon, sometimes upstage the main course. If it's available, order the chocolate panna cotta topped with espresso gel and shortbread. **TIP→ If you're dining with a local, make sure to ask for the 10% "neighborhood discount."** [$] *Average main: $30* ✉ *1819 Columbia Rd. NW, Adams Morgan* ☎ *202/797–1819* 🌐 *www.cashionseatplace.com* ✍ *Reservations essential* ⏲ *Closed Mon. No lunch weekdays* [M] *Woodley Park/Zoo* ✣ *1:F1.*

$$$ FRENCH 🍴 **Mintwood Place.** Visitors to D.C. from more cosmopolitan confines tend to scoff at the city's high-minded cultural aspirations, but only in a smaller urban center could European cooking this exemplary be found in such an unhurried setting. *Condé Nast Traveler* magazine ranked this as one of the world's best new restaurants last year—you will see why when diving into Chef Cedric Maupillier's sensuous tangle of tagliatelle in a rich bolognese sauce, topped with a fairy-tale dusting of Parmesan. Even a humble-sounding starter like "mountain pie" arrives elegantly, its geometric layers of goat cheese and beets peeking through emerald butter-lettuce leaves. At brunch, try the unique bacon-and-onion *flammekueche* tarts. [$] *Average main: $29* ✉ *1813 Columbia Rd. NW, Adams Morgan* ☎ *202/234–6732* 🌐 *mintwoodplace.com* ✍ *Reservations essential* ⏲ *Closed Mon. No lunch weekdays* ✣ *1:F1.*

$ RAMEN 🍴 **Sakuramen.** After the small plates, artisanal burgers, and cupcake fads, gourmet versions of Japanese ramen soup became the latest trend to storm the city, and this spot strikes the perfect balance between keep-it-simple affordability and adventurous flair. Embodying both of those traits in one bowl: the D.C. Miso, which pairs traditional fish cake and seaweed with a shot of—and it's the best part—monterey jack cheese. Beyond the ramen bowls, other memorable fuel for a night on the town or a long winter's walk includes juicy marinated *bulgogi* beef buns and crispy fresh dumplings. [$] *Average main: $14* ✉ *2441 18th St. NW, Adams Morgan* ☎ *202/656–5285* 🌐 *www.sakuramen.net* ⏲ *Lunch Fri.–Sun. only* ✣ *1:F1.*

U STREET CORRIDOR

U Street links Shaw, centered near Howard University's campus, to Adams Morgan, and is known for indie rock clubs, edgy bars, and trendy restaurants. Although the urban hipster vibe is being threatened by skyrocketing rents and the intrusion of chain stores, you'll still find more tattoos and sneakers than pinstripes and pearls here.

$$ ECLECTIC 🍴 **1905.** In a neighborhood crowded with many Next Big Things, the antique key in this spot's logo is the perfect symbol for a dining experience so intimate you'll want to keep it a closely guarded secret. Young chef Matthew Richardson adds a Continental touch to his lineup of intelligent Southern comfort food. The pork belly is smoked in-house and served with truffled grits, while the seemingly ubiquitous kale salad gets a dose of local color from pickled Virginia peanuts. The dining

room's refurbished Victorian-era fixtures and wallpaper create a romantic buzz that recalls the Moulin Rouge—in fact, canoodling couples like to sip absinthe in the more private window booths. $ *Average main: $23* ✉ *1905 9th St. NW, U Street Corridor* ☎ *202/332-1905* ⊕ *www.1905dc.com* ☽ *Closed Mon. No lunch; brunch Sun. only* Ⓜ *U St./Cardozo* ✛ *1:H2.*

$
AMERICAN
FAMILY

✗ **Ben's Chili Bowl.** Long before U Street became hip, Ben's was serving chili. Chili on hot dogs, chili on Polish-style sausages, chili on burgers, and just plain chili. Add cheese fries if you dare. The shiny red-vinyl stools give the impression that little has changed since the 1950s, but don't be fooled: This favorite of President Obama and his aides has rocketed into the 21st century with renewable energy powering its new iPhone app and kiosks at Nationals baseball games. Turkey burgers and meatless chili are the menu's more upscale nods to modern times. Ben's closes at 2 am Monday through Thursday, at 4 am on Friday and Saturday. It serves no breakfast on Sunday but stays open until 11 pm. Southern-style breakfast is served from 6 am weekdays and from 7 am on Saturday. $ *Average main: $6* ✉ *1213 U St. NW, U Street Corridor* ☎ *202/667-0909* ⊕ *www.benschilibowl.com* ▬ *No credit cards* Ⓜ *U St./Cardozo* ✛ *1:H2.*

$$
WINE BAR

✗ **Cork.** This rustic, dimly lighted slip of a wine bar brings chic cuisine to the still-gentrifying streets of the city's hippest neighborhood. The wine list features rare varietals—with a dozen still under $10 per glass. Even teetotalers will find much to love among the menu's classic dishes. The duck confit, lately garbed in pickled cherries, and avocado bruschetta with pistachio oil are particular standouts, while the goat cheesecake has made its inventor locally famous. The one thing missing: intimacy. Expect to stand uncomfortably close to fellow tipplers at the bar and have a minimum of room to move even with a reserved table. $ *Average main: $22* ✉ *1720 14th St. NW, U Street Corridor* ☎ *202/265-2675* ⊕ *www.corkdc.com/resthome.html* 🍴 *Reservations essential* ☽ *Closed Mon. No lunch; brunch on Sun.* Ⓜ *U Street/Cardozo* ✛ *1:H3.*

$$
RAMEN

✗ **Daikaya.** This quirky, gorgeously decorated split-level party for gourmands is *Lost in Translation* in restaurant form, a sexy-quirky tour of modern Japanese flavors that serves ramen on the ground floor and small plates one flight above that would be right at home in New York City's world-famous Momofuku. The dreamy cream-based burrata cheese adds depth to arugula salad, while pork-and-Brussels-sprout skewers run the texture and taste gamut thanks to crunchy bonito flakes and lush, creamy sauce. Bet you can't eat just one—or resist coming back to try both floors' menus, not to mention the marvelous, affordable brunch and lunch options. $ *Average main: $23* ✉ *705 6th St. NW, U St. Corridor* ☎ *202/589-1600* ☽ *No brunch or lunch Sat.* ✛ *2:D2*

$$$
MODERN ASIAN

✗ **Doi Moi.** The rise of foodie culture can leave adventurous diners feeling like they've turned over every culinary stone, but this pilgrimage into the Southeast Asian unknown will wow even the most jaded. Smoked sour sausage from Northeastern Thailand, the juicy Chinese wilted green known as "morning glory," and the brothy, light-but-hot "jungle" curry are leading lights at this white-tiled taste of the tropics. With so many unexpected delights on offer, it's easy to look past the predictable joys of spicy roasted cashews and fried rice woven with fresh blue crab, but feel free to stay predictable. Vegetarians, vegans, and the gluten-free will be pleased to see their own special menus here. $ *Average main: $31* ✉ *1800 14th St. NW, U Street Corridor* ☎ *202/733–5131* ⊕ *doimoidc. com* ⚘ *Reservations essential* ⊙ *No lunch* ✛ *1:H3.*

$$ ✕ **Etete.** Among the best-loved spots in "Little Ethiopia," a mini-corri-
AFRICAN   dor of expatriate-run restaurants, Etete doesn't hold back on the spices.
FAMILY   Savory pastries known as *sambusas* are filled with fiery lentils, and gin-
ger brightens a stew of vegetables. The sharing of dishes and the mode of eating—rather than using utensils diners tear off pieces of *injera,* a spongy pancakelike bread to scoop up stews and sautées—make for exotic and adventurous dining at this style-conscious eatery. $ *Aver-age main: $19* ✉ *1942 9th St. NW, U Street Corridor* ☎ *202/232–7600* ⊕ *www.eteterestaurant.com* Ⓜ *U St./Cardozo* ✛ *1:H2.*

$$$$ ✕ **Le Diplomate.** Even award-winning chef and owner Stephen Starr was
BRASSERIE   surprised by how revered his first D.C.-area concept became within days of its opening in early 2013. A faithful recreation of the convivial Parisian bistro on a row where new kitchens try their luck nearly every week, his attention to detail—perfectly spreadable butter atop fresh loaves cut in the center of the kitchen, their aroma tantalizing customers half a football field away in the dining room—makes a night here into more than just a meal. This excellent spot prizes quality above all, from graceful martinis to hand-stuffed ravioli to succulent, textbook-worthy steak frites and roasted chicken. $ *Average main: $42* ✉ *1610 14th St. NW, U Street Corridor* ☎ *202/332–3333* ⊕ *www.lediplomatedc.com* ⚘ *Reservations essential* ⊙ *Brunch and lunch weekends only* ✛ *1:H4.*

$$ ✕ **Marvin.** The owner of this quirky club and restaurant named after soul
BELGIAN   singer Marvin Gaye is Eric Hilton, a D.C. local who became a national celebrity as half of the DJ supergroup Thievery Corporation. Inspired by Gaye's sojourn to Belgium in the 1980s, the menu combines soul food with traditional French classics—think chicken and waffles and pork chop with a white bean cassoulet. The food is so good it'll bust your belt. After dinner, sample a Belgian beer and shake your booty on the upstairs dance floor. At Sunday brunch, try the stellar shrimp and grits or a simple waffle with fruit. $ *Average main: $23* ✉ *2007 14th St. NW, U Street Corridor* ☎ *202/797–7171* ⊕ *www.marvindc.com* ⊙ *No lunch. Brunch Sun. only* Ⓜ *U St./Cardozo* ✛ *1:H2.*

$$$$ ✕ **Minibar.** Once a legendarily hard-to-reserve spinoff in the back of a
MODERN   bigger sibling, this critically beloved experimental laboratory of super-
AMERICAN   chef José Andrés now has about a half-dozen more seats in its new location. Yet Andrés remains as committed to pushing limits, as he puts it, using the magic of molecular gastronomy. Expect to pay more than you can imagine but leave amazed. Previous hits have included a foie-gras "lollipop" coated with cotton candy. ∎**TIP➜ For those not lucky enough to snag a table, try reserving online for a spot at barmini next door—the entrance is on 9th Street, north of E Street—where top-secret, creative, and already beloved cocktails are served with a rotating crop of small plates.** $ *Average main: $225* ✉ *855 E St. NW, Chinatown*

☎ 202/393–0812 🌐 www.minibarbyjoseandres.com ✍ Reservations essential 👔 Jacket and tie 🕒 Typically closed Aug., Sun., and Mon. No lunch ✣ 2:D3.

$$ SOUTHERN 🍴 **Oohhs & Aahhs.** No-frills soul food is what you can find at this friendly eat-in/take-out place where the price is right and the food is delicious. Ultrarich macaroni and cheese, succulent baked chicken, and smoky-sweet shortribs just beg to be devoured. Collard greens are mercifully cooked with vinegar and sugar rather than the traditional salt pork—this may leave your stomach room for banana pudding. Smack in the middle of the U Street area, the place is both a neighborhood hangout and destination for those missing the perennial dishes that Mama always made best. [$] *Average main: $22 ✉ 1005 U St. NW, U Street Corridor ☎ 202/667–7142 🌐 www.oohhsnaahhs.com 💳 No credit cards [M] U St./Cardozo ✣ 1:H2.*

$$$ CREOLE 🍴 **Pearl Dive Oyster Palace.** Chef Jeff Black does serve three kinds of po'boys, but that's about as working-class as it gets at this dazzlingly decorated homage to the bivalve. Oysters come raw, with a pair of perfect dipping sauces—for about $1 each, during happy hour—or warm in five irresistible guises, from bacon-wrapped to crusted in cornmeal and sprinkled with sweet potato. If you eschew shellfish, Black has you covered with a grass-fed steak lovingly bedecked in blue cheese. Expect to get the best and pay for it here, where craft cocktails are $12 and each warm apple pie serving comes baked into its own miniskillet. Upstairs, the well-heeled crowd endures lengthy table waits with Peroni on tap at the breezy Black Jack bar. [$] *Average main: $27 ✉ 1612 14th St. NW, U Street Corridor ☎ 202/319–1612 🌐 www.pearldivedc.com ✍ Reservations not accepted 🕒 No lunch; brunch Fri.–Sun. only [M] U St./Cardozo ✣ 1:H4.*

6

$$$ WINE BAR 🍴 **Proof.** Chef Haidar Karoum grew up traveling throughout Europe, acquiring a Continental polyglot's sensibility that serves him perfectly wearing the toque at Proof. Like a wine lover's tour of the Mediterranean, diners can stop by France for the grilled flatiron steak with sautéed spinach and bacon, or try the Turkish foray that is lamb chops with pistachio, apricot and sumac. This is the rare restaurant and wine bar that plays both roles to the hilt, with an expertly curated cheese and charcuterie list as well as an array of small pickled plates that pair with pinots or a craft cocktail such as the unique gin-and-wine "Dark Side." The décor is soothing and chic, perfect for a post-museum retreat. [$] *Average main: $32 ✉ 775 G St. NW, Chinatown ☎ 202/737–7663 🌐 www.proofdc.com ✍ Reservations essential 🕒 No lunch Sat.–Mon. ✣ 2:D2*

$$ WINE BAR 🍴 **Room 11.** You're invited to the coolest house party in the city, where deft hands in a tiny kitchen turn out urbane plates that go down like a designer outfit hidden on the sale rack. From the preserved-lemon risotto at dinner to the tahini-cauliflower salad for lunch to the refined Korean take on steak and eggs, this small wonder has a dish for every mood and every hour. The indoor space is small, lined in bistro tile and tailor-made for knocking knees on date night, but the patio is ample and anchored by outdoor heating in winter. Save room for the baked wonders of local pastry consortium Paisley Fig and a cocktail or two.

[$] *Average main: $20* ✉ *3234 11th St. NW, Chinatown* ☎ *202/332–3234* 🌐 *www.room11dc.com* ✣ *1:H1.*

$ CAFÉ Fodor's Choice ★ 🍴 **Taylor Gourmet.** Sandwiches crafted with attention to detail and fine ingredients are the hallmark of this Philadelphia-inspired classic. Taylor's substitution-friendly staff piles fresh roasted turkey, ham, chicken cutlets, and cold cuts beneath emerald arugula, juicy roasted red peppers, and waves of provolone so finely aged it snaps on the palate. If the Vine Street Expressway (chicken, prosciutto, pesto) or the Callowhill (spicy house-made meatballs in marinara sauce) doesn't grab you, the delicate pasta salads will make you a believer. Other locations can be found on H Street NE in the shadow of the White House, in the heart of Chinatown, and on K Street NW, in the bottom of the massive CityVista complex. [$] *Average main: $11* ✉ *1908 14th St. NW, U Street Corridor* ☎ *202/588–7117* 🌐 *www.taylorgourmet.com* [M] *U St./Cardozo* ✣ *2:B1.*

$$ WINE BAR 🍴 **Vinoteca.** This Euro-chic wine bar has one of the best patios in D.C. With a Tuscan vibe and a bocce court to match, the inviting outdoor plaza allows happy-hour revelers and casual diners to nosh on an abbreviated menu of smaller plates from the increasingly impressive kitchen, which turns out delicate goat-cheese gnocchi and mushroom crostini to go with a fine trio of specialty burgers. In the colder months, belly up to the bar for a refreshing take on the Moscow mule or one of several beers on tap, if the endless wine list isn't enough. Bottomless mimosas and whole-wheat pancakes with ginger butter make brunch equally satisfying. [$] *Average main: $23* ✉ *1940 11th St. NW, U Street Corridor* ☎ *202/332–9463* 🌐 *www.vinotecadc.com* ⏲ *No lunch weekdays* [M] *U St./Cardozo* ✣ *1:H2.*

UPPER NORTHWEST

After the requisite cooing over the pandas and other cuddly creatures at the National Zoo, consider wandering around this popular neighborhood to observe locals eating, drinking, and playing. Many Hill staffers, journalists, and other inside-the-Beltway types live along this hilly stretch of Connecticut Avenue. Eateries and shops line the few blocks near each of the Red Line Metro stops. Restaurants in Cleveland Park range from tiny takeout spots to upscale restaurants where you stand a good chance of spying your favorite Sunday-morning talk-show guests at a nearby table. Ethnic dining is also abundant here, especially in Cleveland Park. Lined up along the stately stretch of modern row houses are diverse dining options ranging from Afghan to Thai.

$$ PIZZA FAMILY 🍴 **2 Amys.** Call it the Brando of D.C. pizzerias, because this Neapolitan sensation has played godfather to a number of throne-stealing wood ovens elsewhere in town since it opened more than a decade ago. Simple recipes allow the ingredients to shine through and make the "wine bar" menu of small Italian plates as exemplary as the pies. You may be tempted to go for the D.O.C. pizza (it has *Denominazione di Origine Controllata* approval for Neapolitan authenticity), but don't hesitate to try the smoked salmon or anchovy crostini. At busy times the wait for a table can exceed an hour, and the noisy din of a packed house may discourage some diners. [$] *Average main: $18* ✉ *3715 Macomb*

St. NW, Upper Northwest ☎ *202/885–5700* 🌐 *www.2amyspizza.com* ✍ *Reservations not accepted* ⏲ *No lunch Mon.* ✥ *1:A2.*

$$$ MODERN AMERICAN 🍴 **Ardeo.** The trendy American Ardeo and its loungelike counterpart, the wine bar Bardeo, sit side by side in the ever-popular culinary strip of Cleveland Park. Ardeo is known for its clean design, professional and knowledgeable staff, and creative menu. Everything is skillfully prepared, from gnocchi with kale pesto to roasted trout and a vegetable-studded chicken pot pie assembled in-house. The two-course brunch, served with all-you-can-drink champagne, is a steal at $28. [$] *Average main: $29* ✉ *3311 Connecticut Ave. NW, Upper Northwest* ☎ *202/244–6750* 🌐 *www.ardeobardeo.com* ⏲ *Brunch weekends only* [M] *Cleveland Park* ✥ *1:D1.*

$$$ FRENCH 🍴 **Bistrot Lepic.** Relaxed and upbeat, with bright yellow walls and colorful paintings, this small, crowded neighborhood bistro is French in every regard—starting with the flirty servers. Traditional bistro fare has been replaced with potato-crusted salmon served with grapes and ouzo sauce. Some standards, like braised veal cheeks, remain. The wine is all French, with many available by the glass. The wine bar on the second floor has a menu of small plates such as foie gras in port wine sauce, grilled trout, and onion-bacon tart. On this level, seating is first-come, first-served, with a smaller menu than the one available to downstairs customers with reservations. [$] *Average main: $29* ✉ *1736 Wisconsin Ave. NW, Glover Park* ☎ *202/333–0111* 🌐 *www.bistrotlepic.com* ✥ *1:A3.*

$$$ SEAFOOD 🍴 **Black Salt.** Just beyond Georgetown in the residential neighborhood of Palisades, Black Salt is part fish market, part gossipy neighborhood hangout, part swanky restaurant. Fish offerings dominate, and vary from classics like oysters Rockefeller and fried Ipswich clams to more-offbeat fixings like Pacific butterfish with mango, shrimp in a coconut-lime stew, and a butterscotch *pot de crème* for dessert. The place can get crowded and loud, and reservations are often de rigueur for weekends. Regulars consider a meal at the bar a good fallback—especially for brioche French toast during the out-of-this-world brunch. [$] *Average main: $31* ✉ *4883 MacArthur Blvd., Upper Northwest* ☎ *202/342–9101* 🌐 *www.blacksaltrestaurant.com* ⏲ *Brunch Sun. only* ✥ *1:A2.*

$$ BISTRO 🍴 **Chez Billy.** The development boom that has reshaped D.C. in recent years leaves more than a few up-and-coming neighborhoods short of commendable culinary choices, which made this French bistro's arrival even more welcome in the new residential hotspot of Petworth, just northeast of Columbia Heights. Juicy steak frites and melt-in-your mouth risotto share menu space with a pair of refreshingly light salads and expert charcuterie. The interior is as sumptuous as the chocolate mousse, bathed in dark wood and antique fixtures from the space's former life as Billy Simpson's, where African-American luminaries used to make the scene in days gone by. [$] *Average main: $24* ✉ *3815 Georgia Ave. NW, Petworth* ☎ *202/506–2080* 🌐 *www.chezbilly.com* ⏲ *Closed Mon. No lunch* ✥ *1:H1.*

$$ MODERN AMERICAN 🍴 **New Heights.** This inviting restaurant has 11 large windows that overlook nearby Rock Creek Park. The sophisticated contemporary

6

cooking has changed hands multiple times in recent years, so frequently that the owners now describe it as "a showcase for young, creative chefs," but all blend bold flavors into the traditional American dishes. Cod takes Pan-Asian form with miso and black rice, while homemade fettuccine gets the carbonara treatment with a slow-cooked egg and bacon. Desserts tend towards the traditionally American, while the chic bar gets its own array of casual small plates. [$] *Average main: $25* ✉ *2317 Calvert St. NW, Upper Northwest* ☎ *202/234–4110* 🌐 *www.newheightsrestaurant.com* ⏲ *No lunch* [M] *Woodley Park/Zoo* ✣ *1:D1.*

$ VIETNAMESE 🍴 **Pho 14.** As the city's population of upwardly mobile strivers migrates north, so do affordable, crowd-pleasing gems like this outpost for huge bowls of soothing (or spicy, depending on your preference) Vietnamese noodle soup. Standing-room-only crowds for the watermelon-size servings of beef, vegetable, shrimp, or chicken eased after the owners doubled the size of their dining room and opened a spinoff location in the nearby Adams Morgan neighborhood. Hearty *banh mi* sandwiches and stir-fries are worthy choices if *pho* soup doesn't appeal. Suggest this to the Washingtonians you're visiting and watch them be impressed by your local prowess. [$] *Average main: $14* ✉ *1436 Park Rd. NW, Columbia Heights* ☎ *202/986–2326* 🌐 *www.dcpho14.com* ✍ *Reservations not accepted* ✣ *2:B1.*

SUBURBAN VIRGINIA

$$$ MODERN AMERICAN Fodor's Choice ★ 🍴 **2941 Restaurant.** Soaring ceilings, a woodsy lakeside location, and a koi pond make this one of the most striking dining rooms in the area. The playful cooking continually surprises, with plates like lamb pasta with mint sprinkled in the ricotta topping, duck breast in Earl Grey-based sauce, and apple strudel bathed in bright mascarpone sorbet. Chef Bertrand Chemel's introduction to cooking came as an apprentice at a French baker, and his flair for rising dough shows. You can order à la carte or splurge on an $85 five-course tasting menu. Those seeking a thriftier experience can head to the bar, where an abridged happy hour menu is offered. [$] *Average main: $27* ✉ *2941 Fairview Park Dr., Falls Church, Virginia* ☎ *703/270–1500* 🌐 *www.2941.com* ⏲ *No lunch weekends* ✣ *1:A6.*

$$$$ AMERICAN 🍴 **Ashby Inn.** If there's a recipe for a perfect country inn restaurant, Chef David Dunlap and co-owner/sommelier Neil Wavra have it. Head an hour or so west from D.C., and your reward is extraordinary comfort food. Dishes are made with eclectic pairings of fresh local ingredients and presented in an intimate setting. Quail is smoked in hickory chips and mated with meaty hedgehog mushrooms, while chocolate fudge is emboldened by herbal chai spices and a candied crouton garnish. A tasting menu is available for $99, or $159 with wine pairings. [$] *Average main: $42* ✉ *692 Federal St., Paris, Virginia* ☎ *540/592–3900* 🌐 *www.ashbyinn.com* ⏲ *Closed Mon. and Tues. Brunch Sun. only* ✣ *1:A6.*

$$$ MODERN AMERICAN 🍴 **Fyve Restaurant Lounge.** Chefs may cycle in and out as often as guests breeze through the adjoining Ritz-Carlton, but this dining room remains anything but staid or predictable despite its shopping-mall environs. Warm tones of red and orange accentuate the autumnal notes of

butternut squash soup or the unexpected duo of roasted beets and crisped chickpeas. Other standout dishes include the lemon ricotta pancakes at breakfast and the pumpkin ravioli, its sweetness balanced by wilted bitter greens. Head to the lounge for a "$5 at fyve" menu of quick bites. [$] *Average main: $30* ✉ *Ritz-Carlton, 1250 S. Hayes St., Pentagon City, Arlington, Virginia* ☎ *703/415–5000* 🌐 *www.fyverestaurant.com* [M] *Pentagon City* ⊕ *2:B6.*

$$$$ AMERICAN Fodor's Choice ★

🍴 **Inn at Little Washington.** A 90-minute drive from the District takes you past hills and farms to this English-style country manor, where the service matches the setting. A four-course dinner, which can easily top $200 with wine pairings, might begin with a "trinity" of beets presented three ways or raw lamb in a Caesar salad "ice cream" straight out of the high-wire kitchens of Las Vegas or Manhattan. Poached trout might come next, then roasted lobster or a carefully curated vegetarian entree. Desserts are fanciful, and the cheese plate is delivered on a life-size, mooing faux cow. A "gastronaut" menu, including wine pairings, takes the foodie fun to more acrobatic heights, beginning with an amuse bouche such as truffle-dusted popcorn. [$] *Average main: $175* ✉ *Middle and Main sts., Washington, Virginia* ☎ *540/675–3800* 🌐 *www.theinnatlittlewashington.com* ✍ *Reservations essential* 🕒 *Closed Tues. Jan.–Apr., and June–Sept. No lunch* ⊕ *2:A6.*

$$$ MODERN INDIAN

🍴 **Rasika West End.** Fans of the fanciful flourishes that made Rasika the jewel in the local crowd of restaurateur Ashok Bajaj will find even more to love at this sequel, where built-in bookcases and pagoda-shaped booths cast an intellectual spell matched by the broccoli dosa in coconut chutney and summer-weight grouper curry with kaffir lime. The original variety's crowd-pleasing wine list is done one better here with a list of unique cocktails, such as rum with pumpkin soda and a chili-spiked Pimm's cup. But one thing will be familiar: the daunting wait for a table if you lack a reservation. [$] *Average main: $28* ✉ *1190 New Hampshire Ave. NW, Foggy Bottom* ☎ *202/466–2500* 🌐 *www.rasikarestaurant.com/westend* ✍ *Reservations essential* 🕒 *No lunch weekends* ⊕ *1:E5.*

$ BURGER Fodor's Choice ★

🍴 **Ray's to the Third.** The ambience is nothing to write home about, comparable to a mall food court, but the succulent beef—freshly ground in-house every day—at this unassuming suburban spot is nothing short of sublime. Owner Michael Landrum pioneered the dirt-cheap foodie-mecca concept at his nearby Ray's the Steaks, and while run-ins with landlords may keep him on the move throughout the area, his fanaticism over quality and variety justifies the sacrifice on ambience. Burgers can be ordered blackened, Cajun, or grilled, but the "big poppa" combination of blue cheese and mushrooms is tops. Spice lovers should try the "diablo," and everyone should try the perfect sweet potato fries. [$] *Average main: $12* ✉ *1650 Wilson Blvd., Arlington, Virginia* ☎ *703/974–7171* 🌐 *www.raystothethird.com* ✍ *Reservations not accepted* 🕒 *No lunch Mon.* [M] *Court House or Rosslyn* ⊕ *1:A6.*

$$$ STEAKHOUSE

🍴 **Ray's The Steaks.** Washington foodies know Ray's owner Michael Landrum as a mercurial meat genius, quick with new concepts that turn out classic American cooking of the deviled-eggs and iceberg-wedge genre with affordable wines to match. This no-frills, dark-wood ode to dry-aged beef is the old reliable in Landrum's ever-changing empire, frequented by the eater-in-chief himself (i.e. President Obama). The ambience is meager compared to more bank-breaking steakhouses in town, but the style and sensibility here are unbeatable. Where else can you get a generous local cut of juicy top sirloin, Cajun-seasoned and kicked up with blue-cheese-and-onion garnishes, with complimentary sides of mashed potatoes and creamed spinach, for $23.99? $ *Average main: $27* ✉ *2300 Wilson Blvd., Arlington, Virginia* ☎ *703/841–7297* ⊕ *www.raysthesteaks.com* ⌂ *Reservations essential* ⊙ *No lunch* Ⓜ *Courthouse* ✢ *1:A6.*

DINING AND LODGING ATLAS

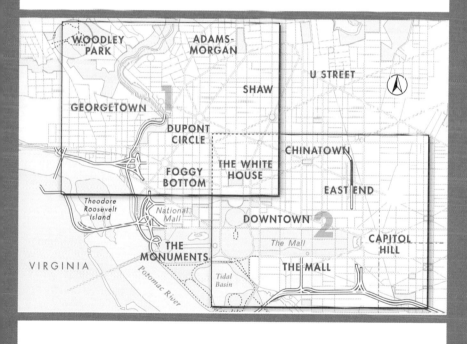

WOODLEY PARK

ADAMS-MORGAN

U STREET

GEORGETOWN

SHAW

DUPONT CIRCLE

CHINATOWN

FOGGY BOTTOM

THE WHITE HOUSE

EAST END

Theodore Roosevelt Island

National Mall

DOWNTOWN

CAPITOL HILL

VIRGINIA

THE MONUMENTS

The Mall

THE MALL

Tidal Basin

Potomac River

KEY	
☐	Hotels
■	Restaurants
■	Restaurant in Hotel
Ⓜ	Metro Station

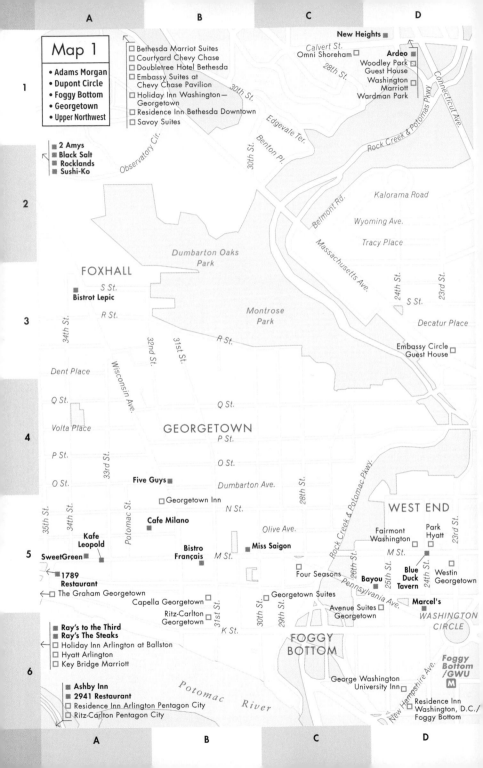

Map 1

- Adams Morgan
- Dupont Circle
- Foggy Bottom
- Georgetown
- Upper Northwest

☐ Bethesda Marriot Suites
☐ Courtyard Chevy Chase
☐ Doubletree Hotel Bethesda
☐ Embassy Suites at Chevy Chase Pavilion
☐ Holiday Inn Washington—Georgetown
☐ Residence Inn Bethesda Downtown
☐ Savoy Suites

■ 2 Amys
■ Black Salt
■ Rocklands
■ Sushi-Ko

New Heights ■

Calvert St.
Omni Shoreham ☐

28th St.

Ardeo ■
Woodley Park ☐
Guest House
Washington ☐
Marriott
Wardman Park

Connecticut Ave.

Rock Creek & Potomas Pkwy.

Edgevale Ter.

30th St.

30th St.

Benton Pl.

Kalorama Road

Belmont Rd.

Wyoming Ave.

Tracy Place

Massachusetts Ave.

24th St.

23rd St.

FOXHALL

Observatory Cir.

Dumbarton Oaks Park

S St.
Bistrot Lepic ■

R St.

Montrose Park

S St.

Decatur Place

34th St.

32nd St.

31st St.

R St.

Embassy Circle ☐
Guest House

Dent Place

Wisconsin Ave.

Q St.

Q St.

Volta Place

GEORGETOWN

P St.

34th St.

33rd St.

P St.

O St.

O St.

O St.

Five Guys ■

Dumbarton Ave.

28th St.

☐ Georgetown Inn

N St.

WEST END

Cafe Milano ■

Olive Ave.

Fairmont
Washington ☐

Park
Hyatt ☐

23rd St.

35th St.

34th St.

Potomac St.

33rd St.

**Bistro
Français** ■

■ **Miss Saigon**

M St.

M St.

**Kafe
Leopold** ■

**Blue
Duck Tavern**

24th St.

Westin ☐
Georgetown

SweetGreen ■

Four Seasons ☐

Bayou

26th St.

25th St.

■ **1789
Restaurant**

←☐ The Graham Georgetown

Capella Georgetown ☐

Ritz-Carlton ☐
Georgetown

Georgetown Suites ☐

31st St.

30th St.

29th St.

Rock Creek & Potomac Pkwy.

Pennsylvania Ave.

Avenue Suites ☐
Georgetown

Marcel's ■

*WASHINGTON
CIRCLE*

■ **Ray's to the Third**
■ **Ray's The Steaks**
☐ Holiday Inn Arlington at Ballston
☐ Hyatt Arlington
☐ Key Bridge Marriott

K St.

**FOGGY
BOTTOM**

*Foggy
Bottom
/GWU*
Ⓜ

Foggy
Bottom
/GWU

■ **Ashby Inn**
■ **2941 Restaurant**
☐ Residence Inn Arlington Pentagon City
☐ Ritz-Carlton Pentagon City

Potomac River

George Washington
University Inn ☐

New Hampshire Ave.

Residence Inn ☐
Washington, D.C./
Foggy Bottom

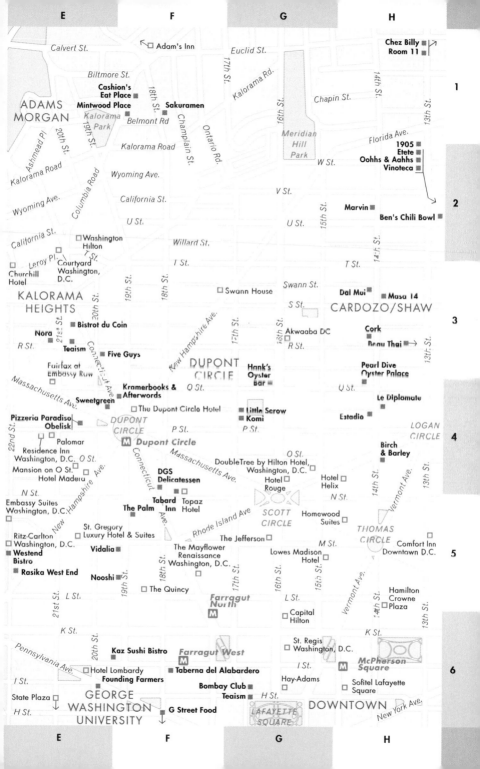

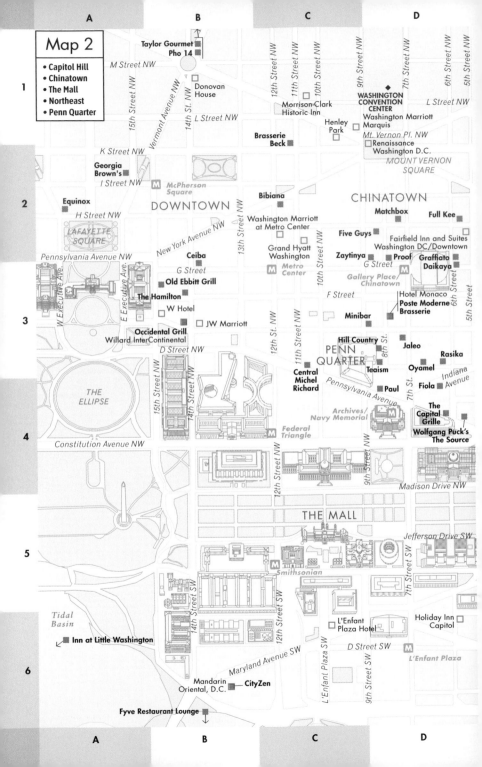

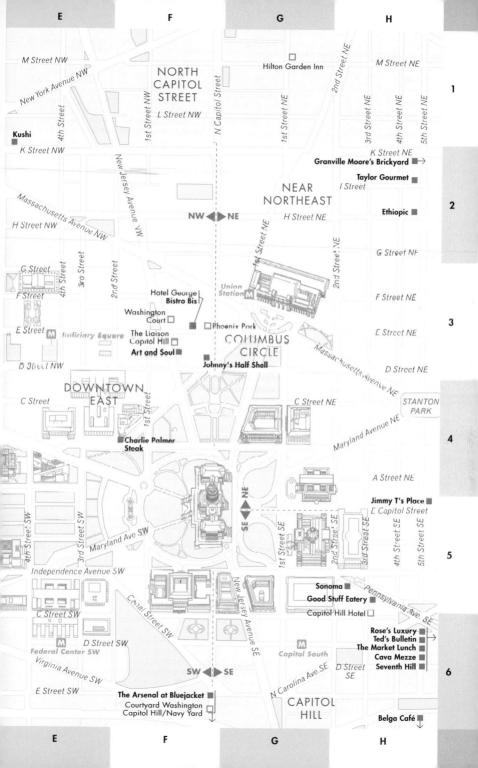

Dining

1789 Restaurant, 1:A5
1905, 1:H2
2 Amys, 1:A2
2941 Restaurant, 1:A6
Ardeo, 1:D1
The Arsenal at Bluejacket, 2:F6
Art and Soul, 2:F3
Ashby Inn, 1:A6
Bayou, 1:D5
Beau Thai, 1:H3
Belga Café, 2:H6
Ben's Chili Bowl, 1:H2
Bibiana Osteria and Enoteca, 2:C2
Birch & Barley, 1:H4
Bistro Bis, 2:F3
Bistro Français, 1:B5
Bistrot Lepic, 1:A3
Bistrot du Coin, 1:E3
Black Salt, 1:A2
Blue Duck Tavern, 1:D5
Bombay Club, 1:G6
Brasserie Beck, 2:C1
Cafe Milano, 1:A5
The Capital Grille, 2:D4
Cashion's Eat Place, 1:F1
Cava Mezze, 2:H6
Ceiba, 2:B3
Central Michel Richard, 2:C3
Charlie Palmer Steak, 2:F4
Chez Billy, 1:H1
CityZen, 2:B6
Cork, 1:H3
Dai Moi, 1:H3
Daikaya, 2:D3DGS Delicatessen, 1:F4
Equinox, 2:A2
Estadio, 1:H4
Etete, 1:H2
Ethiopic, 2:H2
Fiola, 2:D4
Five Guys, 1:B4, 1:E3
Founding Farmers, 1:E6
Full Kee, 2:D2
Fyve Restaurant Lounge, 2:B6
G Street Food, 1:F6
Georgia Brown's, 2:A2
Good Stuff Eatery, 2:H5
Graffiato, 2:D2
Granville Moore's Brickyard, 2:H2
The Hamilton, 2:B3
Hank's Oyster Bar, 1:G4
Hill Country, 2:D3
Inn at Little Washington, 2:A6

Jaleo, 2:D3
Jimmy T's Place, 2:H5
Johnny's Half Shell, 2:F3
Kafe Leopold, 1:A5
Kaz Sushi Bistro, 1:F6
Komi, 1:G4
Kramerbooks & Afterwords, 1:F4
Kushi, 2:E1
Le Diplomate, 1:H4
Little Serow, 1:G4
Marcel's, 1:D5
The Market Lunch, 2:H6
Marvin, 1:H2
Masa 14, 1:H3
Matchbox, 2:D2
Minibar, 2:D3
Mintwood Place, 1:F1
Miss Saigon, 1:B5
New Heights, 1:D1
Nooshi, 1:F5
Nora, 1:E3
Obelisk, 1:E4
Occidental Grill, 2:B3
Old Ebbitt Grill, 2:B3
Oohhs & Aahhs, 1:H2
Oyamel, 2:D3
The Palm, 1:F5
Paul, 2:D4
Pearl Dive Oyster Palace, 1:H4
Pho 14, 2:B1
Pizzeria Paradiso, 1:E4
Poste Moderne Brasserie, 2:D3
Proof, 2:D2
Rasika, 2:D3
Rasika West End, 1:E5
Ray's The Steaks, 1:A6
Ray's to the Third, 1:A6
Rocklands, 1:A2
Room 11, 1:H1
Rose's Luxury, 2:H6
Sakuramen, 1:F1
Seventh Hill, 2:H6
Sonoma, 2:H5
Sushi-Ko, 1:A2
Sweetgreen, 1:A5, 1:E4
Tabard Inn, 1:F4
Taberna del Alabardero, 1:F6
Taylor Gourmet, 2:B1, 2:H2
Teaism, 1:E3, 1:G6, 2:D3
Ted's Bulletin, 2:H6
Vidalia, 1:F5
Vinoteca, 1:H2
Westend Bistro, 1:E5
Wolfgang Puck's The Source, 2:D4
Zaytinya, 2:D2

Lodging

Adam's Inn, 1:F1
Akwaaba DC, 1:G3
Avenue Suites Georgetown, 1:D5
Bethesda Marriott Suites, 1:A1
Capella Georgetown, 1:B5
Capital Hilton, 1:G6
Capitol Hill Hotel, 2:H5
The Churchill Hotel, 1:E3
Comfort Inn Downtown D.C., 1:H5
Courtyard Chevy Chase, 1:A1
Courtyard Washington Capitol Hill/Navy Yard, 2:F6
Courtyard Washington, D.C./Dupont Circle, 1:E2
Donovan House, 2:B1
DoubleTree by Hilton Hotel Washington, D.C., 1:G4
Doubletree Hotel Bethesda, 1:A1
The Dupont Circle Hotel, 1:F4
Embassy Circle Guest House, 1:D3
Embassy Suites Washington D.C.-at Chevy Chase Pavilion, 1:A1
Embassy Suites Washington, D.C., 1:E5
The Fairfax at Embassy Row, 1:E4
Fairfield Inn & Suites Washington DC/Downtown, 2:D2
The Fairmont, Washington, D.C., Georgetown, 1:D5
Four Seasons Hotel, Washington, D.C., 1:C5
The George Washington University Inn, 1:D6
Georgetown Suites, 1:C5
The Graham Georgetown, 1:A5
Grand Hyatt Washington, 2:C2
Hamilton Crowne Plaza, 1:H5
Hay-Adams Hotel, 1:G6
Henley Park Hotel, 2:C1
Hilton Garden Inn/U.S. Capitol, 2:G1
Holiday Inn Arlington at Ballston, 1:A6
Holiday Inn Capitol, 2:D6
Holiday Inn Washington–Georgetown, 1:A1
Homewood Suites by Hilton, Washington, 1:H5

The Hotel George, 2:F3
Hotel Helix, 1:H4
Hotel Lombardy, 1:E6
Hotel Madera, 1:E4
Hotel Monaco, 2:D3
Hotel Rouge, 1:G4
Hyatt Arlington, 1:A6
JW Marriott, 2:B3
The Jefferson, 1:G5
Key Bridge Marriott, 1:A6
L'Enfant Plaza Hotel, 2:C6
The Liaison Capitol Hill, An Affinia Hotel, 2:F3
Loews Madison Hotel, 1:G5
Mandarin Oriental, 2:B6
Mansion on O Street, 1:E4
The Mayflower Renaissance Washington, D.C. Hotel, 1:F5
Morrison-Clark Historic Inn, 2:C1
Omni Shoreham Hotel, 1:C1
Palomar, Washington, D.C., 1:E4
Park Hyatt Washington, 1:D5
Phoenix Park Hotel, 2:F3
The Quincy, 1:F5
Renaissance Washington, D.C., Downtown Hotel, 2:D2
Residence Inn Arlington Pentagon City, 1:A6
Residence Inn Bethesda Downtown, 1:A1
Residence Inn Washington, D.C./Dupont Circle, 1:E4
Residence Inn Washington, D.C./Foggy Bottom, 1:D6
The Ritz-Carlton Georgetown, 1:B6
The Ritz-Carlton Pentagon City, 1:A6
The Ritz-Carlton Washington, D.C., 1:E5
Savoy Suites Hotel, 1:A1
Sofitel Washington, D.C., Lafayette Square, 1:H6
St. Gregory Luxury Hotel & Suites, 1:E5
The St. Regis Washington, D.C., 1:G6
State Plaza, 1:E6
Swann House, 1:F3
Topaz Hotel, 1:F4
W Washington, D.C., 2:B3
Washington Court Hotel, 2:F3
Washington Hilton, 1:E2

Washington Marriott Marquis, 2:C1
Washington Marriott Wardman Park, 1:D1
Washington Marriott at Metro Center, 2:C2
Westin Georgetown, Washington D.C., 1:D5
Willard InterContinental, 2:B3
Woodley Park Guest House, 1:D1

WHERE TO STAY

Updated
by Robert
Michael Oliver The Capital City's hotel scene befits Washington's image as a world-class destination. With so much variety in lodging, the city has something for everyone, from historic properties to modern designer hotels to urban inns. You can pick your hotel based on the type of experience you set out to have when you arrive.

If you are seeking an experience steeped in pomp and circumstance consider one of the city's grand hotels: the Jefferson, the Hay-Adams, the Fairfax at Embassy Row, the Willard, the Mayflower, or the St. Regis, to name but a few. When you check in at any of these beautifully kept and storied properties, it is near impossible to forget the rich history that defines D.C.

If you prefer a more urban vibe, you have a variety of choices: from Hotel George, Hotel Monaco, and Topaz Hotel to contemporary inside-the-Beltway gems like the Palomar, Hotel Rouge, the W, and the Dupont Circle Hotel.

For a more traditional hotel experience consider checking into a first-rate chain located in strategic locations throughout the city and beyond.

Visitors in search of more intimate lodging may do well to cross the threshold at one of the city's many bed-and-breakfasts. The Swann House and Akwaaba DC offer exceptional, personalized service, art-filled guest rooms, and the pleasure of waking up to a home-cooked morning meal. Over the years, the Embassy Circle Guest House and the Woodley Park Guest House have been luring guests back time and again for very good reasons.

PLANNING

LODGING STRATEGY

With hundreds of D.C. metropolitan hotels, it may seem like a daunting task to choose one. Our experts have done most of the legwork, however; the 80-plus selections here represent the best this city has to offer, from the best budget motels to the sleekest designer hotels. ⇨ *Also check out the Side Trips chapter for lodging in Alexandria and Annapolis.*

RESERVATIONS

With more than 95,000 guest rooms available in the area, you can usually find a place to stay, but it's always prudent to reserve. Hotels fill up with conventioneers, politicians in transit, families, and—in the spring—school groups. Hotel rooms in D.C. can be particularly hard to come by in late March or early April during the Cherry Blossom Festival, and in May, when students at the many local colleges graduate. Late October's Marine Corps Marathon also increases demand for rooms. Never forget that when the time comes to celebrate the presidential inauguration every four years, rooms book up fast and prices increase.

FACILITIES

You can assume that all rooms have private baths, phones, TVs, and air-conditioning, unless otherwise indicated. Breakfast is noted when it is included in the rate, but it's not a typical perk at most Washington hotels, and one feature you may want to consider for a summertime visit is a pool *(⇨ see our Best Bets list for some of the most notable)*, especially if you're traveling with kids.

WITH KIDS

From the free Smithsonian museums on the Mall to the cuddly pandas at the National Zoo, D.C. is a very family friendly town. Major convention hotels don't always cater to families, so we recommend looking Downtown, in Foggy Bottom, or in Upper Northwest; in the latter, many hotels offer special panda packages for the zoo-bound. Also, the closer your hotel is to a Metro stop, the quicker you can get on the sightseeing trail. The Metro itself often ranks as a favorite attraction among the under-12 set. Consider a stay at an all-suites hotel, which will allow you to spread out and, if you prepare your meals in a kitchenette, keep costs down. It also gives the grown-ups the option of staying up past bedtime.

A number of well-known chains, including **Embassy Suites, Fairmont, Four Seasons, Ritz-Carlton,** and **St. Regis** offer special programs or packages for kids and—stars be praised—have babysitting services. **Holiday Inns** allow kids under 12 to eat free in their restaurants and several of the Kimpton properties offer family-friendly rooms complete with bunk beds and child-size bathrobes.

PARKING

Hotel parking fees range from free to $50 per night, which involves valet parking and its usual gratuities. Street parking is free on Sunday and after 10 pm other nights. There are often far more cars searching than there are spaces available, particularly Downtown, in Georgetown, and in the upper Connecticut Avenue area.

During weekday rush hours, many streets are unavailable for parking; illegally parked cars are towed, and reclaiming a car is expensive and inconvenient. Read signs carefully; some are confusing, and the ticket writers are quick.

PRICES

If you're interested in visiting Washington at a calmer, less expensive time—and if you can stand semitropical weather—come in August, during the congressional recess. Rates also drop in late December and January, except around inaugurations. Weekend, off-season, and special rates, such as AAA discounts and online-only promotions, can make rooms more affordable. Hotels that cater to government workers and businesspeople, especially properties in the Virginia and Maryland suburbs, offer especially sizable discounts on weekends, even in busy tourist seasons. A little bit of research can pay off in big savings.

WHAT IT COSTS

	$	$$	$$$	$$$$
For Two People	under $210	$210–$295	$296–$400	over $400

Prices are for a standard double room in high season, excluding room tax (14.5% in D.C., 7% in MD, and 6.5% plus one dollar in VA).

HOTEL REVIEWS

Listed alphabetically within neighborhoods. Use the coordinate (✣ 1:B2) at the end of each listing to locate a property on the Where to Eat and Stay map.

The following reviews have been condensed for this book. Please go to Fodors.com for full reviews of each property.

THE WHITE HOUSE AREA

With the White House standing like a guard to the city's Monumental Core, this historic area exudes gravitas and stately visions, even though it also bristles with the same energy as D.C.'s vibrant Downtown. If your interests lie, however, in less commercial pursuits, or if you like to jog or even promenade, then the Mall stretches east and west past memorials and museums and lots of green space.

$$$$ HOTEL Fodor's Choice ★ 🏨 **Hay-Adams Hotel.** Given the elegant charm and refined style, with guest rooms decorated in a class above the rest, it's no wonder that the Obamas chose this impressive Washington landmark as their temporary home when they were preparing to move into 1600 Pennsylvania Avenue. **Pros:** plush guest rooms; impeccable service; packages for families; almost in the shadow of the White House. **Cons:** expensive; no pool. [$] *Rooms from: $599* ✉ *800 16th St. NW, White House Area* ☎ *202/638–6600, 800/424–5054* 🌐 *www.hayadams.com* 🛏 *124 rooms, 21 suites* 🍴 *No meals* [M] *McPherson Sq. or Farragut North* ✣ *1:G6.*

$$$$ HOTEL Fodor's Choice ★ 🏨 **Mandarin Oriental.** Asian accents, an impressive art collection in the public areas and guest rooms, views of the waterfront or the Mall, and beds so comfortable they make you want to ignore your wake-up call all set a standard of sophisticated luxury. **Pros:** excellent spa; beautiful views; best location for cherry-blossom viewing. **Cons:** expensive;

WHERE SHOULD I STAY?

	Neighborhood Vibe	Pros	Cons
The White House Area	Pleasant residential and office area along Pennsylvania Avenue. Stately early-20th-century buildings.	Safe area; close to Downtown's commercial sites and to halls of government, and the Mall.	Parking is always difficult and lots of traffic; older hotels with few budget rates.
Foggy Bottom	Bustling with college students most of the year. Its 18th- and 19th-century homes make for pleasant views.	Safe area; walking distance to Georgetown and the Kennedy Center; good Metro access.	Somewhat removed from other areas of city; paltry dining options.
Capitol Hill and Northeast D.C.	Charming residential blocks of Victorian row houses on Capitol Hill populated by members of Congress and their staffers.	Convenient to Union Station and Capitol. Stylish (if not cheap) hotels. Fine assortment of restaurants and shops.	Some streets iffy at night; parking takes some work; hotels are pricey. Blocks around Capitol and Union Station are chock-full of tourists.
Downtown	A vibrant, bustling modern mix of commercial and residential properties, packed during the day and rowdy in places at night.	Right in the heart of the Metro system; easy access to the White House. Large selection of hotels, shops, and restaurants.	Crowded; busy; daytime street parking near impossible.
Georgetown	Wealthy neighborhood bordered by the Potomac and a world-class university. Filled with students, upscale shops, and eateries.	Safe area. Historic charm on every tree-lined street. Wonderful walking paths along river.	Crowded; no nearby Metro access; lots of traffic. Almost no parking. Lodging options tend to be expensive.
Dupont Circle and Logan Circle	Cosmopolitan, lively neighborhood filled with bars and restaurants; beautiful city sights.	Plenty of modern hotels; easy Metro access; good selection of bars and restaurants.	Few budget hotel options; very limited street parking; crowded in summer months.
Adams Morgan	The center of the late-night activity; eclectic and down to earth; languages galore.	Fabulous selection of ethnic bars and restaurants; vibrant, hip nightlife.	Few lodging options; 10-minute walk to Metro; very hard to park.
Upper Northwest	A pleasant residential neighborhood with a lively strip of good restaurants.	Safe, quiet; easy walk to zoo, Metro, restaurants; street parking easier than Downtown.	A long ride to attractions other than the zoo; feels like an inner suburb. Few new hotels.

7

a bit out of the way; few nearby dining options. $ *Rooms from: $520* ✉ *1330 Maryland Ave. SW, White House Area* ☎ *202/554–8588,* *888/888–1778* ⊕ *www.mandarinoriental.com/washington* ⌨ *347 rooms, 53 suites* 🍴 *No meals* Ⓜ *Smithsonian* ⊹ *2:B6.*

BEST BETS FOR WASHINGTON, D.C. LODGING

Fodor's offers a selective listing of quality lodging, from the city's best budget motel to its most sophisticated luxury hotel. Here are our top recommendations by price and experience. The properties that provide a particularly remarkable experience in a price range are designated with a Fodor's Choice logo.

Fodor's Choice ★

Capella Georgetown, $$$$, p. 237

Courtyard Chevy Chase, $$, p. 246

The Dupont Circle Hotel, $$$$, p. 240

Embassy Circle Guest House, $$, p. 240

The Fairmont, Washington, D.C., Georgetown, $$$, p. 230

Four Seasons Hotel, Washington, D.C., $$$$, p. 238

Hay-Adams Hotel, $$$$, p. 226

The Hotel George, $$$, p. 232

Hotel Monaco, $$$ p. 234

The Jefferson, $$$$, p. 234

Mandarin Oriental, $$$$, p. 226

The Mayflower Renaissance Washington, D.C. Hotel, $$$, p. 235

Omni Shoreham Hotel, $$, p. 245

Palomar, Washington, D.C., $$$ p. 242

Park Hyatt Washington, $$$$, p. 238

Residence Inn Arlington Pentagon City, $$, p. 247

The Ritz-Carlton Georgetown, $$$$, p. 239

Sofitel Washington, D.C. Lafayette Square, $$$, p. 230

Swann House, $$, p. 242

W Washington, D.C., $$$$, p. 236

Willard InterContinental, $$$, p. 236

Woodley Park Guest House, $$, p. 245

Best by Price

$

Courtyard Washington Capitol Hill/Navy Yard, p. 232

The George Washington University Inn, p. 230

$$

Avenue Suites Georgetown, p. 230

Courtyard Chevy Chase, p. 246

Embassy Circle Guest House, p. 240

Henley Park Hotel, p. 237

Omni Shoreham Hotel, p. 245

Residence Inn Arlington Pentagon City, p. 247

Swann House, p. 242

Woodley Park Guest House, p. 245

$$$

The Fairmont, Washington D.C., Georgetown, p. 230

The Hotel George, p. 232

Hotel Madera, p. 241

Hotel Monaco, p. 234

The Mayflower Renaissance Washington, D.C. Hotel, p. 235

Palomar, Washington, D.C., p. 242

Sofitel Washington, D.C. Lafayette Square, p. 230

Willard InterContinental, p. 236

$$$$

Capella Georgetown, p. 237

The Dupont Circle Hotel, p. 240

Four Seasons Hotel, Washington, D.C., p. 238

Hay-Adams Hotel, p. 226

The Jefferson, p. 234

Mandarin Oriental, p. 226

Park Hyatt Washington, p. 238

The Ritz-Carlton Georgetown, p. 239

W Washington, D.C., p. 236

Best by Experience

BEST BOUTIQUE HOTELS

Capella Georgetown, $$$$, p. 237

The Dupont Circle Hotel, $$$$, p. 240

The Hotel George, $$$, p. 232

Hotel Monaco, $$$, p. 234

The Jefferson, $$$$, p. 234

Topaz Hotel, $$, p. 242

BEST DESIGN

The Dupont Circle Hotel, $$$$, p. 240

The Graham Georgetown, $$$$ p. 238

The Hotel George, $$$, p. 232

Hotel Monaco, $$$, p. 234

Hotel Rouge, $$, p. 241

Park Hyatt Washington, $$$$, p.238

BEST FOR KIDS

Courtyard Chevy Chase, $$, p. 246

The Fairmont, Washington, D.C., Georgetown, $$$, p. 230

Four Seasons Hotel, Washington, D.C., $$$$, p. 238

Omni Shoreham Hotel, $$, p. 245

BEST POOL

Donovan House, $$$, p. 234

Doubletree Hotel Bethesda, $$, p. 246

The Liaison Capitol Hill, An Affinia Hotel, $$, p. 233

Omni Shoreham Hotel, $$, p. 245

Washington Marriott at Metro Center, $$$$, p. 236

BEST VIEW

Hay-Adams Hotel, $$$$, p. 226

JW Marriott, $$$$, p. 235

Key Bridge Marriott, $$, p. 247

Mandarin Oriental, $$$$, p. 226

Omni Shoreham Hotel, $$, p. 245

The Ritz-Carlton Georgetown, $$$$, p. 239

BUSINESS TRAVEL

Grand Hyatt Washington, $$$, p. 234

Park Hyatt Washington, $$$$, p. 238

Renaissance Washington, D.C. Downtown Hotel, $$$, p. 237

The St. Regis Washington, D.C., $$$$, p. 236

W Washington, D.C., $$$$, p. 236

GRANDEST GRANDES DAMES

Hay-Adams Hotel, $$$$, p. 226

The Jefferson, $$$$, p. 234

The Mayflower Renaissance Washington, D.C. Hotel, $$$, p. 235

The St. Regis Washington, D.C., $$$$, p. 236

Willard InterContinental, $$$, p. 236

HOT SCENE

The Dupont Circle Hotel, $$$$, p. 240

Hotel Madera, $$$, p. 241

Hotel Rouge, $$, p. 241

The Liaison Capitol Hill, An Affinia Hotel, $$, p. 233

Palomar, Washington, D.C., $$$, p. 242

Topaz Hotel, $$, p. 242

W Washington, D.C., $$$$, p. 236

MOST ECO-FRIENDLY

Capitol Hill Hotel, $$$, p. 232

Courtyard Chevy Chase, $$, p. 246

Willard InterContinental, $$$, p. 236

Washington Marriott Marquis, $$$$, p. 237

MOST ROMANTIC

The Fairmont, Washington, D.C., Georgetown, $$$, p. 230

Hotel Monaco, $$$, p. 234

Hotel Rouge, $$, p. 241

Mandarin Oriental, $$$$, p. 226

Swann House, $$, p. 242

PET-FRIENDLY

L'Enfant Plaza Hotel, $, p. 233

The Fairmont, Washington, D.C., Georgetown, $$$, p. 230

Hamilton Crowne Plaza, $$$, p. 234

Hay-Adams Hotel, $$$$, p. 226

Hotel Helix, $$$, p. 241

Hotel Rouge, $$, p. 241

The Jefferson, $$$$, p. 234

The Liaison Capitol Hill, An Affinia Hotel, $$, p. 233

Loews Madison Hotel, $$$$, p. 235

Palomar, Washington, D.C., $$$, p. 242

Savoy Suites Hotel, $$, p. 245

Topaz Hotel, $$, p. 242

Westin Georgetown, Washington D.C., $$$, p. 231

WASHINGTON-INSIDER BARS

The Dupont Circle Hotel, $$$$, p. 240

Hay-Adams Hotel, $$$$, p. 226

The Hotel George, $$$, p. 232

The Liaison Capitol Hill, An Affinia Hotel, $$, p. 233

W Washington, D.C., $$$$, p. 236

7

$$$
HOTEL
FAMILY
Fodor's Choice
★

[🛏] **Sofitel Washington, D.C. Lafayette Square.** Only a minute's walk from the White House, the French luxury chain could not have landed a better location, and its caring, multilingual staff offers a warm welcome and great service. **Pros:** prestigious location; highly rated restaurant; lovely rooms; nice fitness center and patio. **Cons:** lobby on the small side; expensive parking. [$] *Rooms from: $326* ☒ *806 15th St. NW, White House Area* ☎ *202/730–8800* ⊕ *www.sofitel.com* ↪ *237 rooms, 16 suites* ⎪⦾⎪ *No meals* Ⓜ *McPherson Sq.* ✛ *1:H6.*

FOGGY BOTTOM

With the Kennedy Center for the Performing Arts anchoring its southwestern side and the George Washington University campus to the north, this D.C. community is hopping with youth, even though most of its residents are longtime Washingtonians and most of its homes hearken back to the 18th and 19th centuries. Additionally, nothing beats the early morning views of the Potomac River, where sculls and shells race along the surface as crews prepare for upcoming races.

$$
HOTEL
FAMILY

[🛏] **Avenue Suites Georgetown.** Luxurious and practical at the same time, this is a great choice for families and groups because all the suites have separate bedrooms and full kitchens, and some have views of the city and the Potomac River. **Pros:** centrally located; service-oriented; small gym. **Cons:** a long walk away from the Mall (but close to Georgetown). [$] *Rooms from: $270* ☒ *2500 Pennsylvania Ave. NW, Foggy Bottom* ☎ *202/333–8060* ⊕ *www.avenuesuites.com* ↪ *124 rooms* ⎪⦾⎪ *No meals* Ⓜ *GWU/Foggy Bottom* ✛ *1:D5.*

$$$
HOTEL
FAMILY

[🛏] **Embassy Suites Washington, D.C.** All accommodations at this pleasant and convenient hotel within walking distance of Georgetown and Dupont Circle have a living room and bedroom and surround an atrium filled with classical columns, plaster lions, wrought-iron lanterns, waterfalls, and tall palms. **Pros:** family-friendly; in-house restaurant serves lunch and dinner; pool to keep the little ones—and sweaty tourists—happy. **Cons:** not a lot of character; museums not in walking distance; four blocks from Metro. [$] *Rooms from: $299* ☒ *1250 22nd St. NW, Foggy Bottom* ☎ *202/857–3388, 800/362–2779* ⊕ *www.embassysuites.com* ↪ *318 suites* ⎪⦾⎪ *Breakfast* Ⓜ *Foggy Bottom/GWU or Dupont Circle* ✛ *1:E5.*

$$$
HOTEL
FAMILY
Fodor's Choice
★

[🛏] **The Fairmont, Washington, D.C., Georgetown.** Well placed for exploring Georgetown, this hotel, with good family and fitness amenities, centers on an elegant central courtyard and gardens, overlooked by the large glassed-in lobby and about a third of the bright, spacious rooms. **Pros:** fitness fanatics will love Balance Gym and 50-foot indoor pool; lots of kid- and pet-friendly features; business center; easy walk to Georgetown. **Cons:** pricey; far from most major attractions. [$] *Rooms from: $329* ☒ *2401 M St. NW, Foggy Bottom* ☎ *202/429–2400, 866/540–4505* ⊕ *www.fairmont.com* ↪ *415 rooms, 30 suites* ⎪⦾⎪ *No meals* Ⓜ *Foggy Bottom/GWU* ✛ *1:D5.*

$
HOTEL

[🛏] **The George Washington University Inn.** Wrought-iron gates lead into a pleasant courtyard, setting the tone of this intimate, quiet getaway where the traditionally styled guest rooms are a few blocks from the

Kennedy Center, the State Department, and the George Washington University and Hospital. **Pros:** good price; close to Metro; restaurant. **Cons:** accommodations in need of an upgrade; far from museums. $ *Rooms from: $189* ⊠ *824 New Hampshire Ave. NW, Foggy Bottom* ☎ *800/426–4455, 202/337–6620* ⊕ *www.gwuinn.com* ↴ *64 rooms, 31 suites* ❍ *No meals* Ⓜ *Foggy Bottom/GWU* ✛ *1:D6.*

$$$ ⌂ **Hotel Lombardy.** This romantic spot, three blocks from the White
HOTEL House and Metro, is ideal for couples seeking a peaceful retreat. **Pros:** homey rooms; beautiful lounge. **Cons:** old-fashioned; expensive breakfast; on busy street. $ *Rooms from: $300* ⊠ *2019 Pennsylvania Ave. NW, Foggy Bottom* ☎ *202/828–2600* ⊕ *www.hotellombardy.com* ↴ *140 rooms, 21 suites* ❍ *No meals* Ⓜ *Foggy Bottom/GWU* ✛ *1:E6.*

$$ ⌂ **Residence Inn Washington, D.C./Foggy Bottom.** Formerly a Doubletree,
HOTEL this all-suites hotel is close to the Kennedy Center, George Washington University, and Georgetown. **Pros:** near Metro; rooftop pool overlooks the Watergate; quiet neighborhood; good online deals available. **Cons:** far from the museums; too quiet for some. $ *Rooms from: $220* ⊠ *801 New Hampshire Ave. NW, Foggy Bottom* ☎ *202/785–2000, 800/222–8733* ⊕ *www.marriott.com* ↴ *105 suites* ❍ *Breakfast* Ⓜ *Foggy Bottom/GWU* ✛ *1:D6.*

$$$$ ⌂ **The Ritz-Carlton Washington, D.C.** Luxury oozes from every polished
HOTEL marble surface at one of Washington's most upscale hostelries, and personalized service makes you feel pampered. **Pros:** attentive service; convenient to several parts of town; attached to fabulous health club (fee) and pool. **Cons:** pricey room rates; expensive valet parking. $ *Rooms from: $469* ⊠ *1150 22nd St. NW, Foggy Bottom* ☎ *202/835–0500, 800/241–3333* ⊕ *www.ritzcarlton.com/hotels/washington_dc* ↴ *267 rooms, 32 suites* ❍ *No meals* Ⓜ *Foggy Bottom/GWU* ✛ *1:E5.*

$$ ⌂ **St. Gregory Luxury Hotel & Suites.** Business and leisure travelers alike
HOTEL enjoy these spacious accommodations that include fully stocked kitchens and extra touches like turndown service, complimentary newspaper, and shoe shine. **Pros:** big rooms; good for long-term stays; central location near business district of K Street. **Cons:** far from museums; older; area is sleepy at night. $ *Rooms from: $210* ⊠ *2033 M St. NW, Foggy Bottom* ☎ *202/530–3600, 800/829–5034* ⊕ *www.capitalhotelswdc. com* ↴ *54 rooms, 84 suites* ❍ *No meals* Ⓜ *Dupont Circle* ✛ *1:E5.*

$ ⌂ **State Plaza Hotel.** The surroundings are neither luxurious nor ter-
HOTEL ribly atmospheric, but no Washington hotel gets you quicker access to the State Department, which sits across the street, and the spacious suites have kitchenettes and lighted dressing tables. **Pros:** all suites; free Internet access; walk to Metro; close to GWU; safe neighborhood at night. **Cons:** far from museums; not a lot of character; slow elevators. $ *Rooms from: $199* ⊠ *2117 E St. NW, Foggy Bottom* ☎ *202/861–8200, 800/424–2859* ⊕ *www.stateplaza.com* ↴ *230 suites* ❍ *No meals* Ⓜ *Foggy Bottom/GWU* ✛ *1:E6.*

$$$ ⌂ **Westin Georgetown, Washington D.C.** Not really in Georgetown (but
HOTEL it's nearby), this Westin is in a busy West End location and convenient
FAMILY for the business district, but is equally popular with leisure travelers. **Pros:** quiet neighborhood; excellent bathrooms; family-friendly. **Cons:** 10-minute walk to Metro; a bit out of the way for sightseeing. $ *Rooms*

from: $400 ✉ *2350 M St. NW, Foggy Bottom* ☎ *301/429–0100* 🌐 *www.westingeorgetown.com* 🛏 *263 rooms* 🍴 *Multiple meal plans* [M] *Foggy Bottom* ✣ *1:D5.*

CAPITOL HILL AND NORTHEAST D.C.

To be sure, politics and commerce like oil and water don't mix, but they sure make a great neighborhood. With the dome of the Capitol hovering above and the bustle of Eastern Market teeming below, this District neighborhood is guaranteed to keep you entertained. Plus, Folger Shakespeare is but a walk away from the dome. If that's not enough, then head north for an edgy evening along the H Street corridor with its bars and Atlas Performing Arts Center.

$$$ HOTEL FAMILY 🏨 **Capitol Hill Hotel.** A great choice if you want to stay on the Hill and need some extra room to spread out: All Federalist-chic-style units are suites, with kitchenettes, large work desks, flat-screen TVs, and spacious closets. **Pros:** good for extended stays; close to Metro; continental breakfast included. **Cons:** limited street parking. [$] *Rooms from: $350* ✉ *200 C St. SE, Capitol Hill* ☎ *202/543–6000* 🌐 *www.capitolhillhotel-dc.com* 🛏 *152 suites* 🍴 *Breakfast* [M] *Capitol South* ✣ *2:H5.*

$ HOTEL 🏨 **Courtyard Washington Capitol Hill/Navy Yard.** The location is a bit out of the way, but rooms are large and nicely done in "Federalist" blue and gold, and amenities include an indoor pool. **Pros:** close to Metro and Capitol; popular bar. **Cons:** popular with groups, so some nights may be noisy; neighborhood construction. [$] *Rooms from: $180* ✉ *140 L St. SE, Navy Yard, Capitol Hill* ☎ *202/479–0027* 🌐 *www.marriott.com* 🛏 *192 rooms, 12 suites* 🍴 *No meals* ✣ *2:F6.*

$$$ HOTEL 🏨 **Hilton Garden Inn/U.S. Capitol.** Soothing, well-kept guest rooms are just a block away from the Metro stop and a short walk from Union Station and the Washington Convention Center. **Pros:** near Metro; outdoor pool; business center. **Cons:** some reports of noise at night; not in the center of town; in a gritty neighborhood. [$] *Rooms from: $340* ✉ *1225 First St. NE, Capitol Hill* ☎ *202/408–4870* 🌐 *www.hiltongardeninn.com* 🛏 *204 rooms* 🍴 *Breakfast* [M] *Noma/Galludet U.* ✣ *2:G1.*

$ HOTEL FAMILY 🏨 **Holiday Inn Capitol.** One block from the National Air and Space Museum, this family-friendly hotel is in a great location for those bound for the Smithsonian museums, and, with Old Towne Trolley Tours stopping here, getting around town is a snap. **Pros:** family-friendly; rooftop pool; close to museums. **Cons:** limited dining options nearby; not much going on in the neighborhood at night. [$] *Rooms from: $200* ✉ *550 C St. SW, Capitol Hill* ☎ *202/479–4000* 🌐 *www.hicapitoldc.com* 🛏 *532 rooms, 13 suites* 🍴 *Breakfast* [M] *L'Enfant Plaza* ✣ *2:D6.*

$$$ HOTEL Fodor's Choice ★ 🏨 **The Hotel George.** We cannot tell a lie: D.C.'s first contemporary boutique hotel is still one of its best, and the public areas and stylishly soothing guest quarters still excel at providing a fun and funky alternative to the cookie-cutter chains. **Pros:** close to Union Station; wine hour nightly; popular in-house restaurant; updated fitness center. **Cons:** small closets; some reports of street noise; ultramodern feel not everyone's cup of tea. [$] *Rooms from: $400* ✉ *15 E St. NW, Capitol*

Hill ☎ *202/347–4200, 800/576–8331* 🌐 *www.hotelgeorge.com* 🛏 *139 rooms, 1 suite* 🍴 *No meals* [M] *Union Station* ✛ *2:F3.*

$ HOTEL 🏨 **L'Enfant Plaza Hotel.** Guest rooms are worn, but large and functional, and you can't get much closer to the National Mall—and some rooms have spectacular views of the river and the monuments. **Pros:** short walk to Smithsonian; nice pool and fitness center; pet-friendly. **Cons:** a bit shabby; area is sleepy at night; few nearby restaurants. [$] *Rooms from: $200* ✉ *480 L'Enfant Plaza SW, Capitol Hill* ☎ *202/484–1000, 800/635–5065* 🌐 *www.lenfantplazahotel.com* 🛏 *370 rooms, 102 suites* 🍴 *No meals* [M] *L'Enfant Plaza* ✛ *2:C6.*

$$ HOTEL 🏨 **The Liaison Capitol Hill, An Affinia Hotel.** If the city's most stately buildings weren't steps away, you could easily think you had checked into a sleek Manhattan hotel, with a trendy buzz and guest rooms defined by modern chic. **Pros:** fantastic rooftop pool and deck; pet-friendly; gym. **Cons:** some street noise at night; no great room views; expensive parking. [$] *Rooms from: $270* ✉ *415 New Jersey Ave. NW, Capitol Hill* ☎ *202/638–1616, 866/233–4642* 🌐 *www.affinia.com* 🛏 *343 rooms* 🍴 *No meals* [M] *Union Station* ✛ *2:F3.*

$ HOTEL 🏨 **Phoenix Park Hotel.** If you prefer to be near the Hill but not in a convention hotel, the small but cozy guest rooms in this European-style inn across the street from Union Station may fit the bill. **Pros:** pleasant guest rooms; comfy beds with good linens; friendly service. **Cons:** no swimming pool; small rooms; some rooms are noisy. [$] *Rooms from: $180* ✉ *520 N. Capitol St. NW, Capitol Hill* ☎ *202/638–6900, 800/824–5419* 🌐 *www.phoenixparkhotel.com* 🛏 *146 rooms, 3 suites* 🍴 *No meals* [M] *Union Station* ✛ *2:F3.*

$$ HOTEL 🏨 **Washington Court Hotel.** If you're searching for the city's newest "It" hotel, keep looking, but these soothing guest rooms done in soft grays and browns fit the bill for a reliable, clean, comfortable place to stay. **Pros:** good location; Capitol views from many rooms; executive king rooms have sofa beds. **Cons:** some reports of mixed service; wear and tear is showing; expensive parking. [$] *Rooms from: $280* ✉ *525 New Jersey Ave. NW, Capitol Hill* ☎ *202/628–2100* 🌐 *www.washingtoncourthotel.com* 🛏 *252 rooms, 12 suites* 🍴 *No meals* [M] *Union Station* ✛ *2:F3.*

DOWNTOWN

For those who have not visited Washington for a decade or so, throw away your expectations. Downtown rocks with energy and excitement. Whether you want theater—from the latest musical to the hardest-hitting drama—clubs, restaurants, or museums, this revitalized D.C. neighborhood, with its proximity to the Mall, is the place to settle in for your stay.

$$$ HOTEL 🏨 **Capital Hilton.** The choice of many celebrities and dignitaries since it opened in 1943, the Hilton has modern perks like a health club and spa and is well located for shopping and eating out. **Pros:** nice guest rooms; desirable location; great gym. **Cons:** expensive parking; reports of street noise. [$] *Rooms from: $400* ✉ *1001 16th St. NW, Downtown*

☎ *202/393–1000* ⊕ *www.capital.hilton.com* ⤳ *544 room, 32 suites* |◎| *No meals* Ⓜ *Farragut N* ✛ *1:G6.*

$$$
HOTEL

🔳 **Donovan House.** You won't find anything remotely close to a colonial reproduction here amid the hanging egg chairs, iPod docking stations, spiral showers and bowl-like bathtubs—perfect if you're seeking an out-of-the-box-style lodging. **Pros:** evening wine hour; rooftop pool; near clubs; good service; close to the White House. **Cons:** smallish rooms; 10-minute walk to Metro. Ⓢ *Rooms from: $300* ✉ *1155 14th St. NW, Downtown* ☎ *202/737–1200* ⊕ *www.donovanhousehotel.com* ⤳ *193 rooms, 17 suites* |◎| *No meals* Ⓜ *McPherson Sq.* ✛ *2:B1.*

$$$
HOTEL

🔳 **Grand Hyatt Washington.** A city within the city is what greets you as you step inside the Hyatt's doors and gaze upward to the balconies overlooking the blue lagoon and the many conveniences within the atrium. **Pros:** great location for sightseeing and shopping; often has weekend deals; nice gym and indoor pool. **Cons:** often filled with conventioneers; chain-hotel feel. Ⓢ *Rooms from: $319* ✉ *1000 H St. NW, Downtown* ☎ *202/582–1234, 800/233–1234* ⊕ *www.grandwashington.hyatt.com* ⤳ *851 rooms, 37 suites* |◎| *No meals* Ⓜ *Metro Center* ✛ *2:C2.*

$$$
HOTEL

🔳 **Hamilton Crowne Plaza.** A short walk from the White House and the Mall, this appealing Art Deco hotel is a good choice for visitors doing the sights as well as business guests who come for top-notch meeting rooms and the nearby Convention Center. **Pros:** central location near White House; well-equipped fitness center; women's floor; personal service. **Cons:** some street noise; small rooms; no pool. Ⓢ *Rooms from: $305* ✉ *1001 14th St. NW, Downtown* ☎ *202/682–0111* ⊕ *www.hamiltonhoteldc.com* ⤳ *301 rooms, 17 suites* |◎| *No meals* Ⓜ *McPherson Square* ✛ *1:H5.*

$$$
HOTEL
Fodor's Choice
★

🔳 **Hotel Monaco.** Here's a perfect marriage of whimsy and elegance—the hotel, designed by Robert Mills (of Washington Monument fame), hosts a nightly wine reception, and will even deliver a goldfish to your room for the duration of your stay. **Pros:** fun Penn Quarter location next to the Spy Museum; near great restaurants and shops; convenient to the Metro. **Cons:** noisy part of town; no pool. Ⓢ *Rooms from: $380* ✉ *700 F St. NW, Downtown* ☎ *202/628–7177, 800/649–1202* ⊕ *www.monaco-dc.com* ⤳ *167 rooms, 16 suites* |◎| *No meals* Ⓜ *Gallery Pl./Chinatown* ✛ *2:D3.*

$$$$
HOTEL
Fodor's Choice
★

🔳 **The Jefferson.** Every inch of this 1923 Beaux Arts landmark exudes refined elegance, from the intimate seating areas that take the place of a traditional check-in counter to the delicate blooms and glass atrium at the entryway to Plume, the fine-dining restaurant. The Jefferson is also extremely pet-friendly, and has no weight limit on four-legged guests, which is a rare, especially in a luxury hotel. (The hotel even has a pet butler on hand to walk and feed your dog, and a pet room service menu.) **Pros:** exquisite historic hotel; impeccable service; prestigious location; free Wi-Fi and domestic calls; short walk to Metro. **Cons:** expensive; some rooms have views of other buildings. Ⓢ *Rooms from: $600* ✉ *1200 16th St. NW, Downtown* ☎ *202/448–2300* ⊕ *www.jeffersondc.com* ⤳ *99 rooms, 20 suites* |◎| *No meals* Ⓜ *Farragut North* ✛ *1:G5.*

CLOSE UP

The Mayflower Renaissance: Did You Know?

■ President Franklin D. Roosevelt wrote, "The only thing we have to fear is fear itself." in Room 776.

■ J. Edgar Hoover ate lunch at the Mayflower restaurant almost every weekday for 20 years. He almost always brought his own diet salad dressing.

■ Walt Disney once dined on the Mayflower's roof.

■ The state dinner celebrating the 1979 Arab-Israeli peace treaty was held here.

■ Winston Churchill sat for a portrait here.

■ Members of Congress interviewed Monica Lewinsky in the 10th-floor Presidential Suite while pursuing the impeachment of President Bill Clinton.

■ Former New York Governor Eliot Spitzer was allegedly visited by a high-priced call girl at his room here in 2008. The resulting scandal led to his resignation.

$$$$
HOTEL
JW Marriott. From the location near the White House to the views from the top floors, it's hard to forget you are in the nation's capital when you stay in one of the beautifully furnished rooms here. **Pros:** in the heart of town, spiffy rooms with a luxurious, traditional feel; good views from top floors; indoor pool and fitness center. **Cons:** very busy; expensive for what you get; staff sometimes seems overwhelmed. $ *Rooms from: $500* ✉ *1331 Pennsylvania Ave. NW, Downtown* ☎ *202/393-2000, 800/393-2503* ⊕ *www.jwmarriottdc.com* ⟿ *737 rooms, 35 suites* ⦶ *No meals* Ⓜ *Metro Center* ✛ *2:B3.*

$$$$
HOTEL
Loews Madison Hotel. The signatures of presidents, prime ministers, sultans, and kings fill the guest register at this classic Washington address, noted for polite service and stylish comfort. **Pros:** central location; pet-friendly; pretty guest rooms with plush furnishings and linens. **Cons:** no pool; 20-minute walk from the Mall; many rooms are a bit dark with no views. $ *Rooms from: $490* ✉ *1177 15th St. NW, Downtown* ☎ *202/862-1600, 800/424-8577* ⊕ *www.loewshotels.com* ⟿ *356 rooms, 9 suites* ⦶ *No meals* Ⓜ *McPherson Sq.* ✛ *1:G5.*

$$$
HOTEL
FAMILY
Fodor'sChoice
★
The Mayflower Renaissance Washington, D.C. Hotel. With its magnificent block-long lobby filled with antique crystal chandeliers, layers of gold trim, and gilded columns, there's little wonder that this luxurious landmark has hosted presidential balls since its opening in 1925, as well as historic news conferences and even, for a short time, the Chinese Embassy. **Pros:** historic 1925 building; near dozens of restaurants; a few steps from Metro. **Cons:** rooms vary greatly in size; no pool; expensive parking and pet fees. $ *Rooms from: $370* ✉ *1127 Connecticut Ave. NW, Downtown* ☎ *202/347-3000, 800/228-7697* ⊕ *www.marriott. com* ⟿ *657 rooms, 74 suites* ⦶ *No meals* Ⓜ *Farragut N* ✛ *1:F5.*

$
HOTEL
Morrison-Clark Historic Inn. A fascinating history makes these beautiful 1864 Victorian town houses an interesting as well as a comfortable and well located choice. **Pros:** charming alternative to cookie-cutter hotels; historic feel throughout; near Convention Center; fitness room and

7

outdoor pool. **Cons:** some street noise; four blocks to Metro; room size and style varies considerably. [$] *Rooms from: $188* ✉ *1015 L St. NW, Downtown* ☎ *202/898–1200, 800/332–7898* 🌐 *www.morrisonclark.com* 🛏 *54 rooms, 12 suites* 🍴 *Breakfast* [M] *Metro Center* ✥ *2:C1.*

$$$$ HOTEL FAMILY 🏨 **The St. Regis Washington, D.C.** Just two blocks from the White House, this 1926 Italian Renaissance-style landmark attracts a business and diplomatic crowd, but families will love the F.A.O. Schwarz teddy bears and kid-size robes issued to young guests. **Pros:** close to White House; historic property; exceptional service; easy walk to sights and eateries. **Cons:** no pool; small gym; most rooms don't have great views; very expensive. [$] *Rooms from: $650* ✉ *923 16th St. NW, Downtown* ☎ *202/638–2626* 🌐 *www.stregis.com/washington* 🛏 *175 rooms, 25 suites* 🍴 *No meals* [M] *Farragut N* ✥ *1:G6.*

$$$$ HOTEL Fodor's Choice ★ 🏨 **W Washington, D.C.** A DJ spins tunes in the living room–style lobby; an oversize flat-screen TV near the doorway broadcasts an image of a flickering fireplace; rooms contain ultramodern furnishings—every detail here screams urban chic, and does so with style. **Pros:** hip; individualized and attentive service; fabulous location; good restaurant and rooftop bar; nice spa; car service available. **Cons:** pricey; too modern for some; no pool; guest rooms vary from spacious and light to smallish and dark. [$] *Rooms from: $485* ✉ *515 15th St. NW, Downtown* ☎ *202/661–2400* 🌐 *www.starwoodhotels.com/whotels* 🛏 *317 rooms, 32 suites* 🍴 *No meals* [M] *McPherson Sq.* ✥ *2:B3.*

$$$$ HOTEL 🏨 **Washington Marriott at Metro Center.** The big-chain feel is offset by a good location just steps away from the monuments and museums; attractive, comfortable guest rooms; and an indoor pool and health club. **Pros:** great location; updated guest rooms. **Cons:** expensive; busy location; generic. [$] *Rooms from: $550* ✉ *775 12th St. NW, Downtown* ☎ *202/737–2200, 800/393–2100* 🌐 *www.marriott.com/wasmc* 🛏 *454 rooms, 5 suites* 🍴 *Breakfast* [M] *Metro Center* ✥ *2:C2.*

$$$ HOTEL FAMILY Fodor's Choice ★ 🏨 **Willard InterContinental.** Favored by American presidents and other newsmakers, this Washington landmark offers superb service, a wealth of amenities, and guest rooms filled with period detail and Federal-style furniture. **Pros:** luxurious historic hotel; great location two blocks from the White House; impeccable service; luxurious spa. **Cons:** expensive; no pool. [$] *Rooms from: $340* ✉ *1401 Pennsylvania Ave. NW, Downtown* ☎ *202/628–9100, 800/827–1747* 🌐 *www.washington.intercontinental.com* 🛏 *335 rooms, 40 suites* 🍴 *No meals* [M] *Metro Center* ✥ *2:B3.*

CHINATOWN

This is by far one of D.C.'s most vibrant commercial neighborhoods, with a seemingly endless variety of local and national chains offering not only the best in Asian cuisine but also African, Mediterranean, and pub food. The Verizon Center offers visitors an array of entertainment and the nationally recognized Shakespeare Theatre Company presents audiences with the best in classical fare.

$$$ HOTEL 🏨 **Fairfield Inn & Suites Washington DC/Downtown.** Bold, contemporary design provides a soothing retreat in a busy part of town, near many

of the top attractions like the Verizon Center, the National Portrait Gallery, and the Mall. **Pros:** complimentary breakfast; lots of restaurants, entertainment, and attractions nearby. **Cons:** some complaints about street noise; pricey for level of service; small gym; part of town not for everyone. [$] *Rooms from: $299* ✉ *500 H St. NW, Chinatown* ☎ *202/289–5959* 🌐 *www.marriott.com* 🛏 *189 rooms, 9 suites* 🍴 *No meals* [M] *Gallery Pl./Chinatown* ⊕ *2:D2.*

$$ HOTEL 🏨 **Henley Park Hotel.** A Tudor-style building adorned with gargoyles, this National Historic Trust property has the cozy feel of an English country house, and the atmosphere extends to charming rooms that were once the choice of senators and notables from Washington society. **Pros:** welcoming; historic building; privileges at nearby pool. **Cons:** little parking; nearby construction. [$] *Rooms from: $250* ✉ *926 Massachusetts Ave. NW, Chinatown* ☎ *202/638–5200, 800/222–8474* 🌐 *www.henleypark.com* 🛏 *83 rooms, 13 suites* 🍴 *No meals* [M] *Metro Center* ⊕ *2:C1.*

$$$ HOTEL 🏨 **Renaissance Washington, D.C. Downtown Hotel.** Large rooms with views, extensive business services, such touches as fine linens, and a lavish fitness center and spa elevate this chain hotel into the luxury realm. **Pros:** convenient to Convention Center; near Metro; popular part of town with many shops and restaurants; nice lobby and rooftop terrace. **Cons:** convention crowds; chain-hotel feel; expensive. [$] *Rooms from: $379* ✉ *999 9th St. NW, Chinatown* ☎ *202/898–9000, 800/228–9898* 🌐 *www.marriott.com* 🛏 *794 rooms, 13 suites* 🍴 *No meals* [M] *Gallery Pl./Chinatown* ⊕ *2:D2.*

$$$ HOTEL 🏨 **Washington Marriott Marquis.** Opened in May 2014, this eco friendly hotel, directly adjacent to the Washington Convention Center, spans an entire city block, capped with an enormous atrium skylight, and houses restaurants, a sports bar, an extensive health club, a lounge, and retail shops. **Pros:** new hotel; location near Metro; large health club. **Cons:** connected to Convention Center, which may make it more city-centric than retreat; expensive parking. [$] *Rooms from: $389* ✉ *901 Massachussetts Ave. NW, Chinatown* ☎ *202/962–4482 pre-sales* 🌐 *www.marriott.com* 🛏 *1,179 rooms, 49 suites* 🍴 *No meals* [M] *Gallery Place/Chinatown* ⊕ *2:C1.*

GEORGETOWN

Even to other native Washingtonians, this high-end neighborhood—home to Washington's elite—represents a tourist destination in itself. Historic homes on quiet streets with plenty of trees and a canal make this area ideal for strolling. Yet M Street and Wisconsin Avenue restaurants and shops make it the hottest spot in town for those with money to burn. Georgetown University students keep this area bustling into the early hours.

$$$$ HOTEL Fodor's Choice ★ 🏨 **Capella Georgetown.** The most expensive accommodations in town come with superlative standards, and the pampering begins even before you arrive—a personal assistant will make arrangements for tickets, tours, transportation, personal shopping, behind-the-scenes access to events, or whatever. **Pros:** unparalleled service; sumptuous guest rooms and public areas; prime Georgetown location. **Cons:** incredibly

7

expensive; far from Metro and Mall. [$] *Rooms from: $850* ✉ *1050 31st St. NW, Georgetown* ☎ *202/617–2400* 🌐 *www.capellahotels.com* 🛏 *49 rooms* 🍴 *No meals* [M] *Foggy Bottom/GWU* ✥ *1:B5.*

$$$$ HOTEL FAMILY Fodor's Choice ★ 🏨 **Four Seasons Hotel, Washington, D.C.** An army of valets, doormen, and bellhops, plus a wealth of amenities, make one of Washington's leading hotels a favorite with celebrities, hotel connoisseurs, and families. **Pros:** edge of Georgetown makes for a fabulous location; lap-of-luxury feel; impeccable service. **Cons:** astronomically expensive; challenging street parking; far from Metro. [$] *Rooms from: $725* ✉ *2800 Pennsylvania Ave. NW, Georgetown* ☎ *202/342–0444, 800/332–3442* 🌐 *www.fourseasons.com/washington* 🛏 *164 rooms, 58 suites* 🍴 *No meals* [M] *Foggy Bottom* ✥ *1:C5.*

$$ HOTEL FAMILY 🏨 **Georgetown Suites.** If you're looking for plenty of space in a top location, these suites vary in size, but all come with fully equipped kitchens and separate sitting rooms. **Pros:** spacious rooms; good choice for a family that wants to spread out. **Cons:** parking can be challenging; not a lot of character or style. [$] *Rooms from: $280* ✉ *1111 30th St. NW, Georgetown* ☎ *202/298–7800, 800/348–7203* 🌐 *www.georgetownsuites.com* 🛏 *216 suites* 🍴 *Breakfast* [M] *Foggy Bottom/GWU* ✥ *1:C5.*

$$$$ HOTEL 🏨 **The Graham Georgetown.** Alexander Graham Bell, the inventor who once lived in Georgetown, would be honored to lend his name to these luxurious and stylish quarters with panoramic views of the Kennedy Center, the Washington Monument, and the Rosslyn skyline. **Pros:** great Georgetown location; quiet and extremely attractive surroundings; nice water and city views. **Cons:** expensive parking; no pool. [$] *Rooms from: $420* ✉ *1075 Thomas Jefferson St. NW, Georgetown* ☎ *855/341–1292* 🌐 *www.thegrahamgeorgetown.com* 🛏 *57 rooms* 🍴 *No meals* [M] *Foggy Bottom/GWU* ✥ *1:A5.*

$$ HOTEL FAMILY 🏨 **Holiday Inn Washington–Georgetown.** On the northern edge of Georgetown, this no-surprises chain hotel is a short walk from Dumbarton Oaks, the National Cathedral, and Georgetown University, and some rooms offer a scenic view of the Washington skyline. **Pros:** easy walk to restaurants; pretty outdoor pool; friendly staff. **Cons:** not near a Metro; far from Downtown; generic chain feel. [$] *Rooms from: $230* ✉ *2101 Wisconsin Ave. NW, Georgetown* ☎ *202/338–4600, 800/423–0908* 🌐 *www.ihg.com* 🛏 *281 rooms, 4 suites* 🍴 *No meals* [M] *Foggy Bottom* ✥ *1:A1.*

$$$$ HOTEL FAMILY Fodor's Choice ★ 🏨 **Park Hyatt Washington.** Understated elegance and refined service are much in evidence at this soothing city getaway, where the earth-tone guest rooms are a minimalist tribute to the American experience and feature walnut floors, hard-covered books, and folk art accent pieces. **Pros:** spacious rooms; good for entertaining; lull-you-to-sleep beds; destination in-house restaurant. **Cons:** expensive valet parking; 10-minute walk to Foggy Bottom Metro. [$] *Rooms from: $595* ✉ *1201 24th St. NW, Georgetown* ☎ *202/789–1234* 🌐 *www.parkwashington.hyatt.com* 🛏 *216 rooms, 28 suites* 🍴 *No meals* [M] *Foggy Bottom* ✥ *1:D5.*

HOT HOTEL BARS AND LOUNGES

Some of the most iconic examples of power bars, where inside-the-Beltway decision makers talk shop and rub elbows, are housed in many of this town's historic hotels. So grab a snifter of single malt and begin your people-watching at these classic D.C. hotel bars.

The **Jockey Club Lounge** at the **Fairfax at Embassy Row** made a comeback when it reopened after a long absence on the power bar scene. The original club started serving diplomats, politicians, lobbyists, and other notable individuals in the 1920s, and the reborn club continues that tradition today.

The **Off the Record** bar at the **Hay-Adams** advertises itself as the place to be seen and not heard. Being just steps from the White House, that couldn't be more true. Tucked away in the historic hotel's basement, you really never know who you might run into here.

Although they don't boast the same old-world dark wood and red-leather charm of the bars at the historic hotels, the lobby bar at the decidedly more modern **Liaison Capitol Hill** and **P.O.V.** on the roof of the **W Hotel** hold their own as stops on the see-and-be-seen hotel bar scene.

$$$$
HOTEL
Fodor's Choice
★

☆ **The Ritz-Carlton Georgetown.** Once an incinerator dating from the 1920s, this building, still topped with a smokestack, might seem the most unlikely of places for upscale lodgings, but settle into one of the large and chicly designed guest rooms (upper level suites overlook the river) and you'll agree the concept works. **Pros:** quiet; steps away from restaurants and shopping; polished service; good spa and fitness center. **Cons:** far from the Metro; very expensive. $ *Rooms from: $650* ✉ *3100 South St. NW, Georgetown* ☎ *202/912-4200* ⊕ *www.ritzcarlton.com/hotels/georgetown* ⤵ *86 rooms, 29 suites* ⦿ *No meals* Ⓜ *Foggy Bottom/GWU* ✚ *1:B6.*

DUPONT CIRCLE AND LOGAN CIRCLE

Around the Dupont traffic circle spins everything that makes D.C. what it is: embassies from all over the world with their ethnically diverse communities, and a vibrant Connecticut Avenue and 14th Street with their panoply of restaurants, bars, and shops. Add to that an assortment of theaters, museums, and galleries—seemingly on every block—and this rich Washington neighborhood has something for everyone. And, of course, the Circle is also known for its fabulously eclectic gatherings of people. The upwardly mobile Logan Circle area includes a historic district with some fine buildings, plus shops, galleries, and nightlife.

$
B&B/INN

☆ **Akwaaba DC.** If your perfect vacation includes having a good book, warm fire, and soft bed, then this charming bed-and-breakfast is your dream come true. **Pros:** neighborhood location; nice breakfasts; well-kept historic home; non-intrusive service. **Cons:** smallish bathrooms; older; some noise in street-facing rooms. $ *Rooms from: $200* ✉ *1708 16th St. NW, Dupont Circle* ☎ *877/893-3233* ⊕ *www.akwaaba.com* ⤵ *7 rooms, 1 apartment* ⦿ *Breakfast* Ⓜ *Dupont Circle* ✚ *1:G3.*

7

The Fairfax at Embassy Row: Did You Know?

The Fairfax at Embassy Row has a long connection to D.C. politics. Here are a few fun facts about the historic property.

■ Al Gore lived here as a child (it was not a hotel at the time).

■ Hillary Clinton held press conferences here when she was running for president.

■ The Steinway piano in the lounge was a gift from the Kennedy family.

■ Nancy Reagan was a Jockey Club regular (she liked the corner table) and back in the day had a chicken salad named for her.

■ The Jockey Club opened for business in 1961 on the day John F. Kennedy took the presidential oath of office.

$$
HOTEL

Comfort Inn Downtown D.C. The location near the Washington Convention Center makes this a popular choice for business travelers, while rooms with pull-out couches and attractive rates appeal to families. **Pros:** fresh cookies at check-in; pleasant staff; excellent breakfast. **Cons:** some street noise at night; a bit out of the way. $ *Rooms from: $250* ⊠ *1201 13th St. NW, Logan Circle* ☎ *202/682–5300* ⊕ *www. comfortinn.com* ⤳ *100 rooms* ⦿| *Breakfast* Ⓜ *McPherson Sq.* ✛ *1:H5.*

$$
HOTEL
FAMILY

DoubleTree by Hilton Hotel Washington, D.C. Centrally located at the crossroads of Downtown, Adams Morgan, and Dupont Circle, with their host of nightlife options, these spacious guest rooms will provide you with comfortable beds and well-equipped workstations. **Pros:** child-friendly; good location just off Scott Circle and near White House; newly renovated rooms. **Cons:** no pool; small bathrooms; showing signs of wear and tear; limited street parking. $ *Rooms from: $280* ⊠ *1515 Rhode Island Ave. NW, Logan Circle* ☎ *202/785–2000, 800/222–8733* ⊕ *www.washington.doubletree.com* ⤳ *220 rooms, 9 suites* ⦿| *No meals* Ⓜ *Dupont Circle* ✛ *1:G4.*

$$$$
HOTEL
Fodor's Choice
★

The Dupont Circle Hotel. With its contemporary furniture, sleek color scheme, and clean lines, the Dupont pulls off *Mad Men* chic without so much as a hint of kitsch. **Pros:** right on Dupont Circle; especially luxurious rooms on concierge level. **Cons:** traffic and noise on Dupont Circle; some guest rooms are on the small side; limited closet space. $ *Rooms from: $440* ⊠ *1500 New Hampshire Ave. NW, Dupont Circle* ☎ *202/483–6000, 800/423–6953* ⊕ *www.doylecollection.com/dupont* ⤳ *295 rooms, 32 suites* ⦿| *No meals* Ⓜ *Dupont Circle* ✛ *1:F4.*

$$
B&B/INN
Fodor's Choice
★

Embassy Circle Guest House. Owners Laura and Raymond Saba have lovingly restored this former embassy, transforming it into a warm and friendly home away from home. **Pros:** lovely hosts; personal service; good location; laundry services. **Cons:** no bathtubs; too intimate for some. $ *Rooms from: $280* ⊠ *2224 R St. NW, Dupont Circle* ☎ *202/232–7744, 877/232–7744* ⊕ *www.dcinns.com* ⤳ *11 rooms* ⦿| *Breakfast* Ⓜ *Dupont Circle* ✛ *1:D3.*

$$$ HOTEL **The Fairfax at Embassy Row.** Light-filled hallways, invitingly bright guest rooms, soft bed linens, marble baths, and impeccable service make this hotel, formerly Al Gore's childhood home *(⇨ see The Fairfax at Embassy Row: Did You Know?)*, a bastion of comfort. **Pros:** historic hotel; large rooms; great location. **Cons:** no pool; challenging street parking. [$] *Rooms from: $305* ✉ *2100 Massachusetts Ave. NW, Dupont Circle* ☎ *202/293–2100, 888/625–5144* 🌐 *www.fairfaxhoteldc.com* 🛏 *259 rooms, 27 suites* 🍴 *No meals* [M] *Dupont Circle* ✣ *1:E4.*

$$$ HOTEL FAMILY **Homewood Suites by Hilton, Washington.** Suites with kitchens, a free grocery-shopping service, and complimentary dinner buffet Monday through Thursday make this a popular choice for tourists, but the large family room–style lobby may well also be abuzz with people in suits preparing presentations. **Pros:** roomy suites; reduced weekend rates; breakfast included. **Cons:** no pool; difficult street parking; 10 minutes to Metro. [$] *Rooms from: $359* ✉ *1475 Massachusetts Ave. NW, Logan Circle* ☎ *202/265–8000* 🌐 *www.homewoodsuites.com* 🛏 *175 suites* 🍴 *Breakfast* [M] *McPherson Sq.* ✣ *1:H5.*

$$$ HOTEL **Hotel Helix.** A hip vibe prevails in these contemporary-style guest quarters with flat screens, colorful furnishings, and huge photos of surfing scenes and pop-culture icons ranging from Little Richard to Jackie O. **Pros:** funky feel; excellent service; afternoon champagne "Bubbly Hour"; pet friendly and allows large dogs. **Cons:** a schlep to the Metro; some rooms are small; no pool; small gym. [$] *Rooms from: $340* ✉ *1430 Rhode Island Ave. NW, Logan Circle* ☎ *202/462–9001, 866/508–0658* 🌐 *www.hotelhelix.com* 🛏 *160 rooms, 18 suites* 🍴 *No meals* [M] *McPherson Sq.* ✣ *1:H4.*

$$$ HOTEL **Hotel Madera.** Located just south of a vibrant Dupont Circle, this tranquil hotel provides the perfect respite after an evening restaurant and club hopping along P Street and Connecticut Avenue. **Pros:** fun place to stay; convenient to Metro, restaurants, and clubs; friendly staff. **Cons:** no pool or gym; small bathrooms. [$] *Rooms from: $309* ✉ *1310 New Hampshire Ave. NW, Dupont Circle* ☎ *202/296–7600, 800/430–1202* 🌐 *www.hotelmadera.com* 🛏 *82 rooms* 🍴 *No meals* [M] *Dupont Circle* ✣ *1:E4.*

$$ HOTEL **Hotel Rouge.** You'll be seeing red and loving it. Rooms are a sleek postmodern tribute to the color, from the red platform beds to the red velvet curtains, offset with chic gray and white accent pieces. **Pros:** gay-friendly vibe; good location near two Metro stations. **Cons:** no pool; the scene is not for everyone; not ideal for young children. [$] *Rooms from: $250* ✉ *1315 16th St. NW, Dupont Circle* ☎ *202/232–8000, 800/738–1202* 🌐 *www.rougehotel.com* 🛏 *137 rooms* 🍴 *No meals* [M] *Dupont Circle* ✣ *1:G4.*

$$$ B&B/INN **Mansion on O Street.** Rock 'n' roll palace meets urban thrift shop in this unique guesthouse, a scramble of five connected townhouses crammed with art, kitsch, and everything in between—it's the most unusual sleep in town. **Pros:** one-of-a-kind; serious about privacy; glamorous common areas; sumptuous buffets. **Cons:** layout makes for many dark rooms; eccentric staff and service. [$] *Rooms from: $380* ✉ *2020 O St. NW, Dupont Circle* ☎ *202/496–2020* 🌐 *www.omansion.com* 🛏 *18 rooms, 11 suites* 🍴 *Breakfast* [M] *Dupont Circle* ✣ *1:E4.*

$$$
HOTEL
Fodor'sChoice
★

⚏ **Palomar, Washington, D.C.** Aside from the hard-to-beat location, these muted, chocolate-beige rooms are some of the largest in town and are decorated with cool animal prints (think tiger-striped robes, crocodile-patterned carpets, and faux-lynx throws) and plush purple and fuchsia furnishings. **Pros:** spacious rooms; outdoor pool; good for pet owners. **Cons:** busy public areas get crowded. Ⓢ *Rooms from: $300* ✉ *2121 P St. NW, Dupont Circle* ☎ *202/448–1800* ⊕ *www.hotelpalomar-dc.com* ⤢ *315 rooms, 20 suites* ⦿ *No meals* Ⓜ *Dupont Circle* ✛ *1:E4.*

$$
HOTEL
FAMILY

⚏ **The Quincy.** It's good for business guests too, but if you're traveling with kids, this city-center retreat could really fit the bill. Kids (and the kid inside you) will certainly get a kick out of the hotel's game library, and the studio apartment–style rooms with kitchenettes are family friendly. **Pros:** central location; convenient to Metro; lower weekend rates; pet-friendly. **Cons:** complaints of street noise; much of the area shuts down at end of the workday; no pool or gym (but free use of facility nearby). Ⓢ *Rooms from: $249* ✉ *1823 L St. NW, Dupont Circle* ☎ *202/223–4320, 800/424–2970* ⊕ *www.thequincy.com* ⤢ *100 suites* ⦿ *No meals* Ⓜ *Farragut N or Farragut W* ✛ *1:F5.*

$$$
HOTEL
FAMILY

⚏ **Residence Inn Washington, D.C./Dupont Circle.** It's remarkable that a commercial chain can feel so cozy—a small fireplace sitting room is right off the lobby, kitchens come stocked with everything you need, and sleeper sofas are an added bonus for families looking for more room to spread out. **Pros:** free breakfast; two blocks from Metro; good choice for families. **Cons:** chain-hotel rooms; small gym; no pool. Ⓢ *Rooms from: $380* ✉ *2120 P St. NW, Dupont Circle* ☎ *202/466–6800, 800/331–3131* ⊕ *www.marriott.com/wasri* ⤢ *107 suites* ⦿ *Breakfast* Ⓜ *Dupont Circle* ✛ *1:E4.*

$$
B&B/INN
Fodor'sChoice
★

⚏ **Swann House.** You'll be hard-pressed to find a more charming inn or hosts more delightful than innkeeper Rick Verkler and his staff. **Pros:** perfect location; beautiful, immaculate, and lavish rooms; fireplaces in winter, a pool in summer. **Cons:** intimate atmosphere not for everyone; less expensive rooms are small. Ⓢ *Rooms from: $250* ✉ *1808 New Hampshire Ave. NW, Dupont Circle* ☎ *202/265–4414* ⊕ *www.swannhouse.com* ⤢ *9 rooms, 4 suites* ⦿ *Breakfast* Ⓜ *Dupont Circle* ✛ *1:F3.*

$$
HOTEL

⚏ **Topaz Hotel.** A marriage of cozy and whimsy lulls visitors with funky purple couches, green-and-white striped walls, plush bedding, and contemporary accent pieces. **Pros:** spacious rooms; good location near two Metro stops; pet friendly; individual feel. **Cons:** funky style not for everyone; no pool. Ⓢ *Rooms from: $275* ✉ *1733 N St. NW, Dupont Circle* ☎ *202/393–3000, 800/775–1202* ⊕ *www.topazhotel.com* ⤢ *91 rooms, 8 suites* ⦿ *No meals* Ⓜ *Dupont Circle* ✛ *1:F4.*

ADAMS MORGAN

This thriving multiethnic community is the place to be for a fabulous assortment of aromas, languages, tastes, and late-night entertainments. A short walk from a nearby hotel or Metro stop gives you salsa, hip-hop, jazz, or the latest in experimental performance art. Its neighborhoods of 19th- and early-20th-century homes and row houses and its proximity to Rock Creek Park provide this bustling area with a tranquil shell.

$ B&B/INN **Adam's Inn.** Live like a local at this cozy, Victorian-style bed-and-breakfast spreading through three residential townhouses near Adams Morgan, the zoo, and Dupont Circle. **Pros:** affordable rates; near Metro; lively neighborhood. **Cons:** tight parking; some shared baths; steps to climb. [$] *Rooms from: $145* ✉ *1746 Lanier Pl. NW, Woodley Park, Adams Morgan* ☎ *202/745–3600, 800/578–6807* 🌐 *www.adamsinn.com* 🛏 *26 rooms* 🍴 *Breakfast* [M] *Woodley Park/Zoo* ✣ *1:F1.*

$$ HOTEL **The Churchill Hotel.** One of the Historic Hotels of America, this Beaux Arts landmark built in 1906 has spacious guest rooms that are comfortable and elegant, include small work and sitting areas, and many have excellent views. **Pros:** good-size rooms; relaxed and quiet; comfortable walking distance to Adams Morgan and northern Dupont Circle. **Cons:** a busy Connecticut Avenue; older building. [$] *Rooms from: $270* ✉ *1914 Connecticut Ave. NW, Adams Morgan* ☎ *202/797–2000, 800/424–2464* 🌐 *www.thechurchillhotel.com* 🛏 *91 rooms, 82 suites* 🍴 *No meals* [M] *Dupont Circle* ✣ *1:E3.*

$$$ HOTEL **Courtyard Washington, D.C./Dupont Circle.** The standard Courtyard amenities come with a big plus here: some of the newly renovated south-facing rooms on higher floors enjoy fantastic panoramic views of the city that take in the Washington Monument and other historic landmarks through the floor-to-ceiling windows. **Pros:** great views from some rooms; good location for restaurants and shopping; friendly, helpful staff. **Cons:** a busy location on Connecticut Avenue; chain-hotel feel with few unique touches. [$] *Rooms from: $300* ✉ *1900 Connecticut Ave. NW, Adams Morgan* ☎ *202/332–9300* 🌐 *www.marriott.com* 🛏 *146 rooms, 1 suite* 🍴 *Breakfast* [M] *Dupont Circle* ✣ *1:E2.*

$$$ HOTEL **Washington Hilton.** With its range of restaurants, outdoor pool, and fancy new health club, this historic 1965 hotel, at the intersection of Dupont Circle, Adams Morgan, and Woodley Park, is a great place to unwind after a day of business or seeing the sights. **Pros:** great lobby; plenty of services; recent renovations. **Cons:** corporate feel; busy, noisy location. [$] *Rooms from: $299* ✉ *1919 Connecticut Ave. NW, Adams Morgan* ☎ *202/328–2080* 🌐 *www.washington.hilton.com* 🛏 *1,070 rooms, 47 suites* 🍴 *No meals* ✣ *1:E2.*

UPPER NORTHWEST

Whether you travel north through Rock Creek Park on a scenic jaunt, or head up Connecticut Avenue past the National Zoo, or take Wisconsin Avenue starting at the Washington National Cathedral, you see a diverse collection of prosperous neighborhoods with single-family homes, apartment high-rises, and shopping districts. These Upper Northwest communities won't have as many museums or as much history as the other parts of D.C., but they still have plenty of sights, movie theaters, and minimalls.

$$$ HOTEL FAMILY **Embassy Suites Washington D.C.–at Chevy Chase Pavilion.** If you are looking for an easy, family-friendly place to unpack your bags, these spacious two-room suites right at the D.C./Maryland border may be ideal.

LODGING ALTERNATIVES

APARTMENT RENTALS

D.C. is a notoriously transient town, with people hopping on and off the campaign trail at a moment's notice, often listing their apartments in the sublets and long-term rental columns of local newspapers and websites. If you can't stomach the idea of another family vacation with you and the kids squeezed into a single hotel room with no kitchen, or if you are traveling with others, a furnished rental might be for you. Often these rentals wind up saving you money, especially on meals and snacks. Be warned, the allure of a full kitchen and room to spread out might get you hooked on apartment rentals for life. Here are some websites to help you find hotel alternatives, short-term apartment rentals, apartment exchanges, and other alternative ways to stay in town.

vrbo.com

thehill.com/resources/classifieds

militarybyowner.com

dcdigs.com

cyberrentals.com

International Agents Hideaways International. An annual membership fee of $195 provides access to listings around the world. ⊠ *767 Islington St., Portsmouth, New Hampshire* ☏ *603/430–4433, 800/843–4433* ⊕ *www.hideaways.com.*

Rental Listings Washington CityPaper (⊕ *www.washingtoncitypaper.com*). **Washington Post** (⊕ *www.washingtonpost.com*).

BED-AND-BREAKFASTS

Bed and Breakfast DC. This well-run organization handles about 45 different properties in the area, from reasonably priced accommodations in small guesthouses and bed-and-breakfasts to short- and long-term rentals in private homes. ⊠ *1339 14th St. NW, Downtown* ☏ *877/893–3233* ⊕ *www.bedandbreakfastdc.com.*

HOME EXCHANGES

If you would like to exchange your home for someone else's, join a home-exchange organization, which will send you its updated listings of available exchanges for a year and include your own listing in at least one of them. It's up to you to make specific arrangements.

Exchange Clubs HomeLink International. Established in 1953, this organization helps travelers arrange to exchange houses in 80 countries around the world and in the United States. Members don't pay to stay, but the fee is $130 for a listing published in a directory and on the website. ☏ *800/638–3841* ⊕ *www.homelink.org.* **Intervac U.S.** Families, singles, and retired people can get help planning vacations by exchanging homes with other members throughout the world; $199.99 yearly for a listing, online access, and a catalog; $99.99 without catalog. Free trial memberships are available. ☏ *800/756–4663* ⊕ *www.intervacus.com.*

Pros: eco- and family-friendly; close to Metro; updated guest rooms. **Cons:** small bathrooms; chain feel. $ *Rooms from: $340* ✉ *4300 Military Rd., Upper Northwest* ☎ *202/362–9300, 800/760–6120* ⊕ *www. embassysuitesdcmetro.com* ⤴ *198 suites* ⦿ *Breakfast* Ⓜ *Friendship Heights* ✛ *1:A1.*

$$
HOTEL
FAMILY
Fodor'sChoice
★

⊡ **Omni Shoreham Hotel.** The venue of inaugural balls since its opening in 1930, this elegant landmark overlooking Rock Creek Park has welcomed heads of state and celebs like the Beatles, and is still luring guests with light-filled guest rooms. **Pros:** historic property; great pool and sundeck; good views from many rooms; close to Metro. **Cons:** not Downtown; noisy at times; extremely large. $ *Rooms from: $275* ✉ *2500 Calvert St. NW, Woodley Park, Upper Northwest* ☎ *202/234–0700, 800/834–6664* ⊕ *www.omnihotels.com* ⤴ *836 rooms, 16 suites* ⦿ *No meals* Ⓜ *Woodley Park/Zoo* ✛ *1:C1.*

$$
HOTEL

⊡ **Savoy Suites Hotel.** Be the Vice President's neighbor in the heart of Embassy Row, in a traditional, classic style room, with a nice view of the city. **Pros:** near Georgetown; enthusiastic service; spacious rooms. **Cons:** distance from Metro and Downtown; far from sightseeing; older hotel. $ *Rooms from: $250* ✉ *2505 Wisconsin Ave. NW, Glover Park, Upper Northwest* ☎ *202/337–9700* ⊕ *www.savoysuites.com* ⤴ *150 rooms* ⦿ *No meals* Ⓜ *Woodley Park* ✛ *1:A1.*

$$$
HOTEL
FAMILY

⊡ **Washington Marriott Wardman Park.** In a pleasant neighborhood, this is a good choice for families—kids will love the outdoor pool and the proximity to the pandas at the zoo—and is popular with groups. **Pros:** on top of Metro; light-filled sundeck and pool; pretty residential neighborhood with restaurants; some city views. **Cons:** busy and hectic public areas; poor soundproofing; massive; many groups; a bit worn. $ *Rooms from: $330* ✉ *2660 Woodley Rd. NW, Woodley Park, Upper Northwest* ☎ *202/328–2000, 800/228–9290* ⊕ *www.marriott.com* ⤴ *1,175 rooms, 125 suites* ⦿ *No meals* Ⓜ *Woodley Park/Zoo* ✛ *1:D2.*

$$
B&B/INN
Fodor'sChoice
★

⊡ **Woodley Park Guest House.** Experience the height of hospitality at this warm, peaceful bed-and-breakfast on a quiet residential street near the zoo. **Pros:** close to Metro; near the zoo; excellent breakfast. **Cons:** a Metro ride away from Downtown; some shared baths; communal breakfast table doesn't suit everyone; limited privacy. $ *Rooms from: $215* ✉ *2647 Woodley Rd. NW, Woodley Park, Upper Northwest* ☎ *202/667–0218, 866/667–0218* ⊕ *www.dcinns.com* ⤴ *13 rooms* ⦿ *Breakfast* Ⓜ *Woodley Park/Zoo* ✛ *1:D2.*

SUBURBAN MARYLAND

Although you won't find too many sights in these inner suburbs, both downtown Bethesda and downtown Silver Spring offer a plethora of unique eating and shopping possibilities. With a sprinkle of movie houses and theaters to spice up the surroundings, and their centrally located Metro stops, these rapidly developing neighborhoods are a viable choice for those wanting a wee bit of distance from the urban rush.

$$
HOTEL

⊡ **Bethesda Marriott Suites.** Although the focus here is on business travelers, families enjoy the variety of the spaces and the heated indoor/outdoor pool. **Pros:** excellent service (Mariott headquarters is next door);

7

close to Beltway, shops, and restaurants; free parking; free shuttle to Metro. **Cons:** far from Downtown and Metro; chain hotel. [$] *Rooms from: $230* ✉ *6711 Democracy Blvd., Bethesda* ☎ *301/897–5600* 🌐 *www.marriott.com* 🛏 *272 suites* 🍴 *No meals* [M] *Grosvenor* ✥ *1:A1.*

$$ HOTEL FAMILY Fodor's Choice ★ 🏨 **Courtyard Chevy Chase.** Everything about this chain hotel is bright and shiny, from the sleek lobby that features "media pods" for quiet work sessions to good-size, stylish, scarlet and amber rooms with tree motifs, all equipped with high-tech amenities. **Pros:** close to Metro, shopping, and restaurants; outdoor pool; good for business travelers. **Cons:** a distance from Downtown; chain feel. [$] *Rooms from: $229* ✉ *5520 Wisconsin Ave., Chevy Chase* ☎ *301/656–1500* 🌐 *www.marriott.com* 🛏 *225 rooms, 1 suite* 🍴 *Breakfast* [M] *Friendship Hts.* ✥ *1:A1*

$$ HOTEL 🏨 **Doubletree Hotel Bethesda.** Everything here is geared to business: larger-than-typical guest rooms equipped with firm, comfortable beds and ample working space include amenities such as free morning newspapers and free shuttles to the Metro, the National Institutes of Health, and the Naval Medical Center. **Pros:** rooftop pool; hypoallergenic rooms; good value. **Cons:** outside the city; far from major attractions; fee for parking; a bit of a walk to Metro. [$] *Rooms from: $235* ✉ *8120 Wisconsin Ave., Bethesda* ☎ *301/652–2000* 🌐 *www.doubletreebethesda.com* 🛏 *269 rooms, 7 suites* 🍴 *No meals* [M] *Bethesda* ✥ *1:A1.*

$$ HOTEL 🏨 **Residence Inn Bethesda Downtown.** If you're looking for an affordable home away from home, these studios and one- and two-bedroom suites all come with fully equipped kitchens with a standard-size refrigerator and dishwasher, plates, and utensils. **Pros:** dozens of restaurants within walking distance; rooftop pool; walk to Metro; complimentary dinner some nights. **Cons:** far from monuments; $20-a-day valet parking fee; chain-hotel feel. [$] *Rooms from: $270* ✉ *7335 Wisconsin Ave., Bethesda* ☎ *301/718–0200, 800/331–3131* 🌐 *www.marriott.com* 🛏 *187 suites* 🍴 *Breakfast* [M] *Bethesda* ✥ *1:A1.*

SUBURBAN VIRGINIA

Across the Potomac and Anacostia rivers, along Metro's Blue Line, you'll find Old Town Alexandria and its historic port; Pentagon City and its Fashion Centre Mall, Crystal City and underground network of corridors linking offices and shops to high-rise apartments; and Rosslyn, a former ferry landing turned transportation hub for rail, car, and bike. These thriving communities might not offer as much as D.C. proper, but they have everything the weary traveler might need in cuisine and fun entertainment.

$$ HOTEL 🏨 **Holiday Inn Arlington at Ballston.** While rooms are typical chain-style, you can get into Washington quickly via the Metro, and Arlington National Cemetery and the Iwo Jima Memorial are nearby. **Pros:** refrigerators in rooms; near shopping mall and restaurants; five-minute walk from Metro. **Cons:** outside the city; chain-hotel feel. [$] *Rooms from: $235* ✉ *4610 N. Fairfax Dr., Arlington* ☎ *703/243–9800* 🌐 *www.hiarlington.com* 🛏 *221 rooms, 2 suites* 🍴 *No meals* [M] *Ballston* ✥ *1:A6.*

$$ HOTEL 🏨 **Hyatt Arlington.** If you're feeling energetic, it's just a five-minute walk to Georgetown over Key Bridge from this solid over-the-Potomac

choice; but if energy is lacking, the hotel is just across from the Metro. **Pros:** across from Metro; fitness center; well-maintained. **Cons:** outside the city; dull neighborhood; not great for kids; no pool. $ *Rooms from: $259* ✉ *1325 Wilson Blvd., Rosslyn, Arlington* ☎ *703/525–1234, 800/908–4790* ⊕ *www.arlington.hyatt.com* ☎ *312 rooms, 5 suites* ⦿ *No meals* Ⓜ *Rossyln* ✢ *1:A6.*

$$

HOTEL

⌖ **Key Bridge Marriott.** Camera-ready views and proximity to Georgetown, which is just across Key Bridge, may help you overlook the '60s style and small rooms here. **Pros:** near the Metro; nice pool. **Cons:** outside the city; area dull at night; chain-hotel ambience. $ *Rooms from: $239* ✉ *1401 Lee Hwy., Rosslyn, Arlington* ☎ *703/524–6400, 800/228–9290* ⊕ *www.marriott.com* ☎ *571 rooms, 11 suites* ⦿ *No meals* Ⓜ *Rosslyn* ✢ *1:A6.*

$$

HOTEL

FAMILY

Fodor's Choice

★

⌖ **Residence Inn Arlington Pentagon City.** The view across the Potomac of the D.C. skyline and the monuments is magnificent from these suites in a high-rise adjacent to the Pentagon and two blocks from The Fashion Centre at Pentagon City. **Pros:** family-friendly; indoor pool; easy walk to Metro; airport shuttle. **Cons:** parking fee; neighborhood dead at night. $ *Rooms from: $275* ✉ *550 Army Navy Dr., Arlington* ☎ *703/413–6630, 800/331–3131* ⊕ *www.marriott.com* ☎ *299 suites* ⦿ *Breakfast* Ⓜ *Pentagon City* ✢ *1:A6.*

$$$$

HOTEL

⌖ **The Ritz-Carlton Pentagon City.** The feel is more contemporary and casually chic than generally associated with this luxury chain, and it's convenient for both the Ronald Reagan National Airport, a short cab ride away, and downtown D.C. via the Metro. **Pros:** indoor walk to Metro; indoor pool; connected to shops and restaurants; fitness center. **Cons:** outside D.C.; lots of hidden fees, less ritzy than other Ritz properties; expensive, given the location. $ *Rooms from: $469* ✉ *1250 S. Hayes St., Arlington* ☎ *703/415–5000, 800/241–3333* ⊕ *www.ritzcarlton. com/PentagonCity* ☎ *351 rooms, 15 suites* ⦿ *No meals* Ⓜ *Pentagon City* ✢ *1:A6.*

7

NIGHTLIFE

Updated by
Will O'Bryan

From buttoned-down political appointees who've just arrived to laid-back folks who've lived here their whole lives, Washingtonians are always looking for a place to relax. And they have plenty of options when they head out for a night on the town. Most places are clustered in several key neighborhoods, making a night of barhopping relatively easy.

Georgetown's dozens of bars, nightclubs, and restaurants radiate from the intersection of Wisconsin and M streets, attracting crowds that include older adults and college students. Many restaurants here turn into bars after the dinner crowd leaves. Georgetown is one of the safest neighborhoods in D.C., with a large police presence on weekends.

Those seeking a younger and less inhibited nightlife may prefer the 18th Street strip in Adams Morgan, between Columbia Road and Florida Avenue, which offers a wide variety of places for dancing, drinking, eating, and everything else you can imagine. The best part of Adams Morgan is that there are so many bars and clubs around 18th Street that if you don't like one, there's another next door. At night the streets are so crowded you will have trouble weaving your way through the swarms of revelers. AdMo, as it's affectionately called, is best known as a drinking hot spot, but there are some underappreciated restaurants that make the strip worth the trip for those in search of a good meal.

The U Street Corridor (U Street NW between 9th and 17th streets NW), historically D.C.'s hippest neighborhood and a regular stop for jazz greats, has undergone a revival and is now the hottest spot in town, with bars that appeal to all types. Down 14th Street you will also find an explosion of new bars and restaurants, spilling revelers out on the street on weekends. Wine bars, dive bars, hipster bars, gastropubs, and dance clubs make for a full night out.

Ibiza draws a dance crowd to Northeast D.C., where the capital's construction boom continues. Other hot spots include Capitol Hill and Downtown. The stretch of Pennsylvania Avenue between 2nd and 4th streets has a half-dozen bars. And thanks to massive redevelopment, Penn Quarter/Chinatown is burgeoning with squeaky-clean new bars and music venues orbiting the Verizon Center and Gallery Place. The newest center of gravity for D.C. nightlife is the burgeoning H Street Corridor, still tricky to get to, but home to some of the city's most dynamic venues.

PLANNING

ADMISSION

Most nightlife venues in D.C. have cover charges for bands and DJs, especially those performing on Friday and Saturday. Expect to pay from $10 to $20 for most dance clubs. Jazz and comedy clubs often have higher cover charges along with drink minimums.

DRESS CODE

Despite how formally they might have to dress during the week, on the weekend Washingtonians really let their hair down. Although many of the high-end clubs require you to "dress to impress," including dress shoes for men, most bars and pubs are slightly more casual. This is especially true during the summer, when shorts can be considered acceptable on an oppressively humid night.

HOURS

Last call in D.C. is 2 am, and most bars and clubs close by 3 am on the weekend and between midnight and 2 am during the week. The exceptions are after-hours dance clubs and bars with kitchens that stay open late.

NIGHTLIFE INFORMATION

To survey the local scene, consult Friday's "Weekend" section in the *Washington Post* and the free weekly *Washington CityPaper*. A terrific website (with an accompanying cell-phone app) for local happenings is the *Post*'s Going Out Guide (⊕ *www.washingtonpost.com/gog*). The free publications *Metro Weekly* and *Washington Blade* offer insights on LGBT nightlife. Local blog DCist (⊕ *www.dcist.com*) posts daily on D.C. events. It's a good idea to call clubs ahead of time, as last week's punk-rock party might be this week's merengue marathon.

WHITE HOUSE AREA AND FOGGY BOTTOM

The area near the White House and Foggy Bottom once offered a less frantic nightlife environment as the city center emptied out during the weekends. Today, some interesting clubs and restaurants have reenergized the area. Many are near—or in—major hotels, making the area more attractive to the going-out crowd.

WHITE HOUSE AREA

BARS AND LOUNGES

The Hamilton. From the street, it looks like a swanky downtown D.C. restaurant with a high-ceilinged power bar to match. The magic really happens, however, with live shows in The Hamilton's cavernous basement space. Care in equal parts has focused on acoustics, comfort, and

ADAMS MORGAN
18th and Columbia is a nightlife nexus

U STREET CORRIDOR
live rock and jazz, hipster bars

DUPONT CIRCLE AND LOGAN CIRCLE
gay-friendly; trendy clubs

GEORGETOWN
college kids and well-heeled grownups

FOGGY BOTTOM
farmers' market

WHITE HOUSE AREA
more subdued; hotel bars

DOWNTOWN
upscale drinking and dancing

CAPITOL HILL AND NORTHEAST D.C.
the Atlas District is a hotspot for music and dance clubs

Florida Ave.

16th St.

U St.

Columbia Rd.

Florida Ave.

Vermont Ave.

Sheridan Circle

Massachusetts Ave.

New Hampshire Ave.

Dupont Circle

Logan Circle

Rock Creek

Rhode Island Ave.

Connecticut Ave.

Scott Circle

M St.

M St.

Thomas Circle

Whitehurst Fwy.

Washington Circle

Pennsylvania Ave.

K St.

New York Ave.

23rd St.

15th St.

14th St.

Theodore Roosevelt Island

Virginia Ave.

Constitution Ave.

THE MALL

Reflecting Pool

THE MONUMENTS

Independence Ave.

Arlington Memorial Br.

Columbia Island

Tidal Basin

Francis Case Memorial Br.

Washington Canal

Potomac River

VIRGINIA

| 0 | 500 yards |
| 0 | 500 meters |

FIVE GREAT NIGHTLIFE EXPERIENCES

9:30 Club: The best live music venue in D.C., the club showcases new and legendary performers from across the nation.

The Birchmere: Known for bluegrass, the club offers a variety of genres, with something for everybody—from Kelly Willis to Aaron Neville to Tom Rush and Jerry Jeff Walker.

Blues Alley: D.C.'s classiest jazz club is the place to enjoy outstanding performers and Cajun food in an intimate setting.

P.O.V: At the top of the W hotel, the picture-perfect views are matched by the expert cocktails.

Rock and Roll Hotel: Experience the H Street Corridor with locals-in-the-know, while enjoying indie acts and a great dance party.

tiered seating that makes it hard to find a bad seat. For more intimate acts, there is secondary space above the bar-restaurant. ✉ *600 14th St. NW, White House Area* ☎ *202/787–1000* ⊕ *www.thehamiltondc.com* Ⓜ *Metro Center.*

P.O.V. For decades, the perfect way to end a night out in Washington was a trip up to the Sky Tavern on the Hotel Washington's 11th-floor rooftop. The W hotel has replaced the Hotel Washington, and the Sky Tavern has been reincarnated as P.O.V. ("Point of View"), a trendy indoor lounge and outdoor terrace offering a tremendous view over D.C.'s low skyline. Enjoy the unique view of the Washington Monument and the White House while enjoying a cocktail or a bite from Jean-Georges Vongerichten's menu. While the view here is no secret, meaning waits are common, P.O.V. does take reservations. Popping by in the late afternoon may be a more relaxed option. ■**TIP→** After 7 pm, the venue only allows 21 and older. ✉ *515 15 St. NW, White House Area* ☎ *202/661–2400* ⊕ *www.pointofviewdc.com* Ⓜ *McPherson Sq.*

DANCE CLUBS

Science Club. Quiet and relaxed early in the evening, this nerd-chic-inspired, upscale dive starts with a mellow happy hour that runs weekdays from 4 until 8 pm, and then gets loud and crowded after 10 pm. DJs spin on two floors, and music styles change depending on the night. ✉ *1136 19th St. NW, White House Area* ☎ *202/775–0747* ⊕ *www.scienceclubdc.com* Ⓜ *Farragut W.*

FOGGY BOTTOM

DANCE CLUBS

Eden. This four-floor hot spot near the White House attracts Washington celebrities, foreign visitors, and the sophisticated elite. The club hosts a variety of local and big-name DJs and is famous for its rooftop deck, attracting big crowds in the summer. Bottle service is available. ✉ *1716 I St. NW, Foggy Bottom* ☎ *202/785–0270* ⊕ *www.edendc.com* Ⓜ *Farragut W.*

CAPITOL HILL AND NORTHEAST D.C.

Seemingly overnight, Capitol Hill has become a hot location. Great new restaurants and bars match time-tested steadies, allowing nighttime crowds to enjoy food from celebrity chefs and then dance away the night or relax in a casual dive bar. A four-block area in the H Street Corridor, known as the Atlas District, is home to some great music venues and plenty of D.C.'s new hipster bars. Keep in mind, though, that the H Street area is not easily accessed by public transport, so be ready to take a cab.

Northeast's industrial environment can be intimidating, and caution is warranted for safety reasons. Make use of the premium parking—for about $20—that will put you close to the entrance. Even parking a few blocks away on neighborhood streets is risky at night. Taxis are another good option.

CAPITOL HILL

BARS AND LOUNGES

Dubliner. This Washington institution offers cozy paneled rooms, rich pints of Guinness and other authentic fare. It's especially popular with Capitol Hill staffers and Georgetown law students. While offering live Irish music seven nights a week, this charming spot never charges a cover, save for St. Patrick's Day. ⊠ *4 F St. NW, Capitol Hill* ☎ *202/737–3773* ⊕ *www.dublinerdc.com* Ⓜ *Union Station.*

Phase One. Since 1970 this legendary lesbian club has attracted an eclectic, laid-back clientele of all ages. The small dance floor and pool tables make it an intimate and comfortable spot, although sometimes the place gets very crowded. Cash only, but there's an on-site ATM. ⊠ *525 8th St. SE, Capitol Hill* ☎ *202/544–6831* ⊕ *www.phaseonedc. com* Ⓜ *Eastern Market.*

The Pour House. This neighborhood sports bar is a place to grab some brewskies and watch a game with friends. Or head to the basement for live-action sports, with skeeball, Wii and shuffleboard. On the second floor, the Top of the Hill lounge hits a more subdued note. ⊠ *319 Pennsylvania Ave. SE, Capitol Hill* ☎ *202/546–0779* ⊕ *www.pourhousedc. com* Ⓜ *Capitol S.*

Sona Creamery and Wine Bar. Along Pennsylvania Avenue, below the looming Capitol, there's a venue that takes wine and cheese at least as seriously as those nearby legislators take lawmaking. Husband-and-wife team Conan and Genevieve O'Sullivan have created the perfect spot for those wanting to learn more about wine—particularly from the Northwest—or cheese, boasting the city's sole on-site creamery. Or simply enjoy an evening in the friendly, uncluttered and calm space with insightful pairings and a quiet that allows for easy conversation. ⊠ *660 Pennsylvania Ave. SE, Capitol Hill* ☎ *202/758–3556* ⊕ *www. sonacreamery.com* Ⓜ *Eastern Market.*

MUSIC CLUBS

Mr. Henry's. Opened in 1966, this laid-back club is the last holdout of a once-thriving live-music scene on Capitol Hill. Roberta Flack got her start in the upstairs performance space, where a dozen or so tables are scattered around the wood-paneled room. There's never a cover. ✉ *601 Pennsylvania Ave. SE, Capitol Hill* ☎ *202/546–8412* ⊕ *www. mrhenrysrestaurant.com* Ⓜ *Eastern Market.*

NORTHEAST D.C.

BARS AND LOUNGES

Biergartenhaus. Step off of H Street and into a boisterous bit of Bavaria. There might be football on TV, but that's not enough to break the spell of a place so genuinely Germanic. With about a dozen draughts on offer, along with other authentic specialties—apfel schnapps?—and a full bar, there's something for everyone, including a variety of spaces. Get cozy inside, or head for the courtyard, heated in winter. In pleasant weather, the second-story terrace also packs them in. Best accessed by taxi. ✉ *1355 H St. NE, Northeast D.C.* ☎ *202/388-4085* ⊕ *www. biergartenhaus.com.*

Granville Moore's. Beer and mussels: The appeal is that simple, and they're that satisfying. The Belgian-themed gastropub has its own "beverage director" and one of the largest selections of beer, from ilsners to Flemish reds, in Washington. Offerings in this cozy spot go beyond mussels, and the chef has been featured on the Food Network. The narrow, rustic bars on two floors attract more than a dinner crowd. ✉ *1238 H St. NE, Northeast D.C.* ☎ *202/399-2546* ⊕ *www.granvillemoores. com* Ⓜ *Union Station.*

H Street Country Club. The only D.C. bar to offer indoor miniature golf, Big Buck Hunter, and skeeball has a friendly, laid-back vibe. Margaritas, fish tacos and an impressive tequila list round out the fun mix at this popular nightspot. Big-screen sports line the walls downstairs, but you can usually catch a breath of fresh air on the roof deck. ✉ *1335 H St. NE, Northeast D.C.* ☎ *202/399-4722* ⊕ *www.thehstreetcountryclub. com* Ⓜ *Union Station.*

DANCE CLUBS

Ibiza. One of D.C.'s most popular dance clubs is a great space, but only if you like your dance floor crowded—which it tends to be, despite the cavernous space and seven bars. When you need a breath of fresh air, enjoy the rooftop deck. Saturday is 18-and-over night, which can attract a younger crowd; expect long lines. Dress code calls for fashionable attire, no athletic wear. DJs and special guests are announced a week in advance on the radio and online. ✉ *1222 1st St. NE, Northeast D.C.* ☎ *888/424-9232* ⊕ *www.ibizadc.com* Ⓜ *New York Ave./Florida Ave./ Gallaudet U.*

MUSIC CLUBS

HR-57. This place is all about the music. Named after a congressional resolution proclaiming jazz a "rare and valuable national treasure," HR-57 isn't just a club, it's a nonprofit cultural center. It spotlights musicians based in the D.C. area, many of whom have national followings. Enjoy the Caribbean menu anytime, or enjoy it with your own wine ($7 per person corkage) during the weeknight jam sessions by local artists. Big names sometimes join in on the weekends. The warm and relaxed atmosphere makes this place well worth a visit. ⊠ *1007 H St. NE, Northeast D.C.* ☎ *202/253–0044* ⊕ *www.hr57.org* Ⓜ *Union Station.*

Fodor'sChoice ★ **Rock and Roll Hotel.** A former funeral home hosts some of the nation's best indie acts. Live bands are in the main room and DJs spin on the second floor, called the Hotel Bar, hosting some of the most enthusiastic dance parties in town—and the dance floors can get very crowded. The rooftop bar is festive, too.

LIVE MUSIC INFO

D.C. Blues Society. This clearinghouse for information on upcoming shows, festivals, and jam sessions in the metropolitan area also publishes a monthly newsletter and welcomes volunteers. ⊕ *www.dcblues.org.*

Folklore Society of Greater Washington. At more than 200 events a year, the society presents folk and traditional musicians and dancers from all over the country. Venues around the D.C. area host events ranging from contra dancing to storytelling to open group singing. ☎ *202/546–2228* ⊕ *www.fsgw.org.*

Notable acts include the Walkmen, Lost in the Trees, and Juliette and the Licks. It's a 15-block walk from the Union Station metro and, in this still-up-and-coming area, it's best to take a taxi. ⊠ *1353 H St. NE, Northeast D.C.* ☎ *202/388–7625* ⊕ *www.rockandrollhoteldc.com* Ⓜ *Union Station.*

DOWNTOWN

You'll find plenty of bars and lounges in the Downtown area, which has been wonderfully revitalized, compared to years past. Development around Chinatown and the Verizon Center has turned this into a lively neighborhood, especially when there's a sports or musical event at the arena. A few blocks south, the formerly quiet Penn Quarter is seeing larger evening crowds, thanks to the opening of several terrific new restaurants, cafés, bars, and a world-class theater scene. Conveniently, especially if you plan to imbibe, you can easily get to Downtown on the Metro, exiting at the Archives/Navy Memorial/Penn Quarter station (Green and Yellow lines) or at the Gallery Place/Chinatown stop (Green, Yellow, and Red lines).

BARS AND LOUNGES

The Passenger. D.C.'s craft cocktail scene has exploded in recent years, and this speakeasy with a frenetic vibe is a magnet for cocktail connoisseurs and food critics alike. No longer the best-kept secret in Washington, the dark and crowded space retains its welcoming vibe. Inside, the intimate Columbia Room provides seating for about a dozen in a private area in the back of the bar for a unique mixology experience— you need a reservation for its two-hour seating, and with its high price tag it's a special-occasion type of place. ⊠ *1021 7th St. NW, Downtown*

☎ *202/393–0220* ⊕ *www.passengerdc.com* Ⓜ *Mount Vernon/Convention Center.*

COMEDY CLUBS

Capitol Steps. Putting the "mock" in democracy, the musical political satire of this group—many of whom are current or former Hill staffers—is presented in the amphitheater of the Ronald Reagan Building every Friday and Saturday at 7:30 pm and occasionally at other spots around town. This Washington classic is fun for the whole family, no matter on which side of the aisle you sit! Tickets are available through Ticketmaster and online. ✉ *Ronald Reagan Bldg. and International Trade Center, 1300 Pennsylvania Ave. NW, Downtown* ☎ *703/683–8330* ⊕ *www. capsteps.com* Ⓜ *Federal Triangle.*

DC Improv. The Improv, as everyone calls it, offers a steady menu of well-known and promising stand-up headliners—recent acts have included Christian Finnegan, Dick Gregory, and Wanda Sykes—as well as a bevy of funny amateurs. ✉ *1140 Connecticut Ave. NW, Downtown* ☎ *202/296–7008* ⊕ *www.dcimprov.com* Ⓜ *Farragut N.*

DANCE CLUBS

The Park at Fourteenth. A high-end crowd includes visiting basketball players and R&B stars, who dance on four levels. The fancy and formal dress code is strictly enforced by the bouncers. You can arrange in advance to get a table or brave the long lines that develop later in the night. ✉ *920 14th St. NW, Downtown* ☎ *202/737–7275* ⊕ *www. park14.com* Ⓜ *McPherson Sq.*

GEORGETOWN

Due to its proximity to the university, weekends (and even weeknights) are a happening affair in Georgetown. A number of bars serve as restaurants by day, until the college and intern crowds take over at night. Although most venues here tend to attract a younger set, the neighborhood still offers many options for patrons over thirty, such as the legendary Blues Alley. There's little parking here, and no easy Metro access, so if you're not staying nearby your best bet is a taxi. In late spring and summer, head to the Washington Harbour for drinks and a riverside stroll.

BARS AND LOUNGES

Degrees. Hidden away inside the Ritz-Carlton hotel, in what was once the Georgetown Incinerator, this modern bar exudes elegance from all corners and is a breath of fresh air in the neighborhood's rather monotone scene. There's an extensive wine and cocktail selection behind the black granite bar and a hip, well-dressed set of patrons in front of it. If there's too much attitude in the bar, head out to the hotel's lovely lobby and sit by the fireplace. This is a perfect pre-movie, post-date, mid-shopping stop. ✉ *Ritz-Carlton, 3100 South St. NW, Georgetown* ☎ *202/912–4100* ⊕ *www.ritzcarlton.com.*

Nick's Riverside Grille. A perch on the Georgetown waterfront affords a great view of the Potomac and, in winter, the ice-skating rink. When the weather's nice, crowds of college students flock to the outdoor tables. The food is fine but the draw is location, location, location. ✉ *3050 K St. NW, Georgetown* ☎ *202/342-3535* ⊕ *www.nicksriver sidegrill.com.*

The Tombs. Visitors to Georgetown University looking for a pint or some pub grub head down the stairs below 1789 restaurant to this traditional, half-century-old collegiate watering hole adorned with rowing paraphernalia and steeped in charming Georgetown boosterism. One block from the main gate, it's the closest bar to campus so it gets crowded with students at night. ✉ *1226 36th St. NW, Georgetown* ☎ *202/337-6668* ⊕ *www.tombs.com.*

EARLY TO BED

During a performance at Georgetown's Blues Alley, the headliner noted that the 8 pm shows at the club sell out, while the later 10 pm shows beg for patrons. She attributed this to the fact that "people in Washington have to get up at 5:30 am every morning and turn on the TV to see what is happening with the world." That remark is close to the truth, and explains D.C.'s sometimes-lackluster nightlife during the workweek.

Tony and Joe's. Right on Georgetown's waterfront, this restaurant has a large outdoor patio where you can enjoy a drink alfresco on a spring or summer evening. The cocktails are a little pricey, but you can't beat the view of the Potomac River and Kennedy Center at night. ✉ *3000 K St. NW, Georgetown* ☎ *202/944-4545* ⊕ *www.tonyandjoes.com.*

MUSIC CLUBS

Fodor'sChoice **Blues Alley.** Head here for a classy evening in an intimate setting, com-
★ plete with great music from well-known performers such as Mose Allison and Wynton Marsalis and outstanding New Orleans–style grub. Expect to pay a cover charge as well as a food or drink minimum. ■ TIP→ You can come for just the show, but those who enjoy a meal get better seats. ✉ *1073 Wisconsin Ave. NW, near M St., Georgetown* ☎ *202/337-4141* ⊕ *www.bluesalley.com* Ⓜ *Foggy Bottom.*

DUPONT CIRCLE AND LOGAN CIRCLE

Dupont Circle is a long-standing weekend hot spot, with numerous bars and lounges for all ages and preferences. Home to some legendary classics, like Russia House and Kramerbooks & Afterwords, the expansion toward Logan Circle has introduced new favorites like Church-Key. P Street, especially between 17th and 14th streets, is Washington's answer to San Francisco's Castro Street, and remains the vibrant focal point of the city's gay and lesbian nightlife scene. And, as Dupont's boom expanded east to Logan, that expansion continues into the Shaw neighborhood, adding a new wonderland of nightlife between the Convention Center and U Street. The Dupont Circle Metro (Red Line) is the western jumping-off point, while the Shaw/Howard University and Mount Vernon Square/7th Street/Convention Center stops (Green and Yellow lines) cover the east.

D.C.'S PARTY ANIMALS: INTERNS

GENERAL DESCRIPTION
Migratory species, aged 16 to 25, present in the region in great abundance in summer.

IDENTIFYING MARKS
Eager expression, drained complexion suggesting a hangover. Can be confused with law students, but interns are almost always spotted in groups of four or more, do not carry books, and wear badges marked *intern*—a dead giveaway. The male is nearly uniform in khakis, blazer, and tie. Female shows greater variety of plumage, but look for sundresses in spring and summer and pearls year-round. They also look about 10 years younger than everyone else.

DIET
A fairly regular daily diet of Starbucks in the morning, Chinese takeout at lunch, and pizza, burritos, and the like in the evening is enriched by many pitchers of draft beer, often consumed in groups.

HABITAT
During the day interns flock with other political species to the Capitol and White House, and are most easily spotted inside these buildings, Republican and Democratic subspecies sometimes intermingling. After hours, they congregate both at bars like **Capitol Lounge** (mostly Republicans) and the **Stetson's** (mostly Democrats), and also farther afield, at **The Tombs** in Georgetown. On weekends, look for interns at **Open City** in Woodley Park, gathering in great numbers to feed on pancakes.

BEHAVIOR
When among their own, Washington interns are known for late-night parties and beer pong. In the presence of other political species (staffers, legislators), behavior is markedly more subdued. Interns are nearly always single while in Washington, and their mating rituals are particularly showy; coupling up between Republican and Democratic subspecies is not unusual, and occasionally interns have been known to pair temporarily with legislators and others.

DUPONT CIRCLE

BARS AND LOUNGES

Fodor's Choice ★ **Eighteenth Street Lounge.** This multilevel space's division into an array of sofa-filled rooms makes an evening at this home away from home for Washington's hipper globalists seem like a chill house party. Jazz musicians often entertain on the top floor of the former mansion, and the luxe back deck, complete with hanging chandeliers, provides summer visitors with two extra bars and a fresh-air dance floor. Fans of ambient house music flock here as it's the home of the ESL record label and the renowned musical duo Thievery Corporation. ■TIP→ The dress code here is strictly enforced by the doorman: no khakis, baseball caps, sneakers, or light-colored jeans. For men: no shorts or open-toed shoes. ⊠ *1212 18th St. NW, Dupont Circle* ☏ *202/466–3922* ⊕ *www.eighteenthstreetlounge.com* Ⓜ *Dupont Circle.*

Black Fox Lounge. Without drawing much attention to itself, this relaxed neighborhood bar with a great Dupont address has an ace up its sleeve: loads of live entertainment. With a tiny stage on the ground floor, a cabaret space below, and rarely a cover charge, it's easy to find yourself stumbling into some piano ballads or a little jazz. Whatever the lineup, Black Fox keeps the mood warm and low-key. ⊠ *1723 Connecticut Ave. NW, Dupont Circle* ☎ *202 1723* ⊕ *www.blackfoxlounge. com* Ⓜ *Dupont Circle.*

Hank's Oyster Bar. A small, sleek and unpretentious nautical-themed bar offers a half-price raw bar after 10 every night of the week, here and at its Capitol Hill location. The bartenders are friendly, giving you tastes of different wines or drinks to try, along with recommendations on the daily catch. Also a neighborhood favorite at its Old Town Alexandria location. ⊠ *1624 Q St. NW, Dupont Circle* ☎ *202/462–4265* ⊕ *www. hanksoysterbar.com* Ⓜ *Dupont Circle.*

JR's Bar & Grill. A popular institution on the 17th Street strip packs in a mostly male, mostly professional gay crowd. Various nights offer showtune singalongs, trivia contests and the like. For the "Sunday Funday" daylong happy hour or any time the federal government shuts down, expect a festive, wall-to-wall crowd in this narrow, window-lined space. ⊠ *1519 17th St. NW, Dupont Circle* ☎ *202/328–0090* ⊕ *www. jrsbar-dc.com* Ⓜ *Dupont Circle.*

Quill. At this *Mad Men* flashback fantasy bar tucked inside the Jefferson Hotel, the drinks are stiff and complicated, while the mood is a quiet celebration of all things civilized. The dimly lit, two-room, wood-paneled Art Deco space provides an intimate atmosphere made even more welcoming by the friendly and expert service of the bartenders. A pianist quietly serenades patrons throughout the evening. Pricey, but worth it. ⊠ *1200 16th St. NW, Dupont Circle* ⊕ *www.jeffersondc.com/ dining-lounge/quill* Ⓜ *Farragut N.*

Russia House Restaurant and Lounge. Transport yourself by sampling vodka flights from an entire menu devoted to Russia's signature spirit. The brooding vibe, bizarre old-world charm, and authentic food might feel kitschy until you see real Eastern European revelers dancing it up late at night in one of the lounges (there are four floors, though they are not all open all the time). While the DJ reigns supreme Saturday night, the live music in the lounge may be preferable for Tatar-esque tippling. ⊠ *1800 Connecticut Ave. NW, Dupont Circle* ☎ *202/234–9433* ⊕ *www.russiahouselounge.com* Ⓜ *Dupont Circle.*

St. Arnold's Mussel Bar on Jefferson. This cozy space in the heart of Dupont is named after the patron saint of brewing, and it's certainly blessed with its choice of hard-to-find Belgian beers. The Belgian theme continues in the menu, and mussels (half-price during happy hour) are prepared in numerous ways. It all makes for a casual evening out or a comfortable happy-hour spot, and the wood-lined basement is sure to transport you to the old world. There is a second location in Cleveland Park. ⊠ *1827 Jefferson Pl. NW, Dupont Circle* ☎ *202/833–1321* ⊕ *www. starnoldsmusselbar.com* Ⓜ *Dupont Circle.*

D.C.'S PARTY ANIMALS: STAFFERS

GENERAL DESCRIPTION
Prolific species endemic to the Washington area; similar species are present in state capitals throughout the country, but the Washington staffer is notably more rapacious. Republican and Democratic subspecies are distinct; Congressional, White House, and departmental varieties are less so, due in part to migration between offices every two to four years.

IDENTIFYING MARKS
BlackBerry or iPhone; security badge, usually worn around neck. Dark suits, bland ties, hair neatly coiffed. Republican subspecies have been harder to find in the past few years and the males have extremely neat hair; Democratic subspecies is younger, with big idealistic eyes.

DIET
The bulk of the staffer's diet is coffee, but it also consumes takeout and martinis. Although staffers are technically omnivores, their actual intake depends on their environment and which other species are present. A staffer may eat lo mein with legislators or lobster with lobbyists, or both, in the same day.

HABITAT
Like other political species, staffers tend to stick close to the Capitol and White House during the day, although they can also be spotted at the **Union Pub** and the **Capital Grille** at lunchtime. After hours, the best places to watch Republican staffers are **Bullfeathers, Tune Inn,** and **Tortilla Coast,** all on the Hill. Democratic staffers now enjoying proximity to the White House can be found at **Le Bar** at the **Sofitel Hotel,** and **BlackFinn. George** in Georgetown is also popular among both species, for those with the financial means. As populations of GOP and Democratic staffers shift, turf wars sometimes erupt; observe Democratic staffers moving in on Republican territory at the **Capitol Lounge** on the Hill, and the reverse at **Stetson's,** in Adams Morgan

BEHAVIOR
Remarkably intelligent and adaptable, though notoriously young, staffers are some of Washington's most interesting species to observe. It is not uncommon to observe a staffer simultaneously sending email, talking on a cell phone, and ordering in a restaurant or bar (the scientific name for this behavior is formulating policy).

DANCE CLUBS

Cafe Citron. Mojitos are the specialty at this Latin bar and dance club, where the salsa, merengue, bachata, and Latin rock continues late into the night. With two floors to get your groove on, Citron encourages revelers to dance on the tables and take a whirl at the bongos. The sign above the bar sets the tone: "Be Nice Or Go Away." Free salsa lessons offered weekly. ✉ *1343 Connecticut Ave. NW, Dupont Circle* ☎ *202/530–8844* ⊕ *www.cafecitrondc.com* Ⓜ *Dupont Circle.*

Cobalt. Popular among the gay and lesbian crowd, this venue anchors the 17th Street strip with three distinct floors: At the bottom, it's the Level One restaurant, topped by the cool 30 Degrees lounge, and crowned by the booming dance club, Cobalt. The weekends get wild on the top floor with guest DJs, celebrity drag queens and a monthly ladies night. ✉ *1639 R St. NW, Dupont Circle* ☎ *202/232–4416* ⊕ *www.cobaltdc. com* Ⓜ *Dupont Circle.*

LOGAN CIRCLE

BARS AND LOUNGES

A&D Neighborhood Bar. From the street, A&D seems camouflaged with a front window brimming with houseplants and an old bicycle. Don't be fooled. Inside, you'll find a friendly bar serving a young, fashionably relaxed crowd some of the best cocktails in town. Happy hour starts off mellow, but the place is often jumping in the later hours. And while other trendy spots are still offering the game on TV, A&D's only sports action is the foosball table in the back room. If you're hungry, bring in a sandwich from the gourmet Sundevich in the adjacent alley. Closed Sunday. ✉ *1314 9th St. NW, Shaw* ☎ *202/290–1804* ⊕ *www.andbardc. com* Ⓜ *Mt. Vernon Sq./Convention Center.*

Churchkey. There's an astounding selection of beers here—more than 500 varieties from more than 30 countries, including 50 beers on tap and exclusive draught and cask ales. There's even a Beer Director on staff. If you have trouble making a choice, bartenders will offer you 4-ounce tasters. The urban-vintage vibe balances unassuming and pretentious in pretty much equal measure, reflected in a menu that ranges from tater tots through artisan cheeses to porkbelly carbonara. The size of the weekend crowds attests to the popularity of this beer mecca. ✉ *1337 14th St. NW, Logan Circle* ☎ *202/567–2576* ⊕ *www.churchkeydc.com* Ⓜ *McPherson Sq.*

Dacha. Sometimes the feng shui is just right. Dacha is one of those times. Part pop-up, all beer garden, this German expression with a bit of Russian flavor is the transformation of a nondescript corner into an outdoor spot locals love. Afternoon and night, it's often standing-room only as beer lovers—beer, German and otherwise, is the only beverage on offer aside from water—take over the dozen picnic tables and champion good cheer. Though the portopotties may be too rustic for some, the two-story mural of Elizabeth Taylor overlooking the festivities is proof that Dacha is nonetheless sophisticated. Closed in winter. ✉ *Q and 7th sts. NW, Shaw* ☎ *202/524–8790* Ⓜ *Shaw/Howard U.*

El Centro D.F. A sunny addition—whatever the weather—to D.C.'s ongoing 14th Street redevelopment, this Richard Sandoval outpost celebrates tequila with a ridiculously expansive selection and an expert staff to guide you, particularly in crafting a personalized flight. The real draw, however, is the roof deck, where the young and boisterous keep the fiesta going. Great nightly happy hour. ✉ *1819 14th St. NW, U Street Corridor* ☎ *202/328–3131* ⊕ *www.richardsandoval.com/elcentrodf* Ⓜ *U St./Cardozo.*

Number Nine. In the heart of Logan Circle nightlife, Number Nine is a predominently male gay bar attracting guests of all ages. The downstairs lounge offers plush banquettes and street views, while big-screen viewing is offered upstairs at the "9½" video bar. The daily happy hour (5–9 pm) offers two-for-one drinks. At any time this is a great place for a cocktail and some good conversation in a bustling neighborhood. ✉ *1435 P St. NW, Logan Circle* ☎ *202/986–0999* ⊕ *www. numberninedc.com* Ⓜ *Dupont Circle.*

ADAMS MORGAN

Adams Morgan is Washington's version (albeit much smaller) of New Orleans's French Quarter. The streets are jammed on the weekends with people of all ages and descriptions. Bars and restaurants of all types line the streets, making it easy to find one that will suit your tastes. Be prepared for crowds on the weekends and a much tamer vibe on weeknights. Getting there is easy, with four nearby Metro stops: Woodley Park/Adams Morgan (Red Line), Dupont Circle (Red Line), Columbia Heights (Green and Yellow lines), and U Street/Cardozo (Green and Yellow lines). Taxis also are easy to find, except after last call when the crowds pour out of bars.

BARS AND LOUNGES

Bourbon. A more mature Southern-tinged drinking and dining experience diverges from the typical Adams Morgan scene. Though you can dance on the second floor into the wee hours Friday and Saturday, earlier in the evening you'll find interesting whiskey, scotch, and bourbon options coupled with Southern goodies like barbeque chicken salads, grits, and mac 'n' cheese. It's casual, sometimes crowded, and the outdoor porch in summer is a welcome respite from the 18th Street crowd. ✉ *2321 18th St. NW, Adams Morgan* ☎ *202/332 0800* ⊕ *www. bourbondc.com* Ⓜ *Adams Morgan/ Woodley Park.*

Chief Ike's Mambo Room. A wild and eccentric crowd enjoys some of the best dance-your-pants-off parties in town, with DJs Saturday and Sunday. Wednesday and Sunday offer live music. There's plenty of room to hang out, chat, and sip a cool cocktail. You can't miss the gaudy entrance. ✉ *1725 Columbia Rd. NW, Adams Morgan* ☎ *202/332–2211* ⊕ *www.chiefikes.com* Ⓜ *Columbia Hts.*

L'Enfant Cafe. This French-flavored café boasts the most sidewalk seating in Adams Morgan, superb for watching the world go by at the intersection where Adams Morgan meets Dupont Circle. Inside, things get very intimate with a corner transformed on occasion to offer cabaret. The mood is downright bacchanalian, however, during Saturday's "La Boum" brunch that gets the nightlife started long before the sun goes down and has D.C.'s bohemian set clamoring to get in, making reservations mandatory. Dancing on the bar during La Boum with a sparkler in one hand and a tambourine in the other remains optional. ✉ *2000 18th St. NW, Adams Morgan* ☎ *202/319–1800* ⊕ *www.lenfantcafe com* Ⓜ *Dupont Circle.*

Madam's Organ. Neon lights behind the bar, walls covered in kitsch, and works from local artists add to the gritty feel of three levels that play host to an eclectic clientele that listens to live music performed every night (open-mic night is Tuesday) and soaks up rays on the roof deck by day. This is a place that's hard not to like. ✉ *2461 18th St. NW,*

Adams Morgan ☎ *202/667–5370* ⊕ *www.madamsorgan.com* Ⓜ *Woodley Park/Zoo.*

Tryst. Bohemian and unpretentious, this coffeehouse/bar serves fancy sandwiches and exotic coffee creations. Comfy chairs and couches fill the big open space, where you can sit for hours sipping a cup of tea—or a martini—while chatting or clacking away at your laptop. Some of D.C.'s many bloggers make this their home base during the day, and the management has no problem letting people relax for an hour or two . . . or eight. Tryst is best in the warm months, when the front windows swing open and the temperature matches the temperament. ⊠ *2459 18th St. NW, Adams Morgan* ☎ *202/232–5500* ⊕ *www.trystdc. com* Ⓜ *Woodley Park/Zoo.*

MUSIC CLUBS

Columbia Station. An unpretentious retreat on the 18th Street strip attracts a diverse crowd, many of whom were pulled in off the street by the good vibes emanating from this place. Amber lights and morphed musical instruments adorn the walls, and high-quality live local jazz and blues fills the air. The large, open windows up front keep the place cool—much like the music—in summer months. Reservations are available, though the tunes, and not the mediocre food, are the real draw. ⊠ *2325 18th St. NW, Adams Morgan* ☎ *202/462–6040* ⊕ *www. columbiastationdc.com* Ⓜ *Woodley Park/Zoo.*

U STREET CORRIDOR

Decades ago, the U Street Corridor was famous as D.C.'s Black Broadway. After many dormant years, today the neighborhood has come roaring back with a lively bar, club, and music scene that's expanding both north and south along 14th Street. The U Street Corridor is easily accessible from the U Street/Cardozo Metro stop, on the Green and Yellow lines. Taxis also are easy to find.

BARS AND LOUNGES

Black Jack. A red-velvet, almost vaudeville-like interior around the bar offers a saucy experience upstairs from the highly rated Pearl Dive Oyster Palace. In the back, you'll find a bocce court surrounded by stadium-style seats so onlookers can recline, imbibe, and cheer simultaneously. Though the most exquisite cocktail confections can be pricey, there's also an impressive beer lineup and a worthwhile menu ranging from mussels to pizza. ⊠ *1612 14th St. NW, Logan Circle* ☎ *202/319–1612* ⊕ *www.blackjackdc.com* Ⓜ *U St./Cardozo.*

Fodor's Choice ★ **The Brixton.** An English pub with an upscale D.C. twist offers three levels of fun in the heart of the U Street bustle. The menu is inspired by the Commonwealth's reach, including Indian, some Caribbean spice, and outstanding English, right down to the fish and chips. The sprawling roof deck changes pace with two bars, great views and weekend DJs. In between, the second floor is wide open. Brixton also offers trivia contests and comedians. ⊠ *901 U St. NW, U Street Corridor* ☎ *202/560–5045* ⊕ *www.brixtondc.com* Ⓜ *U. St./Cardozo.*

D.C.'S PARTY ANIMALS: LOBBYISTS

GENERAL DESCRIPTION

Though currently plentiful, the lobbyist is a threatened species in Washington. Ironically, recent legislation and public awareness of the species have only deepened its endangerment.

IDENTIFYING MARKS

Lobbyists may look familiar to New Yorkers, due to their marked resemblance to investment bankers (the latter are extremely rare in Washington). Easy to identify by custom-made suits, stylish haircuts, and the occasional suspender or cigar (males only), they are distinguishable from lawyers by their habit of picking up the check and by the gaggle of out-of-towners that they often escort. Be warned: They are also exceptionally friendly and good at engaging in conversations with strangers.

DIET

Studies of lobbyists' expense reports indicate a particularly voracious appetite, heavy on red meat, sushi, whiskey, and fine wine. It is interesting to note, however, that lobbyists take virtually all their meals in restaurants, and thus have a limited ability to find food on their own; without an expense account, the lobbyist may starve.

HABITAT

The lobbyist's habitat is shrinking rapidly and is a source of some concern. Washington lobbyists are native only to K Street, but in recent years their normal range had extended to the Capitol, with a vast migratory range encompassing Scottish golf courses, Mississippi casinos, and the Mariana Islands. As pressure increases on the species, it is being driven back to K Street, but can still be reliably spotted at **Charlie Palmer, Sonoma, Bistro Bis, Central, The Source,** and **Capital Grille.** Follow the sommelier.

BEHAVIOR

Lobbyists coexist symbiotically with legislators, each reliant on the other for protection and sustenance. Thus, the two species are often spotted together: the lobbyist feeding the legislator with food, trips, and campaign cash, the legislator reciprocating with spending bills and business-friendly rhetoric. In such company, the lobbyist is at its most resplendent—charming and expansive. When alone or with members of their own species, however, lobbyists can be gruff and temperamental. Watch for them on cell phones in expensive restaurants.

Busboys and Poets. Part eatery, part bookstore, and part event space, this popular local hangout draws a diverse crowd and hosts a wide range of entertainment, from poetry open mikes to music to guest authors and activist speakers. The name is an homage to Langston Hughes, who worked as a busboy in D.C. before becoming a famous poet. This original location is open until 2 am on weekends—there's another downtown (at 1025 5th Street NW), as well as outposts in Maryland and Virginia. ✉ *2021 14th St. NW, U Street Corridor* ☎ *202/387–7638* ⊕ *www.busboysandpoets.com* Ⓜ *U St./Cardozo.*

Café Saint-Ex. Named for Antoine de Saint-Exupéry, French pilot and author of *The Little Prince*, this bilevel bar has a split personality. The upstairs brasserie has pressed-tin ceilings and a propeller hanging over the polished wooden bar. Downstairs is the Gate 54 nightclub, designed to resemble an airplane hangar, with dropped corrugated-metal ceilings and backlit aerial photographs. The downstairs DJs draw a fairly young crowd, while the upstairs menu attracts a more subdued clientele for dinner. ⊠ *1847 14th St. NW, U Street Corridor* ☎ *202/265–7839* ⊕ *www.saint-ex.com* Ⓜ *U St./Cardozo.*

Chi-Cha Lounge. Groups of young professionals relax on sofas and armchairs in this hip hangout modeled after an Ecuadorian hacienda, while Latin jazz mingles with pop music in the background and old movies run silently behind the bar. The place gets packed on weekends, so come early to get a coveted sofa along the back wall. Down the tasty tapas as you enjoy the namesake drink—think sangria with a bigger kick. Or try a hookah filled with a range of flavored tobaccos, from apple to watermelon. A dress-to-impress dress code is strictly enforced. ⊠ *1624 U St. NW, U Street Corridor* ☎ *202/234–8400* ⊕ *www.chichaloungedc. com* Ⓜ *U St./Cardozo.*

Fodor's Choice ★ **Cork Wine Bar.** On weekends, the crowds can spill onto 14th Street, and one of the best wine bars in D.C. is worth the wait. An outstanding wine list (mainly French and Italian) is matched with delectable small plates (especially notable are the avocado-pistachio bread and goat-cheese cheesecake). ⊠ *1720 14th St. NW, U Street Corridor* ☎ *202/265–2675* ⊕ *www.corkdc.com* ☞ *U St./Cardozo.*

Marvin. Young crowds cram in on the weekend, but even if that's not your scene this trendsetter is still worth a visit. The excellent gastropub—moules frites, shrimp and grits—and a chill lower level offer respite from the dance floors above. The outdoor back porch (heated in chillier months) provides an additional outlet for the partying masses. ⊠ *2007 14th St. NW, U Street Corridor* ☎ *202/797–7171* ⊕ *www.marvindc.com* Ⓜ *U St./Cardozo.*

Nellie's Sports Bar. This popular sports bar with a gay following makes everyone feel welcome. Catch the games on multiple screens, or try your luck with "drag bingo" or trivia games. Spaces in this eclectic two-story venue range from roof deck to cozy pub room to a dining area serving all-American meets Venezuelan. ⊠ *900 U St. NW, U Street Corridor* ☎ *202/332–6355* ⊕ *www.nelliessportsbar.com* Ⓜ *U St./Cardozo.*

The Saloon. A classic watering hole has no TVs, no light beer, and no martinis. What you can find are locals engaged in conversation—a stated goal of the owner—and some of the world's best beers, including the rare Urbock 23, an Austrian brew that is rated one of the tastiest and strongest in the world, with 9.6% alcohol content (limit one per customer). The Saloon is now offering a broader bar menu, too. ⊠ *1207 U St. NW, U Street Corridor* ☎ *202/462–2640* Ⓜ *U St./Cardozo.*

Satellite Room. Pre- and postconcert patrons of the adjacent 9:30 Club can enjoy alcoholic milkshakes—think avocado with tequila or a more traditional chocolate with Kahlúa—which taste much better than they sound. Delicious, albeit greasy, Mexican-inspired fare is also on offer. An open-air patio and dark, hip vibe can provide the perfect complement to a musical night out. ✉ *2047 9th St. NW, U Street Corridor* ☎ *202/506–2496* ⊕ *www.satellitedc.com* Ⓜ *U St./Cardozo.*

U Street Music Hall. This basement dance hall hosts both DJs and live bands playing indie, dance, dub-step, and electro music. The diverse crowd really mirrors the night, with club kids on DJ nights and young hipsters for the bands (cover charge), so check the website to make sure it's your kind of crowd. ✉ *1115 U St. NW, U Street Corridor* ☎ *202/588–1880* ⊕ *www.ustreetmusichall.com* Ⓜ *U St./Cardozo.*

Vinoteca. The sophisticated set flocks here for a solid list of around 100 wines, a menu of delicious small bites, and weekend brunches. There's a daily happy hour (5–7 pm), and the flights of wine to sample are attractively priced. On Sunday nights there are live flamenco performances. In good weather you can dine on the front patio, and out back there's a large bar and a bocce court. Vinoteca also offers wine classes for small groups in the private rooms upstairs. ✉ *1940 11th St. NW, U Street Corridor* ☎ *202/332–9463* ⊕ *www.vinotecadc.com* Ⓜ *U St./Cardozo.*

DANCE CLUBS

Local 16. When they have to remove all the chairs in the joint to make more room for dancing, you know you've picked a good spot. Locals and out-of-towners alike pack in on weekends to enjoy the joyful pop music, multiple dance rooms, and the outdoor-deck bar perched one story above 16th Street. Luxe couches, chandeliers, vintage pieces, and winding staircases enhance the atmosphere of a Victorian house party with a modern twist. Outstanding $5 happy hour. ✉ *1602 U St. NW, U Street Corridor* ☎ *202/265–2828* ⊕ *www.localsixteen.com* Ⓜ *U St./Cardozo.*

Town Danceboutique. Two stories of drag shows, international DJs, go-go boys and a "chill-out room" keep the crowds coming to this U Street Corridor party place. With a largely young (18 and older on Friday), gay, and festive atmosphere, expect lines, but not too much attitude. Regular hours are Friday and Saturday, but some weeks see special events on other nights. There are two adjacent parking lots—a plus in Washington. ✉ *2009 8th St. NW, U Street Corridor* ☎ *202/234–8696* ⊕ *www.towndc.com* Ⓜ *U St./African-American Civil War Memorial/Cardozo.*

MUSIC CLUBS
JAZZ AND BLUES

Bohemian Caverns. The cramped stairway delivers you to a performance space designed to look like a cave, a complete and accurate renovation of the Crystal Caverns, once a mainstay of D.C.'s "Black Broadway" and the place to see Miles Davis and Charlie Parker. The club rightfully calls itself "the Sole Home for Soul Jazz." These days Friday and Saturday are given over to jazz, and open-mic night on Wednesday brings jazz-influenced poets to the stage. ✉ *2001 11th St. NW, U Street Corridor* ☎ *202/299–0800* ⊕ *www.bohemiancaverns.com* Ⓜ *U St./Cardozo.*

Twins Jazz. For more than 25 years, twin sisters Kelly and Maze Tesfaye have been offering great jazz, featuring some of D.C.'s strongest straight-ahead jazz players, as well as groups from as far away as New York. The food is nothing to write home about but it's easy to meet the

D.C.'S PARTY ANIMALS: LEGISLATORS

GENERAL DESCRIPTION

The legislator's life cycle is one of migration, from its home state to Washington and back, during weekends, congressional recesses, and finally, election years. Natural selection has made it thus a particularly hardy and dynamic species; its struggles for dominance are among Washington's most dramatic and powerful.

IDENTIFYING MARKS

Prominent smile, entourage, American flag pin. Legislators are rarely alone, but outside the Capitol are seldom seen in the company of other legislators, preferring the company of staffers, lobbyists, and (sometimes) interns. They often travel in black SUVs and tend to be hard to catch, but can sometimes be lured by cameras and microphones.

DIET

While in Washington, legislators eat a rich diet of porterhouse steak, Chinese takeout, and french fries. But in election years a legislator's epic journey of campaign migration results in significant culinary hardship, and during this time many subsist on doughnuts and pie.

HABITAT

Observe legislators in the Capitol itself, and around the Hill and White House at the **Source, Capital Grille,** and the **Caucus Room,** as well as in Georgetown at **Cafe Milano.** On Friday afternoon and Monday morning, you may catch a glimpse of legislators migrating through Reagan National Airport. In election years their habitat changes dramatically, and although hard to find in Washington, they're easy to spot at county fairs and senior citizens' homes.

BEHAVIOR

This species is known for noisy and complex displays of principle, called speechifying. These displays are meant to simultaneously attract voters and intimidate competitors; occasionally, they also result in legislation.

nightly minimum with drinks. Connections with local universities bring in new and experimental talent. ⊠ *1344 U St. NW, U Street Corridor* ☎ *202/234–0072* ⊕ *www.twinsjazz.com* Ⓜ *U St./Cardozo.*

ROCK AND POP

Fodor'sChoice
★
9:30 Club. When they come to town, the best indie performers, and a few of the bigger acts, play this large but cozy space wrapped by balconies on three sides. Recent acts have included current sensations such as Mogwai as well as groups with a long history, such as George Clinton, OAR, Mos Def, and Joe Jackson. Bands and singers often make way for DJ-fueled dance parties. ■TIP→ For the best view, arrive at least an hour before the doors open, typically at 8:30. ⊠ *815 V St. NW, U Street Corridor* ☎ *202/265–0930* ⊕ *www.930.com* Ⓜ *U St./Cardozo.*

Fodor'sChoice
★
Black Cat. Come here to see the latest local bands as well as indie stars such as Neko Case, Modest Mouse, Arcade Fire, and the Pizza Underground. Or check out some edgy burlesque and comedy. There's also plenty of ironic dueling-DJ action—think The Cure vs. The Smiths. The post-punk crowd whiles away the time in the Red Room, a side bar with pool tables, an eclectic jukebox, and no cover charge. The club

also is home to Food for Thought, a legendary vegetarian café. ✉ *1811 14th St. NW, U Street Corridor* ☎ *202/667–4490* ⊕ *www.blackcatdc. com* Ⓜ *U St./Cardozo.*

DC9. With live music seven days a week, this small two-story rock club hosts up-and-coming indie bands and the occasional nationally known act. There's a narrow bar on the ground floor and a sizable concert space upstairs. DJs take the controls for Friday night indie dance parties. ✉ *1940 9th St. NW, U Street Corridor* ☎ *202/483–5000* ⊕ *www. dcnine.com* Ⓜ *U St./Cardozo.*

SUBURBAN VIRGINIA

Just across the Potomac, Arlington and Alexandria boast some top-notch bars and lounges—with considerably more parking and less hectic traffic than D.C. Also accessible by the Metro, revitalized Ballston and Clarendon are interesting and enjoyable places, though more laid-back, to visit at night.

BARS AND LOUNGES

Carpool. "Andy Warhol meets General Motors" is how one magazine described this former-garage-turned-bar. Enjoy a brew and standard bar fare, from Caesars to sliders. Amenities include eight pool tables, as well as skeeball, shuffleboard and darts. Carpool also boasts more sports screens than you can shake a foam finger at. Fun and games aside, keep in mind it's 21 and older after 4 pm. ✉ *4000 Fairfax Dr., Arlington* ☎ *703/532–7665* ⊕ *www.gocarpool.com* Ⓜ *Ballston.*

PX. Reservations are accepted for this swanky speakeasy, but if the blue light is lit that's the sign they've got room for some walk-ins. It's hard to say what's the best part—the intimate setting, the attentive service, or the otherworldly drinks. Jackets are preferred for gents, and a pocket square wouldn't hurt. ✉ *728 King St., Old Town, Alexandria* ☎ *703/299–8385* ⊕ *www.eamonnsdublinchipper.com/PX* Ⓜ *King St.*

State Theatre. This is the place to go to see current comics and famous bands from the past like Leon Russell, the Smithereens, and Jefferson Starship. You have the choice of sitting or standing in this renovated movie theater, which is about 10 miles south of D.C. The popular 1980s Retro Dance Parties, featuring the Legwarmers tribute band, draw locals who like to dress the part. ✉ *220 N. Washington St., Falls Church* ☎ *703/237–0300* ⊕ *www.thestatetheatre.com* Ⓜ *East Falls Church.*

MUSIC CLUBS

Fodor's Choice ★ **The Birchmere.** A legend in the D.C. area, the Birchmere is one of the best places outside the Blue Ridge Mountains to hear acoustic folk, country, and bluegrass. Enthusiastic crowds have enjoyed performances by artists such as Mary Chapin Carpenter, Lyle Lovett, Béla Fleck, and Emmylou Harris. More recently, the club expanded its offerings to include jazz performers such as Diane Schuur and Al Jarreau, and blues artists like Robert Cray and Buddy Guy. Tickets are available online. ✉ *3701 Mt. Vernon Ave., Alexandria* ☎ *703/549–7500* ⊕ *www.birchmere.com.*

8

PERFORMING ARTS

Updated
by Robert
Michael Oliver

Whether you're looking for theater, jazz, dance, cinema, cabaret, comedy, or something classical, Washington, D.C., has some of the most exciting and thought-provoking entertainment in the country. Since the opening of the John F. Kennedy Center for the Performing Arts in 1971, the city's performing arts culture has grown steadily. So much so that Washington now hosts the third-largest theater scene in the country, as well as a rich offering of nightly music opportunities featuring local, national, and international talent, and so much more. No city outshines the District on the magnificence and variety of its arts venues.

A wealth of theaters offers everything from Rodgers and Hammerstein to experimental fare. The Kennedy Center and the historic National Theatre bring in primarily big time touring shows, but the 64-year-old Arena Stage offers the best in regional theater. Meanwhile, relative newcomers like the Studio Theatre, Woolly Mammoth, and Northern Virginia's Signature Theatre offer a palette of performances as varied as any in the country.

The city also has its share of every kind of music imaginable, from classical quartets to the most current raving sensation. With venues ranging from DAR Constitution Hall to the Verizon Center near D.C.'s Chinatown to Northern Virginia's Birchmere Music Hall and Maryland's Music Center at Strathmore, music can be found wherever you are, both in the city and its many suburbs.

Those looking for cinema can catch unusual foreign fare, rare documentaries, independent features, and classics. As for dance, Washington has more than enough to help you remember what it is like to watch bodies gracefully move through space.

PLANNING

TICKETS

Tickets to most events are available by calling or visiting the venue's box office and website or through the following ticket agencies:

Ticketmaster. You can buy tickets for events at most large venues by phone, online, or in person at the Verizon Center and other select locations. ☎ 800/745–3000, 866/448–7849 ⊕ www.ticketmaster.com.

Ticketplace. This web-based organization sells discount tickets for select theater and performing arts events throughout metro D.C. ☎ 202/393–2161 ⊕ www.ticketplace.org Ⓜ Archives/Navy Memorial.

Tickets.com. Reservations for many larger events around town are available online. ☎ 800/955–5566 ⊕ www.tickets.com.

EVENTS INFORMATION

For information on events in D.C., the best listings are found at the *Washington Post Going Out Guide* (⊕ www.washingtonpost.com/gog) and the free weekly *Washington CityPaper* (⊕ www.washingtoncitypaper.com). Other events listings are found in the daily "Guide to the Lively Arts" and the Friday "Weekend" sections in the *Washington Post*, and the "City Lights" section in the monthly *Washingtonian* magazine. For theater and other arts activities, you can also check out Theatre Washington (⊕ www.theatrewashington.org), which keeps a weekly listing of theatrical performances, and the Culture Capital (⊕ www.culturecapital.com). DCist (⊕ www.dcist.com), a popular local blog, the MD Theatre Guide (⊕ www.mdtheatreguide.com), and DC Theatre Scene (⊕ www.dctheatrescene.com) post daily on D.C. events.

WHITE HOUSE AREA

Surrounding the president's home and the nation's monumental core is a wealth of concerts, films, music, and dance, not to mention galleries of the world's most famous art and relics displayed in the Smithsonian Institution's many exhibits. The best part of all, many of these treasures are free and open to the public.

MAJOR VENUES

DAR Constitution Hall. Acts ranging from Steve Harvey to Josh Groban to B.B. King perform at this 3,700-seat venue, one of Washington's grand old halls. DAR is well worth a visit for both the excellent performers it attracts as well as its awesome architecture and acoustics. ⊠ 1776 D St. NW, White House Area ☎ 202/628–4780 ⊕ www.dar.org/conthall Ⓜ Farragut West.

National Gallery of Art. On Friday from Memorial Day through Labor Day, local jazz groups perform to packed crowds in the sculpture garden from 5 to 9 pm. Listeners dip their feet in the fountain, sip sangria, and let the week wash away. From October to June free concerts by the National Gallery Orchestra and performances by visiting recitalists and ensembles are held in the West Building's West Garden Court on Sunday nights. Entry is first-come, first-served, with doors opening at 6 pm and concerts starting at 6:30. On Wednesday, free midday performances of classical music begin around noon. Also check out their film series. ⊠ *6th St. and Constitution Ave. NW, White House Area* ☎ *202/842–6941* ⊕ *www.nga.gov* Ⓜ *Archives/Navy Memorial.*

Fodor's Choice **Smithsonian Institution.** Throughout the year the Smithsonian Associates

★ sponsor programs that offer everything from a cappella groups to Cajun zydeco bands; all events require tickets and locations vary. For an especially memorable music experience, catch a performance of the Smithsonian Jazz Masterworks Orchestra in residence at the National Museum of American History. Children and adults will enjoy the two IMAX theatres, at the Museum of Natural History and at the Air and Space Museum. The Smithsonian's annual summer Folklife Festival, held on the Mall, highlights the cuisine, crafts, and day-to-day life of several different cultures. ⊠ *1000 Jefferson Dr. SW, The Mall* ☎ *202/357–2700, 202/633–1000 for recording, 202/357–3030 for Smithsonian Associates* ⊕ *www.si.edu* Ⓜ *Smithsonian.*

FILM

National Archives. Historical films, usually documentaries, are shown here regularly. Screenings range from Robert Flaherty's 1942 coverage of the plight of migrant workers to archival footage of Charles Lindbergh's solo flight from New York to Paris. ⊠ *Constitution Ave. between 7th and 9th sts. NW, The Mall* ☎ *202/501–5000* ⊕ *www. archives.gov* Ⓜ *Archives/Navy Memorial.*

National Gallery of Art, East Building. Free classic and international films, often complementing the exhibits, are shown in this museum's large auditorium each weekend. Pick up a film calendar at the museum or online. ⊠ *Constitution Ave. between 3rd and 4th sts. NW, The Mall* ☎ *202/842–6799* ⊕ *www.nga.gov* Ⓜ *Archives/Navy Memorial.*

PERFORMANCE SERIES

Armed Forces Concert Series. In a Washington tradition, bands from the four branches of the armed services perform June to August on Monday, Tuesday, Wednesday, and Friday evenings on the west steps of the U.S. Capitol. Concerts usually include marches, patriotic numbers, and some classical music. Other performances take place at 8 pm from June to August, on Tuesday, Thursday, Friday, and Sunday nights at various locations throughout the Metro area. The Air Force celebrity series features popular artists such as Earl Klugh and Keiko Matsui on Sunday in February and March at DAR Constitution Hall. ⊠ *U.S. Capitol, Capitol Hill* ☎ *202/767–5658 for Air Force, 703/696–3718 for Army, 202/433–4011 for Marines, 202/433–2525 for Navy* Ⓜ *Capitol S.*

Screen on the Green. Every July and August this weekly series of classic films turns the Mall into an open-air cinema. People arrive as early as 5 pm to picnic, socialize, and reserve a spot. The show starts at dusk. ⊠ *The Mall at 7th St., The Mall* ☎ *877/262–5866* Ⓜ *Smithsonian.*

FOGGY BOTTOM

South of Downtown D.C. and north of Georgetown, Foggy Bottom is home to the John F. Kennedy Center for the Performing Arts and George Washington University's Lisner Auditorium—two great venues for the performing arts. Both facilities present drama, dance, and music, offering a platform for some of the most famous American and international performers. Hungry and thirsty visitors to the Kennedy Center can dine and drink at the Roof Top Terrace Restaurant and Bar.

MAJOR VENUES

Fodor's Choice
★

John F. Kennedy Center for the Performing Arts. On the bank of the Potomac River, the gem of the Washington, D.C., performing arts scene is home to the National Symphony Orchestra, the Suzanne Farrell Ballet, and the Washington National Opera. The best out-of-town acts perform at one of three performance spaces—the Concert Hall, the Opera House, or the Eisenhower Theater. An eclectic range of performances is staged at the center's smaller venues, including the Terrace Theater, showcasing chamber groups and experimental works; the Theater Lab, home to cabaret-style performances; the KC Jazz Club; and a 320-seat family theater. But that's not all. On the Millennium Stage in the center's Grand Foyer, you can catch free performances almost any day at 6 pm.

■ TIP→ On performance days, a free shuttle bus runs between the Center and the Foggy Bottom/GWU Metro stop. ✉ *New Hampshire Ave. and Rock Creek Pkwy. NW, Foggy Bottom* ☎ *202/467-4600, 800/444-1324* ⊕ *www.kennedy-center.org* Ⓜ *Foggy Bottom/GWU.*

Lisner Auditorium. A 1,500-seat theater on the campus of George Washington University hosts pop, classical, and choral music shows, modern dance performances, and musical theater, attracting students and outsiders alike. ✉ *730 21st St. NW, Foggy Bottom* ☎ *202/994-6800* ⊕ *www.lisner.org* Ⓜ *Foggy Bottom/GWU.*

DANCE

Suzanne Farrell Ballet. This dance company began as an educational program at the Kennedy Center and has grown into an internationally recognized troupe. The company's Balanchine Preservation Initiative carries forth the legacy of the Bolshoi's famous innovator. ✉ *John F. Kennedy Center for the Performing Arts, 2700 F St. NW, Foggy Bottom* ⊕ *www.kennedy-center.org* Ⓜ *Foggy Bottom.*

Washington Ballet. Classical and contemporary dance is performed from September through May. The main shows take place at the Kennedy Center and at the recently opened THEARC in Southeast D.C. Each December the company performs *The Nutcracker* at the Warner Theatre. ✉ *3515 Wisconsin Ave. NW, Woodley Park* ☎ *202/362-3606* ⊕ *www.washingtonballet.org.*

MUSIC

CHORAL MUSIC

Choral Arts Society of Washington. From fall to late spring, this 200-voice choir performs a musical array, ranging from classical to tango to Broadway, at the Kennedy Center Concert Hall and other venues. Three Christmas sing-alongs are also scheduled each December, and in January or February there's a popular tribute to Martin Luther King, Jr. ✉ *5225 Wisconsin Ave. NW, Friendship Heights, Ste. 603, Foggy Bottom* ☎ *202/244-3669* ⊕ *www.choralarts.org* Ⓜ *Friendship Heights.*

Five Great Arts Experiences

■ **Arena Stage:** Housed in the audience-friendly Mead Center for American Theatre, Arena Stage offers innovative new American plays as well as classic plays and musicals.

■ **John F. Kennedy Center for the Performing Arts:** The gem of the D.C. arts scene, this is the one performance venue you might take with you if you were stranded on a desert isle.

■ **Shakespeare Theatre:** Among the top Shakespeare companies in the world, this troupe excels at both classical and contemporary interpretations.

■ **Studio Theatre:** With its four intimate theaters and its hip urban locale, this 14th Street landmark provides the best in contemporary dramas and comedies.

■ **Woolly Mammoth:** This remarkable theater company stages some of the most creative and entertaining new plays from the nation's best playwrights.

OPERA

Washington National Opera. The Washington National Opera presents eight works a year at the Kennedy Center Opera House in their original languages with English supertitles. In 2014, the WNO will premiere the New American Opera Initiative. ⊠ *John F. Kennedy Center for the Performing Arts, New Hampshire Ave. and Rock Creek Pkwy. NW, Foggy Bottom* ☎ *202/295–2400, 800/876–7372* ⊕ *www.dc-opera.org.*

ORCHESTRA

National Symphony Orchestra. Under the direction of Christoph Eschenbach, the orchestra performs from September to June at the Kennedy Center Concert Hall. In summer the orchestra performs at Wolf Trap and gives free concerts at Rock Creek Park's Carter Barron Amphitheatre. On Memorial and Labor Day weekends and July 4, the NSO can be seen on the West Lawn of the Capitol. ⊠ *John F. Kennedy Center for the Performing Arts, New Hampshire Ave. and Rock Creek Pkwy. NW, Foggy Bottom* ☎ *202/467–4600* ⊕ *www.kennedy-center.org/nso* Ⓜ *Foggy Bottom.*

PERFORMANCE SERIES

Washington Performing Arts Society. One of the city's oldest arts organizations stages classical music, jazz, gospel, world music, modern dance, and performance art in citywide venues. Past artists include Yo-Yo Ma, The Chieftains, Herbie Hancock, and Savion Glover. ⊠ *2000 L St. NW, Ste. 510, Foggy Bottom* ☎ *202/785–9727* ⊕ *www.wpas.org.*

CAPITOL HILL AND NORTHEAST D.C.

The arts scene in Capitol Hill and Northeast D.C. has blossomed in recent years with the opening of several performance venues and the explosion of restaurants, bars, and stages along the emerging H Street Corridor. Leading the charge is the Atlas Performing Arts Center, at the cutting edge of dance, music, and drama. Lovers of classical drama will discover great performances and an intimate atmosphere at the Folger Theatre near the Capitol.

MAJOR VENUES

Atlas Performing Arts Center. Known as the "People's Kennedy Center," this performance venue is located in a restored historic movie theater in one of Washington's up-and-coming neighborhoods. The Atlas's four theaters and three dance studios house a diverse group of resident arts organizations, including theater troupes, dance companies, orchestras, and choral groups. Street parking can be difficult so take the Metro. ⊠ *1333 H St. NE, Northeast D.C.* ☎ *202/399–7993* ⊕ *www.atlasarts. org* Ⓜ *Union Station.*

DANCE

Joy of Motion. Resident companies include El Teatro de Danza Contemporanea El Salvador, Furia Flamenca, and Silk Road Dance Company. They offer drop-in classes in the Atlas; the Jack Guidone Theatre in Upper Northwest; and in Bethesda, Maryland. ⊠ *5207 Wisconsin Ave. NW, Northeast D.C.* ☎ *202/362–3042* ⊕ *www.joyofmotion.org* Ⓜ *Friendship Heights.*

MUSIC

CHAMBER MUSIC

Coolidge Auditorium at the Library of Congress. Over the past 80 years, the Coolidge has hosted most of the 20th-century's greatest performers and composers, including Copland and Stravinsky. Today, the theater draws musicians from all genres, including classical, jazz, and gospel, and the hall continues to wow audiences with its near-perfect acoustics and sightlines. Concert tickets are free, but must be ordered in advance through Tickermaster. ■TIP➜ Because of the Library's security procedures, patrons are urged to arrive 30 minutes before the start of each event. ⊠ *Library of Congress, Jefferson Bldg., 101 Independence Ave. SE, Capitol Hill* ☎ *800/551–7328* ⊕ *www.loc.gov* Ⓜ *Capitol South.*

Folger Shakespeare Library. The library's internationally acclaimed resident chamber music ensemble, the Folger Consort, regularly presents medieval, Renaissance, and Baroque pieces performed on period instruments. The season runs from October to May. ⊠ *201 E. Capitol St. SE, Capitol Hill* ☎ *202/544–7077* ⊕ *www.folger.edu* Ⓜ *Union Station or Capitol South.*

Rorschach Theatre. This company's intimate and passionate performances on the stages of H Street's Atlas Performing Arts Center are some of the most offbeat plays in Washington. The company offers lesser-known works by such playwrights as Fengar Gael, Jennifer Maisel, and José Rivera, as well as imaginative revivals of classics like Thorton Wilder's *The Skin of our Teeth*. ⊠ *1333 H St. NE, Northeast D.C.* ☎ *202/452–5538* ⊕ *www.rorschachtheatre.com* Ⓜ *Union Station.*

CHORAL MUSIC

Basilica of the National Shrine of the Immaculate Conception. Choral and church groups occasionally perform at the largest Catholic church in the Americas. Every summer the Basilica offers recitals featuring the Shrine's massive pipe organ. When there, be sure to go down to the crypt to see the world's many Madonnas. See the website for times and visiting performers. ⊠ *400 Michigan Ave. NE, Northeast D.C.* 🕾 *202/526–8300* ⊕ *www.nationalshrine.com* Ⓜ *Brookland/CUA.*

THEATER AND PERFORMANCE ART

Arena Stage. The first regional theater company to win a Tony Award performs innovative American theater, reviving such classic plays as *Oklahoma* and also showcasing the country's best new writers. The architecturally magnificent Mead Center for American Theatre houses three stages and, after the Kennedy Center, is the second-largest performing arts complex in Washington. Located near the waterfront neighborhood in Southwest D.C., the Mead Center features the Fichandler Stage, a theater-in-the-round seating 680; the Kreeger Theater, a modified thrust seating 514; and the Kogod Cradle, a 200-seat blackbox theater for new or experimental productions. ■ TIP→ Inside the Mead, the Catwalk Café serves meals inspired by the shows playing that evening. ⊠ *1101 6th St. SW, Southwest D.C.* 🕾 *202/554–9066* ⊕ *www.arenastage.org* Ⓜ *Waterfront/SEU.*

Folger Theatre. The library's theater, an intimate 250-seat re-creation of the inn-yard theaters in Shakespeare's time, hosts three to four productions a year of Shakespearean or Shakespeare-influenced works. Although the stage is a throwback, the sharp acting and staging certainly push the envelope. ⊠ *Folger Shakespeare Library, 201 E. Capitol St. SE, Capitol Hill* 🕾 *202/544–7077* ⊕ *www.folger.edu* Ⓜ *Union Station or Capitol South.*

DOWNTOWN

Several of Washington's most prestigious performance centers can be found in Downtown D.C. Woolly Mammoth Theater, the Shakespeare Theatre's Sidney Harmon Hall, and other venues are surrounded by a bustling nightlife where visitors have their choice of cuisines and after performance conversation. Plus, on your way to and fro you will be entertained by a host of street performers and musicians.

FILM

Landmark's E Street Cinema. Specializing in independent, foreign, and documentary films, this theater has been warmly welcomed by D.C. movie lovers both for its selection and its state-of-the-art facilities. The Washington Post has declared it D.C.'s Best Movie Theatre for three years running. Its concession stand is fabulous and it is also one of the few movie theaters that serve alcohol. ⊠ *555 11th St. NW, Downtown* 🕾 *202/452–7672* ⊕ *www.landmarktheatres.com* Ⓜ *Metro Center.*

THEATER AND PERFORMANCE ART

Capital Fringe Festival. Since its founding in 2005, the Capital Fringe Festival has grown each year, and currently offers no fewer than 125 productions over a three-week period in July. Local and national performers display the strange, the political, the surreal, and the avantgarde to eclectic crowds at all times of the day in venues throughout the city. With tickets around $17, this is an affordable theater experience, but don't forget your Fringe Button. ■ TIP→ Not all theaters are air-conditioned and Washington can be torrid in mid-summer. ⊠ *607 New York Ave. NW, Downtown* ☎ *866/811–4111* ⊕ *www.capfringe. org.*

FAMILY **Ford's Theatre.** Looking much as it did when President Lincoln was shot at a performance of *Our American Cousin,* Ford's hosts musicals as well as dramas with historical connections, and stages *A Christmas Carol* every year. The historic theater is now maintained by the National Park Service. Tours of the theater and a renovated museum are available for free, but timed-entry tickets are required. ⊠ *511 10th St. NW, Downtown* ☎ *202/426–6925* ⊕ *www.fordstheatre.org* Ⓜ *Metro Center.*

FAMILY **National Theatre.** Though rebuilt several times, the National Theatre has operated in the same location since 1835. It now hosts touring Broadway shows, such as *Hal Holbrook in Mark Twain Tonight, Blue Man Group,* and *West Side Story.* In November 2013, the National presented *If/Then,* its first pre-Broadway tryout in years. ■TIP→ From September through April, look for free children's shows Saturday mornings and free Monday night shows. ⊠ *1321 Pennsylvania Ave. NW, Downtown* ☎ *800/447–7400* ⊕ *www.nationaltheatre.org* Ⓜ *Metro Center.*

Fodor's Choice
★ **Shakespeare Theatre.** This acclaimed troupe crafts fantastically staged and acted performances of works by Shakespeare and other significant playwrights, offering traditional renditions but also some with a modern twist. Complementing the stage in the Lansburgh Theatre is the Sidney Harman Hall, which provides a state-of-the-art, midsize venue for an outstanding variety of performances, from Shakespeare's *Two Gentleman of Verona* to Racine's tragic *Phèdre* to visiting theatres like South Africa's Baxter Theatre and their production of *Mies Julie.* For two weeks in the summer the group performs Shakespeare for free at Carter Barron Amphitheatre. ⊠ *450 7th St. NW, Downtown* ☎ *202/547–1122* ⊕ *www.shakespearetheatre.org* Ⓜ *Gallery Pl./Chinatown or Archives/Navy Memorial.*

Warner Theatre. One of Washington's grand theaters, the Warner hosts Broadway road shows, dance recitals, high-profile pop music acts, and comedians in a majestic Art Deco performance space. ⊠ *513 13th St. NW, Downtown* ☎ *202/783–4000* ⊕ *warnertheatredc.com* Ⓜ *Metro Center.*

Fodor's Choice
★ **Woolly Mammoth.** Unusual cutting-edge shows with solid acting have earned this company top reviews and 35 Helen Hayes Awards. The theatre performs works for a decidedly urban audience that challenge the status quo. In recent years, they have welcomed Chicago's The Second City for an annual political comedy show as well as the works of Mike Daisey, aka the author of *The Agony and Ecstasy of Steve Jobs.* The troupe's talent is accentuated by its modern 265-seat theater in a bustling downtown D.C. ■TIP→ The Woolies create a unique lobby experience for each show; so bring your iPhones and tweet the experience. ⊠ *641 D St. NW, Downtown* ☎ *202/393–3939* ⊕ *www.woollymammoth.net* Ⓜ *Gallery Pl./Chinatown or Archives/Navy Memorial.*

CHINATOWN

With the Verizon Center drawing people from all across the greater Metropolitan area, this hub of Washington's Asian communities thrives on its assortment of cuisines at reasonable prices. Within its four square blocks, where shoppers of all kinds mingle and cavort, the energy is electric.

MAJOR VENUES

Verizon Center. In addition to being the home of the Washington Capitals hockey and Washington Wizards basketball teams, this 19,000-seat arena also plays host to D.C.'s biggest concerts, ice-skating events, and the circus. If Lady Gaga comes to town, this will be the spot to see her! Drivers need to park in one of the many underground garages close by, but several Metro lines are conveniently located close to the Center. ⊠ *601 F St. NW, Chinatown* ☎ *202/661–5000* ⊕ *www.verizoncenter. com* Ⓜ *Gallery Place/Chinatown.*

THEATER AND PERFORMANCE ART

Sixth & I Historic Synagogue. Known for its author readings, with guests ranging from comedian Tina Fey to Nancy Pelosi, the Sixth & I Historic Synagogue has been named one of the most vibrant congregations in the nation. ⊠ *600 I St. NW, Chinatown* ☎ *202/408–3100* ⊕ *www. sixthandi.org* Ⓜ *Gallery Pl./Chinatown.*

GEORGETOWN

Georgetown entertainment goes far beyond barhopping on a Saturday night. Smaller drama groups stage productions in several of Georgetown's larger churches; check local publications for the latest offerings.

MUSIC

CHAMBER MUSIC

Dumbarton Concerts. A fixture in Georgetown since 1772 (in its current location since 1850), Dumbarton United Methodist Church sponsors a concert series that has been host to such musicians as the American Chamber Players, the St. Petersburg String Quartet, and the Thibaud String Trio. ∎ TIP→ Pre-concert, take a stroll through Dumbarton Oaks estate. ⊠ *Dumbarton United Methodist Church, 3133 Dumbarton Ave. NW, Georgetown* ☎ *202/965–2000* ⊕ *dumbartonconcerts.org* Ⓜ *Foggy Bottom.*

DUPONT CIRCLE AND LOGAN CIRCLE

Dupont Circle's reputation has grown in recent years as a place for good drama, with the Studio Theatre offering outstanding productions from new writers and some of Europe and America's best-known playwrights. Talented troupes in unique venues, including the Keegan Theatre on Church Street and Washington Stage Guild at the Undercroft Theatre, are sprinkled throughout the neighborhood. But a little-known secret is the free concerts offered at the Phillips Collection.

FILM

Filmfest DC. For nearly 30 years running, this annual citywide festival of international cinema (officially known as the D.C. International Film Festival) takes place in April or early May at venues throughout Washington. ⊠ *1700 14th St. NW, Logan Circle* ☎ *202/234-3456* ⊕ *www.filmfestdc.org* Ⓜ *U St./Cardozo.*

National Geographic Society. Documentary films with a scientific, geographic, or anthropological focus are shown regularly at National Geographic's Grosvenor Auditorium. An easy walk from Dupont Circle, "NatGeo" also hosts speakers, concerts, and photography exhibits year round. ⊠ *1145 17th St. NW, Dupont Circle* ☎ *202/857-7700* ⊕ *events.nationalgeographic.com/events* Ⓜ *Farragut N.*

MUSIC

CHAMBER MUSIC

Phillips Collection. Duncan Phillips's mansion is more than an art museum. On Sunday afternoons from October through May, chamber groups from around the world perform in the long, dark-paneled Music Room. Plus, on the first Thursday of the month, from 5:00 to 8:30 pm, the museum offers Phillips After 5, a lively mix of jazz performances, food and drink, gallery talks, films, and more. ■TIP➜ The free Sunday concerts begin at 4 pm; arrive early for good seats. ⊠ *1600 21st St. NW, Dupont Circle* ☎ *202/387-2151* ⊕ *www.phillipscollection.org* Ⓜ *Dupont Circle.*

THEATER AND PERFORMANCE ART

The Keegan Theatre. This 115-seat black-box theater is tucked among the scenic row houses of Dupont Circle and stages both Irish and American plays. An expansion and renovation is scheduled for next year. ■TIP➜ Note that, given the size and age of this unique venue, there is little access for those with limited mobility and long lines form for the bathrooms at intermission. ⊠ *1742 Church St. NW, Dupont Circle* ☎ *703/892-0202* ⊕ *keegantheatre.com* Ⓜ *Dupont Circle.*

Theater J. One of the country's most distinctive and progressive Jewish performance venues offers an ambitious range of programming that includes work by noted playwrights, directors, designers, and actors. Past performances have included one-person shows featuring Sarah Bernhard and Judy Gold as well as more edgy political pieces. Performances take place in the Aaron and Cecile Goldman Theater at the D.C. Jewish Community Center. ⊠ *1529 16th St. NW, Dupont Circle* ☎ *202/518-9400* ⊕ *www.theaterj.org* Ⓜ *Dupont Circle.*

ADAMS MORGAN

Adams Morgan has long been the hub of the city's best avant-garde performances, primarily offered by the District of Columbia Arts Center. You can enjoy an incredible meal at one of many nearby ethnic restaurants, see a performance at the Gala Hispanic Theatre, and then head to one of the neighborhood's colorful bars after the show.

THEATER AND PERFORMANCE ART

District of Columbia Arts Center. Known by area artists as DCAC, this cross-genre space shows changing exhibits in its gallery and presents avant-garde performance art, improv, and experimental plays in its tiny black-box theater. DCAC is the home of Washington's oldest experimental theatre group, Theatre Du Jour. ⊠ *2438 18th St. NW, Adams Morgan* ☎ *202/462–7833* ⊕ *www.dcartscenter.org* Ⓜ *Woodley Park.*

Gala Hispanic Theatre. This company attracts outstanding Hispanic actors from around the world, performing works by such leading dramatists as Federico García Lorca and Mario Vargas Llosa. Plays are presented in English or in Spanish with projected subtitles. The company performs in the newly renovated Tivoli Theatre in Columbia Heights, a hot spot for Latino culture and cuisine. ⊠ *Tivoli Sq., 3333 14th St. NW, at Park Rd., Adams Morgan* ☎ *202/234–7174* ⊕ *www.galatheatre.org* Ⓜ *Columbia Heights.*

U STREET CORRIDOR

The U Street Corridor is enjoying a renaissance and is starting to reclaim its former title of Washington's "Black Broadway." The Howard Theatre offers great productions from diverse sources, and the newly reopened Lincoln Theatre offers music from the best in country, reggae, pop, and more. Try some of the smaller venues in this neighborhood for original and compelling performances.

MAJOR VENUES

Fodor'sChoice
★ **The Howard Theatre.** What was once was "the largest colored theatre in the world" is operating again in the heart of Washington's historic "Black Broadway." The Howard now hosts a regular array of music acts from Chuck Brown to Jefferson Starship to the 50th anniversary tour of El Gran Combo. ⊠ *620 T St. NW, U Street Corridor* ☎ *202/803–2899* ⊕ *thehowardtheatre.com* Ⓜ *Shaw-Howard U.*

MUSIC

OPERA

Lincoln Theatre. Once the host of such notable black performers as Cab Calloway, Lena Horne, and Duke Ellington, the 1,250-seat 1920s-inspired Lincoln is part of the lively U Street Corridor. Today, under its new management, it presents contemporary musical performers such as Jennifer Nettles, Josh Ritter, and Stephen "Ragga" Marley. ⊠ *1215 U St. NW, U Street Corridor* ☎ *202/328–6000* ⊕ *www.thelincolntheatre.org* Ⓜ *U St./Cardozo.*

UPPER NORTHWEST

Summer is when the performing arts come alive in Upper Northwest D.C. One of the city's gems is Carter Barron, an outdoor amphitheater that offers everything from classical music to jazz to rhythm and blues. Other venues include the refurbished Avalon Theatre, which features outstanding documentaries and hard-to-find independent films. Some of the biggest blockbuster films are presented at the historic Loews Cineplex Uptown, which has the largest film screen in town.

FILM

AMC Loews Uptown 1. This is a true movie palace, with art deco flourishes; a wonderful balcony; and—in two happy concessions to modernity—crystal clear Dolby sound and a Christie Dual-Projector 3D system. The theater boasts the town's largest movie screen, almost three times the size of a standard screen with triple the effect. ⊠ *3426 Connecticut Ave. NW, Cleveland Park, Upper Northwest* ☎ *202/966–5400* ⊕ *www.amctheatres.com/uptown1* Ⓜ *Cleveland Park.*

Avalon Theatre. A movie house from 1923 is operated by a nonprofit group and offers some of the best and most unusual in independent and foreign film. The theater offers monthly showcases of the best in French, Israeli, Czech, and Greek cinema, plus family matinees every weekend. ⊠ *5612 Connecticut Ave. NW, Upper Northwest* ☎ *202/966–6000 for info, 202/966–3464 for box office* ⊕ *www.theavalon.org* Ⓜ *Friendship Heights.*

MUSIC

CHORAL MUSIC

Washington National Cathedral. Choral and church groups frequently perform in this breathtaking cathedral. Organ recitals on the massive pipe organ are offered every Sunday afternoon and the choir sings Evensong most weekdays around 5:30. Admission is usually free. ⊠ *Massachusetts and Wisconsin aves. NW, Cathedral Heights, Upper Northwest* ✢ *From the Tenleytown Metro station, take any 30-series bus south* ☎ *202/537–6207* ⊕ *www.nationalcathedral.org* Ⓜ *Tenleytown.*

PERFORMANCE SERIES

Carter Barron Amphitheatre. On Saturday and Sunday nights from June to September, this 3,750-seat outdoor theater in the middle of Washington's historic Rock Creek Park hosts pop, jazz, gospel, and rhythm-and-blues artists such as Chick Corea and Nancy Wilson. The National Symphony Orchestra also performs here, and for two weeks the Shakespeare Theatre presents a free play. ⊠ *Rock Creek Park, 4850 Colorado Ave. NW, Upper Northwest* ☎ *202/426–0486* ⊕ *www.nps.gov/rocr/index.htm* Ⓜ *Van Ness.*

SUBURBAN MARYLAND

Several venues make it worth your while to venture outside the District for entertainment. Glen Echo Park, once an amusement park, is now an arts center; the Music Center at Strathmore, while farther out toward Rockville, is easily accessed by Metro and well worth the trip; and Round House Theatre, with its beautiful Bethesda location, offers theater-lovers high-quality, year-round entertainment.

MAJOR VENUES

Fodor'sChoice ★ **Music Center at Strathmore.** Located just outside the Capital Beltway in North Bethesda, this majestic concert hall receives praise for its acoustics and its audience-friendly design. Major national folk, blues, pop, jazz, Broadway, and classical artists perform here. The center is home to the Baltimore Symphony Orchestra and the National Philharmonic. More-intimate performances are held in the 100-seat Dorothy M. and Maurice C. Shapiro Music Room. ✉ *5301 Tuckerman La., North Bethesda* ☎ *301/581–5200* ⊕ *www.strathmore.org* Ⓜ *Grosvenor/ Strathmore.*

FILM

Fodor'sChoice   **American Film Institute Silver Theatre and Cultural Center.** This state-of-the-
★   art center for film is a restoration of architect John Eberson's Art Deco Silver Theatre, built in 1938. In addition to its many educational offerings, the AFI hosts film retrospectives, festivals, and tributes celebrating artists from Jeanne Moreau to Russell Crowe. ✉ *8633 Colesville Rd., Silver Spring* ☎ *301/495–6700* ⊕ *www.afi.com/silver* Ⓜ *Silver Spring.*

MUSIC

PERFORMANCE SERIES

Institute of Musical Traditions. Emerging, near-famous, and celebrated folk performers such as Si Kahn, John McCutcheon, and the Kennedys perform at the Institute's concerts, held at the St. Mark Presbyterian Church in Rockville, a 30-minute drive from Washington, and at other select locations throughout the D.C. area. ✉ *10701 Old Georgetown Rd., Rockville* ☎ *301/754–3611* ⊕ *www.imtfolk.org.*

THEATER AND PERFORMANCE ART

FAMILY   **Glen Echo Park.** The site of Washington's oldest amusement park (1911–68) is preserved here, as is a stone tower from the village of Glen Echo, founded in 1891 by Edwin and Edward Baltzley, brothers who made their fortune from the invention of a reversible eggbeater. The National Park Service now administers this 10-acre property as a thriving arts center with classes in the arts, two children's theaters, two art galleries with ongoing exhibits, artist demonstrations, and the Living Classrooms Museum with environmental education workshops. Every weekend the Adventure Theater puts on traditional plays and musicals aimed at children ages four and up. Families can spread out on carpeted steps. At the Puppet Company Playhouse, skilled puppeteers perform classic stories Wednesday through Sunday. There's a great playground for kids, and young and old alike can ride on a 1921 Dentzel carousel May through September. ✉ *7300 MacArthur Blvd., Glen Echo* ☎ *301/634–2222, 301/320–5331 for Adventure Theater, 301/320–6668 for Puppet Co.* ⊕ *www.glenechopark.org.*

FAMILY   **Imagination Stage.** Shows like the classic *Dr. Doolittle,* and such original fare as Karen Zacarias and Deborah Wicks LaPuma's *Cinderella Likes Rice and Beans,* are produced here for children ages four and up, but there is programming for people as young as 12 months. The state-of-the-art center in Bethesda includes two theaters and a digital media studio. ✉ *4908 Auburn Ave., Bethesda* ☎ *301/961–6060* ⊕ *www. imaginationstage.org* Ⓜ *Bethesda.*

Round House Theatre. One of Maryland's oldest and most respected theatrical companies offers an eclectic array of plays each season in its 250-seat theater, from world premieres to classic American. Notable productions have ranged from Thorton Wilder's *Our Town* to a multimedia adaptation of *Fahrenheit 451*. ⊠ *4545 East–West Hwy., Bethesda* ☎ *240/644–1100* ⊕ *www.roundhousetheatre.org* Ⓜ *Bethesda*.

SUBURBAN VIRGINIA

Suburban Virginia is home to a number of outstanding performing venues offering Shakespeare, opera, dance, popular music, and more. Arlington's Signature Theatre stages some of the best musical productions in the area and is only a short trip from downtown Washington, while Synetic Theatre, made nationally famous by its production of Silent Hamlet, is but a Metro stop away in Crystal City. You'll need a car to reach the Birchmere Music Hall, but you'll enjoy an array of country, folk, and popular music nightly.

MAJOR VENUES

Center for the Arts. This state-of-the-art performance complex on the suburban Virginia campus of George Mason University satisfies music, ballet, and drama patrons with regular performances in its 1,900-seat concert hall, the 500-seat proscenium Harris Theater, and the intimate 150-seat black-box theater. The 9,500-seat Patriot Center, site of pop acts and sporting events, is also on campus. ⊠ *Rte. 123 and Braddock Rd., Fairfax* ☎ *888/945–2468* ⊕ *cfa.gmu.edu*.

Wolf Trap National Park for the Performing Arts. At the only national park dedicated to the performing arts, the massive, outdoor Filene Center hosts close to 100 performances June through September. They range from pop and jazz concerts to dance and musical theater productions. The National Symphony Orchestra is based here in summer, and the Children's Theatre-in-the-Woods delivers 70 free performances. During the colder months the intimate, indoor Barns at Wolf Trap fill with the sounds of musicians playing folk, country, and chamber music, along with myriad other styles. The park is just off the Dulles Toll Road, about 20 miles from downtown Washington. ■TIP→ Wolf Trap provides round-trip bus service from the West Falls Church Metro stop during events. ⊠ *1645 Trap Rd., Vienna* ☎ *703/255–1900, 703/938–2404 for Barns at Wolf Trap* ⊕ *www.wolftrap.org* Ⓜ *West Falls Church*.

MUSIC

PERFORMANCE SERIES

Fodor's Choice ★ **The Birchmere Music Hall.** One of Northern Virginia's hidden treasures is known as one of the best listening halls in the country. You can eat and drink as you listen to the likes of Merle Haggard, B. B. King, Emmylou Harris, and other music legends crooning from the acoustically wonderful stage. You need a car to get here. ⊠ *3701 Mount Vernon Ave., Alexandria* ☎ *703/549–7500* ⊕ *birchmere.com*.

THEATER AND PERFORMANCE ART

American Century Theatre. Devoted to staging overlooked or forgotten 20th-century American plays, American Century has staged performances of Paddy Chafeysky's *The Tenth Man*, Orson Wells's *Moby Dick Rehearsed*, Eugene O'Neill's *Beyond the Horizon*, and even a rare Mel Brooks production, *Archy and Mehitabel*. ⊠ *2700 Lang St., Arlington* ☎ *703/998–4555* ⊕ *www.americancentury.org*.

9

Signature Theatre. Led by artistic director Eric Schaeffer, the Tony Award–winning Signature has earned national acclaim for its presentation of contemporary plays and groundbreaking American musicals, especially those of Stephen Sondheim. The company performs in a dramatic facility in Arlington, Virginia, with two performance spaces, the 299-seat MAX and the 99-seat ARK. ⊠ *4200 Campbell Ave., Arlington* ☎ *703/820–9771* ⊕ *www.signature-theatre.org.*

Synetic Theatre. One of the most distinctive performing arts groups in the Washington area uses music, dance, high energy, acting, and athleticism to transform the works of Shakespeare, Edgar Allan Poe, and Robert Louis Stevenson into dominantly visual theatrics that are guaranteed to leave audiences fascinated. The theatre is tucked away in Virginia's Crystal City, a short Metro ride away from downtown Washington. ⊠ *1800 S. Bell St., Arlington* ☎ *800/494–8497* ⊕ *www.synetictheater. org* Ⓜ *Crystal City.*

SPORTS AND
THE OUTDOORS

Updated
by Robert
Michael Oliver Although Washington may be best known for what goes on inside its hallowed corridors, what happens outside is just as entertaining. Washingtonians are an active bunch, and the city provides a fantastic recreational backyard, with dozens of beautiful open spaces in the District and the nearby Maryland and Virginia suburbs. The city's residents take full advantage of these opportunities, biking its many trails, running amid the monuments, and sailing up the Potomac. They're also passionate about their local teams—especially the Redskins, the Capitals, and the Nationals, whose games are sold out year after year.

Visitors to Washington can enjoy a wealth of outdoor attractions. Rock Creek Park is one of the city's treasures, with miles of wooded trails and paths for bikers, runners, and walkers that extend to almost every part of the city. The National Mall connects the Lincoln Memorial and the Capitol and is one of the most scenic green spaces in the world. Around the Tidal Basin you can run, tour the monuments, and rent paddleboats. Theodore Roosevelt Island, a wildlife sanctuary, has several paths for hiking and enjoyable spots for picnics. And these places are just a few among dozens.

PLANNING

WHERE THE PROS PLAY
If you're going to a pro sports event, chances are you'll be headed here.

FedEx Field. The perennially popular Redskins play football in the Maryland suburbs at this field that seats 79,000 and was built in 1997, making it one of the older stadiums in the NFL. Several restaurants overlook the field, and the stadium houses the Redskins Hall of Fame.

A large installation of solar panels, including one shaped like a giant quarterback and dubbed "Solar Man," powers the lights. Outside of the football season, the field attracts big-name music acts and college sports. Parking is a hassle, so arrive several hours early if you don't want to miss the kickoff. ⊠ *1600 FedexWay, Landover, Maryland* ☎ *301/276–6000* ⊕ *www.redskins.com/fedexfield* Ⓜ *Morgan Boulevard.*

Nationals Park. D.C.'s baseball team, the Nationals, plays in a spacious, 41,546-seat state-of-the-art park, on the fast-developing Capitol Riverfront in Southeast Washington. Since it's opening in 2008, the park has been a catalyst for the renaissance in this area. Inside the stadium, at various locations, fans witness panoramic views of Washington, including the Capitol and the Washington Monument, and dozens of outstanding food venues and craft beer vendors operate concessions. The stadium offers the option of sitting or standing at a bar within sight of the field. Tours are available. ⊠ *1500 S. Capitol St. SE, Capitol Hill* ☎ *202/675–6287* ⊕ *www.washington.nationals.mlb.com/was/ballpark* ⌖ *Tours, $15* Ⓜ *Navy Yard.*

Robert F. Kennedy Stadium. Soccer is incredibly popular in the nation's capital, finding many of its fans in the international crowds who miss the big matches at home, as well as families whose kids play soccer. Robert F. Kennedy Stadium, the Redskins' and Senators' former residence on Capitol Hill, is now home to Major League Soccer's D.C. United. The Capitol View Club is a pub style eatery with full bar ⊠ *2400 E. Capitol St. NE, at 22nd St., Capitol Hill* ☎ *202/587–5000* ⊕ *www.dcunited.com/stadium* Ⓜ *Stadium*

Verizon Center. This 20,000-seat multipurpose sports and entertainment venue averages more than 200 events each year and has helped to turn the surrounding area into the most vibrant part of Downtown. The Acela Club restaurant is accompanied by a wide range of vendors selling everything including doughnuts, kosher and vegan specialties, craft beers, and Chesapeake Bay crab cakes. The Gallery Place/Chinatown Metro station is directly below the Center, making it extremely convenient for fans to travel here and back. Sporting events include Washington Capitals hockey; Washington Wizards, Washington Mystics, and Georgetown Hoyas basketball; and figure-skating events. ■ TIP➔ Outside, street musicians of all kinds and styles add to the Center experience. ⊠ *601 F St. NW, between 6th and 7th sts., Chinatown* ☎ *202/628–3200* ⊕ *www.verizoncenter.com* Ⓜ *Gallery Pl./Chinatown.*

WASHINGTON FOR EVERY SEASON

With every change of the seasons, D.C. offers new pleasures for sports and outdoor enthusiasts.

In winter you can have an old-fashioned afternoon of ice-skating and hot chocolate in the National Gallery's Sculpture Garden, or go to the Verizon Center to see the Wizards play basketball or the Capitals play hockey.

Come spring, the city emerges from the cold with activities everywhere. Runners throng Rock Creek Park, Frisbee contests and soccer games fill up the Mall, and boats float down the Potomac.

FIVE GREAT OUTDOOR EXPERIENCES

Bird-watch on Theodore Roosevelt Island: Take in the spectacular scenery at this tucked-away wildlife sanctuary.

Get a new perspective on the cherry trees: Take a leisurely trip in a paddleboat around the Tidal Basin in spring.

Get moving with picture-postcard motivation: Run or bike on the Mall with Washington's monuments as a unique background.

See the National Zoo's giant pandas: Washington's love affair with the adorable pandas at the National Zoo has gotten a welcome extension; Mei Xiang and Tian Tian are extending their D.C. stay until December 2015.

Walk or ride along the C&O Canal: An excursion along the historic waterway comes with nice views of the Potomac River; you may even see a bald eagle.

In summer, baseball fans head to Nationals Park for games, and this greenery-laced city seems to become one big outdoor playground.

When fall arrives, the seasonal colors of the trees in Rock Creek Park are a spectacular sight for bikers, hikers, and runners. Tickets to see the Redskins at FedEx Field are among the city's most prized commodities.

PARKS AND NATURE

Washington is more than marble and limestone buildings. The city is blessed with numerous parks and outdoor attractions that provide a break from the museums and government facilities. Rock Creek Park extends through much of the city, with entrances to the park near many hotels. Other outdoor spaces, such as the National Mall, Potomac Park, and Constitution Gardens, offer a chance to see nature, combined with the beauty of nearby waterways and the majesty of the city's beloved monuments.

GARDENS

Constitution Gardens. Many ideas were proposed to develop this 50-acre site near the Reflecting Pool and the Vietnam Veterans Memorial. It once held "temporary" buildings erected by the Navy before World War I and not removed until after World War II. President Nixon is said to have favored something resembling Copenhagen's Tivoli Gardens. The final design was plainer, with paths winding through groves of trees and, on the lake, a tiny island paying tribute to the signers of the Declaration of Independence, their signatures carved into a low stone wall. In 1986 President Reagan proclaimed the gardens a living legacy to the Constitution. In that spirit, naturalization ceremonies for new citizens take place. ⊠ *Constitution Ave., between 17th and 23rd sts. NW, White House Area* ⊕ *www.nps.gov/coga* Ⓜ *Farragut W or Foggy Bottom.*

At the circular snack bar just west of the lake at Constitution Gardens, you can get hot dogs, potato chips, candy bars, soft drinks, and beer at prices lower than those charged by most street vendors.

FAMILY

Fodor'sChoice

★

Dumbarton Oaks. One of the loveliest places for a stroll in Washington is Dumbarton Oaks, the acres of enchanting gardens adjoining Dumbarton House in Georgetown. Planned by noted landscape architect Beatrix Farrand, the gardens incorporate elements of traditional English, Italian, and French styles and include a formal rose garden, an English country garden, and an orangery (circa 1810). A full-time crew of a dozen gardeners toils to maintain the stunning collection of terraces, geometric gardens, tree-shaded brick walks, fountains, arbors, and pools. Plenty of well-positioned benches make this a good place for resting weary feet, too. Public garden tours are at 2:10 pm Tuesday–Thursday and Saturday. ■TIP➔ In May, the peonies and azaleas in full bloom are spectacular. ✉ *31st and R sts, Georgetown* ☎ *202/339–6401, 202/339–6400* ⊕ *www.doaks.org* ✉ *$8 mid-Mar.–Oct., free Nov.–mid-Mar.* ☉ *Mid-Mar.–Oct., Tues.–Sun. 2–6; Nov.–mid-Mar., Tues.–Sun. 2–5.*

Hillwood Estate, Museum and Gardens. Cereal heiress Marjorie Merriweather Post purchased the 25-acre Hillwood Estate in 1955, and devoted as much attention to her gardens as she did to the 40 room Georgian mansion. You can wander through 13 acres of them, including a Japanese rock and waterfall garden, a manicured formal French garden, a rose garden, Mediterranean fountains, and a greenhouse full of orchids. The "Lunar Lawn," where she threw garden parties that were the most coveted invitation in Washington society, is planted with dogwood, magnolia, cherry, and plum trees, as well as azaleas, camellias, lilacs, tulips, and pansies. Tours are offered on a first-come, first-served basis in spring and fall. ■TIP➔ The estate is best reached by taxi or car (parking is available on the grounds); it's a 20- to 30-minute walk from the Metro and there's no bus from the station. ✉ *4155 Linnean Ave. NW, Upper Northwest* ☎ *202/686–5807, 202/686–8500* ⊕ *www. hillwoodmuseum.org* ✉ *House and grounds $15 (suggested donation)* ☉ *Tues.–Sat. 10–5 and two Sun. per month 1–5 (except annual closure around late Jan.; call for details). Tours: Apr.–late June and early Sept.–mid-Nov., Tues.–Sat. at 10:30 and 12:30, Sun. at 2:30* Ⓜ *Van Ness/UDC.*

Kahlil Gibran Memorial Garden. In a town known for it's political combat, this tiny urban park is a wonderful place to find some peace. The shady park combines Western and Arab symbols and is perfect for contemplation. From the Massachusetts Avenue entrance, a stone walk bridges a grassy swale. Farther on are limestone benches, engraved with sayings from Gibran, that curve around a fountain and a bust of the Lebanese-born poet. The garden is near the grounds of the U.S. Naval

Observatory. ⊠ *3100-block of Massachusetts Ave. NW, Upper Northwest* Ⓜ *Woodley Park or Dupont Circle.*

Kenilworth Park and Aquatic Gardens. Exotic water lilies, lotuses, hyacinths, and other water-loving plants thrive in this 14-acre sanctuary of quiet ponds, protected wetlands, and marshy flats. The gardens' wetland animals include turtles, frogs, beavers, spring azure butterflies, and some 40 species of birds. ▪ TIP➜ In May the water lilies and lotus are at their peak. In July nearly everything blossoms; early morning is the best time to visit, when day bloomers are just opening and night bloomers have yet to close. There's a tiny child-friendly museum in the Visitors Center. The nearest Metro stop is a 15-minute walk away, but there is ample free parking. ⚠ Exit gates are locked promptly at 4. ⊠ *1550 Anacostia Ave. at Douglas St. NE, Anacostia* ☎ *202/426–6905* ⊕ *www.nps.gov/keaq* ⌨ *Free* ◷ *Gardens and visitor center daily 8–4. Tours daily at 9, 10, and 11* Ⓜ *Deanwood.*

FAMILY **Tudor Place.** A little more than a block from Dumbarton Oaks in Georgetown is this neighborhood gem, the former home of Martha Washington's granddaughter. The house has 5½ acres of grounds that offer impressive replications of Federal-period gardens and include 19th-century specimen trees and boxwoods from Mount Vernon. The self-guiding tour comes with a map and/or an audio tour. Make time for a one-hour docent-led tour of the house itself, which features many rare possessions of George and Martha Washington. ⊠ *1644 31st Pl. NW, Georgetown* ☎ *202/965–0400* ⊕ *www.tudorplace.org* ⌨ *$10 house and garden, $3 garden only* ◷ *Self-guided garden tours: Feb.–Dec., Mon.–Sat. 10–4, Sun. noon–4. House tours: Feb.–Dec., Tues.–Sat. on the hr 10–3, Sun. on the hr noon–4* Ⓜ *Woodley Park or Dupont Circle.*

FAMILY
Fodor'sChoice
★
United States Botanic Garden. Established by Congress in 1820, this is the oldest botanic garden in North America. The garden conservatory sits at the foot of Capitol Hill, in the shadow of the Capitol building and offers an escape from the stone and marble federal office buildings that surround it. Inside are exotic rain-forest species, desert flora, and trees from all parts of the world. A special treat is the extensive collection of rare and unusual orchids. Walkways suspended 24 feet above the ground provide a fascinating view of the plants. A relatively new addition is the National Garden, opened in 2006, which emphasizes educational exhibits. The garden features the Rose Garden, Butterfly Garden, Lawn Terrace, First Ladies' Water Garden, and Regional Garden. Step outside the building to see the Bartholdi Park, where theme gardens surround a historic fountain. ▪ TIP➜ Ask for a Junior Botanist kid's backpack of exploration for kids nine and above. ⊠ *100 Maryland Ave. SW, at 1st St., Capitol Hill* ☎ *202/225–8333* ⊕ *www.usbg.gov* ⌨ *Free* ◷ *Daily 10–5* Ⓜ *Federal Center SW.*

Fodor'sChoice
★
United States National Arboretum. During azalea season (mid-April through May) this 446-acre oasis is a blaze of color. In early summer, clematis, peonies, rhododendrons, and roses bloom. At any time of year the 22 original Corinthian columns from the U.S. Capitol, re-erected here in 1990, are striking. All 50 states are represented by a

state tree or flower. The arboretum has guided hikes throughout the year, including a Full Moon Hike at night. Check the website for schedules and to register. For a soothing, relaxing outing, visit the Cryptomeria Walk and Japanese Stroll Garden, which are part of the Bonsai and Penjing Museum. Admission to the grounds and the Visitors Center is free. On weekends a tram tours the arboretum's curving roadways at 11:30, 1, 2, 3, and 4. It's a difficult walk from the Metro so driving or biking in is best. The National

WORD OF MOUTH

"I guess the question is whether the point is just to see cherry trees or to see a larger context. The Arboretum is lovely (but not easy to get to if you don't know D.C.) but the Tidal Basin has the advantage, of well, being the Tidal Basin and on the Mall. The cherry trees are part of a larger experience visually. The Arboretum will be much less crowded." —MikeT

Herb Garden and the National Bonsai Collection are also here. ⊠ *3501 New York Ave. NE, Northeast* ☎ *202/245–2726* ⊕ *www.usna.usda.gov* ✉ *Free* ⊙ *Fri.–Mon. 8–5, Bonsai and Penjing Museum Fri.–Mon. 10–4* Ⓜ *Weekends only: Union Station, then X6 bus (runs every 40 mins). Weekdays: Stadium/Armory, then B2 bus to Bladensburg Rd. and R St.*

PARKS

FAMILY
Fodor's Choice
★

C&O Canal. George Washington was one of the first to advance the idea of a canal linking the Potomac with the Ohio River across the Appalachians. Work started on the Chesapeake & Ohio Canal in 1828, and when it opened in 1850 its 74 locks linked Georgetown with Cumberland, Maryland, 185 miles to the northwest (still short of its intended destination). Lumber, coal, iron, wheat, and flour moved up and down the canal, but it was never as successful as its planners had hoped it would be. Many of the bridges spanning the canal in Georgetown were too low to allow anything other than fully loaded barges to pass underneath, and competition from the Baltimore & Ohio Railroad eventually spelled an end to profitability. Today the canal is part of the National Park System; walkers and cyclists follow the towpath once used by mules, while canoeists paddle the canal's calm waters. You could walk or pedal to the end of the canal, nearly 200 miles away in Cumberland, Maryland, but most cyclists stop at Great Falls, Maryland, 13 miles from where the canal starts. ⊠ *Georgetown Canal Visitor Center, 1057 Thomas Jefferson St. NW, Georgetown* ☎ *202/653–5190 for Georgetown, 301/767–3714 for Great Falls* ⊕ *www.nps.gov/choh* ⊙ *Visitor center June–Aug., weekends 9:30–4:30.*

FAMILY
East Potomac Park. This 328-acre finger of land extends south of the Jefferson Memorial from the Tidal Basin between the Washington Channel to the east and the Potomac River to the west. There are playgrounds, picnic tables, tennis courts, swimming pools, a driving range, one 18-hole and two 9-hole golf courses, miniature golf, and a pool. Double-blossoming cherry trees line Ohio Drive and bloom about two weeks after the single-blossoming variety that attracts throngs to the

Tidal Basin each spring. ⊠ *Ohio Dr. SW, Southwest* ☎ *202/426–6841* ⊕ *www.npca.org/parks* Ⓜ *Smithsonian.*

Glover-Archbold Park. Groves of beeches, elms, and oaks flourish at this 183-acre park, part of the Rock Creek system, which begins just west of Georgetown and ends, 3½ miles later, near Van Ness Street. Along the way you'll experience a stream valley with ancient trees, possible bird sightings, and perhaps even a celebrity or two. ⊠ *Wisconsin Ave. at Van Ness St. NW, Upper Northwest* Ⓜ *Tenleytown/American University.*

Pershing Park. A quiet, sunken garden and fountain honors General John J. "Black Jack" Pershing, the first to hold the title General of the Armies, a rank Congress created in 1919 to recognize his military achievements. Engravings on the stone walls recount pivotal campaigns from World War I, when Pershing commanded the American expeditionary force and conducted other military exploits. ⊠ *15th St. and Pennsylvania Ave., White House Area* Ⓜ *McPherson Sq.*

FAMILY
Fodor'sChoice
★

Rock Creek Park. The 1,800 acres surrounding Rock Creek have provided a cool oasis for visitors and D.C. residents ever since Congress set them aside for recreational use in 1890. The bubbling, rocky stream draws nature lovers to the miles of paved walkways. Bicycle routes, jogging and hiking paths, and equestrian trails wind through the groves of dogwoods, beeches, oaks, and cedars, and 30 picnic areas are scattered about. About twice the size of NYC's Central Park, the park bifurcates the length of the city, making entrance and egress easy for short or long exercise excursions.

An asphalt bike path running through the park has a few challenging hills but is mostly flat, and it's possible to bike several miles without having to stop for cars (the roadway is closed entirely to cars on weekends). Bikers can begin a ride at the Lincoln Memorial or Kennedy Center, pass the Washington Zoo, and eventually come to the District line, where the trail separates, with one part continuing to Bethesda and another to Silver Spring. The most popular run in Rock Creek Park is along a trail that follows the creek from Georgetown to the National Zoo, about 4 miles round-trip. In summer there's considerable shade, and there are water fountains and an exercise station along the way. Rangers at the Nature Center and Planetarium introduce visitors to the park and keep track of daily events; guided nature walks leave from the center on weekends at 2. The park is open only during daylight hours. ⊠ *5200 Glover Rd. NW, Nature Center and Planetarium* ☎ *202/895–6070* ⊕ *www.nps.gov/rocr* ☼ *Nature Center Wed.–Sun. 9–5; planetarium shows Wed. at 2, weekends at 1 and 4.*

10

Meridian Hill Park. Landscape architect Horace Peaslee created oft-overlooked Meridian Hill Park, a noncontiguous section of Rock Creek Park, after a 1917 study of the parks of Europe. As a result, the garden contains elements of gardens in France (a long, straight mall bordered with plants), Italy (terraces and wall fountains), and Switzerland (a lower-level reflecting pool based on one in Zurich). John Quincy Adams lived in a mansion here after his presidency in 1829, and the park later served as an encampment for Union soldiers during the Civil War. All 50 states are represented by a state tree or flower. Meridian Hill is

also unofficially known as **Malcolm X Park** in honor of the civil rights leader. On weekends you will find a mix of pickup soccer games, joggers running the stairs, and a weekly (weather permitting) drum circle. A statue of **Joan of Arc** poised for battle on horseback stands above the terrace, and a statue of **Dante** is on a pedestal below. A ranger-led tour and cell-phone tours illuminate the history of the landmarks inside the park. Meridian Hill is open year-round during daylight hours. ⊠ *16th and Euclid sts., Adams Morgan* ⊕ *www.nps.gov/mehi* Ⓜ *U St./Cardozo or Columbia Heights.*

WORD OF MOUTH

"My suggestions would be to spend time in Rock Creek Park, the canal area in Georgetown, as well as possibly Dumbarton Oaks in Georgetown, and/or Hillwood Estate on the edge of Rock Creek Park, both of which have pretty grounds." —Cicerone

FAMILY
Fodor's Choice
★

Tidal Basin. This placid pond was part of the Potomac until 1882, when portions of the river were filled in to improve navigation and create additional parkland. The Tidal Basin is the setting for memorials to Thomas Jefferson, Franklin Delano Roosevelt, Martin Luther King, Jr., and George Mason, and can be enjoyed by strolling along the banks or paddling across the tame waters.

Two grotesque sculpted heads on the sides of the Inlet Bridge can be seen as you walk along the sidewalk that hugs the basin. The inside walls of the bridge also feature two other sculptures: bronze, human-headed fish that spout water from their mouths. The bridge was refurbished in the 1980s at the same time the chief of the park, Jack Fish, was retiring. Sculptor Constantine Sephralis played a little joke: these fish heads are actually Fish's head.

Once you cross the bridge, continue along the Tidal Basin to the right. This route is especially scenic when the **cherry trees** are in bloom. The first batch of these trees arrived from Japan in 1909. The trees were infected with insects and fungus, however, and the Department of Agriculture ordered them destroyed. A diplomatic crisis was averted when the United States politely asked the Japanese for another batch, and in 1912 First Lady Helen Taft planted the first tree. The second was planted by the wife of the Japanese ambassador, Viscountess Chinda. About 200 of the original trees still grow near the Tidal Basin. (These cherry trees are the single-flowering Akebeno and Yoshino variety. Double-blossom Fugenzo and Kwanzan trees grow in East Potomac Park and flower about two weeks after their more famous cousins.)

The trees are now the centerpiece of Washington's two-week **Cherry Blossom Festival,** held each spring since 1935. The festivities are kicked off by the lighting of a ceremonial Japanese lantern that rests on the north shore of the Tidal Basin, not far from where the first tree was planted. The once-simple celebration has grown over the years to include concerts, martial-arts demonstrations, a running race, and a parade. Park Service experts try their best to predict exactly when the buds will pop. The trees are usually in bloom for about 12 days in late

March or early April. When winter will not release its grip, parade and festival take place without the presence of blossoms, no matter how inclement the weather. When the weather complies and the blossoms peak at the time of the festivities, Washington rejoices. ⊠ *Bordered by Independence and Maine aves., The Mall* Ⓜ *Smithsonian.*

West Potomac Park. Between the Potomac and the Tidal Basin, this park is known for its flowering cherry trees, which bloom for two weeks in late March or early April, and for the World War II Memorial, as well as the memorials for Lincoln, Martin Luther King Jr., Franklin Delano Roosevelt, Jefferson, George Mason, and the Korean and Vietnam War Veterans. A nice place to picnic and play ball, families can relax and admire the views of the water. ⊠ *Bounded by Constitution Ave., 17th St., and Independence Ave.* ⊕ *www.npca.org.*

ZOO

FAMILY
Fodor's Choice
★

Smithsonian National Zoological Park. The National Zoo has much to offer in addition to the pandas. Carved out of rolling, wooded hills in Rock Creek Park, it houses 2,000 animals, representing 400 species, in innovative compounds showing animals in their native settings. Step inside the Great Flight Cage to observe the flight of many species of birds; this walk-in aviary is open from May to October (the birds are moved indoors during the colder months). Between 11 and 2 each day you can catch the orangutans traveling on the "O Line," a series of cables and towers near the Great Ape House that allows the primates to swing hand over hand about 35 feet over your head. One of the more unusual exhibits is Amazonia, an amazingly authentic reproduction of a South American rain-forest ecosystem. You feel as if you are deep inside a steamy jungle, with monkeys leaping overhead and noisy birds flying from branch to branch. Exciting new exhibits are always being added, such as the new Asia trail featuring sloth bears, fishing cats, red pandas, a Japanese giant salamander, clouded leopards, and other Asian species.

On the giant panda front, Tian Tian and Mei Xiang have been the zoo's most famous residents since 2000, and a new contract guarantees that they will stay in Washington until December 2015. In 2005 the pandas had their first cub, Tai Shan, who was moved to China in 2010. The new baby, Bao Bao, born in the late summer of 2013, is currently delighting visitors with her bamboo eating and lounging.

Part of the Smithsonian Institution, the National Zoo was created by an Act of Congress in 1889, and the 163-acre park was designed by landscape architect Frederick Law Olmsted, who also designed the U.S. Capitol grounds and New York's Central Park. Before the zoo opened in 1890, live animals used as taxidermists' models were kept on the Mall. ■TIP→ **Visit early in the morning or late afternoon for your best chance of seeing active animals. Many sleep at midday.** ⊠ *3001 Connecticut Ave. NW, Upper Northwest* ☎ *202/673–4800, 202/673–4717* ⊕ *nationalzoo.si.edu* ☯ *Grounds: Apr.–Oct., daily 6 am–8 pm; Nov.–Mar., daily 6–6. Zoo buildings from 10* Ⓜ *Cleveland Park or Woodley Park/Zoo.*

10

Hop on two wheels to give your feet a break and explore the monuments by bike.

SPORTS

Washington is well designed for outdoor sports, with numerous places to play, run, and ride. When the weather is good, it seems all of Washington is out riding a bike, playing softball and volleyball, jogging past monuments, or taking a relaxing stroll. Many of the favorite locations for participation sports are in the shadow of D.C.'s most famous spots, such as Capitol Hill and the White House.

BASEBALL

Washington Nationals. Major League Baseball has returned to D.C., where the Washington Nationals of the National League play in the spectacular 41,546-seat, state-of-the-art Nationals Park. The team has enjoyed winning seasons and are hugely popular with the hometown crowd, although seats are usually available at the gate. The Nationals' mascots, "The Racing Presidents," compete during the fourth inning at every game. Tours of the stadium are available when the Nationals are on the road and in the morning when the team has night games. ■TIP→ The Metro is a hassle-free and inexpensive way to get to the ballpark. Parking is scarce. ⊠ *Nationals Park, 1500 S. Capitol St. SE, Navy Yard* 🕾 *202/675–6287* ⊕ *washington.nationals.mlb.com* ✉ *$7–$598; tours $15* Ⓜ *Navy Yard.*

BASKETBALL

Georgetown University Hoyas. Former NCAA national champions, the Hoyas are the most prominent Division I men's college basketball team in the area. They became a national basketball powerhouse under their coach John Thompson, and remain perennial contenders in the national tourney under their current coach, John Thompson III. The Hoyas play home games at the Verizon Center downtown. ✉ *Verizon Center, 601 F St. NW, between 6th and 7th sts., Chinatown* ☎ *202/687–4692* ⊕ *guhoyas.com* Ⓜ *Gallery Pl./Chinatown*

Washington Mystics. This WNBA team plays at the Verizon Center in downtown Washington and perennially lead the WNBA in attendance, despite a losing record. The games are loud, boisterous events. You can buy Mystics tickets at the Verizon Center box office or through Ticketmaster. The women's season runs from late May to August. ✉ *Verizon Center, 601 F St. NW, between 6th and 7th sts., Chinatown* ☎ *202/432–7328* ⊕ *www.wnba.com/mystics* 🎫 *$18–$300* Ⓜ *Gallery Pl./Chinatown.*

Washington Wizards. From October to April the NBA's Washington Wizards play at the Verizon Center and feature NBA All-Star and 2014 Slam Dunk Contest champion John Wall. For showtime entertainment look for the G-Wiz, the G-Man, the Wiz Kids, and of course the Wizard Girls. Buy tickets from the Verizon Center box office, the Wizards' online, or Ticketmaster. ✉ *Verizon Center, 601 F St. NW, between 6th and 7th sts., Chinatown* ☎ *202/432–7328* ⊕ *www.nba.com/wizards* 🎫 *$18–$2,500* Ⓜ *Gallery Pl./Chinatown.*

BICYCLING

The numerous trails in the District and its surrounding areas are well maintained and clearly marked. Washington's large parks are also popular with cyclists. Plus, with new bike lanes on all major roads and the Capital Bikeshare scheme, it's also a great way to get around town. ⇨ *See also the C&O Canal and Rock Creek Park in Parks, and the National Mall in Running.*

Capital Crescent Trail. Suited for bicyclists, walkers, rollerbladers, and strollers, this paved trail stretches along the old Georgetown Branch, a B&O Railroad line that was completed in 1910 and was in operation until 1985. The 7.5-mile route's first leg runs from Georgetown near Key Bridge to central Bethesda at Bethesda and Woodmont avenues. At Bethesda and Woodmont the trailheads through a well-lighted tunnel near the heart of Bethesda's lively business area and continues into Silver Spring. The 3.5-mile stretch from Bethesda to Silver Spring is gravel. The Georgetown Branch Trail, as this section is officially named, connects with the Rock Creek Trail, which goes to Rockville in the north and Memorial Bridge past the Washington Monument in the south. On weekends when the weather's nice, all sections of the trails are crowded. ☎ *202/234–4874 for Capital Crescent Coalition* ⊕ *www.cctrail.org.*

10

East Potomac Park. Cyclists might try the 3-mile loop around the golf course in East Potomac Park at Hains Point (entry is near the Jefferson Memorial). This peninsula, though somewhat less scenic than a run around the Mall, is a favorite training course for dedicated local racers and would-be triathletes. Hains Point is a great place to view Fort McNair and the National War College, as well as to watch planes take off and land from Reagan National Airport across the river. ⊠ *14th St. SW, Southwest* ☏ *202/485–9874 for National Park Service.*

BIKING THE MALL

A pleasant loop route begins at the Lincoln Memorial, going north past the Washington Monument, and turning around at the Tidal Basin. Along the way you can take a break at some of the small fountains and parks and there are places to get a drink of water.

Mount Vernon Trail. Across the Potomac in Virginia, this riverside trail has two sections. The northern part begins near the causeway at Theodore Roosevelt Island across the river from the Kennedy Center *(⇨ see Hiking)*. Three and a half miles later it passes Ronald Reagan National Airport and continues on to Mount Vernon, a total distance of 18 miles. This section has slight slopes and almost no interruptions for traffic, making it a delightful biking experience. Even inexperienced bikers enjoy the trail, which provides wonderful views of the Potomac. To access the trail from the District, take the Theodore Roosevelt Bridge or the Rochambeau Memorial Bridge, also known as the 14th Street Bridge. South of the airport, the trail runs down to the Washington Marina. The final mile of the trail's northern section meanders through protected wetlands before ending in the heart of Old Town Alexandria. The trail's 9-mile southern section extends along the Potomac from Alexandria to Mount Vernon. No motorized vehicles (including skateboards, bicycles, scooters, and Segways) are allowed, however. ⊠ *Park Headquarters, Turkey Run Park, McLean, Virginia* ☏ *703/289–2500* ⊕ *www.nps.gov/gwmp* Ⓜ *Arlington Cemetery, Ronald Reagan Washington National Airport, or Rosslyn.*

INFORMATION

Washington Area Bicyclist Association. Members conduct local outreach to encourage biking and do advocacy for a better-integrated transportation system linking transit, trails, bicycling, and walking facilities. They also educate the public about bike safety. WABA also provides an institutional structure for those looking for longer organized rides. ⊠ *1803 Connecticut Ave. NW, 3rd fl., Dupont Circle* ☏ *202/518–0524* ⊕ *www.waba.org* Ⓜ *Dupont Circle.*

RENTALS AND TOURS

Big Wheel Bikes. This company near the C&O Canal Towpath rents multispeed and other types of bikes hourly or for the day. Rates range from $7–$10 per hour and $35–$100 per day. There is a three-hour minimum. Tandem bikes, kids' bikes, and bikes with baby carriers are also available. Other locations are in Bethesda, near the Capital Crescent Trail, and Alexandria, if you want to ride the Mount Vernon

Trail. ⊠ *1034 33rd St. NW, Georgetown* ☎ *202/337–0254* ⊕ *www. bigwheelbikes.com.*

Bike and Roll. Three-hour, 4- to 8-mile guided tours of downtown Washington operate between early March and Thanksgiving and range in cost from $35 to $60, including bike rental. Advance reservations are required. Tours start from the Union Station, the Mall, and the Martin Luther King, Jr. Memorial Library, as well as from Alexandria for rides to Mount Vernon. ⊠ *50 Massachusetts Ave. NE, Downtown* ☎ *202/962–0206* ⊕ *www.bikethesites.com* Ⓜ *Union Station.*

Capital Bikeshare. One of the nation's largest bike-share programs, with more than 2,500 bikes, lets you pick up a bike at one of more than 300 stations located around Washington and Arlington, Virginia, and then return it at a location near your destination. Using a credit card to pay the 24-hour, three-day, or annual membership fee at a bike station kiosk, you receive a code to unlock a bike. The membership entitles you to an unlimited number of rides during the 24 hours. The first 30 minutes are free, then different rates apply, depending on the amount of time you have the bike. Bikers provide their own helmets. ■TIP→ Capital Bikeshare is designed for quick, short trips, but you can take as many trips as you want each day, so design your daylong adventures with short trips in mind. ☎ *877/430–2453* ⊕ *www.capitalbikeshare.com.*

BOATING AND SAILING

The Chesapeake Bay is one of the great sailing basins of the world. For scenic and historical sightseeing, take a day trip to Annapolis, Maryland, the home of the U.S. Naval Academy. ■TIP→ The popularity of boating and the many boating businesses in Annapolis make it one of the best civilian sailing centers on the East Coast.

Annapolis Sailing School. Founded in 1959, this organization is the oldest of its kind in the United States and is a great choice for lessons and rentals. It's world-renowned. ⊠ *7001 Bembe Beach Rd., Annapolis, Maryland* ☎ *800/638–9192* ⊕ *www.annapolissailing.com.*

Mather Gorge. Some of the best white-water kayakers and canoeists in the country call Washington home. On weekends they practice below Great Falls in Mather Gorge, a canyon carved by the Potomac River just north of the city, above Chain Bridge. The water is deceptive and dangerous, containing Class I to Class IV rapids. Beginners should watch the experts at play from a post above the gorge. ■TIP→ Great Falls Park is now a trash free zone, so be prepared to carry your trash out of the park with you. ⊠ *Great Falls Park, 9200 Old Dominion Dr., McLean, Virginia* ☎ *703/285–2965 in Virginia, 301/299–3613 in Maryland* ⊕ *www.nps.gov/grfa.*

Potomac River. Canoeing, sailing, and powerboating are popular in the Washington, D.C. area. Several places rent boats along the Potomac River north and south of the city. You can dip your paddle just about anywhere along the river—go canoeing in the C&O Canal, sailing in the widening river south of Alexandria, or even kayaking in the raging rapids at Great Falls, a 30-minute drive from the capital.

10

RENTALS

Belle Haven Marina. South of Reagan National Airport and Old Town Alexandria, the marina, located off George Washington Parkway, rents two types of sailboats: Sunfish are $35 for two hours during the week and $40 for two hours on the weekend; Flying Scots are $50 for two hours during the week and $60 for two hours during the weekend. All-day rentals are also available. Canoes, jon boats, and kayaks are available for rent as well. Rentals are available from April to October. The marina takes reservations, which are useful during peak-season weekends. ✉ *1201 Belle Haven Rd., Old Town, Alexandria, Virginia* ☎ *703/768–0018* ⊕ *www.saildc.com.*

The Boathouse at Fletcher's Cove. In business since the 1850s, the Boat House at Fletcher's Cove, on the D.C. side of the Potomac, rents rowboats, canoes, and bicycles and sells tackle, snack foods, and D.C. fishing licenses. Here you can catch shad, perch, catfish, striped bass, and other freshwater species. Canoeing is allowed on the canal and on the Potomac, weather permitting. There's a large picnic area along the riverbank. ✉ *4940 Canal Rd., at Reservoir Rd., Georgetown* ☎ *202/244–0461* ⊕ *www.fletcherscove.com.*

Thompson's Boat Center. The center rents canoes and kayaks, as well as bikes. The location provides a nice launching point into the Potomac, right in the center of the city. Rowing sculls are also available, but you must demonstrate prior experience and a suitable skill level. Note: Thompson closes Halloween through early March, based on the water's temperature. ✉ *2900 Virginia Ave. NW, Foggy Bottom* ☎ *202/333–4861, 202/333–9543* ⊕ *www.thompsonboatcenter.com* Ⓜ *Foggy Bottom/GWU.*

Tidal Basin Boathouse. Paddleboat rentals are available mid-March through mid-October. The entrance is on the east side of the Tidal Basin. You can rent two-passenger boats at $14 per hour and four-passenger boats at $22 per hour. ✉ *1501 Maine Ave. SW, The Mall* ☎ *202/479–2426* ⊕ *www.tidalbasinpaddleboats.com* Ⓜ *Smithsonian.*

Washington Sailing Marina. Sailboats can be rented from this scenic marina around mid-May to October, or until the water gets too cold. Aqua fins are $15 per hour or $40 for three hours. The 19-foot Flying Scots are $23 per hour and $80 for four hours. All-terrain bikes rent for $8 per hour and $28 per day. The marina is on the Mount Vernon Trail off the George Washington Parkway, south of Ronald Reagan National Airport. ✉ *1 Marina Dr., Alexandria, Virginia* ☎ *703/548–9027* ⊕ *www.washingtonsailingmarina.com.*

FOOTBALL

Washington Redskins. The perennially popular Redskins continue to play football in the Maryland suburbs at 79,000-seat FedEx Field. Under ongoing discussion is a name change for the team, since some deem it insensitive to Native Americans. Super Bowl wins in 1983, '88, and '92 have ensured the Redskins a place as one of the top three most valuable franchises in the NFL. Diehard fans snap up season tickets year after year, especially after the acquisition of the explosive new quarterback,

Robert Griffin III, or RGIII as he's known to the fans. Individual game-day tickets can be hard to come by when the team is enjoying a strong season. Your best bet is to check out StubHub (⊕ *www.stubhub.com*, the official ticket marketplace of the Redskins.) Several restaurants overlook the field, and the stadium houses the Redskins Hall of Fame. A large installation of solar panels, including one shaped like a giant quarterback and dubbed "Solar Man," powers the lights. Parking is a hassle, so take the Metro or arrive several hours early if you don't want to miss the kickoff.

■TIP➜ Game tickets can be difficult to get, but fans can see the players up close and for free at the Bon Secours Training Camp in Richmond, Virginia. Camp begins in late July and continues through mid-August. The practices typically last from 90 minutes to two hours. Fans can bring their own chairs, and the players are usually available after practice to sign autographs. Call ahead to make sure the practices are open that day. A practice schedule is on the team's website. ⊠ *FedEx Field, 1600 FedexWay, Landover, Maryland* 🕾 *301/276–6000 for FedEx Field* ⊕ *www.redskins.com* 🖿 *$75–$1,200.*

HIKING

Great hiking is available in and around Washington. Hikes and nature walks are listed in the Friday "Weekend" section of the *Washington Post*. Several area organizations sponsor outings, and many are guided.

Billy Goat Trail. This challenging trail in the Chesapeake and Ohio Canal National Historical Park starts and ends at the C&O Canal Towpath for a total hike of 4.7 miles, providing some outstanding views of the wilder parts of the Potomac, along with some steep downhills, rock hopping, as well as some climbs. Be prepared—the hike is mostly in the sun, not suitable for small children, and no dogs are allowed. ⊠ *Near Great Falls Tavern Visitor Center, 11710 MacArthur Blvd., Potomac, Maryland* 🕾 *301/413–0720* ⊕ *www.nps.gov/choh.*

Huntley Meadows Park. On this 1,500-acre refuge in Alexandria, you can spot more than 200 bird species—from ospreys to owls, egrets, and ibis. Much of the park is wetlands, a favorite of aquatic species. A boardwalk circles through a marsh, enabling you to spot beaver lodges, and 4 miles of trails wend through the park, making it likely you'll see deer, muskrats, and river otters as well. The park has an observation tower for good wildlife spotting and a small visitor's center and gift shop. ⊠ *3701 Lockheed Blvd., Alexandria, Virginia* 🕾 *703/768–2525* ⊕ *www.fairfaxcounty.gov/parks/huntley.*

Potomac Appalachian Trail Club. Founded in 1927, the club sponsors hikes—usually free—on trails from Pennsylvania to Virginia, including the C&O Canal Towpath and the Appalachian Trail. This is a good resource for books with trail maps, hiking guides, trail cabins, and camping information. ⊠ *118 Park St. SE, Vienna, Virginia* 🕾 *703/242–0315* ⊕ *www.patc.net.*

Fodor's Choice ★ **Theodore Roosevelt Island.** Designed as a living memorial to the environmentally minded president, this wildlife sanctuary is off the George

10

Washington Parkway near the Virginia side of the Potomac—close to Foggy Bottom, Georgetown, East Potomac Park, and the Kennedy Center. Hikers and bicyclists can reach the island by crossing the Theodore Roosevelt Memorial Bridge or walking from the Rosslyn Metro. Many birds and other animals live in the island's marsh and forests. Rangers are available for an Island Safari, where a statue of Teddy greets you with his arm raised. ☎ 703/289–2500 ⊕ www.nps.gov/this.

Woodend Sanctuary. A self-guided nature trail winds through a verdant 40-acre estate that is the suburban Maryland headquarters of the local **Audubon Naturalist Society.** So bring those binoculars! A Georgian Revivalist mansion, designed in the 1920s by Jefferson Memorial architect John Russell Pope, graces the grounds. You're never far from the trill of birdsong here, as the Audubon Society has turned the place into something of a private nature preserve, forbidding the use of toxic chemicals and leaving some areas in a wild, natural state. Programs include wildlife identification walks, environmental education programs, and a weekly Saturday bird walk September through June. A bookstore stocks titles on conservation, ecology, and birds. The grounds are open daily sunrise to sunset, and admission is free. ⊠ 8940 Jones Mill Rd., Chevy Chase, Maryland ☎ 301/652–9188, 301/652–1088 for recent bird sightings ⊕ www.audubonnaturalist. org ☑ Free.

HOCKEY

Fodor's Choice ★ **National Gallery of Art Ice Rink.** One of the most popular outdoor winter venues in Washington is surrounded by the museum's Sculpture Garden. The Art Deco rink is perfect for a romantic date night, a fun daytime kid activity (when it's less crowded), or for just enjoying the wintry views of the National Archives and the sculptures as the sun sets. In spring the rink becomes a fountain. Plus, the Gallery's Pavilion Café is right there. Admission is $8 for adults, skate rental is $3, and lockers are $0.50, plus a $5 deposit. ⊠ Constitution Ave. NW, between 7th and 9th sts., Downtown ☎ 202/216–9397 ⊕ www.nga.gov Ⓜ Archives/ Navy Memorial.

Washington Capitals. One of pro hockey's top teams, the Washington Capitals play loud and exciting home games in October through April at the Verizon Center. The team is led by one of hockey's superstars, Alex Ovechkin, and enjoys a huge, devoted fanbase. Tickets are difficult to find but can be purchased at the Verizon Center box office, StubHub, or Ticketmaster. ⊠ Verizon Center, 601 F St. NW, between 6th and 7th sts., Chinatown ☎ 202/266–2222 ⊕ capitals.nhl.com ☑ $45–$385 Ⓜ Gallery Pl./Chinatown.

RUNNING

Running is one of the best ways to see the city, and several uninterrupted scenic trails wend through Downtown Washington and nearby northern Virginia (including the Mount Vernon Trail; ⇨ see Bicycling). The trails of Rock Creek Park close at nightfall and the ones along the

C&O Canal *(⇨ see Parks for information on both these prime daytime running spots)* and other remote areas—or on the Mall—are not as safe, although the streets are fairly well lit.

Fodor's Choice **National Mall and Memorial Parks.** The most popular running route in
★ Washington is the 4½-mile loop on the Mall. At any time of day hundreds of runners and speed walkers make their way along the gravel pathways. There's relatively little car traffic and, as they travel from the Lincoln Memorial all the way up to the Capitol and back, they can take in some of Washington's finest landmarks, such as the Washington Monument, the Reflecting Pool, and the Smithsonian's many museums. For a longer run, veer south of the Mall on either side of the Tidal Basin and head for the Jefferson Memorial and East Potomac Park, the site of many races. ⊠ *Bounded by Constutution and Independence aves., The Mall* ⊕ *www.nps.gov/nacc.*

INFORMATION AND ORGANIZATIONS

For low-key group runs, check the D.C. Road Runners' website (⊕ *www.dcroadrunners.org*). Pacers (⊕ *www.runpacers.com*), a popular running-store chain, has weekly group runs at its six locations. Information on weekend races around Washington and comprehensive listings of running and walking events are posted online by a local publication, the *Washington Running Report* (⊕ *www.runwashington.com*).

Fleet Feet Sports Shop. Most Sunday mornings this shop sponsors informal runs through Rock Creek Park and other areas. Runners gather at the store just before 9 am to embark on 5-mile Fun Run along the streets and into Rock Creek Park. ⊠ *1841 Columbia Rd. NW, Adams Morgan* ☎ *202/387-3888* ⊕ *www.fleetfeetdc.com* Ⓜ *Woodley Park/Zoo.*

SOCCER

Fodor's Choice **D.C. United.** One of the best Major League Soccer teams has a huge
★ fan base in the nation's capital, finding many of its fans in the international crowds who miss the big matches at home, as well as families whose kids play soccer. International matches, including some World Cup preliminaries, are often played on the grass field of Capitol Hill's RFK Stadium, the Redskins' and Senators' former residence. Games are played March through October. You can buy tickets at the RFK Stadium ticket office or through the team's website, which offers special youth pricing. The DC Talon, the team mascot, entertains the crowd, along with enthusiastic, horn-blowing fans. ⊠ *Robert F. Kennedy Stadium, 2400 E. Capitol St. SE, Capitol Hill* ☎ *202/547-3134* ⊕ *www.dcunited. com* ⌨ *$25-$65* Ⓜ *Stadium.*

10

SHOPPING

Updated by
Catherine
Sharpe

Despite the fact that going to "the Mall" in D.C. doesn't mean you're going shopping, Washington offers fabulous stores that sell serious or silly souvenirs, designer fashions, recycled and green goods, books about almost everything, and handicrafts. Even if you are headed to the mall, our nation's Mall, that is, you'll discover that plenty of collections housed along the famous greensward, such as the Smithsonian museums and the National Gallery of Art, sell interesting keepsakes in their gift shops.

Beyond the Mall, smaller one-of-a-kind shops, designer boutiques, and interesting specialty collections add to Washington's shopping scene alongside stores that have been part of the landscape for generations. Weekdays, Downtown street vendors add to the mix by offering funky jewelry; brightly patterned ties; buyer-beware watches; sunglasses; and African-inspired clothing, accessories, and art. Discriminating shoppers will find satisfaction at upscale malls on the city's outskirts. Of course, T-shirts and Capitol City souvenirs are in plentiful supply.

PLANNING

GALLERY HOPPING
Washington has three main gallery districts—Downtown, Dupont Circle, and Georgetown—though small galleries can be found all over in converted houses and storefronts. Whatever their location, many keep unusual hours and close entirely on Sunday and Monday. The *Washington Post* "Weekend" section (⊕ *www.washingtonpost.com*) and *Washington CityPaper* (⊕ *www.washingtoncitypaper.com*), published on Thursday, are excellent sources of information on current exhibits and hours.

HISTORIC WALKS

Shopping is the perfect way to acquaint yourself with some of D.C.'s distinguished neighborhoods. A quick diversion down a side street in Georgetown reveals the neighborhood's historic charm and current glamour. Peer around a corner in Dupont or Capitol Hill to see a true D.C. architecture classic—the row house. Wandering Downtown you are sure to bump into one of the nation's great Neoclassical structures, whether it is the White House or Ford's Theatre.

HOURS

Store hours vary greatly. In general, Georgetown stores are open late and on Sunday; stores Downtown that cater to office workers close as early as 5 pm and may not open at all on weekends. Some stores extend their hours on Thursday, while some in Adams Morgan and along the U Street Corridor don't open until noon but keep late hours to serve the evening crowds.

HOW TO SAVE MONEY

If you're willing to dig a bit, D.C. can be a savvy shopper's dream. Upscale consignment stores like Secondi in Dupont Circle and discount outlets like Nordstrom Rack in Friendship Heights provide an alternative to the surrounding luxury retail. Secondhand bookstores throughout the city provide hours of browsing and buying at welcoming prices.

WHITE HOUSE AREA

In the area best known for the nation's most famous citizen, you can also shop for official White House Christmas ornaments and Easter eggs, flags from all over the world, and crafts made by living Native American artists and artisans. If you're looking for a tasty treat, grab the fixings for a picnic lunch at the FreshFarm market held every Thursday April through October on the corner of Lafayette Square the produce that's sold here is said to be as fresh as food grown in the White House garden.

BOOKS

InfoShop. You won't find the *New York Times* bestsellers here, but you will find titles on world development issues, poverty, and other weighty issues, along with fiction by writers from Africa, Central and South America, and Asia that are otherwise hard to find. Also at this bookstore stocked and run by the World Bank are desk flags of countries from all over world for $5 each. Students, teachers, and government employees with IDs receive discounts. ⊠ *701 18th St. NW, White House Area* ☎ *202/458-4500* ⊕ *www.worldbank.org/infoshop* ⊙ *Closed weekends* Ⓜ *Farragut W.*

CRAFTS AND GIFTS

Fodor's Choice
★

Indian Craft Shop. Jewelry, pottery, sand paintings, weavings, and baskets from more than 50 Native American tribes, including Navajo, Pueblo, Zuni, Cherokee, and Lakota, are at your fingertips here—as long as you have a photo ID to enter the federal building. Items range from inexpensive jewelry (as little as $5) on up to collector-quality art pieces (more than $10,000). This shop has been open since 1938.

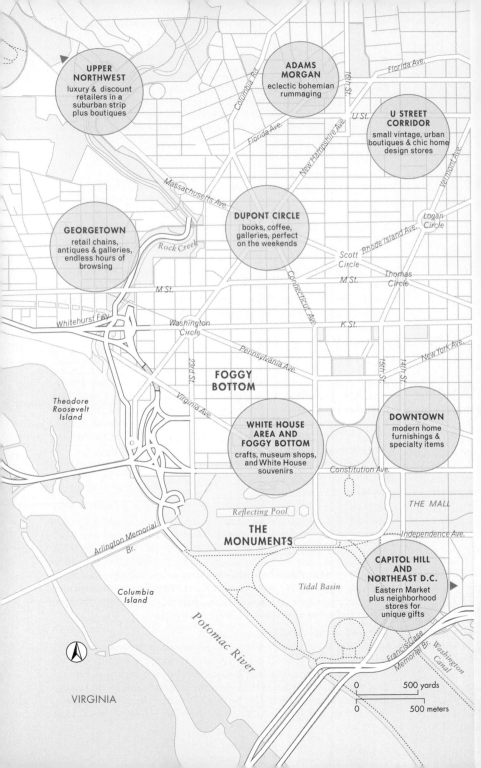

UPPER NORTHWEST
luxury & discount retailers in a suburban strip plus boutiques

ADAMS MORGAN
eclectic bohemian rummaging

U STREET CORRIDOR
small vintage, urban boutiques & chic home design stores

GEORGETOWN
retail chains, antiques & galleries, endless hours of browsing

DUPONT CIRCLE
books, coffee, galleries, perfect on the weekends

WHITE HOUSE AREA AND FOGGY BOTTOM
crafts, museum shops, and White House souvenirs

DOWNTOWN
modern home furnishings & specialty items

CAPITOL HILL AND NORTHEAST D.C.
Eastern Market plus neighborhood stores for unique gifts

Columbia Rd.

Florida Ave.

16th St.

U St.

Florida Ave.

New Hampshire Ave.

Vermont Ave.

Massachusetts Ave.

Rock Creek

Logan Circle

Rhode Island Ave.

Scott Circle

M St.

Thomas Circle

M St.

Connecticut Ave.

Whitehurst Fwy.

Washington Circle

K St.

New York Ave.

23rd St.

Pennsylvania Ave.

15th St.

14th St.

Theodore Roosevelt Island

Virginia Ave.

FOGGY BOTTOM

Constitution Ave.

THE MALL

Reflecting Pool

THE MONUMENTS

Independence Ave.

Arlington Memorial Br.

Columbia Island

Tidal Basin

Francis Case Memorial Br.

Washington Canal

Potomac River

VIRGINIA

0   500 yards
0   500 meters

✉ *U.S. Department of the Interior, 1849 C St. NW, Room 1023, White House Area* ☎ *202/208–4056* ⊕ *www.indiancraftshop.com* ⊘ *Closed weekends (except 3rd Sat. of each month) and federal holidays* Ⓜ *Farragut W or Farragut N.*

National Air and Space Museum Store. Of course, one of the most visited museums in the world has a huge gift shop! The lower level of the three-floor, 12,000-square-foot store has a small clearance section, tons of toys and games, and glow-in-the-dark jewelry and nail polish. The upper level showcases higher quality goods that will appeal to more serious aviation fans, such as hardcover books and authentic flight jackets. Most merchandise is on the middle level. Space pens that work upside down and freeze-dried "astronaut" ice cream are bestsellers. Keep in mind the biggest item in the store, the original model of the USS *Enterprise* from first Star Trek television series, isn't for sale. During the summer, a pop-up space station store near the Independence Avenue exit sells shuttle lollisticks; when the candy's gone, you can play with the shuttle toy. ■**TIP➔** If the main store is too crowded, you can pick up the most popular inexpensive items at small retail outlets on the first and second floors of the museum. ✉ *Independence Ave. and 6th St. SW, The Mall* ☎ *202/633–4510* Ⓜ *L'Enfant Plaza or Smithsonian.*

Fodor's Choice ★ **National Archives Store.** In a town full of museum shops, the National Archives Store stands out, with bespoke merchandise that's only available here. Authentic-looking copies of the Constitution and other historical documents are printed in Pennsylvania and replicas of stationery used in the Civil War come from Maine. The popular "red tape" jewelry is crafted by an Archives employee who works in the building and uses real red tape that bound Government documents: hence the phrase "cut through the red tape." Other popular products feature Rosie the Riveter and presidential pets from Jefferson's bear cubs to the Obamas' dog, Bo. Throughout the store, interactive games associated with special exhibits provide entertainment and education into history—of the United States and even you. Enter your last name into the computer and see how many people in the U.S. share your name and in which states they live. ✉ *Constitution Ave. between 7th and 9th sts., The Mall* ☎ *202/357–5271* ⊕ *www.archives.gov* Ⓜ *Archives/Navy Memorial.*

The Shop at President's Square. Located in the historic Decatur House on Lafayette Square just a block from the White House, this shop sells official merchandise from the White House Historical Association. From the popular Christmas ornaments to jewelry, ties, scarves, and accessories, everything is well made. Ten dollars or less will get you cocktail napkins, bookmarks, or a wooden Easter egg. The more expensive merchandise includes silk scarves, hand-painted enamel boxes, and jewelry with cameos of the White House. ✉ *1610 H St. NW, White House Area* ☎ *202/218–4337* ⊕ *www.whitehousehistory.org/decatur-house* ⊘ *Closed weekends* Ⓜ *Farragut W.*

MARKETS

USDA Farmers' Market. Blueberry popcorn anyone? On Friday early June through October from 10 to 2, pick up fresh fruits, vegetables, breads, baked goods, and flavored popcorn across from the Smithsonian

Metro station. Appropriately, the market is in the parking lot of the U.S. Department of Agriculture building. ✉ *12th St and Independence Ave. SW, White House Area* ⊕ *www.ams.usda.gov* Ⓜ *Smithsonian.*

FOGGY BOTTOM

Home to George Washington University, the Kennedy Center, the famed Watergate complex and row houses owned by diplomats and dignitaries, it's a good spot for people-watching and fine dining, but alas there's very little shopping in this area.

MARKETS

FRESHFARM Market. Pick up a crab cake, an empanada, or a Mexican-style ice pop at this farmers market on Wednesday from 3 to 7, early April through November. Similar fare is available near Lafayette Park (810 Vermont Avenue NW) on Thursday from 11 to 2:30, April through October. Other FRESHFARM markets are in Dupont Circle (year-round on Sunday), H Street NE (April–December, Saturday morning), and at Penn Quarter (Thursday afternoon). All locations sell local fruits and vegetables. ✉ *I St. between New Hampshire and 24th St. NW, Foggy Bottom* ☎ *202/362–8889* ⊕ *www.freshfarmmarkets.org* Ⓜ *Foggy Bottom.*

CAPITOL HILL

Capitol Hill is surprisingly good territory for shopping. Eastern Market and the unique shops and boutiques clustered around the historic redbrick building are great for browsing. Inside Eastern Market are produce and meat counters, plus places to buy flowers and sweets. ■**TIP→ The flea market, held on weekends outdoors, presents nostalgia and local crafts by the crateful. There's also a farmers' market on Saturday.** Along 7th Street you can find a number of small shops selling such specialties as art books, handwoven rugs, and antiques. Cross Pennsylvania Avenue and head south on 8th Street for historic Barracks Row, where shops, bars, and restaurants inhabit the charming row houses leading toward the Anacostia River. The other shopping lure on the Hill is Union Station, D.C.'s gorgeous train station, these days actually a shopping mall that happens to also accommodate Amtrak and commuter trains.

Keep in mind that Union Station and Eastern Market are on opposite sides of the Hill. The Eastern Market Metro stop is the midpoint between the Eastern Market strip and Barracks Row; Union Station is several blocks away. You can certainly walk to Union Station from the Eastern Market stop, but it might be taxing after the time already spent on your feet in the shops.

▌ QUICK
  BITES

The Market Lunch. You might have a tough time choosing what to order at this always-crowded spot in Eastern Market's South Hall. For breakfast, try their "blue bucks" specialty, incredibly light and fluffy buckwheat and blueberry pancakes only available on weekend mornings, or their crab cake benedict with a side of jalapeno grits. If it's lunch, any of the fried-fish sandwiches or platters can't be beat, especially the soft-shell crabs when in season. Just be sure to order a side of fried green tomatoes; you won't be sorry! And as you sit on the long communal table, you're bound to pick up insider tips from the locals sitting next to you. Have cash on hand here, as credit cards aren't accepted. ✉ *Eastern Market, 225 7th St. SE, North corner of market, Capitol Hill* ☎ *202/547–8444* ☉ *Closed Mon.* Ⓜ *Eastern Market.*

SHOPPING MALL

Union Station. Resplendent with marble floors and vaulted ceilings, Union Station is a shopping mall as well as a train station. Tenants include Ann Taylor, Victoria's Secret, Jos. A. Banks, and Godiva, as well as restaurants and a food court with everything from sushi and smoothies to scones. The east hall is filled with vendors of domestic and international wares who sell from stalls. April through October an outdoor market is held Monday to Saturday with dozens of vendors. Christmas brings lights, a train display, and seasonal gift shops. ✉ *50 Massachusetts Ave. NE, Capitol Hill* ☎ *202/289–1908* ⊕ *www. unionstationdc.com* Ⓜ *Union Station.*

BOOKS

Capitol Hill Books. Pop into this three-story maze of used books to browse through a wonderful collection of out-of-print history titles, political and fiction writings, and mysteries. On the 2nd Saturday of every month, this cozy bookstore hosts a free wine and cheese reception from 4–7 and all purchases are discounted 10%. ✉ *657 C St. SE, Capitol Hill* ☎ *202/544–1621* ⊕ *www.capitolhillbooks-dc.com* Ⓜ *Eastern Market.*

FAMILY **Fairy Godmother.** This specialty store, which opened in 1984, features a delightful selection of books for children, from infants through teens, in English, Spanish, and French, including an extensive selection of nonfiction books. It also sells puppets, games, dolls, puzzles, toys, and CDs. ✉ *319 7th St. SE, Capitol Hill* ☎ *202/547–5474* Ⓜ *Eastern Market.*

CHILDREN'S CLOTHING

FAMILY **Dawn Price Baby.** The infant and toddler clothing at this friendly rowhouse boutique has been carefully selected with an eye for super-comfortable fabrics and distinct designs. The shop also stocks toys, gifts, strollers, and bibs for baby Democrats and Republicans. There's a second location in Georgetown. ✉ *325 7th St. SE, Capitol Hill* ☎ *202/543–2920* ⊕ *www.dawnpricebaby.com* Ⓜ *Eastern Market.*

CRAFTS AND GIFTS

Fodor'sChoice **Homebody.** Original artwork, contemporary rugs, delicious-smelling
★ candles, modern kitchen items, furniture, and an eclectic mix of jewelry, bags, and wallets crowd this sophisticated and irreverent boutique. ✉ *715 8th St. SE, Capitol Hill* ☎ *202/544–8445* ⊕ *www.homebodydc. com* Ⓜ *Eastern Market.*

Woven History/Silk Road. Landmarks in this bohemian neighborhood, these connected stores sell gorgeous, handmade treasures from the mountain communities in India, Nepal, Turkey, Iran, Pakistan, and Tibet. You'll find everything from colorful weavings, pillows, and

FIVE GREAT SHOPPING EXPERIENCES

Eastern Market, Capitol Hill Area: Artists, musicians, farmers, and more make this beautifully restored market a feast for the senses. Most vendors accept only cash.

Kramerbooks & Afterwords, Dupont Circle: Meeting up at Kramerbooks for a lazy Sunday afternoon of brunch and browsing is a quintessential D.C. experience.

Miss Pixie's Furnishings & Whatnot, U Street Corridor: The color scheme of the store may be bright pink, but everything for sale is "green." Buyers flock to Miss Pixie's for vintage furniture and home goods.

National Archives Store, The Mall: The hallowed hall where you can see the Declaration of Independence is also home to a store full of all-American gifts, including jewelry made out of real "red tape."

Tiny Jewel Box, Downtown: Since 1930, one family has owned and run this gem of a shop. On the day that her husband was inaugurated, First Lady Michelle Obama presented former First Lady Laura Bush with a custom-made Tiny Jewel Box leather-bound journal and silver pen.

embroidered quilts to exotic jewelry and bags, as well as antique furniture. Woven History's rugs are made the old-fashioned way, with vegetable dyes and hand-spun wool and sizes range from 3-by-5 to 8-by-10. ⊠ *311–315 7th St. SE, Capitol Hill* ☎ *202/543–1705* ⊕ *www.wovenhistory.com* Ⓜ *Eastern Market.*

MARKET

Fodor'sChoice **Eastern Market.** For nearly 145 years, this has been the hub of the Capitol
★ Hill community. Vibrantly colored produce and flowers; freshly caught fish; fragrant cheeses; and tempting sweets are sold at the market by independent vendors. On weekends year-round, local farmers sell fresh fruits and vegetables, and artists and exhibitors sell handmade arts and crafts, jewelry, antiques, collectibles and furniture from around the world. The city's oldest continuously operating public market continues to be a vibrant and lively gathering place, complete with entertainment, art showings, and a pottery studio for residents and visitors alike. ⊠ *7th St. and North Carolina Ave. SE, Capitol Hill* ☎ *202/698–5253* ⊕ *www.easternmarket-dc.com* ☉ *Closed Mon.* Ⓜ *Eastern Market.*

WOMEN'S CLOTHING

Forecast. If you like classic, contemporary styles, Forecast should be in your future. It sells silk and wool-blend sweaters in solid, muted tones and bright colors for women seeking elegant but practical clothing from brands like Lafayette 148 and Eileen Fisher. The housewares and gifts selection on the first floor is colorful and of high quality. ⊠ *218 7th St. SE, Capitol Hill* ☎ *202/547–7337* ⊕ *www.forecaststore.com* ☉ *Closed Mon.* Ⓜ *Eastern Market.*

D.C.'s Museum Shops

11

Would someone in your life love a replica of the Hope diamond? It's waiting for you at the gift shop in the National Museum of Natural History. With a wide range of merchandise and price points, from inexpensive postcards to pricey pottery, museum gift shops allow you the flexibility to bring home a small memento of your visit to the nation's capital or to invest in a piece of American art or history.

Museum gift shops offer everything from period jewelry reproductions to science kits for kids, not to mention prints and postcards of the masterpiece paintings in the permanent collections. Prices are no higher than you'd find in comparable stores. Another bonus: You won't pay tax on anything purchased in a Smithsonian museum.

DOWNTOWN

Downtown D.C. is spread out and sprinkled with federal buildings and museums. Shopping options run the gamut from the Gallery Place shopping center to small art galleries and bookstores. Gallery Place houses familiar chain stores like Urban Outfitters, Bed Bath & Beyond, Ann Taylor Loft, and Aveda; it also has a movie theater and a bowling alley. Other big names in the Downtown area include Macy's and chain stores like H&M, Target, and Banana Republic. With its many offices, Downtown tends to shut down at 5 pm sharp, with the exception of the department stores and larger chain stores. A jolly happy-hour crowd springs up after work and families and fans fill the streets during weekend sporting events at the Verizon Center. The revitalized Penn Quarter has some of the best restaurants in town peppered among its galleries and specialty stores.

The worthwhile shops are not concentrated in one area, however. The Gallery Place Metro stop provides the most central starting point—you can walk south to the galleries and design shops, or west toward the Metro Center and Farragut North, though this trek is only for the ambitious. Although Gallery Place is a nightlife hot spot, the Metro Center and the Farragut area are largely silent after working hours.

CRAFTS AND GIFTS

Fodor's Choice
★

Fahrney's Pens. What began in 1929 as a repair shop and a pen bar—a place to fill your fountain pen before setting out for work—is now a wonderland for anyone who loves a good writing instrument. You'll find pens in silver, gold, and lacquer by the world's leading manufacturers. If you want to improve your handwriting, the store offers classes in calligraphy and cursive. ✉ 1317 F St. NW, Downtown ☎ 202/628-9525 ⊕ www.fahrneyspens.com ☉ Closed Sun. Ⓜ Metro Center.

JEWELRY

Fodor's Choice
★

Tiny Jewel Box. Despite its name, this venerable D.C. favorite contains six floors of precious and semiprecious wares, including unique gifts, home accessories, vintage pieces, and works by such well-known designers as David Yurman, Penny Preville, and Alex Sepkus. The Federal Collection on the sixth floor features handmade boxes and paperweights with decoupages of vintage prints of Washington commissioned by the Tiny Jewel Box. *InStore Magazine* has named this family-run store "America's Coolest Jewelry Store." ✉ *1147 Connecticut Ave. NW, Downtown* ☎ *202/393-2747* ⊕ *www.tinyjewelbox.com* ⊙ *Closed Sun.* Ⓜ *Farragut N.*

SPAS AND BEAUTY SALONS

Andre Chreky. Housed in an elegantly renovated Victorian town house, this salon offers complete services—hair, nails, facials, waxing, and makeup. Because it's a favorite of the Washington elite, you might just overhear a tidbit or two on who's going to what black-tie function with whom. Adjacent whirlpool pedicure chairs allow two friends to get pampered simultaneously. ✉ *1604 K St. NW, Downtown* ☎ *202/293-9393* ⊕ *www.andrechreky.com* Ⓜ *Farragut N.*

WOMEN'S CLOTHING

Coup de Foudre. The name translates to "love at first sight," and that may be the case when you step into this inviting, elegant boutique. All the upscale lingerie hails from France, Belgium, and Italy, and the specialty is friendly, personalized bra fittings. Appointments accepted. ✉ *1001 Pennsylvania Ave. NW, Downtown* ☎ *202/393-0878* ⊕ *www.shopcdf. com* ⊙ *Closed Sun.* Ⓜ *Metro Center.*

Rizik Bros. This tony, patrician Washington institution offers designer women's clothing and expert advice. The sales staff will help find just the right style from the store's inventory, which is particularly strong in formal dresses. Take the elevator up from the northwest corner of Connecticut Avenue and L Street. ✉ *1100 Connecticut Ave. NW, Downtown* ☎ *202/223-4050* ⊕ *www.riziks.com* ⊙ *Closed Sun.* Ⓜ *Farragut N.*

GEORGETOWN

Although Georgetown is not on a Metro line and street parking is tough to find, people still flock here to shop. This is also the capital's center for famous residents, as well as being a hot spot for restaurants, bars, and nightclubs.

National chains and designer shops now stand side by side with the specialty shops that first gave the district its allure, but the historic neighborhood is still charming and its street scene lively. Most stores lie east and west on M Street and to the north on Wisconsin Avenue. The intersection of M and Wisconsin is the nexus for chain stores and big-name designer shops. The farther you venture in any direction from this intersection, the more eclectic and interesting the shops become. Some of the big-name stores are worth a look for their architecture alone; several shops blend traditional Georgetown townhouse exteriors with airy modern showroom interiors.

Shopping in Georgetown can be expensive, but you don't have to add expensive parking lot fees to your total bill. ■TIP→ The DC Circulator is your best bet for getting into and out of Georgetown, especially if it's hot or if you are laden down with many purchases. This $1 bus runs along M Street and up Wisconsin Avenue, passing the major shopping strips. The nearest Metro station, Foggy Bottom/GWU, is a 10- to 15-minute walk from the shops.

QUICK
BITES

DolceZZa. The handmade gelato and sorbet at this all-white storefront are divine, and especially welcome during the heat of summer. The flavors, such as Valrhona chocolate amargo, are endlessly inventive. Strawberry-, peach-, apple-, and clementine-flavored sorbets are available seasonally. Espresso and churros will warm winter afternoons. ⊠ *1560 Wisconsin Ave. NW, Georgetown* ☎ *202/333–4646* ⊕ *www.dolcezzagelato.com.*

SHOPPING MALL

Shops at Georgetown Park. There's a good mix of retailers at this indoor mall in the center of Georgetown including Anthropologie, Dean & DeLuca, DSW, H&M, HomeGoods, J. Crew, and T.J. Maxx. If you need a break from shopping, visit Olivia Macaron's for a coffee and luscious raspberry macaron. You can even try your hand at bocce at Pinstripes, Georgetown's new bistro and entertainment spot which also offers bowling and a wonderful outdoor patio. ⊠ *3222 M St. NW, Georgetown* ☎ *202/342–8190* ⓦ *www.shopsatgeorgetownpark.com* Ⓜ *Foggy Bottom/GWU.*

ANTIQUES AND COLLECTIBLES

Cherub Antiques Gallery and Michael Getz Antiques. You might want to keep your sunglasses on as you enter this shop, where the sterling silver is polished to perfection. Two dealers have shared this Victorian row house since 1983. Michael Getz Antiques carries fireplace equipment and silver. Cherub Antiques Gallery specializes in Art Nouveau and Art Deco. A glass case by the door holds a collection of more than 100 cocktail shakers, including Prohibition-era pieces disguised as penguins, roosters, and dumbbells. ⊠ *2918 M St. NW, Georgetown* ☎ *202/337–2224 for Cherub Gallery, 202/338–3811 for Michael Getz Antiques* ⊕ *www.trocadero.com/cherubgallery* Ⓜ *Foggy Bottom/GWU.*

Fodor's Choice ★ **Jean Pierre Antiques.** Very Georgetown, but fairly close to Dupont Circle, this gorgeous shop sells antique 18th- to 20th-century European furniture and gifts from France, Germany, Sweden, and Italy. The charming owner's vintage bar carts and American Lucite tables are simply sublime. Jean Pierre's Facebook friends will find plenty of pictures to "ooh la la" over. ⊠ *2601 P St. NW, Georgetown* ☎ *202/337–1731* ⊕ *www.jeanpierreantiques.com* Ⓜ *Dupont Circle.*

Marston Luce. House and garden accessories are in the mix here, but the emphasis is on 18th- and 19th-century French and Swedish painted furniture, discovered by the owner on yearly buying trips in Europe. ⊠ *1651 Wisconsin Ave. NW, Georgetown* ☎ *202/333–6800* ⊕ *www.marstonluce.com* ☉ *Closed Sun.* Ⓜ *Foggy Bottom/GWU.*

Old Print Gallery. Here you can find the capital's largest collection of old prints, with a focus on maps and 19th-century decorative prints (including Washingtoniana). ⊠ *1220 31st St. NW, Georgetown* ☎ *202/965–1818* ⊕ *www.oldprintgallery.com* ☉ *Closed Sun. and Mon.* Ⓜ *Foggy Bottom/GWU.*

Fodor's Choice ★ **Opportunity Shop of the Christ Child Society.** This gem of a consignment/thrift store has been a Georgetown landmark since 1954. You'll find gorgeous fine jewelry, antiques, crystal, silver, and porcelain. Prices are moderate, and profits go to a good cause—the Christ Child Society provides for the needs of local children and young mothers. ⊠ *1427 Wisconsin Ave. NW, Georgetown* ☎ *202/333–6635* ⊕ *www.christchilddc.org* ۞ *Closed Sun.* Ⓜ *Foggy Bottom/GWU.*

ART GALLERIES

Many of Georgetown's galleries are on side streets. Their holdings are primarily work by established artists.

Addison Ripley. Contemporary work by national and local artists, including painters Manon Cleary and Wolf Kahn and photographer Frank Hallam Day, is exhibited at this well-respected gallery. ⊠ *1670 Wisconsin Ave. NW, Georgetown* ☎ *202/338–5180* ⊕ *www.addisonripleyfineart.com* ۞ *Closed Sun. and Mon.* Ⓜ *Foggy Bottom/GWU.*

Appalachian Spring. Traditional and contemporary American-made crafts—including art glass, pottery, jewelry, homewares, and toys—fill this lovely shop. The glossy wooden jewelry boxes displayed here are treasures in their own right. There's an outpost in Union Station's East Hall. ⊠ *1415 Wisconsin Ave. NW, Georgetown* ☎ *202/337–5780* ⊕ *www.appalachianspring.com* Ⓜ *Foggy Bottom.*

Maurine Littleton Gallery. Even if the prices are as untouchable as the art in this gallery devoted to glass, it's worth a look to see work by some of the world's finest glass artists. The intimate, bright space is owned and managed by the daughter of Harvey K. Littleton, founder of the American Studio Glass movement. ⊠ *1667 Wisconsin Ave. NW, Georgetown* ☎ *202/333–9307* ⊕ *www.littletongallery.com* ۞ *Closed Sun. and Mon.* Ⓜ *Foggy Bottom.*

Susan Calloway Fine Arts. Latte, the Maltese, may wag his tail as if you came to see him, but it's the art that draws people into this two-floor gallery where a mix of vintage, contemporary, and classical paintings are hung salon-style. You'll find large abstract oils and a lovely selection of landscapes, but don't miss the box full of small original paintings in the back, most priced under $100. ⊠ *1643 Wisconsin Ave., Georgetown* ☎ *202/965–4601* ⊕ *www.callowayart.com* ۞ *Closed Mon. and Tues.* Ⓜ *Foggy Bottom or Dupont Circle.*

BOOKS

Bridge Street Books. This charming independent store focuses on politics, history, philosophy, poetry, literature, film, and Judaica. ⊠ *2814 Pennsylvania Ave. NW, Georgetown* ☎ *202/965–5200* ⊕ *www.bridgestreetbooks.com* Ⓜ *Foggy Bottom/GWU.*

CHILDREN'S CLOTHING

Egg by Susan Lazar. Adorable. That's the word that instantly comes to mind when you step foot into this boutique from designer Susan Lazar. There are clothes for newborns to size 8 in organic and environmentally friendly material with simple and colorful eye-catching patterns and designs. ⊠ *1661 Wisconsin Ave. NW, Georgetown* ☎ *202/338–9500* ⊕ *www.egg-baby.com* Ⓜ *Foggy Bottom.*

DID YOU KNOW?

Georgetown, one of D.C.'s oldest and most storied neighborhoods, is a great spot for political celebrity sightings. Heavyweights like Secretary of State John Kerry, former Secretary of State Madeleine Albright, and journalist Bob Woodward live here.

FAMILY **Tugooh Toys.** You might have a difficult time getting your children to leave this fun toy store filled with educational and eco-friendly toys. From puzzles, games, and building toys to dolls, puppets, and dress-up clothes; you're bound to find the perfect gift for youngsters. ⊠ *1355 Wisconsin Ave.* NW, *Georgetown* ☎ *202/338–9476* ⊕ *www.tugoohtoys. com* Ⓜ *Foggy Bottom.*

HOME FURNISHINGS

Fodor'sChoice **A Mano.** The name is Italian for "by hand," and it lives up to its name,
★ stocking colorful hand-painted ceramics, hand-dyed tablecloths, blown-glass stemware, hand embroidered bed linens, and other home and garden accessories by American, English, Italian, and French artisans. Some of the jewelry pieces are simply stunning, and the kids' gifts are adorable. ⊠ *1677 Wisconsin Ave.* NW, *Georgetown* ☎ *202/298–7200* ⊕ *www.amano.bz.*

MUSIC

Hill & Dale Records. Georgetown's only vinyl record store carries a wonderful collection of new vinyl LPs (yes, it's true, they are new; nothing used at this store) including jazz, country, pop, folk, blues, rock, and electronica. From Billie Holiday's "Body and Soul" and Dick Dale & His Del-Tones' "Summer Surf" to Rush's "Clockwork Angels," the selection is bound to delight any music lover. Also on display in this bright and airy spot are photos and posters that celebrate music. ⊠ *1054 31st St.* NW, *Georgetown* ☎ *202/333–5012* ⊕ *www.hillanddalerecords. com* ۞ *Closed Mon.*

SHOES

Fodor'sChoice **Hu's Shoes.** This cutting-edge selection would shine in Paris, Tokyo, or
★ New York. Luckily for Washingtonians, it brings ballet flats, heels, and boots from designers like Chloé, Givenchy, Manolo Blahnik, Proenza Schouler, and Valentino right to Georgetown. ⊠ *3005 M St.* NW, *Georgetown* ☎ *202/342–0202* ⊕ *www.husonline.com* Ⓜ *Foggy Bottom/GWU.*

SPAS AND BEAUTY SALONS

Bluemercury. Hard-to-find skin-care lines—Laura Mercier, Trish McEvoy, among others—are what set this homegrown, now national, chain apart. The retail space up front sells soaps, lotions, perfumes, cosmetics, and skin- and hair-care products. Behind the glass door is the "skin gym," where you can treat yourself to facials, waxing, and oxygen treatments. ⊠ *3059 M St.* NW, *Georgetown* ☎ *202/965–1300* ⊕ *www. bluemercury.com* Ⓜ *Foggy Bottom/GWU.*

SPECIALTY STORES

Fodor'sChoice **M29 Lifestyle.** Located at the entrance to the Four Seasons Georgetown,
★ this gorgeous store is far from the run-of-the-mill hotel gift shop. You'll find a small collection of women's clothing and accessories from American and international designers Marika Charles, Chan Luu, and Tylho; gorgeous decoupage plates and cake stands from John Darian; and framed stitched art from k studio that would add a charming touch of whimsy to any child's room. The custom-made D.C. notecards and eco-friendly tote bags make great gifts for yourself or friends.

✉ *2800 Pennsylvania Ave. NW, Georgetown* ☎ *202/342–0444* ⊕ *www. fourseasons.com.*

WOMEN'S CLOTHING

Hu's Wear. Ladies looking for just off the runway looks to go with their Hu's Shoes just need to cross the street to find designs by The Row, Isabel Marant, and Proenza Schouler. ✉ *2906 M St. NW, Georgetown* ☎ *202/342–2020* ⊕ *www.husonline.com* Ⓜ *Foggy Bottom.*

The Phoenix. All under one roof (with 30 solar panels) in a delightful shop owned and operated by the Hays family since 1955, you can find contemporary clothing in natural fibers by designers such as Eileen Fisher, White+Warren, Cut Loose, and Lilla P. There's also a stunning selection of jewelry from Germany, Turkey, Israel, and Italy; gorgeous leather handbags; whimsical pewter kitchen accessories from South African-designer Carrol Boyes; and fine- and folk-art pieces from Mexico. ✉ *1514 Wisconsin Ave. NW, Georgetown* ☎ *202/338–4404* ⊕ *www.thephoenixdc.com* Ⓜ *Foggy Bottom.*

relish. In fashionable Cady's Alley, this dramatic space holds a women's collection handpicked seasonally by the owner. Modern, elegant, and practical selections include European classics and well-tailored modern designers, such as Jill Sander, Marni, and Dries Van Noten. ✉ *3312 Cady's Alley NW, Georgetown* ☎ *202/333–5343* ⊕ *www.relishdc.com* ☉ *Closed Sun.* Ⓜ *Foggy Bottom/GWU.*

Urban Chic. It's hard to imagine a fashionista who wouldn't find something here. Gorgeous silk blouses, jeans, cocktail dresses, and accessories from Shoshanna, Joie, Ella Moss, Rebecca Taylor, and Equipment are to be had. The handbags are a highlight. ✉ *1626 Wisconsin Ave. NW, Georgetown* ☎ *202/338–5398* ⊕ *www.urbanchiconline.com* Ⓜ *Foggy Bottom.*

Wink. While the clientele and styles skew toward the young and trendy, women of all ages shop in this subterranean space for coveted jeans and colorful, sparkly tops, dresses, and jewelry. Theory, Joie, and Rebecca Taylor are among the labels. ✉ *3109 M St. NW, Georgetown* ☎ *202/338–9465* ⊕ *www.shopwinkdc.com* Ⓜ *Foggy Bottom/GWU.*

DUPONT CIRCLE AND LOGAN CIRCLE

You might call Dupont Circle a younger, less staid version of Georgetown—almost as pricey but with more apartment buildings than houses. Its many restaurants, offbeat shops, and specialty stores give it a cosmopolitan air. The street scene here is more urban than Georgetown's, with bike messengers and chess aficionados filling up the park. The Sunday farmers' market attracts shoppers with organic food, fresh cheese, homemade soap, and hand-spun wool. To the south of Dupont Circle proper are several boutiques and familiar retail stores close to the Farragut and Farragut North Metro stops. Burberry and Thomas Pink both have stores in this area of Dupont.

Kramerbooks & Afterwords. Serving brunch in the morning, snacks in the afternoon, cocktails in the evening, and coffee all day long, Kramer's is the perfect spot for a break. Try to snag an outside table, drop your shopping bags, and watch the world go by. "Sharezies," appetizers served on tiered plates, are custom-made for sharing. ⊠ *1517 Connecticut Ave. NW, Dupont Circle* ☎ *202/387–1400* ⊕ *www.kramers.com* Ⓜ *Dupont Circle.*

> **OPEN HOUSE FOR ART**
>
> **The Galleries of Dupont Circle.** Check out this Dupont Circle arts blog for information on arts-related events. ⊕ *www. dupontcirclearts.blogspot.com.*

ART GALLERIES

Burton Marinkovich Fine Art. You know you've reached this gallery when you spot the small front yard with a cast bronze Lesley Dill sculpture titled *Poem Dress.* The specialties are painting and sculpture by modern and contemporary masters, including Ross Bleckner, Richard Diebenkorn, David Hockney, Pablo Picasso, Helen Frankenthaler, and others. Rare, modern illustrated books and British linocuts from the Grosvenor School are also featured. ⊠ *1506 21st St. NW, Dupont Circle* ☎ *202/296–6563* ⊕ *www.burtonmarinkovich.com* ☾ *Closed Sun. and Mon.* Ⓜ *Dupont Circle.*

Fodor's Choice ★ **Hemphill Fine Arts.** This spacious showcase for contemporary art shows mid-career and established artists in all media, such as William Christenberry, John Dreyfuss, Linling Lu, and Julie Wolfe. ⊠ *1515 14th St. NW, 3rd fl., Logan Circle* ☎ *202/234–5601* ⊕ *www.hemphillfinearts. com* ☾ *Closed Sun. and Mon.* Ⓜ *Dupont Circle.*

BOOKS

Fodor's Choice ★ **Kramerbooks & Afterwords.** One of Washington's best-loved independent bookstores has a choice selection of fiction and nonfiction. Open all night on Friday and Saturday, it's a convenient meeting place. Kramerbooks shares space with a café that has late-night dining and live music from Wednesday to Saturday. ■TIP➔ There's a computer with free Internet access available in the bar. ⊠ *1517 Connecticut Ave. NW, Dupont Circle* ☎ *202/387–1400* ⊕ *www.kramers.com* Ⓜ *Dupont Circle.*

Second Story Books. A used-books and CDs emporium, this place stays open late and bibliophiles may be enticed to browse for hours. ⊠ *2000 P St. NW, Dupont Circle* ☎ *202/659–8884* ⊕ *www.secondstorybooks. com* Ⓜ *Dupont Circle.*

CRAFTS AND GIFTS

Beadazzled. A rainbow of ready-to-string beads fills the cases, and the stock also includes jewelry as well as books on crafts history and techniques. Check their website for a class schedule. ⊠ *1507 Connecticut Ave. NW, Dupont Circle* ☎ *202/265–2323* ⊕ *www.beadazzled.com* Ⓜ *Dupont Circle.*

The Chocolate Moose. This store is simple, sheer fun for adults and kids alike. Looking for clacking, windup teeth? You can find them here, along with unusual greeting cards, whimsical and colorful socks, and unique handicrafts. If playing with all those fun toys makes you hungry, you can pick up a select line of premium European chocolates. ⊠ *1743 L St. NW, Dupont Circle* ☎ *202/463–0992* ⊕ *www.chocolatemoosedc. com* ☾ *Closed Sun.* Ⓜ *Farragut N.*

HOME FURNISHINGS

Tabletop. Evoking a museum gift shop, this is a delightful place to find tiles by Canadian designer Xenia Taler; colorful Joseph Joseph kitchen gadgets; Anorak tote and toiletry bags with kissing stags, hedgehogs or robins; and Daphne Olive jewelry. Gifts for the hard-to-please man include handsome leather wallets and elegant flasks. For the younger set, there are charming Velvet Moustache sleepy panda pillows and Food Face dinner plates that will make even the pickiest eater clean his or her plate. ⊠ *1608 20th St. NW, Dupont Circle* ☎ *202/387–7117* ⊕ *www.tabletopdc.com* Ⓜ *Dupont Circle.*

JEWELRY

lou lou. A "blingful" boutique, jam-packed with costume jewelry and bags at price points that please the purse, draws lots of ladies looking for the latest trendy item. Lou Lou Clothing, a few doors down at 1623 Connecticut, sells boho-contemporary apparel, arranged by color and style. ⊠ *1601 Connecticut Ave. NW, Dupont Circle* ☎ *202/588–0027* ⊕ *www.loulouboutiques.com* Ⓜ *Dupont Circle.*

MEN'S AND WOMEN'S CLOTHING

Fodor's Choice ★ **Betsy Fisher.** Catering to women of all ages and sizes in search of contemporary and trendy styles, the selection includes one-of-a-kind accessories, clothes, shoes, and jewelry by well-known designers like Trina Turk. A wonderful selection of European and up-and-coming designs is also available. ⊠ *1224 Connecticut Ave. NW, Dupont Circle* ☎ *202/785–1975* ⊕ *www.betsyfisher.com* Ⓜ *Dupont Circle.*

J. Press. Like its flagship store, founded in Connecticut in 1902 as a custom shop for Yale University, this Washington outlet is resolutely traditional: Shetland and Irish wool sport coats are a specialty. ⊠ *1801 L St. NW, Dupont Circle* ☎ *202/857–0120* ⊕ *www.jpressonline.com* ☾ *Closed Sun.* Ⓜ *Farragut N.*

Fodor's Choice ★ **Proper Topper.** As its name suggests, this gem of a boutique carries a delightful collection of hats for women, men and children for any occasion or season. But upon entering, you'll find so much more: unusual gifts for the home, delightful clothes and shoes for the young ones in your life, funky jewelry, clothing from designers like Tracy Reese and Plenty, and a wonderfully varied assortment of accessories for men and women. ⊠ *1350 Connecticut Ave. NW, Dupont Circle* ☎ *202/842–3055* ⊕ *www.propertopper.com.*

Fodor's Choice ★ **Secondi.** One of the city's finest consignment shops carries a well-chosen selection of women's designer and casual clothing, accessories, and shoes. The brands carried include Marc Jacobs, Louis Vuitton, Donna Karan, Prada, and Chanel. ⊠ *1702 Connecticut Ave. NW, 2nd fl., Dupont Circle* ☎ *202/667–1122* ⊕ *www.secondi.com* Ⓜ *Dupont Circle.*

ADAMS MORGAN

Scattered among the dozens of Latin, Ethiopian, and international restaurants in this most bohemian of Washington neighborhoods is a score of eccentric shops. If quality is what you seek, Adams Morgan and nearby Woodley Park can be a minefield; tread cautiously. Still, this is good turf for the bargain hunter. ■TIP➜ **If bound for a specific shop, you may wish to call ahead to verify hours.** Adams Morganites are often not clock-watchers, although you can be sure an afternoon stroll on the weekend will yield a few hours of great browsing. The evening hours bring scores of revelers to the row, so plan to go before dark unless you want to couple your shopping with a party pit stop.

How to get there is another question. Though the Woodley Park/Zoo/Adams Morgan Metro stop is relatively close to the 18th Street strip (where the interesting shops are), getting off here means that you will have to walk over the bridge on Calvert Street. Five minutes longer, the walk from the Dupont Circle Metro stop is more scenic; you cruise north on 18th Street through tree-lined streets of row houses and embassies. You can also easily catch Metrobus No. 42 or a cab from Dupont to Adams Morgan.

QUICK BITES

Tryst Coffeehouse. Relax with a latte on one of the couches or cushiony chairs at this neighborhood hangout. The surprisingly large menu includes sandwiches and salads; tarts and crostinis; flatbreads; nachos; Belgian-style waffles; alcoholic drinks; and great coffee and tea selections. Save room for one of Tryst's fabulous chocolate chip cookies! Free Wi-Fi on weekdays is an added bonus. ⊠ *2459 18th St. NW, Adams Morgan* ☎ *202/232–5500* ⊕ *www.trystdc.com* Ⓜ *Woodley Park/Zoo.*

BOOKS

Idle Time Books. Since 1981, this multilevel used-book store has been selling "rare to medium rare" books with plenty of meaty titles in all genres, especially out-of-print literature. ⊠ *2467 18th St. NW, Adams Morgan* ☎ *202/232–4774* ⊕ *www.idletimebooks.com* Ⓜ *Woodley Park/Zoo.*

CHOCOLATE

Cocova. For chocoholics with a gourmet palate, this is one-stop shopping. Offerings are both foreign (Valrhona from France and Vestri from Italy) and domestic (Recchiuti from San Francisco and Vosges Haut Chocolat from Chicago). Selections from D.C.-area chocolatiers make for tasty souvenirs. ⊠ *1904 18th St. NW, Adams Morgan* ☎ *202/903–0346* ⊕ *www.cocova.com* Ⓜ *Dupont Circle.*

CRAFTS AND GIFTS

Toro Mata. Stunning black-and-white pottery from the Peruvian town of Chulucana is a specialty of this gallery; they directly represent six different artisans living and working there. The walls are lined with elegant handcrafted wood mirrors, colorful original paintings, alpaca apparel, and other imported Andean crafts, including dramatic silver jewelry. ⊠ *2410 18th St. NW, Adams Morgan* ☎ *202/232–3890* ⊕ *www. toromata.com* ⊙ *Closed Mon.* Ⓜ *Woodley Park/Zoo.*

11

HOME FURNISHINGS

Skynear Designs Gallery. A staff of interior designers is on hand to help you identify and sort through the collection of treasures in this extravagant shop. The owners travel the world to find the unusual, and their journeys have netted not only furniture and home accessories, but also modern art from artists including Campbell Maloney, Romero Britto, and Cheryl Parsons. The shop also carries a line of felt tote bags, purses and jewelry made by local designer Gretchen Cook. ⊠ *2122 18th St. NW, Adams Morgan* ☎ *202/797–7160* ⊕ *www.skyneardesigns.com* Ⓜ *Woodley Park/Zoo.*

CLOTHING

Mercedes Bien Vintage. Carefully selected vintage clothing includes everything from cocktail dresses to cowboy boots. You will also find jewelry and belts, all handpicked by the owner, Mercedes. This small shop offers exceptional, personal service. It's open weekends only. ⊠ *2423 18th St. NW, Adams Morgan* ☎ *202/360–8481* ⊙ *Closed weekdays* Ⓜ *Woodley Park/Zoo.*

Violet Boutique. Young women looking for fashion-forward styles will find plenty to love here at prices that fit their wallets. Alluring dresses, silky wraps and jackets, chic clutches and big funky earrings are sure to turn heads. Purchases are wrapped in—what else?—purple tissue paper. ⊠ *2439 18th St. NW, Adams Morgan* ☎ *202/621–9225* ⊕ *www. violetdc.com* ⊙ *Closed Mon.*

SHOES

Fleet Feet Sports Shop. The expert staff at this friendly shop will assess your feet and your training schedule before recommending the perfect pair of new running shoes. Shoes, along with apparel and accessories for running, swimming, soccer, and cycling, crowd the small space. ⊠ *1841 Columbia Rd. NW, Adams Morgan* ☎ *202/387–3888* ⊕ *www. fleetfeetdc.com* Ⓜ *Woodley Park/Zoo.*

U STREET CORRIDOR

In the 1930s and 1940s U Street was known for its classy theaters and jazz clubs. After decades of decline following the 1968 riots, the neighborhood has been revitalized. The area has gentrified at lightning speed, but has retained a diverse mix of multiethnic young professionals and older, working-class African-Americans. U Street resident and Associate Justice of the Supreme Court Sonia Sotomayor says, "U Street is the East Village." At night the neighborhood's club, bar, and restaurant scene comes alive. During the day the street scene is more laid-back, with more locals than tourists occupying the distinctive shops.

Greater U Street Neighborhood Visitor Center. Pick up brochures and maps of the neighborhood and souvenir merchandise from Ben's Chili Bowl at this small visitor center next to—you guessed it—Ben's Chili Bowl. Although the center is unstaffed, you can pose for a photo with a life-size picture of D.C.'s Black Broadway's most famous resident, Duke

Ellington. ✉ *1211 U St. NW, U Street Corridor* ☎ *202/661–7581* ⊕ *www.culturaltourismdc.org* ⊙ *Daily 10–6.*

ANTIQUES AND COLLECTIBLES

GoodWood. It's described by its owners as an American mercantile and dry goods store, but when you open the door, you'll feel as if you've been invited into a friend's warm and inviting loft. Displays throughout the store beautifully showcase 19th-century American furniture. You'll also discover leather goods; vintage mirrors and other decorative home items; men's and women's grooming products and perfumes from around the world; Peruvian alpaca and wool scarves; Swedish clogs; comfortable dresses and tops made by a Spanish designer; and a small but gorgeous collection of estate jewelry. ✉ *1428 U St. NW, U Street Corridor* ☎ *202/986–3640* ⊕ *www.goodwooddc.com* Ⓜ *U St./Cardozo.*

Millennium. The "20th-century antiques" here are a unique blend of high-end vintage midcentury-modern furniture and decorative art. ✉ *1528 U St. NW, downstairs, U Street Corridor* ☎ *202/483–1218* ⊕ *www.millenniumdecorativearts.com* ⊙ *Closed Mon.–Thurs.* Ⓜ *U St./Cardozo.*

HOME FURNISHINGS

Fodor'sChoice
★ **Miss Pixie's Furnishings and Whatnot.** The well-chosen collectibles—handpicked by Miss Pixie herself—include gorgeous textiles, antique home furnishings, lamps and mirrors, glass- and silverware, and artwork. The reasonable prices will grab your attention, as will the location, an old car-dealer showroom. ✉ *1626 14th St, NW, U Street Corridor* ☎ *202/232–8171* ⊕ *www.misspixies.com* Ⓜ *U St./Cordozo or Dupont Circle.*

WOMEN'S CLOTHING

Current Boutique. Don't be fooled by the new dresses in the front—this shop is a consignment shopper's dream. "Current" styles from brands such as Tory Burch, Citizens, True Religion, Banana Republic, Free People, and Diane Von Furstenberg just might fit better when you buy them at a third of their original price. ✉ *1809 14th St. NW, U Street Corridor* ☎ *202/588–7311* ⊕ *www.currentboutique.com* Ⓜ *U St./Cardozo.*

Ginger Root Design. Vintage gets revamped at this combination boutique and tailoring shop where eco-minded hipsters look for "new" ties, vests, and dresses, or bring in their own old clothes to give them a fresh start. Bloomers, shorts to wear under skirts while bicycling, and handmade jewelry sell well. ✉ *1530 U St. NW, U Street Corridor* ☎ *202/567–7668* ⊕ *www.gingerrootdesign.com* ⊙ *Closed Wed. and Sun.* Ⓜ *U St./Cardozo.*

Fodor'sChoice
★ **Lettie Gooch Boutique.** Named after the owner's grandmother, this hip boutique attracts many of D.C.'s fashionistas with its wonderful collection of cutting-edge designers including Prairie Underground, Stewart and Brown, AG jeans, OVI, Weston Wear, and 49 Square Miles, among others. Many of the lines are created with environmentally sustainable materials. After you've selected that perfect party dress, check out the bold and colorful jewelry, shoes, and purses for an outfit that is uniquely yours. And if you need a souvenir for friends back home, the shop carries a selection of handmade soaps and candles from D.C.

artisans. ✉ *1517 U St. NW, U Street Corridor* ☎ *202/332–4242* ⊕ *www. lettiegooch.com* ⊘ *Closed Tues.*

Redeem. With street-smart clothes and accessories from all over the globe, women and men who are stuck in a fashion rut can find redemption here with brands like Kai-aakmann, Won Hundred, and the Los Angeles–based denim line THVM. A small partner shop in the front of the store, Mutiny, adds to the fun with an eclectic assortment of men's products including an apothecary line, writing instruments, accessories, and magazines and other literature. ✉ *1734 14th St. NW, U Street Corridor* ☎ *202/332–7447* ⊕ *www.redeemus.com* ⊘ *Closed Tues.* Ⓜ *U St./Cardozo.*

UPPER NORTHWEST

The major thoroughfare Wisconsin Avenue runs northwest through the city from Georgetown toward Maryland. It crosses the border in the midst of the Friendship Heights shopping district, which is also near Chevy Chase. Other neighborhoods in the District yield more interesting finds and offer more enjoyable shopping and sightseeing, but it's hard to beat Friendship Heights for sheer convenience and selection. The upscale lineup includes Bloomingdales, Neiman Marcus, and two Saks Fifth Avenues—the men's and women's collections are in separate buildings. Stand-alone designer stores like Jimmy Choo, Louis Vuitton, Christian Dior, Tiffany and Co., and Cartier up the luxury quotient. Discounters Nordstrom Rack, Loehmann's, and T.J. Maxx hawk the designer names at much lower prices. Lord & Taylor and chains like the Gap, Ann Taylor Loft, and Williams Sonoma occupy the middle ground. There are also a few local gems in the surrounding neighborhoods.

BOOKS

Fodor's Choice
★

Politics and Prose. After being bought by two former *Washington Post* reporters in 2011, this legendary independent continues the tradition of jam-packed author events and signings, but they added another main attraction: Opus, the book-making machine that instantly prints out-of-issue books or self-published manuscripts. In the coffee shop downstairs, you can debate the issues of the day or read a book. The nearest Metro stop is 15 minutes away. ✉ *5015 Connecticut Ave. NW, Upper Northwest* ☎ *202/364–1919* ⊕ *www.politics-prose.com* Ⓜ *Tenleytown.*

FOOD AND WINE

Calvert Woodley Fine Wines and Spirits. In addition to the excellent selection of wine and hard liquor, 200 kinds of cheese and other picnic and cocktail-party fare are on hand. The international offerings have made this a favorite pantry for embassy parties. ✉ *4339 Connecticut Ave. NW, Upper Northwest* ☎ *202/966–4400* ⊕ *www.calvertwoodley.com* ⊘ *Closed Sun.* Ⓜ *Van Ness/UDC.*

GIFTS

Periwinkle Gifts. A panoply of gift options are available in these warm and welcoming surroundings: boutique chocolates, cases of nutty and gummy treats, handmade jewelry, Stonewall Kitchen snacks, hand-designed wrapping paper, scented bath products, and printed note cards. ☒ *3815 Livingston St. NW, Upper Northwest* ☎ *202/364–3076* ⊕ *www.periwinklegiftsdc.com* Ⓜ *Friendship Heights.*

JEWELRY

Ann Hand. Catering to Washington's powerful and prestigious, this jewelry and gift shop specializing in patriotic pins may seem intimidating, but prices begin at $30. Hand's signature pin, The Liberty Eagle, is $200. Photos on the walls above brightly lit display cases showcase "who's who" in Washington wearing you-know-who's designs. ☒ *4885 MacArthur Blvd. NW, Upper Northwest* ☎ *202/333–2979* ⊕ *www. annhand.com* ☽ *Closed weekends.*

WOMEN'S CLOTHING

Catch Can. Bright and breezy clothes made of mostly natural fibers, plus comfortable but playful shoes and funky rain boots, make casual wear as fun as it is practical. The owners' love of color continues with a sizeable collection of jewelry, greeting cards, housewares, and soaps. ☒ *5516 Connecticut Ave. NW, Upper Northwest* ☎ *202/686–5316* ⊕ *www.catchcan.com* Ⓜ *Friendship Heights.*

Julia Farr. Women who lobby on Capitol Hill and lunch at the country club look to Julia for a professional and polished look. Decorated in soothing sea shades, her boutique carries classic styles from emerging and established designers. Farr recently introduced her own fashion line of classic and elegant wardrobe staples including skirts, blouses, jackets, and dresses inspired by D.C.'s historical and cultural landmarks. And, since they're named after these landmarks, any item would make a beautifully practical souvenir. Appointments are welcomed. ☒ *5232 44th St. NW, Upper Northwest* ☎ *202/364–3277* ⊕ *www.juliafarrdc. com* ☽ *Closed Sun. and Mon.* Ⓜ *Friendship Hts.*

Tabandeh. This avant-garde women's collection includes an expertly selected cache of J Brand jeans, Rick Owens tops, and Ann Demeulemeester clothing, along with accessories including stunning leather belts and handbags. The jewelry pieces in the store are dazzling—rings, necklaces, earrings, and pendants made with precious and semiprecious stones—that are sure to add panache to your wardrobe. ☒ *5300 Wisconsin Ave. NW, Upper Northwest* ☎ *202/966–5080* ⊕ *www. tabandehjewelry.com* Ⓜ *Friendship Hts.*

SIDE TRIPS

WELCOME TO SIDE TRIPS

TOP REASONS TO GO

★ **Walk in Washington's Shadow:** The minute you step onto the grounds of Mount Vernon, you'll be transported back in time to colonial America.

★ **Time Travel:** Delve into colonial history in Old Town Alexandria, then fast-forward to the 21st century with funky shops, artists' galleries, hot restaurants, boutiques, and bars. Don't miss Alexandria's farmers' market, held every Saturday year-round from 7 am to noon. Believe it or not, it has been around since George Washington's produce was sold here.

★ **Get Crabby:** Head east to Annapolis on the Chesapeake Bay and feast on a Maryland specialty: blue crabs by the bushel (the bib is optional).

1 Alexandria. Alexandria is across the Potomac and 7 miles downstream from Washington. As a commercial port, it competed with Georgetown in the days before Washington was a city. It's now a big small town loaded with historic homes, shops, and restaurants.

2 Mount Vernon, Woodlawn, and Gunston Hall. Three splendid examples of plantation architecture remain on the Virginia side of the Potomac, 16 miles south of D.C. Mount Vernon, the most-visited historic house in America, was the home of George Washington; Woodlawn was the estate of Martha Washington's granddaughter; and Gunston Hall was the residence of George Mason, a patriot and author of the document on which the Bill of Rights was based.

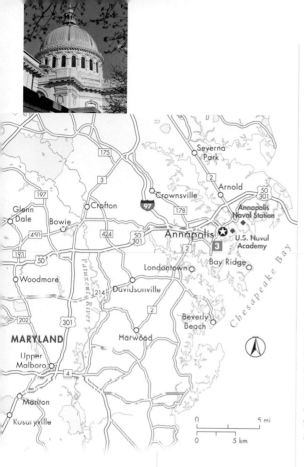

GETTING ORIENTED

There's no question that Washington, D.C., has enough sights, sounds, and experiences to keep you busy for a week or more without seeing everything on your itinerary. The three destinations highlighted here help enrich your experience whether you're a history buff, foodie, outdoor enthusiast, or boater. With just a bit of planning, any one of these trips can be done in a day or even an afternoon. Follow the locals' example and escape the heat of the capital with a trip to the countryside—or the banks of the Potomac or shores of Chesapeake Bay.

2 Annapolis, Maryland. Maryland's capital is a popular destination for seafood lovers and boating fans. Warm, sunny days bring many boats to the City Dock, where they're moored against a background of waterfront shops and restaurants. The city's nautical reputation is enhanced by the presence of the U.S. Naval Academy. It also has one of the country's largest assemblages of 18th-century architecture.

Updated by
Catherine
Sharpe

Within an hour of D.C. are getaway destinations connected to the nation's first president, naval history, and colonial events. Alexandria was once a bustling colonial port, and Old Town preserves this flavor with its cobblestone streets, taverns, and waterfront. Cycle 7 miles downriver along the banks of the Potomac to get here, or hop on the Metro for a quick 30-minute ride.

Mount Vernon, George Washington's plantation, is a mere 16 miles from D.C. on the Virginia side of the Potomac. Make a day of it, and visit two other interesting plantation homes—Woodlawn and Gunston Hall—that are nearby.

Another option is to get out on the water in Annapolis, a major center for boating and home to the U.S. Naval Academy. Feast on the Chesapeake Bay's famous crabs, then watch the midshipmen parade on campus at the academy.

PLANNING

KID TIPS

No matter the ages of your children or the weather, Mount Vernon can keep everyone amused with activities that delight the senses. See where George and Martha Washington and their slaves lived, hear the Revolutionary rifles fired in animated movies, taste hoecakes, and smell the herbs in the garden. A dress-up room in the education center gives children the chance to look like colonial kids.

In Annapolis, find out what it takes to become a midshipman at the **U.S. Naval Academy's** new exhibit in the visitor center.

■TIP→ Even kids who don't "dig" history might like sifting through dirt for artifacts in Alexandria during Family Dig Days at the archaeology museum in the Torpedo Factory.

TO GET TO . . .	BY CAR:	BY METRO OR BUS:
Alexandria	George Washington Memorial Pkwy. or Jefferson Davis Hwy. (Rte. 1) south from Arlington (10 mins)	The Blue or Yellow Line to the King St. Metro stop (25 mins from Metro Center)
Mount Vernon	Exit 1 off the Beltway; follow signs to George Washington Memorial Pkwy. southbound (30 mins)	The Yellow Line to the Huntington Metro stop. From there, take Fairfax County Connector Bus No. 101, 151, or 159 (45–50 mins)
Woodlawn	Rte. 1 southwest to the second Rte. 235 intersection; entrance is on the right at the traffic light (40 mins)	Bus No. 101, 151 , or 159 from Huntington Metro station (45–50 mins)
Gunston Hall	Rte. 1 south to Rte. 242; turn left and go 3¾ miles to entrance (30 mins)	No Metro or bus
Annapolis	U.S. 50 east to the Rowe Blvd. Exit (35–45 mins, except during weekday rush hour when it may take twice as long)	Amtrak from Union Station to BWI; MTA Light Rail from BWI to Patapsco Light Rail Station; transfer to Bus No. 14 (2 hrs)

12

ALEXANDRIA, VIRGINIA

A short drive (or bike ride) from Washington, Alexandria provides a welcome break from the monuments and hustle and bustle of the District. Here you encounter America's colonial heritage. Founded in 1749 by Scottish merchants eager to capitalize on the booming tobacco trade, Alexandria became one of the most important colonial ports and has been associated with the most significant personages of the colonial, Revolutionary, and Civil War periods. In Old Town this colorful past is revived through restored 18th- and 19th-century homes, churches, and taverns; on the cobblestone streets; and on the revitalized waterfront, where clipper ships docked and artisans displayed their wares. Alexandria also has a wide variety of small- to medium-size restaurants and pubs, plus a wealth of boutiques and antiques dealers vying for your time and money.

GETTING HERE AND AROUND

Take either the George Washington Memorial Parkway or Jefferson Davis Highway (Route 1) south from Arlington to reach Alexandria. ■TIP➡ Stop at the Alexandria Visitors Center at Ramsay House (⊠ 221 King Street) to get oriented.

The King Street/Old Town Metro stop (about 25 minutes from Metro Center) is right next to the Masonic Memorial and a 10-block walk on King Street from the center of Old Town. ■TIP➡ There's a free King Street Trolley between the King Street station and the Torpedo Factory Art Center daily from 11:30 am to 10:15 pm.

TOURS

Old Town Experience (⊕ *www.oldtowntour-alexandriava.com*) conducts walking tours at 10:30 am Monday through Saturday and 2 pm Sunday; tickets are $15. Footsteps to the Past (⊕ *www. footstepstothepast.com*) leads 90-minute walking history tours Wednesday through Saturday at 1:30, and historical haunt tours Wednesday through Sunday at 7 pm. A second haunt tour is held on Friday and Saturday at 8:30 pm. Prices are $15 per person for the history tour and $15 per couple for the haunt tour. All of the tours from Old Town Experience and Footsteps to the Past are available April through November. Alexandria Colonial Tours (⊕ *www.alexcolonialtours.com*) leads ghost-and-graveyard tours Friday through Sunday nights March through November (nightly in October); during the summer months there's also a tour on Wednesday and Thursday nights. Tickets cost $13 for adults and $7 for children ages 7 to 17. All tours depart from the Alexandria Visitors Center at Ramsay House.

ESSENTIALS

Visitor Information Ramsay House. The best place to start a tour of Alexandria's Old Town is at the **Alexandria Visitors Center** at Ramsay House, the home of the town's first postmaster and lord mayor, William Ramsay. The unusually helpful staff hands out brochures and maps for self-guided walking tours. You can also use a free computer station to plan your travels. ⊠ *221 King St., Old Town* ☎ *703/746–3301, 800/388–9119* ⊕ *www.visitalexandriava.com* ⊘ *May–Sept., Sun.–Wed. 10–6, Thurs.–Sat. 10–8; Oct.–Apr., daily 10–6* Ⓜ *King St.*

EXPLORING

12

TOP ATTRACTIONS

Appomattox Confederate Statue. In 1861, when Alexandria was occupied by Union forces, the 800 soldiers of the city's garrison marched out of town to join the Confederate Army. In the middle of Washington and Prince streets stands a statue marking the point where they assembled. In 1885 Confederate veterans proposed a memorial to honor their fallen comrades. This statue, based on John A. Elder's painting *Appomattox*, is of a lone soldier glumly surveying the battlefields after General Robert E. Lee's surrender. The names of 99 Alexandria Confederate dead are carved on the base. ⊠ *Washington and Prince sts., Old Town* Ⓜ *King St.*

Boyhood Home of Robert E. Lee. This childhood home of the commander of the Confederate forces of Virginia is a fine example of a 19th-century Federal town house. The house is privately owned and not open to visitors. ⊠ *607 Oronoco St., Old Town* Ⓜ *King St.*

ALEXANDRIA'S FARMERS' MARKET

If it's Saturday and you're up early, join the locals at Alexandria's Farmers' Market, one of the oldest continually operating farmers' markets in the country—open for business since the 1700s. The market is held from 7 am to noon year-round at City Hall (⊠ *301 King St.*). In addition to incredible produce, you'll find artisans selling handmade jewelry, dolls, quilts, purses, sweaters, and more. You'll also find ham biscuits, baked treats, and other snack items for a quick meal on the go or a picnic later in the day.

Carlyle House. Alexandria forefather and Scottish merchant John Carlyle built this grand house, which was completed in 1753 and modeled on a country manor in the old country. Students of the French and Indian War will want to know that the dwelling served as General Braddock's headquarters. The house retains its original 18th-century woodwork and contains Chippendale furniture and Chinese porcelain. An architectural exhibit on the second floor explains how the house was built; outside there's an attractive garden of colonial-era plants. ⊠ *121 N. Fairfax St., Old Town* ☎ *703/549–2997* ⊕ *www.carlylehouse.org* ⊠ *$5* ⊘ *Tues.–Sat. 10–4, Sun. noon–4; guided tour every 30 mins* Ⓜ *King St.*

Christ Church. George Washington and Robert E. Lee were pewholders in this Episcopal church, which remains in nearly original condition. (Washington paid quite a lot of money for pews 59 and 60.) Built in 1773, it's a fine example of an English Georgian country-style church has a Palladian window, an interior balcony, and an English wrought-brass-and-crystal chandelier. Docents give tours during visiting hours. ⊠ *118 N. Washington St., Old Town* ☎ *703/549–1450* ⊕ *www.historicchristchurch.org* ⊠ *$5 donation suggested* ⊘ *Mon.–Sat. noon–4, Sun. 2–4:30* Ⓜ *King St.*

FAMILY **Gadsby's Tavern Museum.** George Washington celebrated his birthdays in the ballroom here, and Thomas Jefferson, John Adams, and the Marquis de Lafayette were other notable patrons of the two buildings—a circa-1785 tavern and the 1792 City Hotel—that were centers of political and social life. They now form a museum, in which the taproom, dining room, assembly room, ballroom, and communal bedrooms have been restored to their original appearances. Special events include costumed reenactments. ⊠ *134 N. Royal St., Old Town* ☎ *703/746–4242* ⊕ *www.gadsbystavern.org* ⊠ *$5* ☾ *Apr.–Oct., Tues.–Sat. 10–5, Sun. and Mon. 1–5 (last tour at 4:45); Nov.–Mar., Wed.– Sat. 11–4, Sun. 1–4 (last tour at 3:45). Tours 15 mins before and after the hr* Ⓜ *King St.*

George Washington Masonic Memorial. Because Alexandria, like Washington, D.C., has no really tall buildings, the spire of this memorial dominates the surroundings and is visible for miles. The building overlooks King and Duke streets, Alexandria's major east–west arteries. Reaching the memorial requires a respectable uphill climb from the King St. Metrorail and bus stations. From the ninth-floor observation deck (reached by elevator) you get a spectacular view of Alexandria and Washington, but access above the first two floors is by guided tour only. The building contains furnishings from the first Masonic lodge in Alexandria. George Washington became a Mason in 1752 in Fredericksburg, and became Charter Master of the Alexandria lodge when it was chartered in 1788, remaining active in Masonic affairs during his tenure as president, 1789–97. ■TIP→ Parking at the Memorial is free and plentiful. ⊠ *101 Callahan Dr., Old Town* ☎ *703/683–2007* ⊕ *www.gwmemorial.org* ⊠ *$5; $8 guided tour (includes observation deck)* ☾ *Apr.–Sept., daily 9–4; Oct.–Mar., daily 10–4. 1-hr guided tours daily at 10, 11:30, 1:30, and 3* Ⓜ *King St.*

Lee-Fendall House Museum and Garden. Built in 1787 at historic Lee Corner, the Lee-Fendall House was, over the course of the next 118 years, home to 37 members of the Lee family and also served as a Union hospital. The house and its furnishings, of the 1850–70 period, present an intimate study of 19th-century family life. Highlights include a splendid collection of Lee heirlooms, period pieces produced by Alexandria manufacturers, and the beautifully restored, award-winning garden, which can be visited without buying a ticket for the museum. ⊠ *614 Oronoco St., Old Town* ☎ *703/548–1789* ⊕ *www.leefendallhouse.org* ⊠ *$5* ☾ *Wed.–Sat. 10–4, Sun. 1–4; sometimes closed for private events* Ⓜ *King St.*

Lyceum. Built in 1839 and one of Alexandria's best examples of Greek Revival design, the Lyceum is also the city's official history museum. Over the years the building has served as the Alexandria Library, a Civil War hospital, a residence, and offices. Restored in the 1970s for the Bicentennial, it has an impressive collection, including examples of 18th- and 19th-century silver, tools, stoneware, and Civil War photographs taken by Mathew Brady. ⊠ *201 S. Washington St., Old Town* ☎ *703/838–4994* ⊕ *www.alexandriava.gov/Lyceum* ⊠ *$2 suggested donation* ☾ *Mon.–Sat. 10–5, Sun. 1–5* Ⓜ *King St.*

FAMILY **Torpedo Factory Art Center.** Torpe-
does were manufactured here by
the U.S. Navy during World War
II, but now the building houses the
studios and workshops of about
160 artists and artisans. You can
observe printmakers, jewelers,
sculptors, painters, potters, textile
artists, and glass makers as they

create original work in their studios. The Torpedo Factory also houses
the Alexandria Archaeology Museum, which displays artifacts such as
plates, cups, pipes, and coins from an early tavern, and Civil War soldiers' equipment. If archaeological activities interest you, call to sign up
for the well-attended public digs (offered once a month in June, August
and September and twice in October). ⊠ *105 N. Union St., Old Town*
☎ *703/838–4565, 703/746–4399 for Archaeology Museum* ⊕ *www.
torpedofactory.org* ⬚*Free* ☉ *Fri.–Wed. 10–6, Thurs. 10–9* Ⓜ *King St.*

WORTH NOTING

Alexandria Black History Museum. This collection, devoted to the history
of African-Americans in Alexandria and Virginia, is housed in part in
the Robert H. Robinson Library, a building constructed in the wake of a
landmark 1939 sit-in protesting the segregation of Alexandria libraries.
The federal census of 1790 recorded 52 free African-Americans living
in the city, but the port town was one of the largest slave-exporting
points in the South, with at least two highly active slave markets. ⊠ *902
Wythe St., Old Town* ☎ *703/746-1356* ⊕ *www.alexblackhistory.org*
⬚*$2* ☉ *Tues.–Sat. 10–4* Ⓜ *King St.*

Athenaeum. One of the most noteworthy structures in Alexandria, this
striking Greek Revival edifice at the corner of Prince and Lee streets
stands out from its many redbrick Federal neighbors. Built in 1852 as
a bank (Robert E. Lee had an account here) and later used as a Union
commissary headquarters, then as a talcum powder factory for the
Stabler-Leadbeater Apothecary, the Athenaeum houses the gallery of
the Northern Virginia Fine Arts Association, which hosts free receptions
throughout the year. This block of Prince Street between Fairfax and
Lee streets is known as **Gentry Row,** after the 18th- and 19th-century
inhabitants of its imposing three-story houses. ⊠ *201 Prince St., Old
Town* ☎ *703/548-0035* ⊕ *www.nvfaa.org* ⬚*Free* ☉ *Thurs., Fri., and
Sun. noon–4, Sat. 1–4* Ⓜ *King St.*

Captain's Row. Many of Alexandria's sea captains once lived on this
block, which gives visitors the truest sense of what the city looked like
in the 1800s. The stone pavement is not original, but nicely replicates
the stones laid down during the Revolution, taken from ships sailing to
America and used to balance the vessels during the passage. ⊠ *Prince
St., between Lee and Union sts., Old Town* ⊕ *King St.*

FAMILY **Friendship Fire House.** Alexandria's showcase firehouse dates from 1855
and is filled with typical 19th-century implements, but the resident
Friendship Fire Company was established in 1774 and bought its first
engine in 1775. Among early fire engines on display is a hand pumper

built in Philadelphia in 1851. Most everything can be seen through the windows even when the firehouse is closed. ⊠ *107 S. Alfred St., Old Town* ☎ *703/746-3891* ⌨ *$2* ☉ *Weekends 1–4* Ⓜ *King St.*

Lloyd House. This fine example of Georgian architecture was built in 1797 and is owned by the City of Alexandria and used for offices for the Office of Historic Alexandria. The interior has nothing on display, so the house is best admired from outside. ⊠ *220 N. Washington St., Old Town* Ⓜ *King St.*

Old Presbyterian Meeting House. Except from 1899 through 1949, the Old Presbyterian Meeting House has been the site of an active Presbyterian congregation since 1772. Scottish pioneers founded the church, and Scottish patriots used it as a gathering place during the Revolution. Four memorial services were held for George Washington here. The tomb of an unknown soldier of the American Revolution lies in a corner of the small churchyard, where many prominent Alexandrians—including Dr. James Craik, physician and best friend to Washington, and merchant John Carlyle—are interred. The original sanctuary was rebuilt after a lightning strike and fire in 1835. The interior is appropriately plain; if you'd like to visit the sanctuary you can borrow a key in the church office, or just peek through the many wide windows along both sides. ⊠ *321 S. Fairfax St., Old Town* ☎ *703/549–6670* ⊕ *www.opmh.org* ⌨ *Free* ☉ *Weekdays 8:15–4:15* Ⓜ *King St.*

Stabler-Leadbeater Apothecary. Once patronized by Martha Washington and the Lee family, the Stabler-Leadbeater Apothecary is among the oldest apothecaries in the country (the reputed oldest is in Bethlehem, Pennsylvania). The shop now houses a museum of apothecary memorabilia, including one of the finest collections of apothecary bottles in the country. In fact, they have so many of these original bottles that it took six years to process them all. Tours include discussions of Alexandria life and medicine, as well as the history of the family that owned and ran the shop for 141 years. ⊠ *105–107 S. Fairfax St., Old Town* ☎ *703/746–3852* ⊕ *www.apothecarymuseum.org* ⌨ *$5* ☉ *Apr.–Oct., Tues.–Sat. 10–5, Sun. and Mon. 1–5; Nov.–Mar., Wed.–Sat. 11–4, Sun. 1–4* Ⓜ *King St.*

WHERE TO EAT

Centuries before the Obamas celebrated at several local restaurants, previous presidents were dining in Alexandria; the first five dined at Gadsby's Tavern. More than 50 restaurants participate in Alexandria's biannual restaurant weeks in January and August, offering either a $35 three-course meal or dinner for two.

$
IRISH
FAMILY
✕ **Eamonn's A Dublin Chipper.** A nod to his native Ireland, this fish-and-chips joint is Chef Cathal Armstrong's most casual outpost in his growing Old Town Alexandria empire—he also runs such other acclaimed spots as Restaurant Eve and Majestic Café. This 20-seat, counter-service, chipper-with-attitude serves up crispy cod and fries with your choice of seven different sauces from classic tartar to curry. Down it with a pint of Guinness or an Irish soda and finish with a piping hot fried Mars bar, a weird-but-wonderful dessert that's the

King Street is the heart of historic Old Town Alexandria, Virginia, with lively restaurants and shops.

perfect end to a battered meal. ■ **TIP→ When the pirate flag is flying and a blue light glows at an unmarked door, head upstairs to the PX, a 21st-century speakeasy operated by Armstrong and his wife.** [$] *Average main: $10* ✉ *728 King St., Alexandria* ☎ *703/299–8384* 🌐 *www.eamonnsdublinchipper.com* [M] *King St.*

$$$ STEAKHOUSE 🍴 **Flat Iron Steak & Saloon.** As its name suggests, beef is the specialty at this lively spot in the heart of Alexandria's busy King Street, with three sauces to accompany any of the steaks on the menu. Seafood specialties include seared scallop risotto, lobster roll, and black-sesame-seed-crusted ahi with delicate rice noodles in an Asian broth embellished with greens. The signature dessert offers a choice of deep fried candy bars. An à la carte brunch is served on weekends 10:30–3. Upstairs in the Saloon there's live music Friday and Saturday nights, happy hour specials weekdays 4–8, and 15 big-screen TVs that attract big crowds on game days. [$] *Average main: $28* ✉ *808 King St.* ☎ *703/299–0777* 🌐 *www.flatironkingstreet.com* [M] *King St.*

$$$ FRENCH 🍴 **Le Refuge.** At this local favorite, run by Jean Fran ois Chaufour and his wife Fran oise for more than 30 years, enjoy lovingly prepared, authentic French country fare with beaucoup flavor; popular selections include trout, bouillabaisse, garlicky rack of lamb, frogs' legs, and beef Wellington. Polish it all off with an order of profiteroles or crème brûlée. [$] *Average main: $30* ✉ *127 N. Washington St.* ☎ *703/548–4661* 🌐 *www.lerefugealexandria.com* 🕒 *Closed Sun.* [M] *King St.*

$$ AMERICAN 🍴 **Majestic Café.** An art deco facade remains, but the stylish interior brings a modern sensibility to a 1930s-era landmark. The cooking style is rustic American, with an emphasis on simplicity, seasonal products, and comfort food—home-style meat loaf and mashed potatoes, Amish

chicken, and fried green tomatoes— that changes seasonally. On Sunday, in addition to the regular menu, the café offers a special family-style dinner. Themes for these dinners include "Summer Lovin'" and "The Harvest." The Majestic is about eight blocks from the Metro. [$] *Average main: $25* ✉ *911 King St.* ☎ *703/837–9117* 🌐 *www.majesticcafe.com* ✍ *Reservations essential* [M] *King St.*

$ BARBECUE FAMILY 🍴 **Rocklands.** This homegrown barbecue stop is known for its flavorful pork ribs smoked over hickory and red oak. Sides like silky corn pudding, rich mac 'n' cheese, and crunchy slaw are as good as the meats, which cover everything from beef brisket and chopped pork barbecue to chicken and fish. The family crowd comes for dinner, but the place also does takeout. There's another branch in D.C. at 2418 Wisconsin Avenue NW. [$] *Average main: $16* ✉ *25 S. Quaker La.* ☎ *703/778–9663* 🌐 *www.rocklands.com* [M] *King St.*

$$$ MODERN GREEK 🍴 **Taverna Cretekou.** Whitewashed stucco walls and colorful macramé tapestries bring a bit of the Mediterranean to the center of Old Town. On the menu are *exohikon* (lamb baked in a pastry shell) and fish sautéed with artichokes, and the extensive wine list includes only Greek choices, such as the special Taverna Cretekou made near Kalamata. In warm weather you can dine in the canopied garden. Thursday evening brings live music, and if you are so moved, plates for breaking are free for the asking—opa! A buffet brunch is served on Sunday. [$] *Average main: $27* ✉ *818 King St.* ☎ *703/548–8688* 🌐 *www.tavernacretekou.com* ⏲ *Closed Mon.* [M] *King St.*

$$$$ MODERN AMERICAN 🍴 **Vermilion.** Be sure to make reservations because foodies flock here for a taste of Chef William Morris's award-winning modern American menu. This upscale establishment puts an emphasis on the casual with its exposed brick walls, ceiling beams, and gas lamps. Morris favors locally sourced, sustainable ingredients, though quality trumps local here so you may find an Alaskan halibut on this Mid-Atlantic menu alongside a braised shortribs and caramelized-onion crespelle. Vermilion is also one of the area's favorite weekend brunch spots. Tuesday and Wednesday evenings bring live music to the first-floor lounge. [$] *Average main: $37* ✉ *1120 King St.* ☎ *703/684–9669* 🌐 *www.vermilionrestaurant.com* ✍ *Reservations essential* ⏲ *No lunch Tues.* [M] *King St.*

WHERE TO STAY

$ HOTEL FAMILY 🏨 **Embassy Suites Old Town Alexandria.** A location across from the Metro station and a free shuttle service to the scenic Alexandria riverfront and any spot along King Street, makes this all-suites hotel a convenient base for city exploring. **Pros:** large rooms; good breakfast; complimentary fitness center; on-site restaurant. **Cons:** just outside Alexandria; small indoor pool is often crowded; popular with school groups. [$] *Rooms from: $139* ✉ *1900 Diagonal Rd., Old Town* ☎ *703/684–5900, 800/362–2779* 🌐 *embassysuites3.hilton.com* 🛏 *288 rooms* 🍽 *Breakfast.*

$ HOTEL FAMILY 🏨 **Hotel Monaco Alexandria.** Charm and modernity are perfectly blended in this boutique hotel in the heart of Old Town Alexandria, and activities for kids make it a great choice for families. **Pros:** central to Old Town sights; complimentary morning coffee and happy-hour wine;

indoor pool and fitness center; complimentary shuttle to Reagan National Airport; pet friendly; 24-hour room service. **Cons:** thin walls mean you might hear conversations in adjoining rooms or barking dogs in the hallway. [$] *Rooms from: $199* ✉ *480 King St.* ☎ *703/549–6080* 🌐 *www.monaco-alexandria.com* 🛏 *241 rooms, 10 suites* 🍴 *No meals* [M] *King St.*

$ HOTEL 🏨 **Morrison House.** You'll feel like you've stepped into a gorgeous Federal-period bed-and-breakfast at this luxurious boutique hotel just off Alexandria's busy King Street. **Pros:** in the heart of Old Town; complimentary morning coffee/tea and newspapers; evening wine hour; pet friendly; free use of bikes; modern building with historic charm. **Cons:** small rooms; about a 15-minute walk from Metro and train stations; can be a bit pricey depending on time of year; fireplaces are decorative only. [$] *Rooms from: $199* ✉ *116 S. Alfred St.* ☎ *703/838–8000, 800/367–0800* 🌐 *www.morrisonhouse.com* 🛏 *42 rooms, 3 suites* 🍴 *No meals* [M] *King St.*

$ HOTEL 🏨 **The Westin Alexandria.** The staff seems genuinely happy to see you come through the door at this hotel just a mile-and-a half from the cobbled streets of Old Town Alexandria, and if you don't need or want to be in D.C.—only 20–25 minutes away by Metro—you'll get more for your travel dollar here. **Pros:** rooms have pretty views; indoor heated pool and 24-hour gym are complimentary; free shuttle service to waterfront and Old Town Alexandria; close to airport and Metro. **Cons:** outside the city; half-hour walk to waterfront. [$] *Rooms from: $129* ✉ *400 Courthouse Sq., Old Town* ☎ *703/253–8600* 🌐 *www.westin.com/alexandria* 🛏 *309 rooms, 10 suites* 🍴 *No meals.*

MOUNT VERNON, WOODLAWN, AND GUNSTON HALL

Long before Washington, D.C., was planned, wealthy traders and gentlemen farmers had parceled the shores of the Potomac into plantations. Most traces of the colonial era were obliterated as the capital grew in the 19th century, but several splendid examples of plantation architecture remain on the Virginia side of the Potomac, 15 miles or so south of D.C. In one day you can easily visit three such mansions: Mount Vernon, the home of George Washington and one of the most popular sites in the area; Woodlawn, the estate of Martha Washington's granddaughter; and Gunston Hall, the home of George Mason, author of the document on which the Bill of Rights was based. (Expect the longest wait times at Mount Vernon, especially in spring and summer.) Set on hillsides overlooking the river, these estates offer magnificent vistas and bring back to vivid life the more palatable aspects of the 18th century.

MOUNT VERNON, VIRGINIA

16 miles southeast of Washington, D.C., 8 miles south of Alexandria.

GETTING HERE AND AROUND

To reach Mount Vernon by car from the Capital Beltway (Route 495), take Exit 1 and follow the signs to George Washington Memorial Parkway southbound. Mount Vernon is about 8½ miles south. From downtown Washington, cross into Arlington on Key Bridge, Memorial Bridge, or the 14th Street Bridge and drive south on the George Washington Memorial Parkway past Ronald Reagan National Airport through Alexandria straight to Mount Vernon. The trip from D.C. takes about a half hour.

THE VIEW OUT BACK

Beneath a 90-foot portico is George Washington's contribution to architecture and the real treasure of Mount Vernon: the home's dramatic riverside porch. The porch overlooks an expanse of lawn that slopes down to the Potomac. In the spring, the river view (a mile wide where it passes the plantation) is framed by redbud and dogwood blossoms. United States Navy and Coast Guard ships salute ("render honors") when passing the house during daylight hours. Foreign naval vessels often salute, too.

Getting to Mount Vernon by public transportation requires that you take both the Metro and a bus. Begin by taking the Yellow Line train to the Huntington Metro station. From here, take Fairfax County Connector Bus No. 101 ($1.80 cash or $1.10 with SmarTrip card). Buses on each route leave about once an hour—more often during rush hour—and operate weekdays from about 5 am to 9:15 pm, weekends from about 6:30 am to 7 pm.

TOURS

BOAT TOURS The *Spirit of Mount Vernon* makes a pleasant day trip from Washington down the Potomac to Mount Vernon mid-March through mid-October. Boarding begins at 8 am for the narrated cruise down the Potomac River. Once you arrive at Mount Vernon, you'll have three hours to tour the estate before re-boarding at 1:15. Tickets cost about $50 and include admission to the estate.

BUS TOURS Gray Line runs a four-hour Mount Vernon tour (with a stop in Alexandria), departing daily at 8 am from Union Station, that costs $55. There's also a 9-hour Mount Vernon and Arlington National Cemetery Tours are priced at $85. Both include admission to the mansion and grounds.

ESSENTIALS

Boat Information *Spirit of Mount Vernon* ⊠ *Pier 4, 6th and Water sts. SW, Southwest* ☎ *866/302-2469 for boat reservations* ⊕ *www.spiritcruises.com.*

Bus Information Fairfax County Connector ☎ *703/339-7200* ⊕ *www. fairfaxconnector.com.*

Bus Tour Information Martz Gray Line ☎ *800/862-1400* ⊕ *www.grayline dc.com.*

U.S. Navy and Coast Guard ships salute ("render honors") when passing Mount Vernon during daylight hours.

Metro Information Washington Metro Area Transit Authority ☎ 202/637–7000 ⊕ www.wmata.com.

EXPLORING

FAMILY

Fodor's Choice

★

Mount Vernon. This plantation and the surrounding lands had been in the Washington family for nearly 70 years by the time the future president inherited it all in 1743. Before taking over command of the Continental Army, Washington was an accomplished farmer, managing the 8,000-acre plantation and operating five farms on the land. He oversaw the transformation of the main house from an ordinary farm dwelling into what was, for the time, a grand mansion. The inheritance of his widowed bride, Martha, is partly what made that transformation possible.

The red-roof main house is elegant though understated, with a yellow-pine exterior that's been painted and coated with layers of sand to resemble white-stone blocks. The first-floor rooms are quite ornate, especially the formal large dining room, with a molded ceiling decorated with agricultural motifs. The bright colors of the walls, which match the original paint, may surprise those who associate the period with pastels. Throughout the house are smaller symbols of the owner's eminence, such as a key to the main portal of the Bastille—presented to Washington by the Marquis de Lafayette—and Washington's presidential chair. As you tour the mansion, guides are stationed throughout the house to describe the furnishings and answer questions.

You can stroll around the estate's 500 acres and three gardens, visiting workshops, kitchen, carriage house, greenhouse, slave quarters, and—down the hill toward the boat landing—the tomb of George and Martha Washington. There's also a pioneer farmer site: a 4-acre hands-on exhibit with a reconstruction of George Washington's 16-side treading barn as its centerpiece.

But some of the most memorable experiences at Mount Vernon, particularly for kids, are in the Museum and Education Center. Interactive displays, movies with special effects straight out of Hollywood, life-size models, and Revolutionary artifacts illustrate Washington's life and contributions.

A National Treasure tour explores behind the scenes and includes a chance to see the basement of the house; the tour sells out quickly so reserve ahead of time.

Actors in period dress who portray General Washington and his wife welcome visitors at special occasions throughout the year, including Presidents' Day, Memorial Day, and July 4th. Evening candlelight tours are offered weekend evenings in late November and early December and during wine festivals held one weekend in May and in October.

MARTHA WASHINGTON: HOT OR NOT?

As hard as it may be to believe from the portraits of her in history books, Martha Washington was a hottie. Far from the frumpy, heavyset woman we know as the *first* First Lady, Martha wore sequined purple high heels on her wedding day, read romance novels, and had many admirers, not to mention a previous husband. A team of forensic anthropologists used a 1796 portrait of Mrs. Washington to digitally create an image of what she might have looked like in her twenties. The image inspired Michael Deas to create a portrait of the young First Lady, which now hangs in the education building at Mount Vernon.

George Washington's **Distillery and Gristmill**—both reproductions—operate on their original sites. Records kept by Washington helped archaeologists excavate the distillery, which was the largest American whiskey producer of its day, in the late 1990s. Today, using the same recipe and processes, small batches of George Washington's whiskey are made and sold at Mount Vernon. During guided tours, led by costumed interpreters, you meet an 18th-century miller and watch the water-powered wheel grind grain into cornmeal and watch the grains being distilled. The mill and distillery, open April through October, are 3 miles from Mount Vernon on Route 235 toward U.S. 1, almost to Woodlawn. General Admission tickets to Mount Vernon include the gristmill and distillery, but the gristmill and distillery can be visited separately. ⊠ *Southern end of George Washington Pkwy., Mount Vernon* ☎ *703/780–2000* ⊕ *www.mountvernon.org* ⊠ *$17, includes admission to Distillery & Gristmill; $5 for Distillery & Gristmill only* ☉ *Mar., Sept., and Oct., daily 9–5; Apr.–Aug., daily 8–5; Nov.–Feb., daily 9–4.*

SPORTS AND THE OUTDOORS

An asphalt bicycle path leads from the Virginia side of Key Bridge (across from Georgetown), past Ronald Reagan National Airport, and through Alexandria all the way to Mount Vernon. Bikers in moderately good condition can make the 16-mile trip in less than two hours. You can rent bicycles at several locations in Washington.

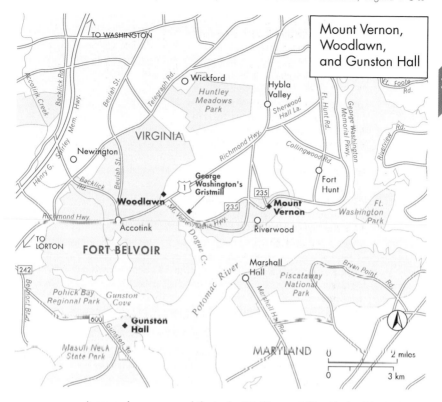

Mount Vernon,
Woodlawn,
and Gunston Hall

12

A great place to rent a bike is the **Washington Sailing Marina** (☎ 703/548–9027 ⊕ *www.washingtonsailingmarina.com*), which is beside the Mount Vernon Bike Trail just past the airport. A 12-mile ride south will take you right up to the front doors of Mount Vernon. Cruiser bikes rent for $8 per hour or $28 per day. The marina is open 9–5 daily.

WOODLAWN, VIRGINIA

3 miles west of Mount Vernon, 15 miles south of Washington, D.C.

GETTING HERE AND AROUND

To drive to Woodlawn, travel southwest on Route 1 to the second Route 235 intersection (the first leads to Mount Vernon). The entrance to Woodlawn is on the right at the traffic light. From Mount Vernon, travel northwest on Route 235 to the Route 1 intersection; Woodlawn is straight ahead through the intersection.

To use public transportation, take Bus No. 101, 151, or 159 ($1.80 cash or $1.10 with SmarTrip card) from Huntington Metro station. Buses returning to the station have the same numbers but are marked Huntington.

EXPLORING

FAMILY **Woodlawn.** This plantation home was once part of the Mount Vernon estate, and from here you can still see the trees of the bowling green that fronted Washington's home. The mansion was built for Martha Washington's granddaughter, Nelly Custis, who married George Washington's nephew, Lawrence Lewis.

Completed in 1805, Woodlawn was designed by William Thornton, a physician and amateur architect who drew up the original plans for the U.S. Capitol and designed Tudor Place and the Octagon House in Washington, DC. Built on a site selected by George Washington, the mansion has commanding views of the surrounding countryside and the Potomac River beyond. In the tradition of mansions from this period, Woodlawn has a central passage that provides a cool refuge in summer.

Woodlawn was once a plantation where more than 100 people, most of them slaves, lived and worked. Guides explain about how the family entertained and architectural details of the house.

Also on the grounds of Woodlawn is the **Pope-Leighey House.** One of Frank Lloyd Wright's "Usonian" homes, the structure was built in 1940 as part of the architect's mission to create affordable housing. It was moved here from Falls Church, Virginia, in 1964, to save it from destruction during the building of Route 66. By design a small and sparsely furnished home, Pope-Leighey provides a stark contrast to Woodlawn. ✉ *9000 Richmond Hwy., Alexandria* ☎ *703/780–4000* ⊕ *www.woodlawnpopeleighey.org* ✉ *$10 for each house or $15 for both* ☉ *Mar.–Nov., Fri.–Mon. noon–4. Tours begin every half hr for each house; last tour at 4.*

GUNSTON HALL, VIRGINIA

12 miles south of Woodlawn, 25 miles south of Washington, D.C.

GETTING HERE AND AROUND

You'll have to use a car to get to Gunston Hall because there is no bus stop within walking distance. Travel south on Route 1, 9 miles past Woodlawn to Route 242; turn left there and go 3½ miles to the plantation entrance.

EXPLORING

FAMILY **Gunston Hall Plantation.** Down the Potomac from Mount Vernon is the
Fodor's Choice home of another important George. Gentleman farmer George Mason
★ was a colonel of the Virginia militia and author of the Virginia Declaration of Rights, the model for the U.S. Bill of Rights, which called for freedom of the press, tolerance of religion, and other fundamental democratic principles. Mason was a framer of the Constitution but refused to sign the final document because it didn't stop the importation of slaves, adequately restrain the powers of the federal government, or include a bill of rights. Mason's objections spurred the movement for the inclusion of the Bill of Rights into the Constitution.

Mason's home was begun about 1755. The Georgian-style mansion has some of the finest hand-carved ornamented interiors in the country and is the handiwork of the 18th century's foremost architect,

William Buckland, who also designed the Hammond-Harwood and Chase-Lloyd houses in Annapolis. The house is built of native brick, black walnut, and yellow pine, and follows the style of the time that demanded absolute symmetry, which explains the false door set into one side of the center hallway and the "robber" window on a second-floor storage room.

12

The interior, with carved woodwork in styles from Chinese to Greek, has been meticulously restored, with paints made from the original formulas and carefully carved replacements for the intricate mahogany medallions in the moldings. Restored outbuildings include a kitchen, dairy, laundry, and smokehouse, and a schoolhouse has also been reconstructed.

The formal gardens, recently under excavation by a team of archaeologists, are famous for their boxwoods—some were planted during George Mason's time, making them among the oldest in the country. The Potomac is visible past the expansive deer park, and Mason's landing road to the river was recently found. Special programs, such as archaeology tutelage and a plantation Christmas celebration, are available. A tour of Gunston Hall takes at least 45 minutes; tours begin on the front porch of the house. Buy tickets at the visitor center, which includes a museum and gift shop. ⊠ *10709 Gunston Rd., Lorton* ☎ *703/550 9220* ⊕ *www.gunstonhall.org* ⎙ *$10* ◷ *Daily 9:30–5, tours every 30 mins until 4:30.*

OFF THE BEATEN PATH

National Museum of the Marine Corps. The glassy atrium of this 118,000 square foot homage to the military's finest soars into the sky next to the Marine Corps Base Quantico. The design was inspired by the iconic photograph of Marines lifting the American flag on Iwo Jima. Inside the museum, visitors are able to see the flag itself, as well as experience the life of a Marine. The museum is completely interactive, from the entrance where drill instructors yell at new "recruits" in surround-sound, to the Korean War exhibit, where visitors walk through a snowy mountain pass and shiver from the cold while listening to the 2nd Platoon fight on the other side of the mountain. The museum also has a staggering collection of tanks, aircraft, rocket launchers, and other weapons. There is even a rifle range simulator, where guests of all ages can learn how to hold a rifle and practice hitting targets. Oohrah! Family Day at the Museum is held the 2nd Saturday of the month with activities and take-home crafts. There also are gallery hunts for children ages 4–10 that encourage exploration of the museum. ⊠ *18900 Jefferson Davis Hwy., Triangle* ☎ *877/635–1775* ⊕ *www.usmcmuseum. org* ⎙ *Free* ◷ *Daily 9–5.*

ANNAPOLIS, MARYLAND

32 miles east of Washington, D.C.

In 1649 a group of Puritan settlers moved from Virginia to a spot at the mouth of the Severn River, where they established a community called Providence. Lord Baltimore, who held the royal charter to settle Maryland, named the area around this town Anne Arundel County, after his wife; in 1684 Anne Arundel Town was established across from Providence on the Severn's south side. Ten years later, Anne Arundel Town became the capital of Maryland and was renamed Annapolis after Princess Anne, who later became queen. It received its city charter in 1708 and became a major port, particularly for the export of tobacco.

In 1774, patriots here matched their Boston counterparts (who had thrown their famous tea party the previous year) by burning the *Peggy Stewart,* a ship loaded with taxed tea. Annapolis later served as the nation's first peacetime capital (1783–84). The city's considerable colonial and early republican heritage is largely intact, and because it's all within walking distance, highly accessible.

Although it has long since been overtaken by Baltimore as the major Maryland port, Annapolis is still a popular pleasure-boating destination. On warm sunny days the waters off City Dock become center stage for an amateur show of power-boaters maneuvering through the heavy traffic. Annapolis's enduring nautical reputation derives largely from the presence of the U.S. Naval Academy, whose strikingly uniformed midshipmen throng the city streets in crisp white uniforms in summer and navy blue in winter.

GETTING HERE AND AROUND

The drive (east on U.S. 50 to the Rowe Boulevard exit) normally takes 35–45 minutes from Washington. During rush hour (weekdays 3:30–6:30 pm), however, it takes about twice as long. Also beware of Navy football Saturdays.

Parking spots on the historic downtown streets of Annapolis are scarce, but there are some parking meters for $2 an hour (maximum two hours). You can park on some residential streets for free. The public parking garage adjacent to the Annapolis Visitors Center charges $2/hr with a $15/day maximum. The Annapolis Circulator offers free trolley transportation within the Historic Area. On Sunday morning from 6 am to 1 pm, most parking is free.

TOURS

Walking tours are a great way to see the historic district. Guides from Watermark wear colonial-style dress and take you to the State House, St. John's College, and the Naval Academy on their very popular, 2-hour "Four Centuries Walking Tour" offered twice daily. The cost is $16. There's also a Historic Ghost Walk on weekends.

Discover Annapolis Tours leads one-hour narrated trolley tours ($18) that introduce you to the history and architecture of Annapolis. Tours leave from the visitor center daily April through November.

To see Maryland's state capital from the water, there are a couple of options. Schooner Woodwind Cruises have two 74-foot sailboats, *Woodwind* and *Woodwind II,* which make daily trips between April and October, with some overnight excursions. Two-hour sails are $39 to $42. Even when it rains, Watermark runs boat tours that last from 40 minutes to 7½ hours and go as far as St. Michaels on the Eastern Shore, where there's a maritime museum, yachts, dining, and boutiques. Prices range from $15 to $75.

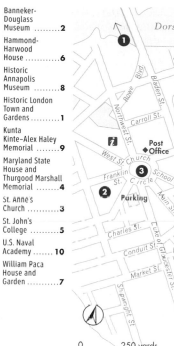

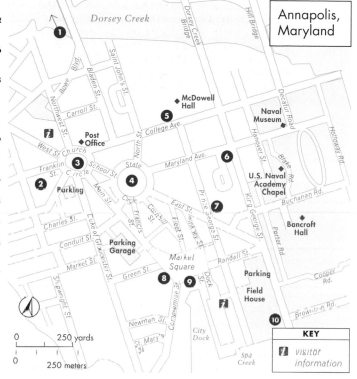

ESSENTIALS

Tour Contacts Discover Annapolis Tours ✉ 26 West St., Historic District ☎ 410/626–6000 ⊕ www.discover-annapolis.com. **Schooner Woodwind Cruises** ✉ Annapolis Marriott Hotel dock, 80 Compromise St. ☎ 410/263–7837 ⊕ www.schoonerwoodwind.com. **Watermark** ✉ 1 Dock St., Historic District ☎ 410/268–7601 ⊕ www.watermarkjourney.com.

Visitor Information Annapolis & Anne Arundel County Conference and Visitors Bureau ✉ 26 West St., West Side ☎ 410/280–0445, 888/302–2852 ⊕ www.visitannapolis.org ⏱ Daily 9–5. **Information Booth** ✉ Dock St. parking lot ☎ 410/280–0445 ⏱ Mar.–Sept. Daily 9–5

EXPLORING

TOP ATTRACTIONS

FAMILY **Banneker-Douglass Museum.** Named for abolitionist Frederick Douglass and scientist Benjamin Banneker, this former church and its next-door neighbor make up a museum that tells the stories of African-Americans in Maryland through performances, lectures, educational programs, and both permanent and changing exhibits. Audio and visual presentations and hands-on exhibits make the museum engaging for kids, while also bringing home the hardships of slave life. ⊠ *84 Franklin St.* ☎ *410/216–6180* ⊕ *www.bdmuseum.com* ✉ *Free* ☉ *Tues.–Sat. 10–4.*

NEED A BREAK? **The Annapolis Bookstore.** This is more than just a bookstore. Relax in the café with a hot or cold beverage, freshly baked pastry, or even a sandwich named after a famous author, and then head to the back to see the charming Fairy Garden and book house, which is literally made of books. Owners Mary Adams and Janice Holmes provide the perfect place for reading, storytelling, and literary adventures. With a carefully selected collection of new, used and rare books, the store is an oasis from the ubiquitous chains. As befits its Annapolis location, the shop specializes in maritime books, as well as classics, poetry, and children's books. ⊠ *35 Maryland Ave.* ☎ *410/280–2339* ⊕ *www.annapolisbookstore.com* ☉ *Sun.–Thurs. 9–6, Fri. and Sat. 9–9.*

Hammond-Harwood House. Based on the Villa Pisani in Stra, Italy, by Andrea Palladio, this 1774 home was designed by premier colonial architect William Buckland and is considered America's greatest colonial high-style residence. Called the architectural "Jewel of Annapolis," the residence was greatly admired by Thomas Jefferson when he sketched the house in 1783. The wood carvings surrounding the front door and enriching the dining room are some of the best surviving of their kind in America. The site today exhibits famous colonial art by Charles Willson Peale, Rembrandt Peale, James Peale, John Trumbull, John Hesselius, Jeremiah Theus, and John Beale Bordley, as well as an extensive decorative arts collection covering everything from Chinese export porcelain to Georgian period silver. Also on display is the world's largest collection of colonial cabinetwork by Annapolis native John Shaw. Noted landscape architect Alden Hopkins from Colonial Williamsburg created the property's Colonial Revival garden. Regular tours may be a bit dry for children under 12. ⊠ *19 Maryland Ave.* ☎ *410/263–4683* ⊕ *www.hammondharwoodhouse.org* ✉ *$7* ☉ *Apr.– Oct., Tues.–Sun. noon–5; Nov. and Dec., Thurs.–Sun. noon–4. Tours begin on the hr; last tour 1 hr before closing.*

Historic London Town and Gardens. The 17th-century tobacco port of London, on the South River a short car ride from Annapolis, was made up of 40 dwellings, shops, and taverns. London all but disappeared in the 18th century, its buildings abandoned and left to decay, but the excavation of the town is underway, and buildings are continually being restored. One of the few original colonial structures is a three-story waterfront brick house, built by William Brown between 1758 and 1764, with dramatic river views. Walk around on your own or take a 30-minute docent-led tour; allow more time to wander the house grounds, woodland gardens, and a visitor center with a new interactive exhibit on the archaeology and history of London Town and Anne Arundel County. ⊠ *839 Londontown Rd., Edgewater* ☎ *410/222– 1919* ⊕ *www.historiclondontown.org* ✉ *$10 Apr.–Nov., $5 Dec.–Mar.* ☉ *Apr.–Nov., Wed.–Sat. 10–4:30, Sun. noon–4:30; Dec.–Mar., weekdays 10–4.*

Fodor'sChoice **Maryland State House.** Originally constructed between 1772 and 1780,
★ the State House is the oldest state capitol in continuous legislative use;
it's also the only one in which the U.S. Congress has sat (1783–84).
General George Washington resigned as commander-in-chief of the
Continental Army here in 1783 and the Treaty of Paris was ratified in
1784, ending the Revolutionary War. Both events took place in the Old
Senate Chamber. The Maryland Senate and House hold their sessions in
two other chambers in the building. Also on the grounds is the oldest
public building in Maryland, the tiny redbrick Treasury, built in 1735.
Visit the Office of Interpretation on the 1st floor to pick up self-guided
tour information. You must have a photo ID to enter the State House.

In the State House Square is the **Thurgood Marshall Memorial,** com-
prising an 8-foot statue of Thurgood Marshall as a young lawyer,
benches with images of students for whom he fought for integration,
and plaques commemorating his achievements. Born in Baltimore, Marshall (1908–93) was the first African-American Supreme Court Justice
and one of the 20th century's foremost leaders in the struggle for equal
rights under the law. He won the decision in 1954's *Brown v. Board
of Education,* in which the Court overturned the doctrine of "separate
but equal." Marshall was appointed as U.S. Solicitor General in 1965
and to the Supreme Court in 1967 by President Lyndon B. Johnson.
✉ *100 State Circle* ⊕ *msa.maryland.gov* ☎ *800/492–7122 ext. 5400*
🎟 *Free* ☉ *Daily 9–5.*

St. John's College. The Annapolis campus of St. John's, the third-oldest
college in the country (after Harvard and William and Mary), once held
the last Liberty Tree, under which the Sons of Liberty convened to hear
patriots plan the Revolution. Damaged in a 1999 hurricane, the 400 year
old tree was removed; its progeny stands to the left of McDowell Hall.
St. John's adheres to a Great Books program, and all students follow
the same four-year, liberal arts curriculum, which includes philosophy,
mathematics, music, science, Greek, and French. Students are immersed
in the classics, through small classes conducted as discussions rather than
lectures. Start a visit here by climbing the gradual slope of the long, brick-
paved path to the cupola of McDowell Hall.

Down King George Street toward the water is the Carroll-Barrister
House, now the college admissions office. Once home to Charles Car-
roll (not the signer of the Declaration but his cousin), the house was
built in 1722 at Main and Conduit streets and moved onto campus in
1955. ✉ *60 College Ave., at St. John's St.* ☎ *410/263–2371* ⊕ *www.
stjohnscollege.edu.*

Fodor'sChoice **United States Naval Academy** *(USNA).* Probably the most interesting
★ and important site in Annapolis, the Naval Academy occupies 328
waterfront acres along the Severn River and abuts Downtown. Men
and women enter the USNA, established in 1845 on the site of a U.S.
Army fort, from every part of the United States and foreign countries
to undergo rigorous study in subjects that include literature, navigation,
and nuclear engineering. Midshipmen (the term used for both women
and men) go to classes, conduct military drills, and practice or compete
in intercollegiate and intramural sports.

FIRST AFRICAN-AMERICAN GRADUATE

In 1949 a man by the name of Wesley Brown made history as the U.S. Naval Academy's first African-American graduate. Five others had tried before him but were forced out by intense racism and violence. Brown also suffered greatly in his years at the academy. A group of upperclassmen tried to force him out by piling him up with unwarranted demerits and ensuring that he was snubbed by his peers, but Brown never gave up. A veteran of World War II and the Korean and Vietnam wars, Brown served another 20 years in the Navy as a lieutenant commander in the Civil Engineering Corps before retiring in 1969. In 2008 the Naval Academy unveiled its $50 million Wesley Brown Field House, a state-of-the-art gymnasium that overlooks the Severn River—a fitting tribute to a man who is credited with not only helping to improve the Navy, but also the country. Today nearly one-fourth of the student body is comprised of minorities. To read more about Brown's fascinating story, check out *Breaking the Color Barrier* by historian Robert J. Schneller Jr.

Your visit to "The Yard" (as the USNA grounds are nicknamed) will start at the **Armel-Leftwich Visitor Center.** Note that all visitors 18 years and older must have a government-issued photo ID to be admitted through the academy's gates. Park on the street or in Annapolis public parking and walk through the Visitor Access Center at Gate 1—only cars on official Department of Defense business are allowed on campus. The Visitor Center features an exhibit, "The Quarter Deck," which introduces visitors to the Academy's mission, including a 13-minute film, "The Call to Serve," and a well-stocked gift shop. From here you can join one of the hour-long guided walking tours of the Academy.

The centerpiece of the campus is the bright copper-clad dome of the interdenominational **U.S. Naval Academy Chapel.** Beneath it lies the crypt of the Revolutionary War naval hero John Paul Jones, who, in a historic naval battle with a British ship, uttered the inspirational words, "I have not yet begun to fight!" Bancroft Hall is one of the largest dormitories in the world—it houses the entire 4,000-member Brigade of Midshipmen. You can't see how shipshape the middies' quarters are, but you can go inside Bancroft and see a sample room and the glorious Memorial Hall, a tribute to Academy grads who died in military operations. In front of Bancroft is the Statue of Tecumseh, a bronze replica of the USS *Delaware*'s wooden figurehead, "Tamanend," which midshipmen decorate for athletics events. ■TIP➜ If you're here at noon on weekdays in fair weather, watch the midshipmen form up outside Bancroft Hall and parade to lunch accompanied by the Drum and Bugle Corps. You also can have lunch on campus either at Drydock in Dahlgren Hall or the Naval Academy Club. ⊠ *Off Prince George St. or Randall St.* 🖀 *410/293–8687* ⊕ *www.navyonline.com* 🖃 *Guided tour $10* ⊙ *Visitor center daily 9–5, tours 10–3.*

U.S. Naval Academy Museum. Displays of model ships and memorabilia from naval heroes and fighting vessels tell the story of the U.S.

Navy. The Rogers Ship Model Collection has 108 models of sailing ships built for the British Admiralty. Kids of all ages will enjoy watching the restoration and building of model ships on the ground level and might even learn a few tricks of the trade should they wish to purchase a model ship kit to build when they get home. ✉ *118 Maryland Ave.* ☎ *410/293–2108* ⊕ *www.usna.edu/ Museum* ✍ *Free* ☉ *Mon.–Sat. 9–5, Sun. 11–5.*

WORD OF MOUTH

"The Naval Academy (there are signs from Rte. 50 to take you directly to the visitor's entrance) is a great bet, full of stately, old marble buildings and midshipmen (and women) in uniform."
—Hannah_reads_for_fun

William Paca House and Garden. A signer of the Declaration of Independence, Paca (pronounced "PAY-cuh") was a Maryland governor from 1782 to 1785. His house was built from 1763 to 1765, and its original garden was finished by 1772. The main floor (furnished with 18th-century antiques) retains its original Prussian blue and soft gray color scheme and the second floor houses more 18th-century pieces. The adjacent two-acre garden provides a longer perspective on the back of the house, plus worthwhile sights of its own: upper terraces, a Chinese Chippendale bridge, a pond, a wilderness area, and formal arrangements. An inn, Carvel Hall, once stood in the gardens, now planted with 18th-century perennials. You can take a self-guided tour of the garden, but to see the house you must go on the docent-led tour, which leaves every hour at half past the hour. The last tour leaves 1½ hours before closing. ✉ *186 Prince George St.* ☎ *410/990–4543* ⊕ *www.annapolis. org* ✍ *House and garden $10, garden only $7* ☉ *Mid-Mar.–Dec., Mon.– Sat. 10–5, Sun. noon–5.*

WORTH NOTING

Historic Annapolis Museum. Light filled and modern, this little museum occupies a historic building that once held supplies for the Continental Army during the Revolutionary War, and is a good place to learn about the people and events that shaped the history of Annapolis and its creation as the state's capitol. The current exhibit, "Freedom Bound: Runaways of the Chesapeake," which runs through 2015, tells the stories of individuals who resisted servitude during the 1760s–1860s. Portions of the exhibit, including artifacts and displays, video, and hands-on activities, also are on display at the Historic Annapolis Waterfront Warehouse at 4 Pinkney Street, which was used in the early 19th century to store tobacco before it was shipped to England. The Museum Store sells history books, ceramics, crafts made by local artisans, and nautical knickknacks. ✉ *99 Main St.* ☎ *410/267–6656* ⊕ *www.annapolis.org* ✍ *Free* ☉ *Mon.–Sat. 10–5, Sun. 11–5.*

Kunta Kinte–Alex Haley Memorial. A series of plaques along the waterfront recounting the story of African-Americans in Maryland lead to a sculpture group depicting Alex Haley, famed author of *Roots,* reading to a group of children. On the other side of the street, a three-sided obelisk and plaque commemorate the 1767 arrival of the African slave immortalized in Haley's novel. This is a lovely place that may inspire you to reflect on African-American history and the importance of family, reading, and passing oral history from one generation to another. ✉ *Market Sq.* 🌐 *www.kintehaley.org.*

St. Anne's Church. Residing in the center of one of the historic area's busy circles, this brick building is one of the city's most prominent places of worship. King William III donated the communion silver when the parish was founded in 1692, but the first St. Anne's Church wasn't completed until 1704. The second church burned in 1858, but parts of its walls survived and were incorporated into the present structure, built the following year. The churchyard contains the grave of the last colonial governor, Sir Robert Eden. ✉ *Church Circle* ☎ *410/267–9333* 🌐 *www.stannes-annapolis.org* 🎟 *Free* 🕒 *Daily 8–6.*

WHERE TO EAT

In the beginning, there was crab: crab cakes, crab soup, whole crabs to crack. This Chesapeake Bay specialty is still found in abundance, but Annapolis has broadened its horizons to include eateries—many in the Historic District—that offer many sorts of cuisines. Ask for a restaurant guide at the visitor center.

$ ECLECTIC 🍴 **49 West Coffeehouse and Gallery.** In what was once a hardware store, this eclectic, casual eatery has one interior wall of exposed brick and another of exposed plaster; both are used to hang art for sale by local artists. Daily specials are chalked on a blackboard. Menu staples include a large cheese-and-pâté plate, deli sandwiches, and soups and salads. There's free Wi-Fi, and live music every night. [$] *Average main: $12* ✉ *49 West St.* ☎ *410/626–9796* 🌐 *www.49westcoffeehouse.com.*

$$ SEAFOOD FAMILY 🍴 **Buddy's Crabs & Ribs.** Family owned and operated since 1988, with a central location overlooking Main Street and City Dock, the biggest restaurant in Annapolis is fun and informal and features all kinds of seafood and shellfish, including their famous "Big Buddy" crab cakes and all-you-can-eat buffets. Not in a crabby mood? There also are pastas, chicken and steak selections, and specialty sandwiches and salads. With each full-price entrée, one child 10 or under can eat free from the kids' menu. [$] *Average main: $20* ✉ *100 Main St.* ☎ *410/626–1100* 🌐 *www.buddysonline.com.*

$$ FRENCH 🍴 **Café Normandie.** Wood beams, skylights, and a four-sided fireplace provide a cozy ambiance, and out of the open kitchen comes an astonishingly good French onion soup, made daily from scratch. Bouillabaisse, puffy omelets, crêpes, and seafood dishes are other specialties. Breakfast is served on weekends. All offerings are sustainable and local. [$] *Average main: $26* ✉ *185 Main St.* ☎ *410/263–3382* 🌐 *www.cafenormandie.com.*

$$ SEAFOOD 🍴 **Cantler's Riverside Inn.** Jimmy Cantler, a native Marylander who worked as a waterman on the Chesapeake Bay, founded this local institution 40 years ago. The no-nonsense interior has nautical items laminated beneath tabletops, and steamed mussels, clams, and shrimp as well as Maryland vegetable crab soup, seafood sandwiches, oysters, crab cakes, and numerous fin fish are served on disposable dinnerware; if you order steamed crabs, they'll come served atop a "tablecloth" of brown paper. Water-view outdoor dining is available seasonally, and boat owners can

DID YOU KNOW?

The Navy's Blue Angels fly over each graduating class at the U.S. Naval Academy in Annapolis to celebrate their accomplishments.

tie up at the dock; there's limited free parking during the busy summer season so be prepared to wait a bit. [$] *Average main: $20* ✉ *458 Forest Beach Rd.* ☎ *410/757–1311* 🌐 *www.cantlers.com.*

> **WORD OF MOUTH**
>
> "Our favorite place in downtown Annapolis is Cafe Normandie. Just look for the French flag outside." —basingstoke2

$$$$ AMERICAN 🍴 **Carrol's Creek.** You can walk, catch a water taxi from City Dock, or drive over the Spa Creek drawbridge to this local favorite in Eastport. Whether you dine indoors or out, the view of historic Annapolis and its harbor is spectacular. The à la carte Sunday brunch is worth checking out, as are the seafood specialties. Any of the entrées, including the herb-encrusted rockfish or filet mignon, can be turned into a four-course meal with the addition of soup, salad, and dessert. [$] *Average main: $45* ✉ *410 Severn Ave., Eastport* ☎ *410/263–8102* 🌐 *www.carrolscreek.com* ⏲ *No brunch Mon.–Sat.*

$ AMERICAN 🍴 **Chick and Ruth's Delly.** Deli sandwiches (named for local politicos), burgers, subs, crab cakes, and milk shakes are the fare at this very busy counter-and-booth institution. Built in 1899, the edifice was just a sandwich shop when Baltimoreans Ruth and Chick Levitt purchased it in 1965. Their son Ted and his wife Beth continue the business today. Don't plan on placing an order at 8:30 am on a weekday or 9:30 am on a weekend— that's when the place stops to say the Pledge of Allegiance. [$] *Average main: $11* ✉ *165 Main St., Annapolis Historic District* ☎ *410/269–6737* 🌐 *www.chickandruths.com.*

$ MEXICAN 🍴 **El Toro Bravo.** The wooden colonial exterior of this local favorite, one block from the visitor center, conceals Mexican tiles and the occasional bull's head on the walls. On weekends, there's often a line for the authentic fajitas, enchiladas, and burritos, but takeout is available. The guacamole is made on the premises, as are the *sopapillas* (light fried dough, coated with honey). There's a children's menu, and the bar offers a staggering range of margaritas along with Mexican beers and sodas. [$] *Average main: $12* ✉ *50 West St.* ☎ *410/267–5949* 🌐 *www.eltorobravoannapolis.com.*

$$$ SEAFOOD 🍴 **Harry Browne's.** In the shadow of the State House, this understated establishment has long held a reputation for quality food and attentive service that ensures bustle year-round, especially during the busy days of the legislative session (early January into early April) and special weekend events at the Naval Academy. The menu clearly reflects the city's maritime culture, but also has seasonal specialties, and in a green approach to dining, everything used is recycled. Live Irish music is performed in the lounge once a month. The sidewalk café is open, weather permitting, April through October. There is a champagne brunch on Sunday. [$] *Average main: $30* ✉ *66 State Circle* ☎ *410/263–4332* 🌐 *www.harrybrownes.com* ⏲ *No brunch Mon.–Sat.*

$$ AMERICAN 🍴 **McGarvey's Saloon and Oyster Bar.** An Annapolis institution since 1975, this dockside eatery and watering hole is full of good cheer, great drink, and grand food. A heritage of seasonal shell- and finfish dishes, the finest burgers and steaks, as well as unstinting appetizers, make McGarvey's

menu one of the most popular in the area. The full menu is available daily until 11 pm; from 11 pm–1 am you can order soups and sandwiches. Choose to eat outside in good weather, at the bar, or in the light-filled atrium. $ Average main: $24 ⊠ 8 Market Space ☎ 410/263-5700 ⊕ www.mcgarveys.net.

$$ ✕**Middleton Tavern.** Horatio Middleton began operating this "inn for
AMERICAN seafaring men" in 1750, and Washington, Jefferson, and Franklin were among his guests. Today four fireplaces, wood floors, paneled walls, and a Colonial theme create a cozy atmosphere and seafood tops the menu; the Maryland crab soup and pan-seared rockfish are standouts. Try the tavern's own Middleton Oyster Ale, perhaps during happy hour or on weekends in the upstairs piano bar where you'll enjoy everything from showtunes and blues to classical pieces. Brunch is served on weekends, and you can dine outdoors in good weather. $ Average main: $24 ⊠ City Dock at Randall St. ☎ 410/263-3323 ⊕ www. middletontavern.com.

$$ ✕**Osteria 177.** This might be the nicest restaurant in the capital that
MODERN ITALIAN doesn't always serve crab cakes. It also might be the only local Italian restaurant that doesn't offer pizza or spaghetti. Instead, Osteria serves seafood from all over the world, meat, and pasta made on the premises. Northern Italian owner and chef Arturo Ottaviano offers sea bass filleted at tableside, lobster bisque served in generous oval-shaped bowls, and his signature dish Linguine all' Osteria 177, surrounded by generous servings of seafood. This is a favorite lunch spot for politicians and lobbyists. $ Average main: $26 ⊠ 177 Main St. ☎ 410/267-7700 ⊕ www.osteria177.com.

$ ✕**Rams Head Tavern.** This traditional English-style pub serves better-
BRITISH than-usual tavern fare, including spicy shrimp salad, crab cakes, beer-battered shrimp, and daily specials, as well as more than 100 beers—30 on tap—including six Fordham beers and others from around the world. Brunch is served on Sunday, and nationally known folk, rock, jazz, country, and bluegrass artists perform most nights. Dinner-show specials are available; the menu also has light fare. $ Average main: $14 ⊠ 33 West St. ☎ 410/268-4545 ⊕ www.ramsheadtavern.com.

WHERE TO STAY

There are many places to stay near the heart of the city, as well as area bed-and-breakfasts and chain motels a few miles outside town. Prices vary considerably. They rise astronomically for "Commissioning Week" at the Naval Academy (late May), the week of July 4, and during the sailboat and powerboat shows in October.

Annapolis Accommodations. Rentals as short as three days or as long as three years are the specialty of this agency, with a range of prices depending on the type of accommodations and length of stay. The office is open weekdays 9–5:30. ⊠ Historic Area, 41 Maryland Ave. ☎ 410/263-3262 ⊕ www.stayannapolis.com.

$$$$ ⊡ **Annapolis Marriott Waterfront.** You can practically fish from your room
HOTEL at the city's only waterfront hotel, where rooms have either balconies
FAMILY over the water or large windows with views of the harbor or the historic

district. **Pros:** a "pure room" is available for the allergy sensitive; accessible for travelers with disabilities; on-site restaurant and bar; complimentary Wi-Fi throughout. **Cons:** some rooms have no waterfront view, some have only partial views; chain hotel lacks charm; parking is pricey. [$] *Rooms from: $429* ✉ *80 Compromise St.* ☎ *410/268–7555* 🌐 *www.annapolismarriott.com* 🛏 *150 rooms* 🍴 *No meals.*

$ HOTEL 🏨 **Country Inn & Suites.** Although this hotel is 5 miles from the historic Annapolis waterfront, there's a free shuttle, and the two-room suites with pull-out sofas are perfect for families. **Pros:** daily hot breakfast included in the price; reliable and inexpensive option; handful of pet-friendly rooms; near shopping; free shuttle services. **Cons:** distance from the dock; small gym; small indoor heated pool can be crowded at times. [$] *Rooms from: $135* ✉ *2600 Housely Rd.* ☎ *410/571–6700, 800/456–4000* 🌐 *www.countryinns.com* 🛏 *45 rooms, 55 suites* 🍴 *Breakfast.*

$ HOTEL 🏨 **Gibson's Lodgings.** Just half a block from the water, the three detached houses that form this hotel come from three centuries—1780, 1890, and 1980—and all the guest rooms are furnished with pre-1900 antiques. **Pros:** conveniently located between the Naval Academy and downtown; free parking in the courtyards. **Cons:** only one of the houses can accommodate children; only one room is handicapped accessible; two of the rooms share a bathroom. [$] *Rooms from: $149* ✉ *110–114 Prince George St.* ☎ *410/268–5555, 877/330–0057* 🌐 *www.gibsonslodgings.com* 🛏 *20 rooms* 🍴 *Breakfast.*

$ B&B/INN 🏨 **Historic Inns of Annapolis.** Three 18th-century properties in the historic district, the Governor Calvert House, Robert Johnson House, and Maryland Inn, are grouped as one inn, all offering guest rooms individually decorated with antiques and reproductions. **Pros:** historic properties; within walking distance of activities; lemonade or spiced cider served daily in the Calvert House. **Cons:** prices vary greatly; some rooms are small. [$] *Rooms from: $169* ✉ *58 State Circle* ☎ *410/263–2641, 800/847–8882* 🌐 *www.historicinnsofannapolis.com* 🛏 *124 rooms, 14 suites* 🍴 *No meals.*

$ B&B/INN 🏨 **Scotlaur Inn.** On the two floors above Chick and Ruth's Delly (⇨ *see Where to Eat*) in the heart of the historic district, this family-owned B&B is cozy and characterful. **Pros:** a chance to stay above one of Annapolis's landmarks right in the center of town; half off in nearby parking garage. **Cons:** not for those who prefer modern style and don't like chintz; rooms are on the small side; no elevator. [$] *Rooms from: $95* ✉ *165 Main St.* ☎ *410/268–5665* 🌐 *www.scotlaurinn.com* 🛏 *10 rooms* 🍴 *Breakfast.*

$$ HOTEL 🏨 **The Westin Annapolis Hotel.** About a mile from City Dock, in a rapidly gentrifying neighborhood, this hotel is the centerpiece of a European-themed planned community, complete with restaurants, shops, and condominiums. **Pros:** the complete Starwood hotel experience; modern hotel with many amenities. **Cons:** parking a bit pricey; distance from the City Dock; Wi-Fi only free in public areas. [$] *Rooms from: $249* ✉ *100 Westgate Circle, Park Place* ☎ *410/972–4300* 🌐 *www.westin.com/annapolis* 🛏 *225 rooms* 🍴 *No meals.*

TRAVEL SMART
WASHINGTON, D.C.

GETTING HERE AND AROUND

Although it may not appear so at first glance, there's a system to addresses in D.C., albeit one that's a bit confusing for newcomers. The city is divided into the four quadrants of a compass (NW, NE, SE, SW), with the U.S. Capitol at the center. Because the Capitol doesn't sit in the exact center of the city, Northwest is the largest quadrant. Northwest also has most of the important landmarks, although Northeast and Southwest have their fair share. The boundaries are North Capitol Street, East Capitol Street, South Capitol Street, and the National Mall.

If someone tells you to meet them at 6th and G, ask them to specify the quadrant, because there are actually four different 6th and G intersections (one per quadrant). Within each quadrant, numbered streets run north to south, and lettered streets run east to west (the letter *J* was omitted to avoid confusion with the letter *I*). The streets form a fairly simple grid—for instance, 900 G Street NW is the intersection of 9th and G streets in the NW quadrant of the city. Likewise, if you count the letters of the alphabet, skipping *J*, you can get a good approximation of an address for a numbered street. For instance, 1600 16th Street NW is close to Q Street, Q being the 16th letter of the alphabet if you skip *J*.

As if all this weren't confusing enough, Major Pierre L'Enfant, the Frenchman who originally designed the city, threw in diagonal avenues recalling those of Paris. Most of D.C.'s avenues are named after U.S. states. You can find addresses on avenues the same way you find those on numbered streets, so 1200 Connecticut Avenue NW is close to M Street, because *M* is the 12th letter of the alphabet when you skip *J*.

▮ AIR TRAVEL

A flight to D.C. from New York takes a little less than an hour. It's about 1½ hours from Chicago, 3 hours from Denver or Dallas, and 5 hours from San Francisco. Passengers flying from London should expect a trip of about 6 hours. From Sydney it's an 18-hour flight.

Airline Contacts AirTran ☎ 800/247-8726 ⊕ www.airtran.com. **American Airlines/American Eagle** ☎ 800/433-7300 ⊕ www.aa.com. **Delta Airlines** ☎ 800/221-1212 ⊕ www.delta.com. **JetBlue** ☎ 800/538-2583 ⊕ www.jetblue.com. **Southwest Airlines** ☎ 800/435-9792 ⊕ www.southwest.com. **United Airlines** ☎ 800/864-8331 ⊕ www.united.com. **US Airways** ☎ 800/428-4322 ⊕ www.usairways.com.

Airline Security Issues Transportation Security Administration ☎ 866/289-9673 ⊕ www.tsa.gov.

Air Travel Resources in Washington, D.C.
U.S. Department of Transportation Aviation Consumer Protection Division ☎ 202/366-2220 ⊕ www.dot.gov/airconsumer.

AIRPORTS

The major gateways to D.C. are **Ronald Reagan Washington National Airport (DCA)** in Virginia, 4 miles south of Downtown Washington; **Dulles International Airport (IAD)**, 26 miles west of Washington, D.C.; and **Baltimore/Washington International–Thurgood Marshall Airport (BWI)** in Maryland, about 30 miles to the northeast.

Reagan National Airport is closest to Downtown D.C. and has a Metro stop in the terminal. East Coast shuttles and shorter flights tend to fly in and out of this airport. Dulles is configured primarily for long-haul flights, although as a United hub, it's also well-connected regionally. BWI offers blended service, with its many gates for Southwest Air, as well as international flights. Although the Metro doesn't serve Dulles or BWI, there is affordable and convenient public transportation to and from each airport. Be aware that the Mid-Atlantic region is prone to quirky weather that can snarl air traffic, especially on stormy summer afternoons.

Airport Information Baltimore/Washington International–Thurgood Marshall Airport (*BWI*). ☎ 800/435-9294 ⊕ www.bwiairport.com. **Dulles International Airport** (*IAD*). ☎ 703/572-2700 ⊕ www.metwashairports.com/dulles. **Ronald Reagan Washington National Airport** (*DCA*). ☎ 703/417-8000 ⊕ www.metwashairports.com/reagan.

GROUND TRANSPORTATION: REAGAN NATIONAL (DCA)

By Car: Take the George Washington Memorial Parkway north for approximately 1 mile. Exit on I–395 North; bear left onto U.S. 1 North toward Downtown. For the city center, turn left on Madison Drive NW and turn right on 15th Street NW. The drive takes 20–30 minutes, depending on traffic and your destination.

By Metro: The Metro station is within easy walking distance of Terminals B and C, and a free airport bus shuttles between the station and Terminal A. The Metro ride to Downtown takes about 20 minutes and costs about $2.40, depending on the time of day and your final destination.

By Shuttle: SuperShuttle, a fleet of bright blue vans, will take you to any hotel or residence in the city. The length of the ride varies, depending on traffic and the number of stops. The approximately 20-minute ride from Reagan National to Downtown averages $14.

By Taxi: Expect to pay $20–$25 to get from National to Downtown. Note that a $2.50 surcharge is added to the metered fare from this airport. Large items of luggage placed in the trunk cost an additional $0.50 per item. Taxi rip-offs have decreased since the District introduced meters, but if the fare seems astronomical, get the driver's name and cab number and contact the D.C. Taxi Commission.

Contacts SuperShuttle ☎ 800/258-3826, 202/296-6662 ⊕ www.supershuttle.com. **Taxicab Commission** ☎ 311, 202/645-6018 ⊕ dctaxi.dc.gov. **Washington Metropolitan Area Transit Authority** ☎ 202/637-7000, 202/638-3780 TTY ⊕ www.wmata.com.

GROUND TRANSPORTATION: BALTIMORE/WASHINGTON INTERNATIONAL (BWI)

By Car: Exit BWI and follow I–95 West. Take Exit 2B to MD–295 South for 24 miles; exit on U.S. 50 West toward Washington. Continue on New York Avenue for about 3 miles; continue on Mount Vernon Place NW for 2 miles. Continue on Massachusetts Avenue NW; turn left on Vermont Avenue NW at Thomas Circle. Turn right on K Street NW; take a left on 17th Street NW and you're now basically in the city center. The distance is about 34 miles and should take 50–60 minutes.

By Public Transit: Amtrak and Maryland Rail Commuter Service (MARC) trains run between BWI and Washington, D.C.'s Union Station from around 6 am to 10 pm. The cost of the 30-minute ride is $11–$93 on Amtrak and $6 on MARC's Penn Line, which runs only on weekdays. A free shuttle bus transports passengers between airline terminals and the train station (which is in a distant parking lot). Washington Metropolitan Area Transit Authority (WMATA) operates express bus service (Bus No. B30) between BWI and the Greenbelt Metro station. Buses run between 6 am and 10 pm. The fare is $6.

By Shuttle: SuperShuttle will take you to any hotel or residence in the city. The ride from BWI, which takes approximately 60 minutes, averages $37.

By Taxi: The fare from BWI is about $90.

Contacts Amtrak ☎ 800/872-7245 ⊕ www.amtrak.com. **Maryland Rail Commuter Service** ☎ 410/539-5000, 410/539-3497 TTY, 866/743-3682 ⊕ www.mtamaryland.com. **SuperShuttle** ☎ 800/258-3826, 202/296-6662 ⊕ www.supershuttle.com. **Washington**

Metropolitan Area Transit Authority
☎ *202/637–7000, 202/638–3780 TTY* ⊕ *www. wmata.com.*

GROUND TRANSPORTATION: DULLES (IAD)

By Car: From Dulles Airport, exit onto Dulles Airport Access Road and follow this for 14 miles; merge onto VA–267 East. Merge onto I–66 East; follow this for approximately 6 miles and exit to the left on E Street Expressway. Take the ramp to E Street NW. Total distance from the airport to Downtown is about 27 miles and should take about 45 minutes.

By Public Transit: Silver Line Express links Dulles International Airport and the Wiehle Avenue station. The 30-minute bus ride is $5 each way for adults, free for children under six. Buses run every half hour from 5:45 am to 10:15 pm. All coaches are accessible to those in wheelchairs. Fares may be paid with cash or credit card at the ticket counter near Door 4 at the Arrivals/Baggage Claim Level. Board the bus just outside the door.

The Washington Metropolitan Area Transit Authority (WMATA) operates express bus service between Dulles and several stops in Downtown D.C., including the L'Enfant Plaza Metro station and Rosslyn Metro station in Arlington, Virginia, just across the river from Georgetown. Bus No. 5A, which costs $6, runs every hour between 5:30 am and 11:30 pm from curb location 2E in the second lane on the (lower) arrivals level in front of the terminal. Make sure to have the exact fare or a rechargeable SmarTrip card, as drivers cannot make change.

By Shuttle: The roughly 45-minute ride from Dulles on the SuperShuttle runs $29 for one person, $10 for each additional person. Sign in with the attendants at the lower-level doors, down the ramp when you exit the terminal.

By Taxi: The fare to Washington D.C. from Dulles is about $50–$60.

Contacts SuperShuttle ☎ *800/258–3826, 202/296–6662* ⊕ *www.supershuttle.com.*

Washington Flyer ☎ *888/927–4359* ⊕ *www. washfly.com.* **Washington Metropolitan Area Transit Authority** ☎ *202/637–7000, 202/638–3780 TTY* ⊕ *www.wmata.com.*

❚ BUS TRAVEL

REGIONAL BUSES

Several bus lines run between New York City and the Washington, D.C., area, including BoltBus, DC2NY, Megabus, Peter Pan Bus Lines, Tripper Bus, Vamoose, and Washington Deluxe. Tripper and Vamoose routes run between NYC and Metro stations in Bethesda, Maryland, and Arlington, Virginia. All the buses are clean, the service satisfactory, and the price can't be beat. Believe it or not, with advance planning, you might be able to get a round-trip ticket for just $2. Megabus also has bus service from Toronto, Canada, and a handful of other U.S. cities. Several of the bus lines offer power outlets, Wi-Fi, and a frequent-rider loyalty program.

Information BoltBus ☎ *877/265–8287* ⊕ *www.boltbus.com.* **DC2NY** ☎ *202/332–2691* ⊕ *www.dc2ny.com.* **Megabus** ☎ *877/462–6342* ⊕ *www.megabus.com.* **Peter Pan Bus Lines** ☎ *800/343–9999* ⊕ *www.peterpanbus. com.* **Tripper Bus** ☎ *877/826–3874* ⊕ *www. tripperbus.com.* **Vamoose** ☎ *877/393–2828* ⊕ *www.vamoosebus.com.* **Washington Deluxe** ☎ *866/287–6932* ⊕ *www.washny.com.*

CITY BUSES

Most of the sightseeing neighborhoods (the Mall, Capitol Hill, Downtown, Dupont Circle) are near Metro rail stations, but a few (Georgetown, Adams Morgan) are more easily reached via Metrobus, blue-and-white buses operated by the Washington Metropolitan Area Transit Authority. Bus No. 42 travels from the Dupont Circle Metro stop to, and through, Adams Morgan. Georgetown is a hike from the closest Metro rail station, but you can take a Georgetown Metro Connection shuttle to any Metrobus stop from the Foggy Bottom or

Dupont Circle Metro stations in D.C. or the Rosslyn Metro station in Arlington, Virginia.

The D.C. Circulator is another option for getting around the city; it has five routes and charges $1. The Potomac Avenue–Skyland via Barracks Row, Union Station–Navy Yard via Capitol Hill, and Woodley Park–Adams Morgan–McPherson Square Metro routes cut a path from north to south; the Georgetown–Union Station and Rosslyn–Georgetown–Dupont routes go east to west.

Complete bus and Metro maps for the metropolitan D.C. area, which note museums, monuments, theaters, and parks, can be picked up free of charge at the Metro Center sales office.

FARES AND TRANSFERS

All regular buses within the District are $1.80; express buses, which make fewer stops, are $4. For every adult ticket purchased, two children under the age of four travel free. Children, ages five and older, pay the regular fare. You'll save $0.20–$0.35 and transfer bus-to-bus for free within a two-hour period by using a SmarTrip card, a rechargeable farecard you can use on buses and the Metro. Just touch the card to the SmarTrip logo on the fare box. You'll also get a $0.50 discount by using a SmarTrip card on bus-to-rail and rail-to-bus transfers.

D.C. Circulator passengers can pay cash when boarding (exact change only) or use Metro SmarTrip cards, and one-day, three-day, or weekly Circulator passes. Passes can be purchased online at ⊕ *www. commuterdirect.com*. You only have to wait about 5–10 minutes at any of the stops for the next bus.

PAYMENT AND PASSES

Buses require exact change in bills, coins, or both. You can eliminate the exact-change hassle by purchasing a seven-day Metrobus pass for $16, or the $5 rechargeable SmarTrip card online before your trip or at the Metro Center sales office, open weekdays from 8 am to 6 pm.

The SmarTrip card can also be used on the Metrorail system.

Information D.C. Circulator ☎ *202/962–1423* ⊕ *www.dccirculator.com*. **Metro Center sales office** ✉ *12th and F sts. NW, Downtown*. **Washington Metropolitan Area Transit Authority** ☎ *202/637-7000, 202/638-3780* TTY ⊕ *www.wmata.com*.

▌ CAR TRAVEL

A car is often a drawback in Washington, D.C. Traffic is awful, especially at rush hour, and driving is often confusing, with many lanes and some entire streets changing direction suddenly during rush hour. Most traffic lights stand at the side of intersections (instead of hanging suspended over them), and the streets are dotted with giant potholes. The city's most popular sights are all within a short walk of a Metro station, so do yourself a favor and leave your car at the hotel. If you're visiting sights in Maryland or Virginia or need a car because of reduced mobility, time your trips to avoid D.C. rush hours, 7–10 am and 3–7 pm.

With Zipcar, an urban car-rental membership service, you can rent a car for a couple of hours or a couple of days from convenient Downtown parking lots. A one-time application fee of $25, an annual membership fee of $60, plus hourly rates starting at $11.50 or daily rates of $84–$117 buys you gas, insurance, parking, and satellite radio. Reserve online or by phone.

Like the comfort of a car but don't want to drive? Uber is your answer. You can request a ride via text message, through the mobile app or the Uber website. Drivers are available seven days a week, 24 hours a day. Once you request your ride, you'll be able to see exactly where the driver is and how long you'll have to wait. The fare for a Black (sedan) is $7 base charge, plus $3.25/mile (traveling more than 11 miles/hour) and $0.75/minute (traveling less than 11 miles/hour); the SUV fare is $14 base charge, plus $4/mile and $0.90/minute. After registering, your credit card information is kept on file and your card is charged upon completion of your ride. When demand is high due to weather, holidays or special events, rates can be considerably higher.

Information Uber ⊕ *www.uber.com.* **Zipcar** 🖃 *866/494-7227* ⊕ *www.zipcar.com.*

GASOLINE

Gas is more expensive in the District than it is in Maryland or Virginia, and gas stations can be hard to find, especially around Pennsylvania Avenue and the National Mall. Your best bets are the BP station at the corner of 18th and S streets NW, the Mobil station at the corner of 15th and U streets NW, the Exxon station at 2150 M Street NW, and the Mobil station at the corner of 22nd and P streets NW. The no-name station at Wisconsin and Q in Georgetown has the cheapest gas in Northwest D.C.—cash only.

LAY OF THE LAND

Interstate 95 skirts D.C. as part of the Beltway, the six- to eight-lane highway that encircles the city. The eastern half of the Beltway is labeled both I–95 and I–495; the western half is just I–495. If you're coming from the south, take I–95 to I–395 and cross the 14th Street Bridge to 14th Street in the District. From the north, stay on I–95 South. Take the exit to Washington, which will place you on the Baltimore–Washington (B–W) Parkway heading south. The B–W Parkway will turn into New York Avenue, taking you into Downtown Washington, D.C.

Interstate 66 approaches the city from the southwest. You can get Downtown by taking I–66 across the Theodore Roosevelt Bridge to Constitution Avenue.

Interstate 270 approaches Washington, D.C., from the northwest before hitting I–495. To reach Downtown, take I–495 East to Connecticut Avenue South, toward Chevy Chase.

PARKING

Parking in D.C. is a question of supply and demand—little of the former, too much of the latter. The police are quick to ticket, tow away, or boot any vehicle parked illegally, so check complicated parking signs and feed the meter before you go. If you find you've been towed from a city street, call 🖃 311 or 202/737–4404 or log on to ⊕ *www.dmv.dc.gov.* Be sure you know the license-plate number, make, model, and color of the car before you call.

Most of the outlying, suburban Metro stations have parking lots, though these fill quickly with city-bound commuters. If you plan to park in one of these lots, arrive early.

Downtown private parking lots often charge around $5–$10 an hour and $25–$40 a day. Most of the streets along the Mall have metered parking and although there are some free, three-hour parking spots on Constitution, Jefferson, and Madison avenues, these spots are almost always filled. There is no parking near the Lincoln or Roosevelt memorials. The closest free parking is in three lots in East Potomac Park, south of the 14th Street Bridge.

RENTAL CARS

If you're staying in D.C., skip it. Public transportation in the city is convenient and affordable, and driving here is no fun.

However, if you're staying in Virginia or Maryland and your hotel doesn't have a shuttle into D.C. and isn't within walking distance of the Metro, then a car may be your best transportation option.

Daily rental rates in Washington, D.C., begin at about $40 during the week and about $22 on weekends for an economy car with air-conditioning, automatic transmission, and unlimited mileage. This does not include airport facility fees or the tax on car rentals.

In Washington, D.C., many agencies require you to be at least 25 to rent a car. However, younger employees of major corporations and military or government personnel on official business should check with rental companies and their employers for exceptions.

Major Rental Agencies Alamo
☏ 877/222-9075 ⊕ www.alamo.com. **Avis**
☏ 800/633-3469 ⊕ www.avis.com. **Budget**
☏ 800/218-7992 ⊕ www.budget.com. **Hertz**
☏ 800/654-3131 ⊕ www.hertz.com. **National Car Rental** ☏ 877/222-9058 ⊕ www. nationalcar.com.

ROADSIDE EMERGENCIES
Dial 911 to report accidents on the road and to reach police, the highway patrol, or the fire department. For police non-emergencies, dial 311.

Emergency Services U.S. Park Police
☏ 202/610-7500.

RULES OF THE ROAD
In D.C. you may turn right at a red light after stopping if there's no oncoming traffic. When in doubt, wait for the green. Be alert for one-way streets, "no left turn" intersections, and blocks closed to car traffic. The use of handheld mobile phones while operating a vehicle is illegal in Washington, D.C. Drivers can also be cited for "failure to pay full time and attention while operating a motor vehicle." The speed limit in D.C. is 25 mph except on the Whitehurst Freeway.

Radar detectors are illegal in Washington, D.C., and Virginia.

During the hours of 6–9 am (inbound) and 3:30–6 pm (outbound), HOV (high-occupancy vehicle) lanes on I–395 and I–95 are reserved for cars with three or more people. From 6:30 to 9 am (inbound) and 4 to 6:30 pm (outbound), all the lanes of I–66 inside the Beltway are reserved for cars carrying two or more, as are some of the lanes on the Dulles Toll Road and on I–270.

Always strap children under a year old or under 20 pounds into approved rear-facing child-safety seats in the backseat. In Washington, D.C., children weighing 20–40 pounds must also ride in a car seat in the back, although it may face forward.

Children cannot sit in the front seat of a car until they are at least four years old and weigh more than 80 pounds.

▐ METRO TRAVEL

The Metro, which opened in 1976, is clean and safe and provides a convenient way to get around the city—if you're staying near a Metro stop. Visit Metro's website and click on Metrorail maps to locate the station nearest your hotel. The Metro operates from 5 am weekdays and fom 7 am weekends, until midnight on Sunday through Thursday nights and until 3 am Friday and Saturday. Don't get to the station at the last minute, as trains from the ends of the lines depart before the official closing time. During the weekday peak periods (5–9:30 am and 3–7 pm), trains come along every three to six minutes. At other times and on weekends and holidays, trains run about every 12–15 minutes. Lighted displays at the platforms show estimated arrival and departure times of trains, as well as the number of cars available. Eating, drinking, smoking, and littering in stations and on the trains are strictly prohibited.

FARES
The Metro's base fare is $2.10; the actual price you pay depends on the time of day and the distance traveled, which means you might end up paying $5.75 if you're traveling to a distant station at rush hour. Your best bet is to use a SmarTrip card, a rechargeable farecard that can be used throughout the Metro, bus, and parking system, to avoid a $2 paper farecard surcharge. Up to two children under age four ride free when accompanied by a paying passenger.

PAYMENT AND PASSES
Buy your ticket at the SmarTrip or farecard machines; they accept coins and crisp $1, $5, or $10 bills. If the machine spits your money out, try folding and unfolding it lengthwise before asking someone for help. Many machines also accept credit and debit cards. You can buy one-day

passes for $14 and seven-day passes for $57.50. To enter the Metro platform, insert your farecard into the slot on the turnstile and take it out again at the back—you'll need it to exit at your destination. With your SmarTrip card, just touch your card to the SmarTrip logo on the turnstile. Passes and SmarTrip cards can be purchased online or at the Metro Center sales office.

Metro Information Washington Metropolitan Area Transit Authority (*WMATA*). ⊠ *12th and F sts. NW, sales center, Downtown* ☏ *202/637-7000, 202/638-3780 TTY, 202/962-1195 for lost and found* ⊕ *www.wmata.com.*

▌ TAXI TRAVEL

Taxis are easy to hail in commercial districts, less so in residential ones. If you don't see one after a few minutes, walk to a busier street. If you call, make sure to have an address—not just an intersection—and be prepared to wait, especially at night. D.C. cabs are independent operators and the various companies' cars all have a different look, some better than others! If you're traveling to or from Maryland or Virginia, your best bet is to call a Maryland or Virginia cab, which generally are more reliable. But they're not allowed to take you from point to point in the District or pick you up there if you hail them, so don't be offended if one passes you by.

FARES
The base rate for the first one-eighth mile is $3.25. Each additional one-eighth mile is $0.27, and each minute stopped or traveling at less than 10 mph is $0.42. The passenger surcharge is $0.25 and each additional passenger is $1.00. There is a $0.50 surcharge per large piece of luggage in the trunk. During D.C.-declared snow emergencies, there is an additional $15 fee. Maryland taxis charge $4 for the first ¼ mile and $0.50 for each successive ¼ mile, plus $1 surcharge for each additional passenger. Virginia cabs charge

$3.25 for the first one-seventh mile, $0.30 for each one-seventh mile thereafter, plus a $1 surcharge for each additional passenger.

Taxi Companies Barwood. (Maryland) ☏ *301/984-1900* ⊕ *www.barwoodtaxi. com.* **Diamond** ☏ *202/387-6200.* **District** ☏ *202/398-0500.* **Red Top.** (Virginia) ☏ *703/522-3333* ⊕ *www.redtopcab.com.* **Yellow** ☏ *202/544-1212* ⊕ *www.dcyellowcab.com.*

▌ TRAIN TRAVEL

More than 80 trains a day arrive at Washington, D.C.'s Union Station. Amtrak's regular service runs from D.C. to New York in 3¼–3¾ hours and from D.C. to Boston in 7¾–8 hours. Acela, Amtrak's high-speed service, travels from D.C. to New York in 2¾–3 hours and from D.C. to Boston in 6½ hours.

Two commuter lines—Maryland Rail Commuter Service (MARC) and Virginia Railway Express (VRE)—run to the nearby suburbs. They're cheaper than Amtrak, but they don't run on weekends.

Amtrak tickets and reservations are available at Amtrak stations, by telephone, or online. Amtrak schedule and fare information can be found at Union Station as well as online.

Amtrak has both reserved and unreserved trains available. If you plan to travel during peak times, such as a Friday night or near a holiday, you'll need to get a reservation and a ticket in advance. Some trains at off-peak times are unreserved, with seats assigned on a first-come, first-served basis.

Information Amtrak ☏ *800/872-7245* ⊕ *www.amtrak.com.* **Maryland Rail Commuter Service** (*MARC*). ☏ *866/743-3682* ⊕ *www.mta.maryland.gov.* **Union Station** ⊠ *50 Massachusetts Ave. NE* ☏ *202/289-1908* ⊕ *www.unionstationdc.com.* **Virginia Railway Express** (*VRE*). ☏ *703/684-1001* ⊕ *www.vre.org.*

ESSENTIALS

■ BUSINESS SERVICES AND FACILITIES

Imagine two Washington monuments laid end to end, and you will have an idea about the size of the Washington Convention Center, the District's largest building. Recognized nationally for its architectural design, the center also has a $4 million art collection featuring 120 sculptures, oil paintings, and photographs from artists around the world.

FedEx Office, across the street from the Convention Center and at many other locations citywide, provides everything from photocopying and digital printing to shipping and receiving packages. In addition, several companies provide translation and interpretation services, including Capital Communications Group, which also offers multilingual city tours, and Comprehensive Language Center.

Business Services FedEx Office Print & Ship Center ⊠ 800 K St. NW, Downtown ☎ 202/682-0349 ⊕ www.fedex.com Ⓜ Mt. Vernon Sq./7th St. Convention Center.

Convention Center Walter E. Washington Convention Center ⊠ 801 Mt. Vernon Pl. NW, Downtown ☎ 202/249-3000 ⊕ www.dcconvention.com Ⓜ Mt. Vernon Sq/7th St. Convention Center.

■ COMMUNICATIONS

INTERNET

Most major hotels offer high-speed access in rooms and/or lobbies and business centers. In addition, dozens of D.C.-area restaurants and coffee shops provide free wireless broadband Internet service, including branches of Starbucks and Così all over town. The Martin Luther King Jr. Memorial Public Library and 23 other branches of the D.C. Library System offer Wi-Fi access free of charge to all library visitors. At Kramerbooks & Afterwords Café you can check your email for free on the computer located at the full-service bar (and it's open all night on Friday and Saturday).

Contacts Così ⊕ www.getcosi.com. **Kramerbooks & Afterwords** ⊠ 1517 Connecticut Ave. NW, Dupont Circle ☎ 202/387-3825 ⊕ www.kramers.com Ⓜ Dupont Circle. **Martin Luther King Jr. Memorial Library** ⊠ 901 G St. NW, Chinatown ☎ 202/727-0321 ⊕ www.dclibrary.org Ⓜ Metro Center or Gallery Place Chinatown.

■ HOURS OF OPERATION

If you're getting around on the Metro, remember that Sunday through Thursday it closes at midnight, and on Friday and Saturday nights it stops running at 3 am. Give yourself enough time to get to the station, because at many stations the last trains leave earlier than the closing times. If it's a holiday, be sure to check the schedule before you leave the station, as trains may be running on a different timetable. Bars and nightclubs close at 2 am on weekdays and 3 am on weekends.

■ MONEY

Washington is an expensive city, comparable to New York. On the other hand, many attractions, including most of the museums, are free.

ITEM	AVERAGE COST
Cup of Coffee	$1–$4
Glass of Wine	$7–$10 and up
Pint of Beer	$5–$7
Sandwich	$5–$7
One-Mile Taxi Ride	$5–$10
Museum Admission	Usually free

Prices in this guide are given for adults. Substantially reduced fees are almost always available for children, students, and senior citizens.

▌PACKING

A pair of comfortable shoes is your must-pack item. This is a walking town, and if you fail to pack for it, your feet will pay. D.C. isn't the most fashionable city in the country but people do look neat and presentable; business attire tends to be fairly conservative, and around college campuses and in hip neighborhoods like U Street Corridor or Adams Morgan, styles are more eclectic.

The most important element to consider, however, is the weather: D.C.'s temperatures can be extreme, and the right clothes are your best defense.

Winters are cold but sunny, with nighttime temperatures in the 20s and daytime highs in the 40s and 50s. Although the city doesn't normally get much snow, when it does, many streets won't be plowed for days, so if you're planning a visit for winter, bring a warm coat and hat and shoes that won't be ruined by snow and salt. Summers are muggy and very hot, with temperatures in the 80s and 90s and high humidity. Plan on cool, breathable fabrics, a hat for the sun, a sweater for overzealous air-conditioning, and an umbrella for daily thunderstorms. Fall and spring are less challenging, with temperatures in the 60s and occasional showers. Pants, lightweight sweaters, and light coats are appropriate.

▌RESTROOMS

Restrooms are found in all of the city's museums and galleries. Most are accessible to people in wheelchairs, and many are equipped with changing tables for babies. Locating a restroom is often difficult when you're strolling along the Mall. There are facilities at the Washington Monument, the Lincoln Memorial, the Jefferson Memorial, and Constitution Gardens, near the Vietnam Veterans Memorial, but these are not always as clean as they should be. The White House Visitors Center at 1450 Pennsylvania Avenue NW has a very nice public restroom.

Restrooms are also available in restaurants, hotels, and department stores. Unlike in many other cities, these businesses are usually happy to help out those in need. There's one state-of-the-art public restroom in the Huntington Station on the Metro. All other stations have restrooms available in cases of emergency; ask one of the uniformed attendants in the kiosks.

▌SAFETY

Washington, D.C., is a fairly safe city, but as with any major metropolitan area it's best to stay alert. Keep an eye on purses and backpacks, and be aware of your surroundings before you use an ATM, especially one that is outdoors. Move on to a different machine if you notice people loitering nearby. Assaults are rare but they do happen, especially late at night in Adams Morgan, Capitol Hill, Northeast D.C., and U Street Corridor. If someone threatens you with violence, it's best to hand over your money and seek help from police later.

Public transportation is quite safe, but late at night, choose bus stops on busy streets over those on quiet ones. The DowntownDC Business Improvement District's free guardian angel SAM service will walk you to a taxi, Metro, or your car until 9:30 pm May to October (until 7:30 pm November to April); just call their dispatch service. They operate in the White House area, part of Capitol Hill, Downtown, Penn Quarter, and Chinatown.

Contact SAM ☎ *202/624-1550.*

▌TAXES

Washington's hotel tax is a whopping 14.5%. Maryland and Virginia charge hotel taxes of 5%–10%. In D.C. and Maryland the sales tax is 6%, and in

Virginia 4% plus 1% in some local municipalities.

TIME

Washington, D.C., is in the Eastern time zone. It's 3 hours ahead of Los Angeles, 1 hour ahead of Chicago, 5 hours behind London, and 15 hours behind Sydney.

TIPPING

TIPPING GUIDES FOR WASHINGTON, D.C.	
Bartender	$1–$5 per round of drinks, depending on the number of drinks
Bellhop	$1–$5 per bag, depending on the level of the hotel
Coat Check	$1–$2 per coat
Hotel Concierge	$5 or more, depending on the service
Hotel Doorman	$1–$5 for help with bags or hailing a cab
Hotel Maid	$2–$5 a day (either daily or at the end of your stay, in cash)
Hotel Room Service Waiter	$1–$2 per delivery, even if a service charge has been added
Porter at Airport or Train Station	$1 per bag
Restroom Attendants	$1 or small change
Skycap at Airport	$1–$3 per bag checked
Spa Personnel	15%–20% of the cost of your service
Taxi Driver	15%, but round up the fare to the next dollar amount
Tour Guide	10% of the cost of the tour
Valet Parking Attendant	$2–$5, each time your car is brought to you
Waiter	15%–20%, with 20% being the norm at high-end restaurants; nothing additional if a service charge is added to the bill

TOURS

GUIDED TOURS

Collette Vacations has a seven-day "Washington D.C. Family Discovery" vacation, which includes a guided bike tour along the National Mall, tours of the U.S. Capitol, Newseum and International Spy Museum and a visit to the Air & Space Museum or National Museum of American History Museum. The trip also includes visits to Mount Vernon; Eastern Market, the city's historic indoor market; and the National Zoo. Mayflower Tours offers a 10-day "America's Heritage" tour featuring D.C., Williamsburg, and New York that includes a visit to Arlington Cemetery, and an evening monuments tour; as well as tours of Mount Vernon, Monticello, Jamestown, and Gettysburg; springtime trips take in the Cherry Blossom Festival, too. Monograms Travel offers itineraries of D.C., some including Boston and/or New York. All trips include a full-day guided trolley tour and free time. Smithsonian Journeys has a three-night "Celebrate Smithsonian" tour that offers an exciting behind-the-scenes look into the preservation and research being conducted by this famed institution. You'll meet with curators from the National Air & Space Museum, Steven F. Udvar-Hazy Center, and more. Tauck has two itineraries that include D.C. "Williamsburg and Washington, D.C." starts in Philadelphia, continues to Amish country, Gettysburg, Williamsburg, and the colony of Jamestown before it concludes with two nights in Washington. Highlights of the six-night, family-focused "National Treasures: Philly to D.C." tour include a kayak adventure on the Potomac River and a scavenger hunt in the National Archives. WorldStrides, which specializes in educational student travel, has Washington programs that are designed to enrich the study of U.S. history and government.

Recommended Companies Collette Vacations ☎ 800/340–5158 ⊕ www.

gocollette.com. **Mayflower Tours**
☎ 800/323–7604 ⊕ www.mayflowertours.com.
Monograms Travel ☎ 866/270–9841 ⊕ www.
monograms.com. **Smithsonian Journeys**
☎ 855/330–1542 ⊕ www.smithsonianjourneys.
org. **Tauck** ☎ 800/788–7885 ⊕ www.tauck.
com. **WorldStrides** ☎ 800/468–5899 ⊕ dn.
educationaltravel.com.

SPECIAL-INTEREST TOURS

Road Scholar, formerly Elderhostel, offers several guided tours for older adults that provide fascinating in-depth looks into the history and beauty of D.C. The non-profit educational travel organization has been leading all-inclusive learning adventures around the world since 1975. In addition to the programs listed here, it has several other world studies and history programs in D.C. All Road Scholar programs include accommodations, meals, and in-town transportation.

Presented in conjunction with the Close Up Foundation, the nation's largest non-profit citizenship education organization, "Monumental D.C." is a four-night program that includes seminars on many of the figures memorialized on and near the National Mall. Prices start at about $1,059 per person.

"Spies, Lies and Intelligence: The Shadowy World of International Espionage" is a fascinating exploration of the country's intelligence operation. Retired CIA agents share secrets of high-profile spying cases on this three-night trip that costs about $998 per person. Highlights include visits to the International Spy Museum and the NSA Cryptologic Museum.

"Signature City Washington, D.C.: Historical & Cultural Gems" lets visitors explore some of the city's lesser-known marvels such as the Scottish Rite of Free Masonry, Georgetown's Tudor Place and Embassy Row, and H Street, one of D.C.'s most historic neighborhoods. This five-night program starts at about $1,399 per person. There's even a four-night "Urban Outdoors Adventure: Bicycling Washington, D.C." tour where you'll explore the

city on two-wheels, including visits to Mount Vernon and Arlington National Cemetery.

Contact Road Scholar ☎ 800/454–5768 ⊕ www.roadscholar.org.

DAY TOURS AND GUIDES

We recommend any of the tours offered by A Tour de Force, D.C. Walkabout, Gross National Product's Scandal Tours, History on Foot, Smithsonian Associates Program, Spies of Washington, and Washington Walks.

For convenience, you can't beat the Old Town Trolley Tours, which take you to all the major historical and cultural landmarks in the city. What's great about these tours is that you can get on and off as you please and stay as long as you like at any spot; you can re-board for free all day long. April through October, Washington Walks has two-hour guided tours that are interesting and, at $15 per person, affordable. Join one of the lively and free tours offered year-round with DC by Foot. And on hot summer days, join Capitol River Cruises for a cool look at the city from the water.

For families we recommend the bike tours (or Segway tours if all kids are over 16), the DC Ducks tour (younger kids will get a kick out of the quackers that are given to all riders), a mule-drawn barge ride on the C&O Canal, and any of Natalie Zanin's historic strolls, especially the Ghost Story Tour of Washington.

BICYCLE TOURS

Bike and Roll has knowledgeable guides leading daily excursions past dozens of Washington, D.C., landmarks. All tours start at L'Enfant Plaza near the National Mall. Bicycles, helmets, snacks, and water bottles are included in the rates, which start at $40. Their Capital Sites and Monuments night tours cost $45, and there's even a Blossoms by Bike tour for $35 during the annual Cherry Blossom Festival. Capital City Bike Tours also offers day and night monuments tours priced at $36 for adults and $26 for children, ages 12 and under. Adventure Cycling Association offers two 330-mile bike tours along the C&O Canal from Washington D.C. to Pittsburgh. The seven-night fall trip is fully supported (vehicles transport riders' gear and meals are catered) and can accommodate up to 65 riders, while the spring trip is a self-contained tour for 14 (riders carry their own gear and cook their meals). Or if you'd like to set out on your own, the Association sells a Tidewater Potomac Heritage Route map for $15.75 with a detailed 378-mile route that starts in D.C. and travels along the Potomac River to the Chesapeake Bay, incorporating many historic sites.

Capital Bikeshare rents bikes by the hour and is a great way to visit the memorials and monuments at your own pace. And, you can return your bike at any of the 300 stations throughout the city, as well as in Alexandria and Arlington, VA, and neighboring Montgomery County, MD.

Contacts Adventure Cycling Association ☎ 800/755-2453 ⊕ www.adventurecycling. org. **Bike and Roll** ☎ 202/842-2453 ⊕ www.bikethesites.com. **Capital Bikeshare** ☎ 877/430-2453 ⊕ www.capitalbikeshare.com. **Capital City Bike Tours** ☎ 877/734-8687 ⊕ capitalcitybiketours.com.

BOAT TOURS

During one-hour rides on mule-drawn barges on the C&O Canal, costumed guides and volunteers explain the waterway's history. The barge rides, which cost $8 and are run by the National Park Service, depart from its visitor center Wednesday through Sunday, April through October.

Capitol River Cruises offers 45-minute sightseeing tours aboard the *Nightingale* and *Nightingale II*, Great Lakes boats from the 1950s. Beverages and light snacks are available. Hourly cruises depart from Washington Harbour noon to 9 pm April through October. Prices are $15 for adults and $7 for children 3 to 12; purchase tickets online and save $1 on each fare.

WORD OF MOUTH

"Take a tour on the hop on and hop off trolley tours. It beats the cost of taxis from one place to another, gives you background information and is very convenient. It will get you closer than the Metro subway ever can." —skigal

Several swanky cruises depart from the waterfront in Southwest D.C. The *Odyssey III*, specially built to fit under the Potomac's bridges, departs from the Gangplank Marina at 6th and Water streets SW. Tickets are approximately $55 for the weekday lunch cruise, $69 for the weekend brunch cruise, and $100–$120 for the daily dinner cruise. As the prices suggest, this is an elegant affair; jackets are requested for men at dinner. The sleek *Spirit of Washington* offers lunch and dinner cruises that range from $45 to $95. Odyssey and Spirit, as well as a handful of other companies, offer sightseeing boat tours from the new National Harbor on the banks of the Potomac River in Maryland. Just minutes from D.C., National Harbor boasts a convention center, hotels, shops, restaurants, condominiums and the National Children's Museum.

Departing from Alexandria, the glass-enclosed *Nina's Dandy* cruises up the Potomac year-round to Georgetown, taking you past many of D.C.'s monuments. Lunch cruises cost $48 weekdays and $53 on Saturday. A Sunday Champagne brunch cruise costs $58. Boarding for these cruises starts at 11:30 am. Depending on the day, dinner cruises start boarding at 6 or 6:30 pm and cost $88 Sunday through Thursday and $98–$108 Friday and Saturday. The *Nina's Dandy* and sister ship *Dandy* also offer special holiday cruises.

The Potomac Riverboat Company, with docks in Alexandria and Georgetown, has a 90-minute Washington by Water Monuments Cruise priced at $26 for adults (one-way tickets also are available should you wish to board at one dock and disembark at another) mid-March through early November. The company also offers sightseeing tours of the Alexandria harbor, a tour to Mount Vernon, and a pirate cruise for mateys young and old alike.

Mid-March through October, DC Ducks offers 90-minute tours in converted World War II amphibious vehicles. After an hour-long road tour of landlocked sights, the tour moves to the water, where for 30 minutes you get a boat's-eye view of the city. Tours depart from Union Station and cost $35.10 for adults and $26.10 for children ages 11 and under for advance online bookings; seating is on a first-come, first-served basis.

If you're a sailing enthusiast, you'll want to hop aboard the 65-foot *American Spirit* schooner with DC Sail, the community sailing program of the National Maritime Heritage Foundation. Sunset cruises aboard this classic-rigged sailing vessel are available every other Friday evenings May through October and cost $50 per person. There also are baseball cruises that include a Nats game after the sailing trip and blossom cruises during the city's annual springtime Cherry Blossom season.

Contacts C&O Canal Barges ⊠ *Canal Visitor Center, 1057 Thomas Jefferson St. NW, Georgetown* ☎ *202/653–5190* ⊕ *www.nps. gov/choh.* **Capitol River Cruises** ⊠ *Washington Harbor, 31st and K sts. NW, Georgetown* ☎ *301/460–7447, 800/405–5511* ⊕ *www. capitolrivercruises.com.* **Dandy Cruises** ⊠ *Prince St., between Duke and King sts., Alexandria, Virginia* ☎ *703/683–6076* ⊕ *www. dandydinnerboat.com.* **DC Ducks** ⊠ *50 Massachusetts Ave. NE, Capitol Hill* ☎ *855/323–8257* ⊕ *www.dcducks.com.* **DC Sail** ⊠ *600 Water St., SW, D.C. Waterfront* ☎ *202/547–1250* ⊕ *www. dcsail.org. Odyssey III and Spirit of Washington* ⊠ *600 Water St. SW, D.C. Waterfront* ☎ *202/488–6010, 866/404–8439* ⊕ *www. entertainmentcruises.com.* **Potomac Riverboat Company** ⊠ *205 The Strand, Alexandria, Virginia* ☎ *877/511–2628, 703/684–0580* ⊕ *www.potomacriverboatco.com.*

BUS AND TROLLEY TOURS

ANC Tours is the only bus company authorized by the National Park Service to offer riding tours through Arlington National Cemetery. Tours depart daily from the Cemetery Visitors Center, 8:30–6:30 April through September, and 8:30–4:30 October through March. Stops include the Kennedy gravesites, the Women in Military Service for America and Robert E. Lee memorials, and the Tomb of the Unknowns, where it is timed to coincide with the Changing of the Guard ceremony; tickets cost $9 for adults and $4.75 for children ages 3–11.

Big Bus Tours offers hop-on, hop-off tours with four different city loops aboard brightly painted red, white, and blue open-top, double-decker buses. The cost is $46 for one day and $57 for a two-day pass and includes all loops. Prices on Tuesday and Wednesday are discounted by 10% if you book in advance online.

Gray Line's nine-hour "D.C. in a Day" tour stops at the White House Visitor Center, U.S. Capitol, World War II Memorial, Martin Luther King Jr. National Memorial, and Smithsonian museums. The cost is $45 for adults and $10 for children ages 3–11; there's also a special family rate of $95 for two adults and two children. The four-hour "Arlington Cemetery Plus a Taste of D.C." includes visits to the Tomb of the Unknowns, Iwo Jima Memorial, and the Lincoln, Korean and Vietnam memorials. It is priced at $45 for adults and $15 for children. Walk in Abraham Lincoln's footsteps on "The Lincoln Experience" tour that includes visits to Ford's Theater and The Cottage, a quiet and unassuming country getaway on the grounds of the Armed Forces Retirement Home where he enjoyed reading, writing and entertaining guests. It was at The Cottage where he developed the Emancipation Proclamation. The 5½-hour tour is priced at $60 for adults and $20 for children.

Gross National Product's Scandal Tours, led by members of the GNP comedy troupe, last 1½ hours and cover scandals from George Washington to Barack Obama. These extremely lively tours, held on Saturday, April through August, at 1 pm ($30 per person); reservations are required.

Old Town Trolley Tours, orange-and-green motorized trolleys, take in the main Downtown sights and also head into Georgetown and the Upper Northwest in a speedy two hours if you ride straight through. However, you can hop on and off as many times as you like, taking your time at the stops you choose. Tickets are $39 for adults, $29 for kids 4–12; purchase tickets online and save $2.90–$3.90 per ticket. Two-day tickets also are available.

On Board D.C. Tours offers a daily six-hour "D.C. It All" tour that lets you hop on and off with the guide at 12 locations. Monday through Thursday the cost is $70 for adults and $60 for children under 12; Friday through Sunday, it's $80 for adults and $60 for children. Mid March through October, a one hour private Potomac River cruise is included in the tour. Their three-hour "D.C. The Lights!" nightlife tour costs $60 for adults and $50 for children.

Contacts ANC Tours ☎ 202/488–1012 ⊕ www.anctours.com. **Big Bus Tours** ☎ 877/332–8689 ⊕ www.bigbustours.com. **Gray Line** ☎ 301/386–8300, 800/862–1400 ⊕ www.graylinedc.com. **Gross National Product** ☎ 202/783–7212 ⊕ www.gnpcomedy. com. **Old Town Trolley Tours** ☎ 202/832–9800, 888/910–8687 ⊕ www.trolleytours. com. **On Board D.C. Tours** ☎ 301/839–5261 ⊕ www.onboarddctours.com.

GOVERNMENT BUILDING TOURS

Special tours of government buildings with heavy security, including the White House and the Capitol, can be arranged through your U.S. representative or senator's office. Limited numbers of these so-called VIP tickets are available, so plan up to six months in advance of your trip. Foreign visitors should contact their embassy in Washington, D.C., as far in advance as possible. Governmental buildings close to visitors when the Department of Homeland Security issues a high alert, so call ahead.

Don't miss the stunning Capitol Visitor Center (⇨ See Chapter 5). Before your tour of the Capitol, you can watch orientation films, view historical documents from the Library of Congress and the National Archives, learn about the history of democracy through interactive touch-screen displays, walk alongside statues of notable historical figures, and see models of the Capitol and the Dome. The Bureau of Engraving and Printing (⇨ See Chapter 5), where U.S. money is made, has some of the most popular tours in the city. Foreign dignitaries are received at the Department of State's lavish Diplomatic Reception Rooms (⇨ See Chapter 5), but everyone else can get a peek on weekdays.

MEDIA TOURS

The Voice of America is the U.S. government's foreign broadcaster, beaming news and current affairs programming around the world in 44 languages. Get a look behind the scenes with tours weekdays at noon and 2:30 pm. Reservations are recommended and can be made either online or by phone.

National Public Radio leads tours of its broadcast facilities on weekdays at 11 am. Register online in advance of your trip and plan to show up 15 minutes beforehand for a security screening.

Contacts National Public Radio ✉ 1111 N. Capitol St. NE, Northeast D.C. ☎ 202/513–2000 ⊕ www.npr.org. **Voice of America** ✉ 330 Independence Ave. SW, Capitol Hill ☎ 202/203–4990 ⊕ www.voatour.com.

ORIENTATION TOURS

Old Town Trolley Tours, orange-and-green motorized trolleys, take in the main Downtown sights and also head into Georgetown and the Upper Northwest in a speedy two hours if you ride straight through. However, you can hop on and off as many times as you like, taking your time at the stops you choose. Tickets are $39 for adults, $29 for kids 4–12; purchase tickets online and save $2.90–$3.90 per ticket. Two-day tickets also are available. ANC Tours is the only bus company authorized by the National Park Service to offer riding tours through Arlington National Cemetery. Tours depart daily from the Cemetery Visitors Center, 8:30–6:30, April through September, and 8:30–5, October through March. Stops include the Kennedy gravesites, the Women in Military Service for America and Robert E. Lee memorials, and the Tomb of the Unknowns, where it is timed to coincide with the Changing of the Guard ceremony; tickets cost $8.75 for adults and $4.50 for children ages 3–11.

PHOTO TOURS

Nationally known photographer Sonny Odom offers custom tours for shutterbugs at $50 per hour, with a four-hour minimum. City Photo Walking Tours, led by portrait photographer M. J. Love, has several two-hour tours priced at $140 per person that guarantee postcard-perfect images of the nation's capital. Washington Photo Safari founder E. David Luria promises opportunities for photographers of all skill levels (even camera phones are OK!) on his half-day ($89 per person) and full-day ($169 per person) "Monuments and Memorials" workshops, held every Wednesday and Saturday. Special themed photo tours, including "A House of Cards: Icons of Capitol Hill," "Washington National Cathedral: An Insider's View," and "Georgetown by Land and Sea," are held on selected weekends. Prices for these half-day tours led by a team of professional photographers range from $74 to $99.

Contacts M. J. Love Photography
☎ 800/737-4051 ⊕ www.mjlovephotography. com. **Sonny Odom** ☎ 703/379-1633 ⊕ www.sonnyodom.com. **Washington Photo Safari** ☎ 877/512-5969 ⊕ www. washingtonphotosafari.com.

PRIVATE GUIDES

A Tour de Force has limo and walking tours of historic homes, diplomatic buildings, and "the best little museums in Washington" led by local historian and author Jeanne Fogle. Award-winning author Anthony Pitch leads two D.C. Sightseeing walking tours: "The Curse of Lafayette Square" and "The Lincoln Assassination." The two-hour tours are $400, no matter the size of your group.

In business since 1964, the Guide Service of Washington puts together half-day and full-day tours of D.C. sights, including some that venture off the beaten path.

Contacts A Tour de Force ☎ 703/525-2948 ⊕ www.atourdeforce.com. **Guide Service of Washington** ☎ 202/628-2842 ⊕ www. dctourguides.com.

SEGWAY AND SCOOTER TOURS

Rest your feet and glide by the monuments, museums, and major attractions aboard a Segway. Guided tours usually last about two hours. D.C. city ordinance requires that riders be at least 16 years old; some tour companies have weight restrictions of 250 pounds. Tours cost around $45–$90 per person and are limited to 6 to 10 people.

City Scooter Tours rents scooters and wheelchairs for self-guided tours. Three-day rental prices start at $175 for scooters and $150 for wheelchairs.

Contacts Capital Segway ☎ 202/682-1980 ⊕ www.capitalsegway.com. **City Scooter Tours** ☎ 888/441-7575 ⊕ www. cityscootertours.com. **City Segway Tours** ☎ 877/734-8687 ⊕ www.citysegwaytours.com. **Segs in the City** ☎ 800/734-7393 ⊕ www. segsinthecity.com.

WALKING TOURS

American-history scholar Steve Livengood, from the Capitol Historical Society, leads guided tours around the grounds of the Capitol every Monday at 10, March through October. The two-hour tours, which start at Union Station, cost $10 per person.

The nonprofit group Cultural Tourism DC has 15 self-guided Neighborhood Heritage Trails, plus a citywide African-American Heritage Trail, all of which are highlighted with historic markers. All the tours can be downloaded from their website. One week each fall, the group leads free, guided walking tours that highlight the history and architecture of certain neighborhoods, from the southwest waterfront to points much farther north. You also can check out other cultural events, many free, happening around the city on the Cultural Tourism DC website.

DC by Foot offers dozens of free tours—the guides work for tips, which makes for a highly entertaining experience—including the Tidal Basin and National Mall, Arlington National Cemetery, Capitol Hill, Georgetown, and U Street. The two- to four-hour tours are available year-round, but days and times vary by season; advance reservations are required.

DC Metro Food Tours explores the culinary heritage of seven neighborhoods, with 3½-hour tours offered year-round on weekends.

DC Walkabout has created a number of engaging and informative audio walking tours including "American Scandal," "Capitol Hill," "The Georgetown Ghost," "Haunted History" and "The Lincoln Assassination," that feature narration, historical recordings, and even music and sound effects. Each tour, ranging from one to two miles, costs $9 and can be downloaded to any mobile device.

You can step back in time on one of Natalie Zanin's interactive theatrical tours, which revisit Washington, D.C., during the Civil War, World War II, or the 1960s. Or you can sign up for a Ghost Story Tour, on which Zanin dresses as Dolley Madison's ghost and shares stories of hauntings around the city, including Lafayette Square Park, where Edgar Allan Poe's spirit is said to wander. Tours cost $12 for adults and $6 for children.

Relive the night of President Abraham Lincoln's assassination with Detective McDevitt on a two-hour "History on Foot" walking tour ($15 per person) from Ford's Theatre to Lafayette Park. You'll follow the escape route taken by assassin John Wilkes Booth on the 1½-mile trek, on Wednesday, Thursday, and Saturday from March to October.

The Smithsonian Associates program offers a range of fascinating guided walks around Washington, D.C., and nearby communities; advance tickets are required.

Spies of Washington Walking Tours, led by a retired Air Force officer and former president of the National Military Intelligence Association, visits sites in Washington associated with espionage over the past 200 years. The approximately two-hour tours cost $15 per person.

One of the more popular tours in the city is the U.S. National Arboretum's Full Moon Hike, offered about three times a month, excluding July and August. It's a brisk 4-mile walk through the grounds and hills by the Anacostia River, which afford beautiful views of the city at night. It costs $22 per person and registration is required. The Arboretum also has a number of other delightful walking tours through the enchanting gardens.

Washington Walks has a wide range of tours for $15 per person, including the self-explanatory "Memorials by Moonlight" and "The Most Haunted Houses"; "Get Local Saturdays," which goes in-depth into Washington neighborhoods; and tours of Georgetown and Dupont Circle.

Contacts Capitol Historical Society
☎ 202/543–8919 ⊕ www.uschs.org.
Cultural Tourism DC ☎ 202/661–7581
⊕ www.culturaltourismdc.org. **DC by Foot**
☎ 202/370–1830 ⊕ www.dcbyfoot.com.
DC Metro Food Tours ☎ 202/683–8847,
800/979–3370 ⊕ www.dcmetrofoodtours.
com. **DC Walkabout** ☎ 202/421–4053
⊕ www.dcwalkabout.com.**History on Foot**
☎ 202/347–4833 ⊕ www.fords.org. **Natalie
Zanin's Historic Strolls** ☎ 301/588–9255
⊕ www.historicstrolls.com. **The Smithsonian Associates** ☎ 202/633–3030 ⊕ www.
smithsonianassociates.org. **Spies of
Washington Tour** ☎ 703/569–1875 ⊕ www.
spiesofwashingtontour.com. **U.S. National
Arboretum** ☎ 202/245–4521 ⊕ www.usna.
usda.gov. **Washington Walks** ☎ 202/484–
1565 ⊕ www.washingtonwalks.com.

▌VISITOR INFORMATION

Destination D.C.'s free, 85-page publication, the *Official Visitors' Guide*, is full of sightseeing tips, maps, and contacts. You can order a copy online or by phone, or pick one up in their office (enter on I Street).

Most of the popular sights in D.C. are run by either the National Park Service (NPS) or the Smithsonian; both of which have recorded information about locations and hours of operation.

**Events and Attractions National Park
Service** ☎ 202/619–7275 for "Dial-a-Park"
⊕ www.nps.gov. **Smithsonian** ☎ 202/633–
1000, 202/633–5285 TTY ⊕ www.si.edu. **White
House Visitor Center** ✉ 1450 Pennsylvania
Ave. NW, White House area ☎ 202/208–1631
⊕ www.nps.gov/whho.

State Information State of Maryland
☎ 866/639–3526 ⊕ www.visitmaryland.org.
Virginia Tourism Corporation ☎ 800/847–
4882 ⊕ www.virginia.org.

Tourist Information Destination DC ✉ 901
7th St. NW, 4th fl., Downtown ☎ 202/789–
7000, 800/422–8644 ⊕ www.washington.org.

ALL ABOUT WASHINGTON, D.C.

The **Smithsonian website** (⊕ *www.si.edu*) is a good place to start planning a trip to the Mall and its museums. The **National Gallery** has its own website, too (⊕ *www.nga.gov*). You can check out the exhibitions and events that will be held during your visit.

Cultural Tourism D.C. (⊕ *www.cultural tourismdc.org*) is a nonprofit coalition whose mission is to highlight the city's arts and heritage. Their website is loaded with great information about sights, special events, and neighborhoods, including self-guided walking tours.

DowntownDC Business Improvement District (⊕ *www.downtowndc.org*) is a nonprofit that oversees the 140-block area from the White House to the U.S. Capitol. The website has special events, shopping, and dining listings and information about the wonderful red, white, and blue uniformed D.C. SAMs, roving hospitality specialists linked to a central dispatcher by radio. In spring and summer, SAMs (which stands for Safety, Administration, and Maintenance) are available to help visitors with directions, information, and emergencies. You'll spot their hospitality kiosks near Metro stops and major attractions.

GAY AND LESBIAN

Washington, D.C., is a very inclusive town, with an active gay community and plenty of gay-friendly hotels, nightlife, and events. In addition to news and features, both *Washington Blade* (⊕ *www.washingtonblade.com*) and *Metro Weekly* (⊕ *www.metroweekly.com*) have guides to gay bars and clubs, including calendars of events.

KIDS AND FAMILIES

Washingtonfamily.com (⊕ *www.washington family.com*) compiles a "Best for Families" feature, as voted on by area families. Families may also want to check out **washingtonparent.com** (⊕ *www. washingtonparent.com*) and **kidfriendlydc. com** (⊕ *www.kidfriendlydc.com*), a blog with loads of kid-friendly events, deals, and activities.

NEWS AND HAPPENINGS

The website of the *Washington Post* (⊕ *www.washingtonpost.com*) has a fairly comprehensive listing of what's going on around town. Also check out the site of *Washington CityPaper* (⊕ *www.washingtoncitypaper.com*), a free weekly newspaper. The *Washingtonian* (⊕ *www.washingtonian.com*) is a monthly magazine.

CultureCapital (⊕ *www.culturecapital. org*), a nonprofit group promoting the city's culture and arts, has an online link (⊕ *www.ticketplace.org*) with dozens of theater, dance, music, and opera performances offering half-price tickets.

For personalized emails of things to do, member reviews, and listings of half-price show and event tickets in D.C. and other major cities nationwide, register for free at ⊕ *www.goldstar.com,* an online entertainment company.

INDEX

PHOTO CREDITS

NOTES

NOTES

NOTES

NOTES

NOTES

NOTES

NOTES